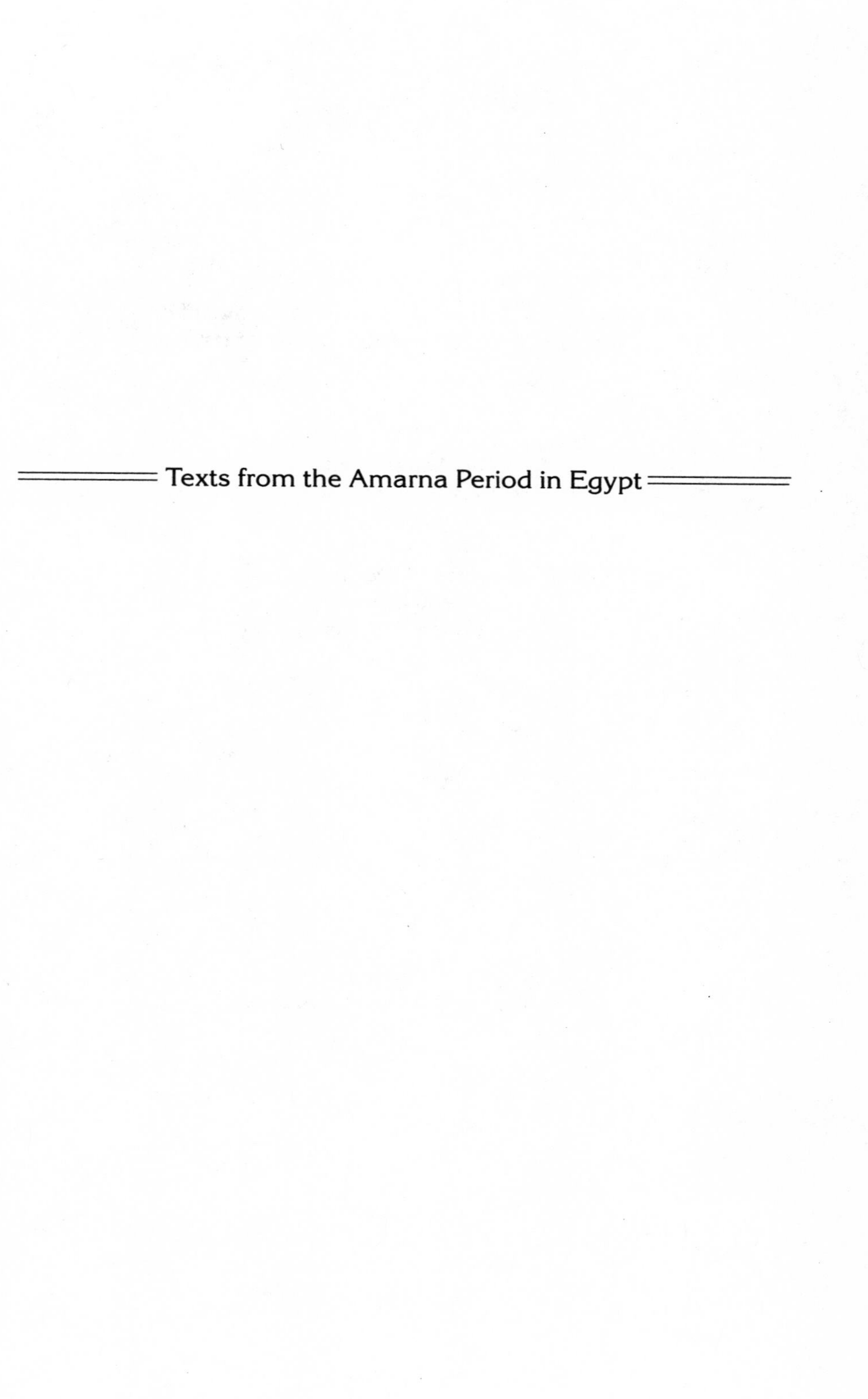

Texts from the Amarna Period in Egypt

Writings from the Ancient World
Society of Biblical Literature

Volume 5
Texts from the Amarna Period in Egypt
by William J. Murnane
Edited by Edmund S. Meltzer

Texts from the Amarna Period in Egypt

by

William J. Murnane

Edited by

Edmund S. Meltzer

Scholars Press
Atlanta, Georgia

The Society of Biblical Literature gratefully acknowledges a grant from the National Endowment for the Humanities to underwrite certain editorial and research expenses of the Writings from the Ancient World series. Published results and interpretations do not necessarily represent the view of the Endowment.

Grateful acknowledgment is also made to the following for permission to reproduce copyrighted material: Yale University Press, for the map of the el-Amarna area, from *The Art and Architecture of Ancient Egypt*, by William Stevenson Smith (Baltimore: Pelican Books, 1958); The Committee of the Egypt Exploration Society, for the figures in chapter 4, from *The Rock Tombs of El-Amarna*, vols. 1–6, by Norman de Garis Davies (London: Egypt Exploration Society, 1903–1908).

Library of Congress Cataloging-in-Publication Data

Murnane, William J.
Texts from the Amarna period in Egypt / by William J. Murnane ;
edited by Edmund S. Meltzer.
p. cm. – (Writings from the ancient world ; no. 05)
Includes bibliographical references and index.
ISBN 1-55540-965-2 (cloth). –ISBN 1-55540-966-0 (pbk.)
1. Egypt–History–Eighteenth dynasty, ca. 1570–1320 B.C.–
Sources. 2. Tell el-Amarna (Egypt). 3. Egypt–Religion–Sources.
I. Meltzer, Edmund S. II. Title. III. Series.
DT87.4.M87 1994
932'.014–dc20 94-5147
CIP

Printed in the United States of America
on acid-free paper.

Contents

Series Editor's Foreword

Writings from the Ancient World is designed to provide up-to-date, readable, English translation of writings recovered from the ancient Near East.

The series is intended to serve the interests of general readers, students, and educators who wish to explore the ancient Near Eastern roots of Western civilization, or compare these earliest written expressions of human thought and activity with writings from other parts of the world. It should also be useful to scholars in the humanities or social sciences who need clear, reliable translations of ancient Near Eastern materials for comparative purposes. Specialists in particular areas of the ancient Near East who need access to texts in the scripts and languages of other areas will also find these translations helpful. Given the wide range of materials translated in the series, different volumes will appeal to different interests. But these translations make available to all readers of English the world's earliest traditions as well as valuable sources of information on daily life, history, religion, etc. in the preclassical world.

The translators of the various volumes in this series are specialists in the particular languages and have based their work on the original sources and the most recent research. In their translations they attempt to convey as much as possible of the original texts in a fluent, current English. In the introductions, notes, glossaries, maps, and chronological tables, they aim to provide the essential information for an appreciation of these ancient documents.

Covering the period from the invention of writing (by 3000 B.C.E.) down to the conquests of Alexander the Great (ca. 330 B.C.E.). the ancient Near East comprised northeast Africa and southwest Asia. The cultures represented within these limits include especially Egyptian, Sumerian, Babylonian, Assyrian, Hittite, Ugaritic, Aramean, Phoenician, and Israelite. It is hoped that Writings from the Ancient World will eventually produce translations of most of the many different genres attested in these cultures: letters—official and private, myths, diplomatic documents, hymns, law collections, monumental inscriptions, tales, and administrative records, to mention but a few.

The preparation of this volume was supported in part by a generous grant from the Division of Research Programs of the National Endowment for the Humanities. Significant funding has also been made available by the Society of Biblical Literature. In addition, those involved in preparing this volume have received financial and clerical assistance from their respective institutions. Were it not for these expressions of confidence in our work, the arduous tasks of preparation, translation, editing, and publication could not have been accomplished or even undertaken. It is the hope of all who have worked on these texts or supported this work that Writings from the Ancient World will open up new horizons and deepen the humanity of all who read these volumes.

Simon B. Parker
Boston University School of Theology

Chronological Table

Archaic Period: Dynasties 1-2	ca. 3100-2675 B.C.E.
Old Kingdom: Dynasties 3-8	ca. 2675-2130
Dynasty 3	ca. 2675-2625
Dynasty 4	ca. 2625-2500
Khafre	ca. 2555-2532
Dynasty 5	ca. 2500-2350
Dynasty 6	ca. 2350-2170
Dynasties 7/8	ca. 2170-2130
First Intermediate Period: Dynasties 9-10 and first half of Dynasty 11	ca. 2130-1980
Middle Kingdom: second half of Dynasty 11 and Dynasties 12-14	ca. 1980-1630
Dynasty 11 (second half)	ca. 1980-1938
Dynasty 12	ca. 1938-1759
Dynasty 13	ca. 1759-1630
Dynasty 14	ca. 1660-1630
Second Intermediate Period: Dynasties 15-17	ca. 1630-1523
New Kingdom: Dynasties 18-20	ca. 1539-1075
Dynasty 18	ca. 1539-1292
Ahmose	ca. 1539-1514

Amenhotep I	ca. 1514-1493
Thutmose I	ca. 1493-1483
Thutmose II	ca. 1483-1479
Thutmose III	ca. 1479-1425
Hatshepsut	ca. 1472-1458
Amenhotep II	ca. 1426-1400
Thutmose IV	ca. 1400-1390
Amenhotep III	ca. 1390-1353
Amenhotep IV/Akhenaten	ca. 1353-1336
Nefernefruaten	ca. 1336-1333
Smenkhkare	ca. 1333-1332
Tutankhamun	ca. 1332-1322
Ay	ca. 1322-1319
Horemheb	ca. 1319-1292
Dynasty 19	ca. 1292-1190
Ramesses I	ca. 1292-1290
Sety I	ca. 1290-1279
Ramesses II	ca. 1279-1213
Third Intermediate Period: Dynasties 21-25	ca. 1075-664
Late Period: Dynasties 26-30	664-332
Macedonian Period	332-305
Ptolemaic Period	305-30
Roman/Byzantine Period	30 B.C.E.-642 C.E.

List of Maps and Figures

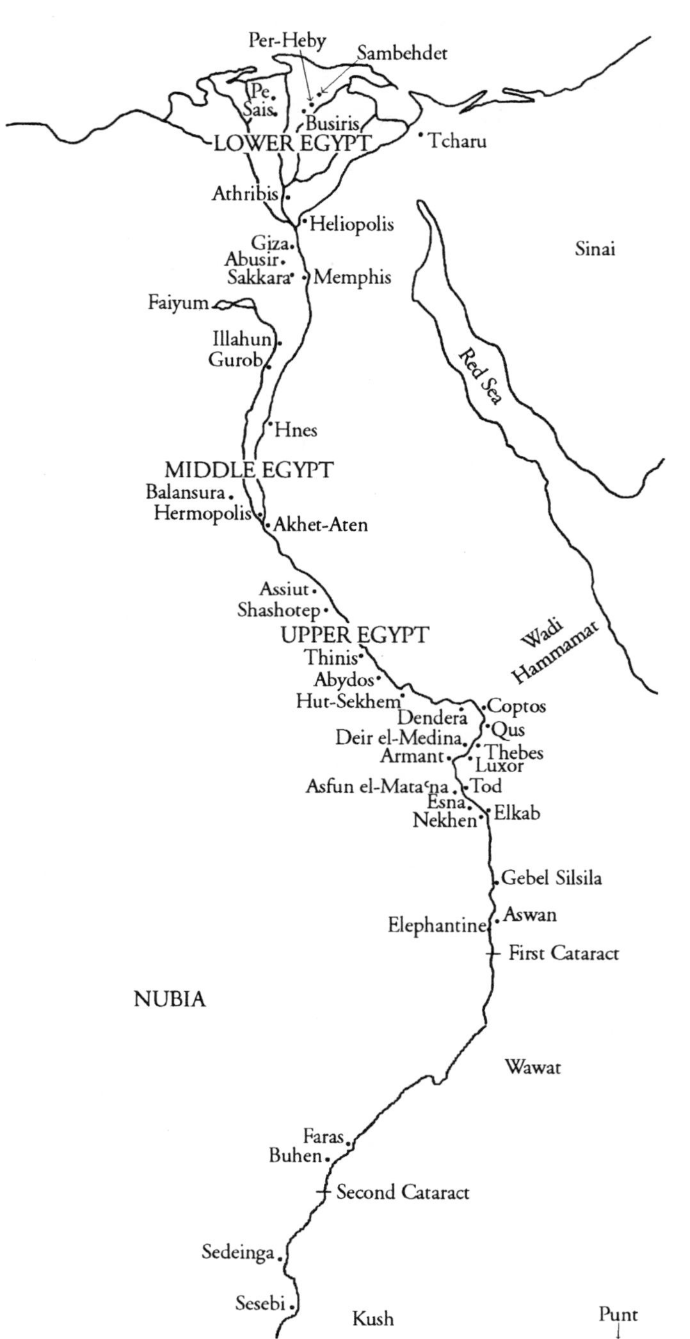
Per-Heby
Sambehdet
Pe
Sais
Busiris
LOWER EGYPT
Tcharu
Djahy
Fenkhu
Kharu
Naharin
Mitanni
Athribis
Heliopolis
Giza
Abusir
Sakkara
Memphis
Sinai
Faiyum
Illahun
Gurob
Red Sea
Hnes
MIDDLE EGYPT
Balansura
Hermopolis
Akhet-Aten
Assiut
Shashotep
UPPER EGYPT
Wadi
Hammamat
Thinis
Abydos
Hut-Sekhem
Coptos
Dendera
Qus
Deir el-Medina
Thebes
Armant
Luxor
Asfun el-Mataʿna
Tod
Esna
Elkab
Nekhen
Gebel Silsila
Aswan
Elephantine
First Cataract
NUBIA
Wawat
Faras
Buhen
Second Cataract
Sedeinga
Sesebi
Kush
Punt

Abbreviations

ÄA	*Ägyptologische Abhandlungen*
AAA	*Annals of Archaeology and Anthropology*
AJSL	*American Journal of Semitic Languages and Literatures*
AMAW	Abhandlungen der Wissenschaften und der Literatur in Mainz
AO	*Acta Orientalia*
AOAT	Alter Orient und Altes Testament
ASAE	*Annales du Service des Antiquités de l'Egypte*
BAe	Bibliotheca Aegyptiaca
BASOR	*Bulletin of the American Schools of Oriental Research*
BdE	Bibliothèque d'Etude (IFAO)
BES	*Bulletin of the Egyptological Seminar*
BIFAO	*Bulletin de l'Institut Français d'Archéologie Orientale*
BiOr	*Bibliotheca Orientalis*
BSEG	*Bulletin de la Societé Egyptologique de Genève*
BSFE	Bulletin de la Société Française d'Egyptologie
CdE	*Chronique d'Egypte*
CG	Catalogue Géneral (Cairo Museum)
DE	*Discussions in Egyptology*
DMOA	Documenta et Monumenta Orientis Antiquii
EES-ASE	Egypt Exploration Society Archaeological Survey of Egypt
EES-TTS	Egypt Exploration Society Theban Tomb Series
GM	*Göttinger Miszellen*
HÄB	Hildesheimer Ägyptologische Beiträge
IFAO	Institut Français d'Archéologie Orientale
JAOS	*Journal of the American Oriental Society*
JARCE	*Journal of the American Research Center in Egypt*
JEA	*Journal of Egyptian Archaeology*
JPK	*Jaarbuch Preussischer Kulturbesitz*

JSSEA	*Journal of the Society for the Study of Egyptian Antiquities*
LÄ	*Lexikon der Ägyptologie*
MÄS	Munchener Ägyptologische Studien
MDAIK	*Mitteilungen des Deutschen Archäologischen Instituts, Kairo*
MDOG	*Mitteilungen der Deutschen Orientgesellschaft*
MEES	Memoirs of the Egypt Exploration Society
MMAF	Mémoires publiées par les membres de la Mission Archéologique Française au Caire
NARCE	*Newsletter of the American Research Center in Egypt*
OIP	Oriental Institute Publications
OLA	*Orientalia Lovaniensa Analecta*
PSBA	*Proceedings of the Society of Biblical Archaeology*
RdE	*Révue d'Egyptologie*
RecTrav	*Recueil de Travaux rélatifs à la philologie et à l'archéologie égyptiennes*
SAK	*Studien zur Altägyptischen Kultur*
SAOC	Studies of Ancient Oriental Civilization
SASAE	Supplement aux Annales du Service des Antiquités de l'Egypte
SBAW	*Sitzungsberichte der Bayerischen Akademie der Wissenschaften, Phil-hist. Klasse*
SBL-WAW	Society of Biblical Literature Writings from the Ancient World
SDAIK	Sonderschrift des Deutschen Archäologischen Instituts
SSEA(P)	Publications of the Society for the Study of Egyptian Antiquities
TRSL	*Transactions of the Royal Society of Literature*
UGAÄ	Untersuchungen zur Geschichte und Altertumskunde Ägyptens
VAB	Vorderasiatische Bibliothek
WVDOG	Wissenschaftliche Veröffentlichungen der Deutschen Orientgesellschaft
ZÄS	*Zeitschrift fur Ägyptische Sprache*

Explanation of Signs

Single brackets [ ] enclose restorations.

Angle brackets < > enclose words or parts of words omitted in the original text.

Parentheses ( ) enclose additions to the English translation.

A row of dots . . . indicates gaps in the text or untranslatable words.

A question mark in parentheses (?) follows words or phrases of which the translation is doubtful.

CAPITAL LETTERS are used to indicate that the word or name is enclosed in the original text by a "cartouche," a name-ring which is normally reserved for royalty.

Underlined words are either duplicated in other selections or were added as replacements for material that was suppressed in the original text: the connotation in each case is indicated in the introduction to the item in question.

Italics in translations (when they are not clearly introductory explanations) indicate restorations or readings which are speculative but probable.

Introduction

In the middle of the fourteenth century B.C.E.[1] Egypt was suddenly wracked by a revolution led, incongruously, by its god-king. Against all precedent, most of the ancient gods were overthrown and their temples closed. In place of the traditional polytheism stood the cult of a single god in the sky, worshiped through and alongside his earthly children, the king and queen. Although this movement barely survived its prime mover, for sheer daring it is unique in ancient history. For nearly two decades a new order held sway in Egypt, as the king and his followers labored to supplant millennia of accumulated tradition. Little evidence for dissent survives from this period, but we can infer how unpopular the program was from the speed with which it was abandoned after its founder died. To make matters worse, its fortunes became entangled in a concurrent change in the balance of power between Egypt and its diplomatic partners in the Near East: for it was at this very time that the Hittites swept away the kingdom of Mitanni, a superpower which adjoined Egypt's empire and with which Egypt had worked out a *modus vivendi* barely three generations before. For the reverses that followed (which would eventually cost Egypt the provinces on its northern border) King Amenhotep IV—or, as he later preferred to call himself, Akhenaten—would receive the lion's share of blame.

The heretic continues to stir passions today. "I don't know why it is, but Akhenaton starts more arguments than any other person or thing in Egyptology. Kindly scholars who would never fight about religion or politics or personal matters get purple in the face over the activities of a man who has been dead for over three thousand years" (Peters 1968: 95). This wry assessment still holds true, for views on the heretic pharaoh are legion, and many of them are mutually exclusive. Akhenaten the monotheist (e.g., Hornung 1982: 244–50) still vies with Akhenaten the henotheist, the politician, and even the atheist (Redford 1984). The "good ruler who loves mankind"

(Aldred 1988: 303–6) emerges in other pages as a pathetic and even sinister figure—not a latter-day St. Francis of Assisi but a foreshadowing of the mad caliph el-Hakim (Ray 1985: 93). Akhenaten the family man seems now to have prevailed, after much controversy, over Akhenaten the homosexual (see Engelbach 1940; Harris 1973a–b, 1974a; Allen 1994a); but there is still enough in dispute to warrant the title of a recent review article, "Akhenaten versus Akhenaten" (Eaton-Krauss 1990). One paradoxical by-product of these debates is that the more sensational theories have been given an extended half-life by that camp follower of scholarship, popular culture: thus, the peculiar physique on display in most of the king's portraits, even though it is now given a theological significance (e.g., Aldred 1988: 231–36), still projects an ambiguous sexuality which haunts modern perceptions—from pulp fiction (Drury 1976) to an opera, in which the heretic's utterances are delivered in the fluting tones of a countertenor (Glass 1987). Given all these problems and the historical significance of the period in which they lie, it is hoped that readers will be in a better position to appreciate both by having within the covers of one book as much of the written evidence as seems pertinent.

The Setting

When Amenhotep IV became king (ca. 1353), Egypt was to all appearances basking in the glow of a golden age. From the divided kingdom of not three centuries earlier, hemmed in by Asiatic overlords—the Hyksos—and their Nubian allies to the south, had emerged a strong and independent nation-state. An effective central administration commanded the resources not only of Egypt but of countries that had previously lain beyond the borders of the "Two Lands." In the south, Egyptian power had expanded far beyond its previous boundary at the second cataract, pushing far beyond the fourth cataract and making these conquered territories into virtual extensions of Egypt. The ruling power might have to chastise disorderly elements on its fringe (see Nos. 55, 56), but Nubia as a whole was secure and, it would seem, not discontented under the pharaohs' governance. In an even greater break with the past, moreover, Egypt now ruled over a hegemonic empire in western Asia. City-states from Canaan to southern Syria acknowledged the pharaoh as their suzerain, paid tribute, and sent their children to Egypt when requested to do so—the girls as member of the royal *harim*, the boys as hostages who would be returned to their homes properly trained in loyalty to their overlord when their turn to rule came. Egypt's prominence was also acknowledged by the other superpowers of the Near East, the "great kings" of Mitanni (once a rival, but bound by ties of diplomatic marriage ever since the time of Amenhotep IV's grandfather, Thutmose IV) and Kassite Babylon. Two other countries that would later upset the balance of this "first internationalism," Assyria and Hatti, were not yet recovered from earlier setbacks. Other secondary and lesser powers were Alashiya (possibly Cyprus) and perhaps even the rulers of Troy and Mycenaean Greece.

The ideological foundation of the pharaoh's rule in Egypt was his relationship with the god of the dynasty's original homeland at Thebes. Amun, "the Hidden One," had risen to national prominence with the Theban dynasts who had reunified Egypt at the end of the First Intermediate Period (ca. 1980). During the Middle Kingdom his temple, the "House (=estate) of Amun," became the region's religious center, while the god's growing prestige was manifested by his absorption of powers associated with other deities: Amun assumed, for example, the ithyphallic form of Min, the fertility god of nearby Coptos; and he was also associated with the creative power of the sun-god, even acquiring a right to share in his name (as "Amun-Re"). Such extensions of Amun's divine personality, which were to become legion by the New Kingdom, expressed in religious terms the real power the god derived from his affiliation with the ruling house. As the deity most intimately associated with the Eighteenth Dynasty's national and imperial policies, Amun profited hugely. The most detailed of surviving records come, unfortunately, from the Twentieth Dynasty, two centuries after the period covered in this book. Even so, the growth of the "Estate of Amun" during the Eighteenth Dynasty, documented by a wealth of anecdotal evidence, is also reflected in the expansion of its Theban headquarters. The core of what survives of Amun's main temple at Karnak, as well as the adjoining precinct of his consort, Mut, and his "southern sanctuary" at Luxor, was built during the four generations that preceded the accession of Amenhotep IV. Moreover, the supemacy of "Amun-Re, King of the Gods" seems to have been more than rhetorical: Amun's high priest was designated "overseer of the priests of all the gods" in the generation before the outbreak of the heresy; and this precedence—if that was all it was—may even extend back for another five generations if a more regular title borne by earlier high priests, "overseer of priests of Upper and Lower Egypt," had a similar meaning (Lefebvre 1929: 228–43).

Recent research has now shown that the power of Amun in the age that preceded Amenhotep IV also reached deeply into the fundamentals of royal legitimacy. The king's divine nature, traditionally expressed by his identity with the falcon-god Horus and his status as the "Son of Re," came to include a subsidiary role as the "Son of Amun." This new identity, while it excluded none of the others, made Amun and the king interdependent in a very public way, for it was effected during the "Opet Festival," one of the great annual feasts of Thebes. The focal point of this celebration, for which Amun came down to the Luxor temple from his residence at Karnak, was a sacred marriage rite (No. 3): assuming the form of the pharaoh's earthly father,

Amun begat the king and his Ka (the divine component of kingship which carried Amun's identity) on the king's mother; and once the young king, reborn as the earthly manifestation of Amun, had been recognized by all the gods inside the temple, he was presented for public acclaim (Bell 1985a). The ritual thus affirmed the interconnection between the dynasty's mortal kings and the divine essence that took possession of them, neatly serving the joint purposes of political and divine legitimation. It was also flexible enough to allow the transition from one royal family to another: thus Horemheb, notoriously of common stock, could be revealed as nursing a secret identity as the eldest son of his hometown god; and once the Eighteenth Dynasty line was defunct and Ay, his immediate predecessor, had died without issue, Horemheb would be adopted by Amun during the Opet Festival (Nos. 106, 107-A). The fact remained, however, that the king in his ceremonially divine role was the image of his father, Amun. Abstractly, this might matter as little as it had historically with the ruler's more traditional role as the "Son of Re." When exploited by a powerful and perhaps overconfident clergy, however, the subordination implied by Amun's official paternity might well have grated on a sensibility, such as Amenhotep IV's, that had been nourished on the conventional rhetoric of kingship. This "royal myth," omnipresent to the point of banality in official pronouncements, stressed the ruler's power and his supremacy as god present on earth. Who could object, then, if the king chose to take these ideas and their implications more seriously than usual? By heightening the divinity already latent in kinship, the regime might not only enhance the pharaoh's prestige; it might also acquire a useful substitute for the image of the warrior king, which had served so well during the age of imperial conquest but was less convincing in a time of imperial maintenance. Akhenaten's father, Amenhotep III, seems already to have moved in this direction (Johnson 1990; cf. Kozloff, Bryan, and Berman 1992). His son would emulate him with a vengeance.

The Reign of Amenhotep IV

Shortly after the beginning of the new reign, Amenhotep IV dispatched an expedition to the sandstone quarry at Gebel Silsila. On the commemorative stela left at the site (No. 5) we see him, conventionally enough, adoring Amun-Re. But in the main text, once past the royal titulary, the king proceeds directly to the expedition's business, which is to obtain stone for a building dedicated not to Amun but to a manifestation of the sun-god. The terms that express this divinity's nature ("Re-Horakhty," "Shu," and "Aten") are conventional enough, but later monuments which began to spring up at Karnak and other places in Egypt reveal a new god with a distinct personality who is presented, against convention, in the manner of a king. Not only is his early name (abbreviated as HOR-ATEN throughout this book) a didactic statement of his nature—"The Living One, Re-Horus-of-the Double Horizon, who is exultantly active in the Horizon, in his name (=identity) which is 'Illumination (=*Shu*) which is from the Solar Orb'"—but it is arbitrarily divided into two parts, which are enclosed in the double name-ring traditionally used by the pharaohs. The Aten (to use the customary abbreviation) is thus presented as the heavenly coregent of his children on earth, the king and queen: official documents of the reign are dated by all three, with the Aten first (Nos. 37, 38, 66.6, 71.1). More will be said about the god's nature below; but the earliest representations show him with a human body and a falcon's head surmounted by a solar disk, which is utterly normal for Horakhty. This, in conjunction with the traditional elements in the early dicactic name, may have been meant to make the new cult more accessible to the orthodox (Assmann 1972); but soon—dates are uncertain—anthropomorphism was abandoned. Instead, the god appears, with seeming literalness, simply as the solar disk, with sunbeams streaming down upon creation, caressing it with little hands and extending life and dominion to the royal figures in the scenes (see figs. 3–5, 7–9).

Amenhotep IV's activities would emerge more clearly as a continuation of his father's policies if he could be shown to have been his father's coregent for any length of time. The matter has been much debated: proponents of a significant coregency have argued for a period of between ten and eleven years (Kitchen 1962; Aldred 1988: 169–94; Johnson 1990), with opponents urging either a very short overlap between the two reigns—two years at most—or none at all (e.g., Redford 1967: 88–169; Murnane 1977: 123ff., 230ff.; Romano 1990). While the weight of recent scholarship has tended toward skepticism (see Eaton-Krauss 1990: 544–55), much of the evidence is so ambiguous that the issue is still far from closed (see No. 35-B).

Study of Amenhotep IV's early reign has been made easier by the discovery of blocks from his Theban temples, which were dismantled after his death and built into later structures at Karnak (Nos. 6–12). While only a fraction of this material has yet been processed, it sheds valuable light on the king's ideas and his *modus operandi* at this point in his reign. One notable feature that is already apparent is the king's personal control over the Aten cult: human servitors the god has in abundance, but even the highest in rank is not described as "high priest" (No. 10-F.1). Rather, it is the king himself who acts in this capacity (No. 12-A; cf. 10-H) while his own divinity is served by a "high priest" (No. 11). His contempt for the old gods is also expressed bluntly (No. 7): needing man-made images, as they do, they are insignificant compared to the one god whose uncreated image is in the sky, "who constructed himself with his own two hands, no craft knowing him" (No. 37.4). Tangible proof of their subservience was now to be imposed on them, as all Egypt, including its temples, was taxed on behalf of the new cult (No. 6). With all due reservations owing to the fragmentary nature of this document in its present semipublished state, the amounts appear to be modest—but even token donations carry with them a symbolic humiliation. Moreover, such paltry gifts could not have supported even the temples at Thebes: surely there were other, more significant diversions of revenue that promoted the king's new cult at the expense of older establishments.

Even in such a diminished state, however, the old gods continued to be recognized and worshiped. Their names were still associated with the king's (No. 18); and although the Amun temple at Karnak might be in direct competition with the Aten temples built nearby, the high priest of Amun was sending an expedition into the quarries of the Wadi Hammamat as late as the fourth year of reign (No. 35-A). Did the rival cults ignore one another? Does continued royal sponsorship of the old temples imply some role for their gods in the new order? An answer is suggested by a hymn, found in a private tomb at Thebes (No. 30-B), which is put into the mouth of Amenhotep IV himself. This curious composition, arranged in the form of a crossword, is addressed to Re-Horakhty (when read vertically) and to Amun (horizontally). Since Amun emerges in both of the resulting texts as one among many possible manifestations of the sun-god (to whom the scene is dedicated in the first instance), it seems most likely that it was this supernumerary role that characterized in principle the old gods' relationship to the Aten. If so, the gist of Amenhotep IV's new dispensation would be a drift not toward monotheism but rather toward a revised hierarchical polytheism, a henotheism with the parts ruthlessly subordinated to the greater whole. This would explain not only Amenhotep IV's continued support for the old cults but the Aten's ability to do without a cult center of his own until the fifth year of the reign—for the sun, which rose over the full length and breadth of creation, had the whole world, "all that Aten encompasses," as his domain. Thus, even at Thebes there could be a "horizon of Aten" (*Akhet-en-Aten*; see Nos. 34-A, 53). We can only speculate as to how this reordering of the religious hierarchy came undone; but early in his fifth year, the king speaks of being violently offended by things that were "worse than those I heard in regnal year 4," or any earlier year of his reign, worse than anything heard by his predecessors, "worse [than] those heard by any kings who had (ever) assumed the White Crown" (No. 37.4). Had the orthodox clergies finally thrown down the gauntlet and declined any further cooperation in the new order? Whatever it was that happened, the king's response was swift. By the time, also early in year 5, that the steward of Memphis submitted his customary report on the condition of the local gods (No. 22), the rift was already past healing: the king was on his way to el-Amarna, and to a new phase of a career that would end by making him "the enemy of Akhet-Aten."

The Reign of Akhenaten

At el-Amarna the hills that hug the eastern edge of the river in this part of Middle Egypt suddenly pull back to form a bay which extends for about 5 km. into the desert at its widest point. Apart from the track that led to the limestone quarry at Hatnub, to the southeast, this desolate expanse had lain unused throughout earlier ages. But this neglect now recommended it to the king, who had just repudiated his orthodox personal name and was now calling himself Akhenaten—meaning either "One Effective on behalf of Aten" or "Illuminated Manifestation of Aten" (see Bilolo 1984). A site such as this, which "belonged to no god, nor to a goddess," nor to any previous ruler, and which was devoid of all previous habitation, could be appropriated for the Aten without embarrassing counterclaims from any of the old divinities. More than that, it could be represented as the place where the sun-god had first become manifest—a spot hitherto undiscovered, until the king had been led to it by the Aten himself (No. 37.2). This was the definitive "Horizon of Aten" (*Akhet-Aten*). Not only would it be the Aten's personal domain, never to be moved to another place; the city that was built here posthaste became the royal residence of choice, the virtual seat of government and (as one final snub directed toward the "City of Amun" at Thebes) the new royal cemetery, to which the king and members of his family would be returned should they die anywhere else in Egypt (No. 37.4).

The city of Akhenaten at el-Amarna, with its ruined buildings and tombs, provides indispensable, if erratic, insights into the heresy in its ascendancy and decline. Events outside the Aten's capital are only dimly reflected. A Nubian war fought in year 12 or 13 (Nos. 55–56), for example, is known only from records found far from the new capital. Similarly, the triumphalism of the "parade of foreign tribute" held at Akhet-Aten in year 12 (Nos. 66.6; 71.1) must be evaluated in light of the volatile conditions revealed by diplomatic archives found at the site (the cuneiform tablets known as the "Amarna Letters"; see Moran 1992). What we know of Egyptian imperialism, while detailed in some respects (e.g., Kemp 1978; Frandsen 1979; Redford 1992: 125–237), is constantly being modified in the light of new discoveries. While it has been long known, for example, that important positions in Egypt's "government of conquests" were held by foreigners, only recently have we learned that this functional cosmopolitanism even allowed a western Asiatic to serve as vizier—one of the prime ministers of Egypt—under Amenhotep III and, apparently, also his son (Zivie 1990). The spottiness of available data still makes it difficult to generalize about such phenomena or to discuss imperial government in much depth. Even so, events in Asia during this period as they are now understood suggest a picture that is less alarming than what contemporary rhetoric and past scholarship have implied. Recent study has exploded the earlier image of an Egypt too paralyzed by religious turmoil to respond to events that affected its interests in western Asia (e.g., Schulman 1964). Even so, the challenges raised by the Hittites' destruction of Egypt's partner, Mitanni, came at an inopportune time; and the eventual outcome, not a happy one for the Egyptians (Murnane 1990), provided a convenient stick with which to beat the heresy and its advocates (see No. 99).

Readers of this book will observe that discussion of the religious revolution is monopolized by the king and his followers: all publicly recorded dissent comes from the years following Akhenaten's death (Nos. 94, 99, 109, 110). While this is no surprise in such an authoritarian setting, it leaves us unable to gauge the nature and extent of the opposition, passive or overt, which the heresy must have encountered. The reality of such dissent can be seen, however, in the persecution of the old gods. With very few exceptions—such as the primeval sun-god Re, the creator Atum, and (more surprisingly) Thoth, the ibis-headed scribe of the orthodox divinities—the gods' figures and their names were hacked off tomb and temple walls. Common terms, moreover, were often purged of hieroglyphs associated with the old divinities (such as the goddess Maʿat, "justice," or the vulture of Mut, used in writing the word "mother") and spelled phonetically. Even the "Amen-" in the personal name of Akhenaten's father was excised, and the entire nomen was sometimes replaced by a reiteration of Amenhotep III's throne name, "Nebmaʿatre." This persecution probably broke out some time after the move to el-Amarna, since passages in the "Earlier Proclamation" (No. 37.2, 4) speak of gods and goddesses as holders of legal rights alongside the Aten. Perhaps it accompanied the adoption of a new didactic name for the god in Akhenaten's ninth year: "The Living One, Sun-Ruler of the double Horizon, who is exultantly active in the Horizon, in his name (=identity) which is 'Light which comes from the Solar Disk.'" (See Bongioanni 1983–4; Allen 1989: 93. This later didactic name is abbreviated as HEKA-ATEN throughout this book.) Notable in the new name is its retreat from the conventional imagery used in the older formulation: neutral terms for the sun's supremacy and his essence as light replace the familiar concepts "Re-Horakhty" and "Shu" used previously. It is hard to dissociate this purge from the persecution of the old gods that was taking place around the same time, or to avoid seeing in it an acknowledgment, even if an unwitting one, that the heresy's earlier attempts to reach a wider audience had failed (see Assmann 1972). From this point on, the Aten cult was the exclusive property of its true believers.

Both royal and private monuments from the Amarna period make much of the "holy family"—usually Akhenaten, Nefertiti, and their children, occasionally joined by queen-mother Tiyi, the deceased Amenhotep III, and other relations. Family scenes on private cult stelae, set up in the garden chapels of officials' villas at Akhet-Aten, are particularly relaxed and intimate (see No. 40); but the function these icons served in private worship suggests that such vignettes existed not merely to charm but to teach. As noted above, the Aten is viewed as the heavenly coregent of his children, Akhenaten and Nefertiti, but the orthodox conception of divine rule, in which kings and queens are children and/or embodiments of all their divine fathers and mothers, the gods (cf. No. 3), is superseded here by something older. Akhenaten and Nefertiti are explicitly compared with the first couple, Shu and Tefnut, whom the primeval god Atum begot in the first stages of creation (see No. 61-B.1 and fig. 3). In Akhenaten's religion, however, the Aten does not exist beside all the other gods who represent different aspects of creation and maintenance in the universe: all these functions are present within himself, enabling him to keep the world in existence as he (re)creates himself constantly every day (Assmann 1975; 1989: 66–68). His childen are his living images on earth—conventional enough in principle, but carried to an extreme when the king is represented not merely as Shu but even on occasion with the indeterminate sexuality of his progenitor, the "undifferentiated totality" (*Atum*) of the primordial creator (Aldred 1988: monochrome illustrations 33–35; cf. Hornung 1971a). Nefertiti's status in this primeval triad receives less attention, but she is not only her husband's female counterpart (Wilson 1973) but fully his equal in the presence of the Aten (see Redford 1984: 76–82). By virtue of their divine natures, then, both king and queen are able to display on earth the life-giving attributes that are also hallmarks of their father's continuing activity in the universe: hence those exuberant scenes on the cult stelae!

Under this placid facade, with its constant round of royal progresses and court life, however, all was not well with the "holy family." Nefertiti, the chief queen, apparently produced no sons; and of her six daughters, only two went on to prominence as adults. The family is last seen intact in year 12, at the "parade of foreign tribute." Sometime after this, Meketaten, the royal couple's second daughter, died and was duly buried in her parents' tomb, perhaps after giving birth to a child (No. 46-B, Room Gamma). Evidence for the burial of one of her younger sisters, Nefernefrure, has recently come to light in one of the other tombs nearby (No. 46-E.4). Moreover, tension between Nefertiti's daughters and Akhenaten's other consort, "the wife and greatly beloved" Kiya—perhaps to be identified as Tadukhepa, daughter of the Mitannian king Tushratta (Helck 1984: 159–60)—precipitated an attack against Kiya's memory and that of her daughter (see No. 45). Was Kiya's crime that she had trumped her competition by producing what the "King's Chief Wife Nefertiti" could not, a male heir (Harris 1974b)? If so, she may be the other royal lady buried in the annex of Akhenaten's tomb at el-Amarna (No. 46-B, Room Alpha)—but this identification remains unproved, along with the parentage of "the king's bodily son, his beloved, Tutankhuaten" (No. 98-A) and his probable brother, the ephemeral king

Smenkhkare. Through all of this, the only continuity, and the life and soul of the heresy, was Akhenaten himself. The manner of his death, like so much else about him, is unknown; but he died no later than his seventeenth year on the throne (No. 93-B; cf. Fairman 1960), leaving his successors to cope with a divided nation and a troubled empire.

The Aftermath

The succession to Akhenaten is no less controversial than the man himself. Smenkhkare, who married the eldest princess, Meritaten, has long been regarded as having followed the heretic onto the throne (e.g., Newberry 1928; Redford 1967: 170–82)—but it is now widely agreed (although see Tawfik 1975; 1981) that the monuments formerly attributed to one king actually belong to two: one with the throne name Ankh-kheprure and the personal name Smenkhkare, and the other called Ankh-kheprure beloved of Akhenaten (or similar) with the personal name Nefernefruaten. Moreover, this King Nefernefruaten might well be female: the throne name has an intrusive feminine ending that turns up too frequently to be accidental; and Nefernefruaten is part of the longer name used by Queen Nefertiti. While an ingenious case has been made for identifying King Nefernefruaten with Princess Meritaten (Krauss 1978), most scholars believe it was her mother who was raised to the kingship (Harris 1973a–b; 1974a; Samson 1978; Allen, 1994a): if so, her change in status was indicated by epithets such as "The Ruler" (No. 93-C), and her daughter Meritaten may have served in the titular role of "king's wife" (No. 92). Whoever King Nefernefruaten was, however, he/she wasted no time in beginning a reconciliation with the deposed gods: by the third year of the reign Amun was being worshiped not only by his votaries at Thebes but in one of the ruler's temples (No. 94). Smenkhkare's reign is even more obscure: his presence is well documented at el-Amarna, but little is known apart from his marriage to Meritaten (No. 95). The secondary royal burial in Tomb 55 in the Valley of the Kings, using a coffin (No. 96-B) and canopic jars that had originally been made for Kiya (Hanke 1978: 171–74; Krauss 1986), might still be attributed to Smenkhkare (most recently Allen 1988). But many questions still remain regarding the identity of the mummy and its ill-matched burial equipment (Wente and Harris 1992: 12–16).

By the time Smenkhkare's successor had ascended the throne, the supporters of orthodoxy had become strong enough to press not merely for an adjustment of the crown's religious policy but for its complete reversal. In the most visible repudiation of the Atenist "rebellion," young King Tutankhaten and his queen, Akhenaten's third daughter, Ankhesenpaaten, were obliged to change their names, becoming "Tutankhamun" and "Ankhesenamun." The city of Akhet-Aten was not abandoned—indeed, parts of it were still quite active (Kemp 1987)—but it ceased being a royal residence before the end of the king's second regnal year (Eaton-Krauss 1985: col. 812 with n. 7). Orthodox cults were restored throughout Egypt, accompanied by the first repairs to the ravaged temples. Even the power of Amun was restored, at least publicly, in all its overweening glory: on the copy of the restoration inscription he set up at Karnak (No. 99), Tutankhamun went out of his way to describe how he sustained Amun's prestige even above that of the greatest of Egypt's other gods, Ptah of Memphis. Not satisfied with reversing Akhenaten's revolution, the forces of orthodoxy now had it in full retreat.

The return of Egypt's old gods was not enough, however, to restore tranquillity. After Akhenaten died, a succession crisis had been averted, perhaps narrowly—for despite the prince's title borne by Tutankhamun (No. 98-A), his royal lineage is still unclear (Wente and Harris 1992: 13–16). The young king seems to have been thoroughly in the shadow of his principal advisers, among them the "God's Father Ay" (Nos. 58, 100-I) and also Horemheb, the commander-in-chief of Egypt's armies (No. 105). It was the latter whose preeminence seemed to mark him as the most likely successor to Tutankhamun, should the king die without an heir (Van Dijk 1993; cf. Martin 1989b). Both of these expectations would be fulfilled, but in a roundabout fashion. When Tutankhamun died (ca. 1322) the army and, most probably, its commander were engaged in western Asia, where the situation was taking a turn for the worse. The Hittites, exasperated by continued resistance from areas that had not submitted when they had overthrown Mitanni, and also by Egypt's repeated efforts to get back the territory it had lost, were consolidating their hold over northern Syria even as the pharaoh's death was creating a political vacuum in Egypt (Bryce 1990). In Horemheb's absence, the coincidence of these two crises permitted a bold initiative. Perhaps at the direction of Ay, Queen Ankhesenamun wrote to the Hittite king, Shuppiluliuma I, offering to wed one of his sons in exchange for peace. The marriage alliance between Egypt and its neighboring superpower would thus be renewed; but instead of an Asiatic princess taking an honored place in the pharaoh's *ḫarim*, a Hittite prince would now rule in the Nile Valley alongside the Egyptian queen. These plans, which so neatly dashed Horemheb's ambitions while they resolved Egypt's other dilemmas, only succeeded in provoking open war between Egypt and Hatti. The Hittite prince died (murdered, his father believed) while in Egyptian hands, and it would take another three generations for the two powers to normalize their relations (Murnane 1990). Even so, the crisis had allowed Ay to take the throne (Nos. 102–4), and Horemheb was relegated to the sidelines (Van Dijk 1993: 58–63) until his rival's death at last permitted him to become king.

Horemheb's accession marks the end of the Amarna period. In later records, which omit Akhenaten and his four successors, it is Horemheb's name which follows that of Amenhotep III in the officially recognized sequence of kings. The extent of this *damnatio memoriae* no doubt reflects Horemheb's personal animus against Tutankhamun and Ay more than any orthodox rage at their previous connections with Akhenaten. Although Horemheb stopped short of vandalizing the tomb of the official restorer of orthodoxy, Tutankhamun, neither the royal tomb of Ay nor the public monuments of Ankhesenamun were treated with any such restraint. Moreover, Horemheb usurped, and in some cases recarved, original inscriptions and restorations made under Tutankhamun and Ay, as if to take for himself all credit for the return to orthodoxy that had begun during their reigns. It was also under Horemheb that the Aten temples at Thebes were dismantled and their blocks recycled into the monuments that the king was building at Karnak (Redford 1984: 227–31). There is, however, a faint possibility that this display of zeal was more a gesture toward Amun's outraged votaries at Thebes than a heartfelt rejection of Akhenaten and his god. The case rests on two fragmentary stone pieces found inside the Great Temple of the Aten and dedicated by Horemheb as king (No. 107-B). While it is possible that they belong with a partial reoccupation of the site contemporary with Ramesses III (Peet and Woolley 1923: 128–29, 160), evidence for this later phase of the city's history occurs at the northern edge of the site, near the river, rather than in the central city, where the two fragments of Horemheb were found. Assuming that Horemheb did make these dedications at el-Amarna, perhaps he did so not to Akhenaten's god, but to the "sanitized" concept of the disk as the physical image of the orthodox sun-god, which appears not infrequently in his inscriptions (see 105-B, C; 108). In any case, this tenuous extension of royal favor could not save Akhet-Aten when hostility to what it represented deepened early in Dynasty XIX. Under Ramesses II, the site was pillaged–its buildings dismantled for stone that was transported elsewhere for current building projects–and Akhenaten himself became "the enemy of Akhet-Aten," the instigator of a "rebellion" that was consigned to the oblivion which, in Egyptian terms, was the ultimate damnation (Nos. 109–10, and cf.111).

Controversies and Reputation

Very little in the voluminous records from the period of Akhenaten's heresy sheds light on the man himself. Too much depends on the context in which diagnostic behaviors occur, and too many of those contexts are either ambiguous (e.g., relating to policy in western Asia) or are shaped by ideological agendas (such as the "human, all too human" poses of the royal family on private and even official monuments). As a result, the individual remains hidden behind the carefully crafted persona. Reactions to Akhenaten are thus most commonly reactions to the ways in which observers perceive his purposes and beliefs. Results are inevitably subjective (at least to some extent) and occasionally tendentious. While an extended survey of opinions and "aberrations about Akhenaten" is beyond the scope of this introduction, the reader may find useful the highlighting of a few main issues, which is attempted here.

Part of the debate regarding Akhenaten's revolution focuses on its ostensible purpose. Was it mainly political, an effort to remove competitors who stood between the king and his subjects, and to restore to him the uncontested status of a living god, which he had held during the Old Kingdom? Or was there a genuine spirituality in what Akhenaten preached? Related to this issue is the question of what Akhenaten believed. His new religion, in its mature form, was certainly different from the henotheism that preceded it (Assmann 1989), with its multitude of gods functioning both as individual receivers of worship and as parts of a greater divine whole. The concept which replaces this, of a unique and solitary god who is manifest in the sky as the sun's disk, appears monotheistic by contrast and has often been treated as such (e.g., Hornung 1982: 244–50; Aldred 1988: 237–48). Yet parts of the older conceptions appear to survive: for example, in the cult of the Mnevis Bull, the earthly embodiment of the Heliopolitan sun-god, which was carried to Akhet-Aten (No. 37.4); and more pervasively, in the divine king and queen, whom their subjects adore as the sky-god's children and who assume to themselves some of the functions of the old gods. Thus, at the corners of Akhenaten's sarcophagus (No. 46-D) appear figures of Nefertiti, whose outstretched arms evoke the wings of the four goddesses who traditionally protect the remains inside, and who here usurps their roles (Wilson 1973: 239; and cf. Eaton-Krauss 1990: 550, n. 66).

Yet even if there is much in the new religion to suggest an austere and pared-down version of the old henotheism, the degree to which the cult focuses on the king has raised questions about its sincerity. The very image of the Aten as a sun-disk, relegated to the tops of scenes in a way that directs attention to the royal figures below, has suggested that for Akhenaten it was merely "the hypostasis of divine kingship, a pale reflection of his own, projected heavenwards" (Redford 1984: 178). In consequence, "what Akhenaten championed was in the truest sense of the word, atheism" (ibid., p. 234). If this is true, then there is nothing in Akhenaten's new order beyond "the absolutism of the disk" (ibid., p. 175), that is, the coercive power of the god-king himself. On the other hand, a less manipulative view of the god's role vis-à-vis the king might be suggested by Akhenaten's rejection of the conventional royal epithet "Good God" midway through his reign, and substitution of "good ruler" (see Eaton-Krauss 1990: 550 with n. 65). This might well indicate an emphasis on the primacy of the sky-god, from whom the king, his son, derived his power. Moreover, the Aten's apparent assimilation of the king's personal qualities seen in the early anthropomorphic images of the god (Redford 1984: 65 [fig. 4.6] and 173) might imply less the submerging of the god into the king than its reverse—that is, the king's sharing of his father's nature, an idea already present before the Amarna period (e.g., Bell 1985b), which adapted itself without strain to the new religion.

A more recent case for Akhenaten's "atheism" springs from the Aten's identity with the fundamental creative forces in nature, which suggests that he was characterized less as a god, conventionally understood, than as a natural principle (Allen 1989). If Akhenaten's alleged monotheism can be characterized with a paraphrase from Islam ("There is no god but Aten, and Akhenaten is his prophet"), then "the true message of Akhenaten's teaching is even more radical" than this, being "there is no natural principle but light, and no god but Akhenaten." If so, however, how did Akhenaten expect the Egyptian public to understand a higher being (the Aten) whose son was their god (the king) but which itself was not understood as divine? The introduction of a concept so new and baffling would seem to be counterproductive, especially given Akhenaten's attempt to encompass traditional concerns (particularly, the all-important relationship of god and king) in his new theology. Moreover, not only is the Aten specifically referred to as a god (Egyptian *nṯr*) in contemporary religious texts; there are also spellings (rare but nonetheless repeated) of the name "Aten" which include the hieroglyph of a seated god—that is, the conventional spelling of a god's name. Clearly, much remains to be said about the nature of Akhenaten's god. It is hoped that these comments, along with the translations in this book, will help readers make up their own minds.

Finally, what was the place of private individuals in the Aten cult? It has been rightly said that the new religion offered rather less than its orthodox competition (e.g., Aldred 1988: 245–48; cf. Redford 1984: 176)—certainly nothing like the divine destiny which awaited the deceased when they took on the identity of Osiris, king of the underworld, or joined the sun-god in his daily round. What Aten worshipers of el-Amarna found in the next world was, to a great extent, a reflection of their lives on earth. Just as they had dwelled in Akhet-Aten when they were alive, so did their Ba-spirits continue to reside in their tombs (Nos. 58-B.8; 66.12). At dawn they rose out of their burial chambers to behold the sunrise at the doors of their tombs (No. 87-D); and through the Aten's rays they cast off the torpor of death (Nos. 70.8; 89.2). Continuing to serve the king within their mortuary chapels (see fig. 9 [=No. 77-B.1] and 58-B.3), they received their rewards by sharing in the offerings he made at the temple of the Aten (e.g., 58-B.8; 70.4-C). Otherwise, although the familiar gods of the next world played no part in the Atenist hereafter, what the deceased could expect was ordinary enough. Funerary rites continued to stress the care and feeding of individuals within their tombs (see fig 6; and cf. 66.12–15), and the dead also received regular offerings at the New Year and the regular monthly feasts (Nos. 62; 87-C). The deceased also enjoyed their usual freedom of movement, along with the ability to return to the places they had enjoyed in life (e.g., No. 80.3). The underworld is mentioned (e.g., No. 70.4-C), but so infrequently that one cannot tell whether it was a normal part of the deceased's environment or merely a survival from earlier modes of expression. In any case, it plays a minor role in the Atenist universe. Survival in the next life depended on a "righteousness" (*ma'at*), which is indistinguishable from loyalty to the king (No. 89.7; and cf. Assmann 1980) as damnation in the hereafter followed rebellion gainst the king (No. 85.11). The central paradox of Akhenaten's religion—the appealing naturalness in an authoritarian setting—persists, for all eternity.

The Translations

In selecting items to be included in this volume it has been my aim to be "intelligently complete." That is, I have not felt obliged to translate every scrap that has come down from the Amarna period, but I have tried to include whatever seemed pertinent to the historical, social, and religious issues of that time, along with a reasonable selection of documents illustrating the period's antecedents and its aftermath. Most of this material comes from public monuments commissioned by royalty and private individuals. The latter are mostly represented by inscriptions on votive statuary (Nos. 4, 20, 21, 105-B) and from their houses and tomb chapels (Nos. 23–34, 58–90), although there are a few letters (Nos. 19, 22) and graffiti (Nos. 13, 35, 63-A, 94) as well. Royal texts are more varied but less well preserved than those that come from private venues, often because of the deliberate breaking up of the monuments of Akhenaten and his successors. Formal inscriptions abound on statues and ritual objects, or in temples or tombs (Nos. 1, 3, 7–12, 15, 41-B, 42–54, 92, 93-A, 95-A, 96, 97–99, 100 A-F, 101A-C, 102, 103 A-B, 104-A, 106–107). For all their numbers, however, such texts (whether royal or private) are highly stylized as a rule; although they sometimes record specific events they are more usually concerned with what is generally or typically true rather than with "history"; and this makes them most useful in defining the religious or ideological framework in which events were seen to occur. More detailed records, which preserve or reflect official decrees (Nos. 5–6, 37–39, 99, 108) or commemorate wars and other outstanding events (Nos. 55–56, 106) are less frequent. In the absence of extensively preserved archives, however, informal dockets on supply jars and other objects can be valuable sources of information about dates, events, personalities, and institutions. The scattering of such useful data among otherwise humdrum minutiae has guided the selection of such material included here (Nos. 17, 47, 93-B, 95-B, 101-D).

I have deliberately excluded from this volume repetitions of the most stereotyped material, as well as items that have been translated elsewhere in this series (i.e., Wente 1990: 94–96 [Nos. 123–27]). I have also left out items of doubtful authenticity, such as the "Aten scarab" attributed to Thutmose IV (Bryan 1991: 354–56), as well as the allusion—probably forged—to a campaign against Carchemish in Horemheb's sixteenth regnal year (Redford 1973; cf. Yoyotte 1981: 44). Later traditions that may preserve authentic materials in garbled form—such as the tale of King Amenophis and "Paapis' son" in Josephus's version of Manetho (Waddell 1940: 121–25; cf. Murnane 1991: 58–59 with n. 43), together with even more speculative possibilities (e.g., Meltzer 1989)—are too uncertain to be of much use, and they have been excluded also.

Among the scholars who have contributed to the making of this volume, it is a pleasure to acknowledge Edward F. Wente for suggesting that I undertake it, as well as Burke O. Long and Simon B. Parker, both patient and supportive series editors. I am also grateful to Edmund S. Meltzer, who made many helpful suggestions from his post halfway across the world, in Manchuria; and I am especially indebted to James P. Allen, whose acuity helped save me from many a slip: any peculiarities that remain are due to my own oversight and/or stubbornness. I would also like to acknowledge the Marcus Orr Center for the Humanities (University of Memphis) for providing me with a fellowship which allowed me to begin working on this project in earnest; and I am grateful to Rolf Krauss, James Romano, and E. F. Wente for sundry suggestions which I hope they will find put to good use in the pages that follow. Finally, for assistance with the manuscript above and beyond the call of any duty, I am very grateful to Annette Webb Lane.

Notes

1. All dates that are not in bibliographical references are before the common era, unless otherwise indicated.

Translations

1

The Prelude to the Amarna Age

1. Statue of Amenhotep III as a Sacred Image

This life-size figure of the king was discovered in 1989, along with a number of other sculptures, buried in a pit at the west side of the "sun court" which Amenhotep III built in front of his temple at Luxor. Now in the Luxor Museum, the statue represents the king as Atum, wearing the double crown and standing upon a sledge of the type used to drag sacred images in procession. The vandalism that this piece suffered at the hands of the Atenists is apparent in the erasures (never repaired) of the names of Amun, both inside the nomen of Amenhotep III and in references to the god himself. The interest of this monument as a precursor of the Amarna period lies in the king's description of himself in association with the solar disk ("Aten") even while professing loyalty to the Theban gods.

Base, Right: Long live the Good God in true fact, the sovereign, ruler of the Nine Bows, king of the Black Land, ruler of the Red Land, who knots together the laws and sets the Two Shores in order; the King of Upper and Lower Egypt, NEBMAATRE, the Son of Re, AMENHOTEP III, given life and dominion.

Base, Left: Long live the Good God, possessor of joy, Lord of Crowns who takes possession of the White Crown and makes many the monuments in the house of his father Amun, who created his beauty; the King of Upper and Lower Egypt, NEBMAATRE, the Son of Re, AMENHOTEP III, given life like Re forever.

Back Pillar: at the rounded top, corresponding to the lunette of a stela, Amenhotep III kneels on the left, with a broad fan at his back giving him the protection of all life behind him. *The king offers a bouquet to the god enthroned on the right side:* Amun, Lord of the Thrones of the Two Lands, ruler of Thebes, as he gives all life and all health. *Below this scene there are four columns of text:*

Re-Harakhty, Mighty Bull who appears in Maat, Good God in true fact, the sovereign, ruler of the Nine Bows, dazzling Aten for all lands, whose sacred cobra has illuminated the Two Shores; functional king, perfect in monuments, master of laws, who sets the Two Shores in order, being one who makes functional the mansions of the gods and makes festive their temples; one who is great in holy and august monuments– never has the like been done! (He is) a king who is watchful toward the one who fashioned him, who does what pleases his Ka– (namely), Amun-Re, Lord of the Thrones of the Two Lands: he is the one who created his beauty, (namely, that of) the King of Upper and Lower Egypt, NEBMAATRE, who is serviceably disposed toward the one who fashioned him, (i.e.) Amun-Re, the one who distinguished him from among millions and decreed valor and victory for him; the Son of Re, AMENHOTEP III, lord of every foreign land–one who acts loyally toward the gods of Thebes,[1] who supplies their offerings. The king, the master of joy, Lord of the Two Lands, NEBMAATRE, the Son of Re, his beloved, AMENHOTEP III, foremost of all living Kas, shall continually be manifest on the throne of his father, Amun-Re, Lord of the Thrones of the Two Lands, his heart joyful as he governs the Two Lands like Re forever continually.

2. Other References to the Aten from the Reign of Amenhotep III

A. The "Lake" Commemorative Scarab

Regnal year 11, third month of the Inundation season, day 1 under the Person of the Horus, "Mighty Bull who appears in Maat"; Two Ladies "Who Establishes Laws and Pacifies the Two Lands"; Golden Horus "Whose Valor is Great, Smiter of Asiatics"; King of Upper and Lower Egypt NEBMAATRE; the Son of Re, AMENHOTEP III, given life; (and) the King's Chief Wife TIYI, may she live. His Person commanded the making of a lake for the King's Chief Wife TIYI–may she live–in her town (called) Djarukha. Its length is 3,700 cubits and its width 700 cubits. His Person celebrated the festival of "Opening the Lakes" in the third month of Inundation, day 16, just as his Person was rowed within it in the royal barge (called) "Aten is Dazzling."

B. Statuette of the Standard-Bearer Kamose

A "boon which the king gives" of Min of Coptos and Isis, mother of the god, that they may give mortuary offerings of bread, beer, oxen, fowl, alabaster, incense, oil, and every good and pure thing on which a god lives and which are received at Min's Progress. For the Ka of the king's follower on water, on land, and on every foreign country, the standard-bearer of the company of "NEBMAATRE, the Dazzling Aten," Kamose.

Made by the (royal) companion, great of love, royal courier upon the foreign country; the seal-bearer of the King of Lower Egypt, the great one in the palace, May, whom the housewife Takhat bore.

On the back pillar: The standard-bearer of the company of "NEBMAATRE, the Dazzling Aten" (*or* "Re") Kamose. Made by the troop captain May.

C. Canopic Jars of Court Ladies

A number of the individuals for whom these objects were made claim affiliation with an institution that is called, in its fullest designation, The House of Dazzling Aten the Great.

D. Tomb of Nefersekheru

Nefersekheru was a palace administrator who played an important role in his master's first jubilee. Among the most important titles listed for this man in his unfinished tomb in West Thebes is Steward of the House of NEBMAATRE, the Dazzling Aten.

E. From Mortuary Temple in West Thebes

On the base of one of the jackal statues from here, the king is described as The image of Re, with a dazzling face, appearing like Aten—the godly falcon of variegated plumage who embraces the Two Lands with his wings.

F. Luxor Temple

Among the many variants of the king's throne name, there is one cartouche that names him as NEBMAATRE THE DAZZLING ATEN. *Elsewhere Amenhotep III is referred to as* sovereign like Aten, lasting as Aten is lasting, *and* a runner like Aten, swift-footed.

G. Karnak, Temple of Montu

The king is one whom [Amun] placed on his throne to be ruler of what Aten encircles, (of) the throne of Geb, the office of Atum and the kingship of Re and Khepri. *Elsewhere he is* the Good God, likeness of Re who illuminates the Two Lands like the Horizon-dweller; master of sunbeams in the face like Aten, because of whom everyone rejoices.

3. The Ritual of the King's Divine Birth from Luxor Temple

This composition grounded the king's divine identity in the paternity of Amun-Re, King of the Gods. Restorations are based in part on an earlier (and substantially different) version in Queen Hatshepsut's mortuary temple, as well as other, more fragmentary parallels.

Scene I: Amun-Re looks on as Amenhotep III's mother, the King's Chief Wife MUTEMWIA, embraces *the goddess Hathor:*

Words spoken [. . .] his mother [. . .] a great, good and pure hecatomb. The person of this god became excited (?) for very love of her [. . .] this god [desired to meet with the king's] mother MUTEMWIA. He was given entry to the palace-dweller, face to face, nose to nose, having changed into the shape [of her husband, while] she [was] exulting (?) [. . .] a great [. . .] which all people desire, and Amun went to impregnate her.

Scene II: Amun-Re faces the king who is Amenhotep III's mortal father.

By King: "[Pray do (?)] what you desire (?) with this young woman, for I say to you [. . . she is more beautiful than any] woman in the entire land, the wife of this sovereign!"

By Amun: [. . .] Go to the Mansion of the Prince in [Karnak . . .] which is in heaven, the great dwelling.

Scene III: Amun-Re, [Lord of the Thrones of] the Two Lands, Lord of Heaven *bids farewell to* [Thoth, Lord of Ashmunein], Preeminent in [Hesret] *as he departs for the palace.*

Scene IV: Amun-Re, Lord of his Inner Sanctuary and [the King's Mother] MUTEMWIA *sit upon the vault of heaven, supported by the goddesses Selkis and Neith.*

Words spoken by Amun-Re, Lord of the Thrones of the Two Lands, Preeminent in his Inner Sanctuary, after he had made his appearance into that of the Person of this husband <of hers>, MENKHEPRURE, given life: "[I have given] to [you] all [life] and dominion." It was resting in the interior of the palace that he found her. At the god's scent she awoke, and she laughed in front of his Person. He went to her at once, for he lusted after her. He caused her to see him in his godly shape after he had come right up to her, so that she rejoiced at seeing his beauty. Love of him coursed through her limbs, and the palace was flooded <with> the god's scent: all his smells were those of Punt![2]

Words spoken [by the King's Mother] MUTEMWIA in front of the Person of this august god, Amun, Lord of the Thrones of the Two Lands: "How great, indeed, is your power! How beautiful is [everything] which you have [done]. How hidden are the plans which you have made. How satisfied is your heart at my Person! Your fragrance is throughout all my body." After this, (i.e.), the Person of this God's doing all that he wanted with her, words spoken by Amun-Re, Lord of the Thrones of the Two Lands in front of her Person: "AMENHOTEP III is the name of this child which I have [placed] in your womb. Let this utterance of words issue from your mouth: 'He shall exercise this effective kingship in this entire land!' My Ba belongs to him, my prestige belongs to him, and my kingly crown belongs to him: he is the one who shall rule the Two Lands like Re forever!"

Scene V: Amun-Re stands before the ram-headed god Khnum, patron of potters.

Words spoken by Amun-Re, Preeminent in his Inner Sanctuary: "I [have] given [you] all . . . before (me). I have given you all life and dominion before me, (O) my beloved son, [O child of] Amun-Re, Lord of his Inner Sanctuary! Make him and his Ka with this body, which is [Amun's], more perfected than any of [the gods']: it is the image of this son whom I have begotten, and to whom I have given all life and dominion, all health, all happiness, all offerings and all sustenance like Re forever."

[Words spoken by Khnum: "My protection is] behind the King of Upper and Lower Egypt NEBMAATRE and all his Kas—may he be given life, stability and dominion—that he may be happy like Re forever. [. . .] heaven [. . .] a genuine [. . .] for [the King of Upper and Lower Egypt] NEBMAATRE, may he live, prosper and be healthy. Health [be to . . .] in [. . .] which he has made for the King of Upper and Lower Egypt."

Scene VI: Khnum models the bodies of the young king and his Ka on the potter's wheel while Hathor gives them life.

[Words spoken by Khnum . . .]: "As one body [. . .] have I shaped you. [I have given (?)] to you (?) all [. . .]. You are to be king of the Black Land and ruler of the Red Land, all lands being under your supervision and the Nine Bows bound together under your sandals. The throne of Geb shall belong to you, and the kingship of Re and Khepri. [The might of the Two Lords] is throughout your body, and their portions shall [belong to you, consisting of] life and dominion when you are risen [on] the throne [of Horus like Re every day]. [. . . your (?)] head [. . . at] every season (?) [. . .] forever."

Scene VII: Thoth announces the impending birth to the hereditary princess whose charm is great, the mistress of Upper and Lower Egypt, the King's Mother MUTEMWIA, may she live and be made young like Re forever."

Words Spoken by Thoth, Lord of [Ashmunein]: "Amun-Re, Lord of the Thrones of the Two Lands, [is satisfied with] <your> genuine rank of hereditary princess whose [favor] is great, [Person sweet of love (?) <like>] Atum, and mistress of all lands."

Scene VIII: The queen, hereditary princess whose charm is great, sweet of love, mistress of all lands, the King's Mother MUTEMWIA, may she live like Re, *is escorted to the birth room by Hathor and Khnum.*

Words spoken by Hathor, Lady of Heaven, Lady of Dendera, the Lady of [. . .]: "I have given you all life, all health, all joy before her [*sic*] forever and ever."

Words spoken by [Khnum the Potter, Lord of] Herwer: "I have given you all life, stability and dominion, and all health before me. Assuredly I shall be <making> protection behind <your> son (?), being [the defender of (?)] <his> limbs forever and ever."

Scene IX: Surrounded by jubilating deities, such as the Souls of Nekhen *and* the Souls of Pe, *the queen gives birth to the king and his Ka. Some of the bystanders' utterances are inscribed at the bottom of the scene:*

"(As for) the hereditary princess whose charm is great, sweet of love, the mistress of all lands, the King's Mother MUTEMWIA, may she live forever: she has taken possession of a torch, whose birth shall be successful. Come forth, O lord of victory, O torch!"

"[. . .] by (?) the one who has come to us from heaven and gives [his office to (?)] his bodily and beloved son, the Lord of the Two Lands, [NEBMAATRE], to [whom has been given all life, stability and dominion], all health and all joy like Re forever."

Scene X: Hathor presents the child to Amun-Re.

[Words spoken by Hathor, Lady of Dendera: "Kiss him, embrace him], and nourish him, for I have loved him more than [. . .]."

Words spoken by Amun-Re, Lord of the Thrones of the Two Lands: "Welcome, welcome in peace, O bodily son of Re, NEBMAATRE, given life [like Re]."

Scene XI: Hathor, followed by Mut (who holds years and jubilees), salutes Amun, as he kisses the child.

Words spoken by Hathor, Lady [of Heaven], Lady of Dendera, as she gives all life, all stability and dominion.

Words spoken by Mut the Great, Lady of [Isheru, . . .], as she gives life, health, and all joy before her, . . . Lady of Heaven: "(O) my beloved son, NEBMAATRE!"

Words spoken by Amun-Re: "Welcome in peace, O bodily son of mine, NEBMAATRE! I have given you the achieving of millions of years like Re."

Scene XII: The King's Mother, MUTEMWIA, may she live like Re *sits on a bed, the goddess Selkis behind her, while in front of her two goddesses each suckle a figure of the child,* Horus NEBMAATRE. *Beside the bed sit nine male deities, each one holding a figure of the infant king. Under the bed are two heavenly cows, each one suckling a kneeling figure of the child ruler. Above the cows,* Words spoken four times: "We nourish you as King of Upper and Lower Egypt. May you live and be joyful upon the Horus Throne; may you guide the living; may you rule the Two Lands in justification like Re forever continually."

By First Cow: As she gives all life, all stability, and dominion before her like Re.

By Second Cow: She who is Preeminent in the House of Fire, as she gives all life and all health before her like Re.

Scene XIII: Two fecundity figures are shown, one bearing symbols of life, the other carrying the infant king and his Ka–the latter carrying on his head a serekh inscribed with the king's Horus name: The Horus, Mighty Bull "Who Appears in Maat."

Above Infant King: The King of Upper and Lower Egypt, NEBMAATRE; the Son of Re, AMENHOTEP III, given life forever.

First Fecundity Figure: Words spoken by Magic, "I am Magic," as he gives all life stability and dominion before him, all health and all joy before <him>.

Second Fecundity Figure: Words spoken by Nile-in-Flood: "I have given you all life and dominion before me."

The action of the scene is described in the label in front of the figures: Presenting (?) AMENHOTEP III and purifying the birth-house (of) Horus and Seth. Words spoken: "The son is guided in."

Scene XIV: Under the spreading wings of the sun, a falcon-headed deity presents the infant king and his Ka to Amun-Re.

Words spoken by [Montu (?) . . .], as he gives all life, stability and dominion, all joy and all valor before him.

Amun-Re, Lord of Heaven, King of the Gods. Words spoken:
"I have given you life, stability, and dominion. I have given you health, I have given you joy. (O) my bodily son, my beloved, NEBMAATRE, whom I made as one body with me inside the palace: I have given you all life and dominion, you having appeared as King of Upper and Lower Egypt upon the throne of Horus. May you be joyful with your Ka like Re!"

Scene XV: Between two pairs of divinities (Khnum and Anubis on the left, Sefkhet-Abwy and Hekau on the right) the infant king and his Ka are first presented to a kneeling deity and then proceed, fully vested with their names, to have these inscribed by the goddess of writing.

Words spoken by [Khnum, Lord of Herwer], Lord of Protection, Preeminent in the House of Life, as he gives [*benefactions to*] NEBMAATRE: "(O) my beloved son, AMENHOTEP III, given life like Re!" Khnum: "I have given you all life and dominion. I have given you all health, I have given you [all joy]."

Anubis, the Great God, Lord of Heaven: "[May he continue to exist] upon the Horus Throne of the Living, that he may be happy with his Ka—that he may rule what Aten encircles, that the Fenkhu-lands may serve him, as Re himself has ordained."

Above goddesses behind the king and his Ka: "We have come, so that we may be protecting the bodily Son of [Amun], NEBMAATRE, to whom we give continuity and for whom we assemble eternity—all flatlands and all hill countries being bound together under his sandals."

The seated children whom these goddesses present are the Royal Ka of the Lord of the Two Lands *and* the bodily Son of Amun, the Good God NEBMAAT-

RE, given life like Re everlastingly. *Kneeling in front of them is* [. . .], as he gives all life, all health, and all joy before him.

Sefkhet-Abwy, Mistress [of Writing], as she gives all life and dominion. Words spoken: "I have given you millions of years, life and dominion."

Hekau, the Great God, Lord of Heaven, as he gives all life, stability and dominion before <him>, all joy and all health before <him>.

4. Hymns from the Stela of the Architects Suty and Hor

Adoration of Amun when he rises as Horakhty by the overseer of the works projects of Amun Suty (and) the overseer of the works projects of Amun Hor. They say:

First Hymn

"Hail to you, (O) beautiful Re of every day who rises at dawn without cease; (O) Khepri who tires himself with works (of creation)! Your rays are manifest, though one may not realize it, and even electrum is not comparable to your brilliance—

(You) who created yourself, gilding your (own) limbs,
(O) fashioner who was not fashioned,
Unique-natured one who sends continuity,
High above the ways, with millions under his guidance.

As your brilliance is, so is the sky's brilliance—more brilliant your complexion than its hues! When you cross heaven all faces see you, and when you depart you are hidden from their sight. When you place yourself (in the sky) daily at dawn, your journey—in your (own) Person—succeeds: in a short day you travel a path (equivalent to) river miles in countless hundreds of thousands! Every day is an instant under you, and when you set it has passed. In the same way you have arranged the night and completed its hours—there is no cease in your labors! By means of you every eye sees, and there is no fulfillment of theirs when your Person sets. When you are moved to rise at dawn, your brightness opens the eyes of cattle; and when you set in Manu, then they sleep in the fashion of death."

Second Hymn

"Hail to you, Aten of the daytime, who has created all and made them live —

Great falcon, with variegated plumage,
Scarab beetle who elevates himself by himself,
Who brought himself into being,[3] who has not his fashioner,
Elder Horus within Nut, for whom rejoicing is made at his appearing and his setting alike,
Modeller of what the ground creates,
Khnum and Amun of the Sun's People, who has taken possession of the Two Lands from great to small,
Effective mother of gods and men,
Patient craftsman, great one who tires himself with making them without number,
Zealous herdsman who herds his cattle,
Their refuge, who makes their life,
Hurrier, runner, racer,
Khepri, whose birth is distinguished,
Who elevates his beauty in the belly of Nut,
Who illuminates the Two Lands with his disk (=Aten),
Primeval one of the Two Lands, who made himself by himself,
Who sees all he has made, alone,
Who reaches the end of the lands every day in the sight of those who tread upon them,
Who rises in heaven, having become Re,
Making the seasons of months with heat as he desires, and coolness as he desires.
And when he makes bodies slack,[4] he gathers them up.

Every land is in adoration at his rising every day in order to worship him."

Notes

1. Literally, "who acts upon the water of" the gods of Thebes, an idiom that is most characteristic of a subordinate's expression of loyalty to a superior.
2. I.e., the incense that was one of that country's chief exports.
3. This clause and the preceding comprise a play on the words for beetle (*ḫprr*) and "bring into being" (*ḫpr*).
4. I.e., when they die. An alternative meaning, however, is that the god "embraces them" when he makes them sleep in the daytime.

2

The Reign of Amenhotep IV

Part I: Royal Documents

5. Stela of Amenhotep IV at Gebel Silsila

This large tablet, cut into the north cliff of the great sandstone quarry on the east bank at Gebel Silsila, commemorates the preparations for what was doubtless the king's first major building projects at Karnak. Their ostensible beneficiary, the god Amun-Re, stands on the right, facing Amenhotep IV. The stela was vandalized–first by the Atenist erasure of Amun, and later when the king's names and figure were attacked during the orthodox reaction–and the monument was never restored. Even so, the figures of the king (who wears the distinctive White Crown) and the god can be discerned clearly in outline.

Above Amun: Words spoken by Amun-Re, King of the Gods: (I) have given you life, stability and dominion.

Above King: King of Upper and Lower Egypt, NEFERKHEPRURE-WAENRE, bodily son of Re, AMENHOTEP IV, long in his lifetime.

Main Text:
The living Horus, mighty bull "Tall-Plumed"; Two Ladies, "Great of Kingship in [Karnak]"; Horus of Gold, "Who Elevates the Crowns in Upper Egyptian Heliopolis"; King of Upper and Lower Egypt, first prophet of Hor-Aten, NEFERKHEPRURE-WAENRE; Son of Re, [AMENHOTEP IV], long in his lifetime—may he live forever continually!—<beloved of> Amun-Re, Lord of Heaven, Ruler of Eternity.

The first occasion that his Person laid a charge on [the king's scribe (?)], the general Amen[. . .] to carry out all the works projects, starting from Elephantine and ending at Sambehdet, and on the leaders of the army to perform a great forced-labor-duty of quarrying sandstone, in order to fashion the great *benben* of "Horakhty in his name, 'Light which is in Aten'"[1] in Karnak, the officials, companions and chief standard-bearers being the taxing-masters for the stone image.

6. A Taxation Decree from the Aten Temple at Karnak

Only fragments of this text are preserved, many of them still unpublished, but there is enough to show that it imposed a tax on temples and municipalities throughout the land for the support of the king's new cult. One group of domains–each described as the House of *Divinity X,* Lord of *City Y–was assessed for the same amount:*

Silver	1 *deben*
Incense	1 *men*-container
Wine	2 *men*-containers
Thick cloth	2 rectangular lengths

Localities in both the Upper and Lower Egypt were taxed with this fixed assessment. Among the gods and goddesses of the north *are* Horus of Tcharu; Horus-Khentekhtay, [Lord of Athribis]; Osiris, Lord of Busiris; Re of the Great Mansion (*Heliopolis?*) and Hathor, Lady of the Field of Re (*Abusir?*). *In the south,* temples of gods and goddesses from Elephantine to [. . .] *which were assessed* with annual taxes *included* the House of Khnum, [Lord of Elephantine]; Nekhbet, Lady of Elkab; [Khnum], Lord of Esna; [Horus (?)], Lord of Mansion-of-Snefru (*Asfun el-Mataʿna*); Montu, [Lord of Armant or Tod]; Horus-the-Great, Lord of [Qus]; Min (?) [of Coptos]; Khnum, Lord of Shashotep *and* [Wepwawet, Lord of] Assiut.

Another section of this composition deals with donations by municipalities and royal domains. These are described either as collections of the mayor of *City X (including localities in Upper and Lower Egypt)* which are dedicated to the House of Aten in Southern Heliopolis, *or* collections of *Royal Domain Y* which the King of Upper and Lower Egypt who lives on Maat, the Lord of the Two Lands NEFERKHEPRURE-WAENRE, the Son of Re AKHENATEN[2] dedicated to his father HOR-ATEN as the tax of each year to the House of Aten in Southern Heliopolis. *Estates endowed for both Amenhotep III and his son are mentioned in this latter group. The individual donations are more extensive than those in the previous section and the amounts are more variable:*

Metals:	Gold (*or* gold vases)	2 deben
	Silver (*or* silver vases)	5 *or* 10 deben
	Bronze (*or* bronze vases)	20, 30 *or* 50 deben

Cloth:	Plain cloth	1 *to* 3 coverlets
		1 *to* 3 wraps
		3 *to* 7 shawls
		3 *to* 7 shirts
		3 *to* 7 underclothes
	Total assorted pieces:	11 *to* 27

Edibles:	[...]	... jars
	Fresh moringa oil	3 (?) jars
	Honey	1 *or* 2 jars
	Wine	10 *or* 50 jars
	Living geese	10 *or* 20

A small number of fragments refer to at least some of the recipients of these revenues, to wit: subordinates of the House of Aten who [are to be supported by these domains, numbering] 6,800 persons, [to whom are assigned] their deliveries for their maintenance [... which are] to be delivered to the House of Aten [in Upper Egyptan Heliopolis]. *A more complete accounting of the institutions, revenues, and recipients affected by this assessment must await the full publication of these blocks.*

7. A Royal Speech from Amenhotep IV's Earliest Building at Karnak

Of this lengthy composition only a fragment (lying in the middle of fourteen columns) is preserved on two blocks from the Tenth Pylon. This part of the king's harangue apparently contrasts the perishable images of orthodox deities with the uncreated and enduring nature of the solar orb: ... Horus (?) ... , ... [their temples (?)] fallen to ruin, [their] bodies (?) shall not ... : ... [since the time of] the ancestors (?). It is the ones who are knowledgeable. ... Look, I am speaking that I might inform [you concerning] the forms of the gods, I know [their (?)] temples [and I am versed in] the writings, (namely) the inventories of their primeval bodies [and I have beheld them] as they[3] cease, one after the other, (whether) consisting of any sort of precious stone ... , [except for the god who begat] himself by himself, no one knowing the mysteries ... : he goes where he pleases and they know not [his] going ... toward him at night. Further, [I] approach. ... [As for the ...]s which he has made, how distinguished they are: ... their [...]s are as stars. Hail to you, in [your ...] rays. ... What would he be like, another one of your sort? It is you [who ...] to them, in your name of. ...

8. Other Fragmentary Inscriptions from Amenhotep IV's Earliest Building at Karnak

Many of the known fragments of this building are still built into the Tenth Pylon at Karnak. The sun-god is generally shown in his traditional guise, that is, in human form, but with a falcon's head surmounted by a sun disk. Only rarely is he shown in what would become his classic image, the radiant sun. The god's name, invariably in its earlier form (HOR-ATEN), is usually not enclosed in a cartouche. The building was still in use after Akhet-Aten became the center of the king's activities in year 5, and the cartouches containing his earlier personal name ("Amenhotep, the god who rules Thebes") were generally altered to read "Akhenaten." What follows is a selection of the more significant texts.

XE 3: . . . in adoration, your place being far, in front of . . . the gods who are settled (?) in every city, without there being one who gives to . . . a dwelling (?) . . . abodes (?). . . .

XE 30: (A column of text behind the god, spoken by him:) "[I have given you] the kingship of the Two Lands and the throne of Geb."

XE 34: HOR-ATEN, resident in the House of Aten.

XE 45: . . . gods (?), Aten who shines and travels . . . , [their (?)] limit not being known [and their (?) . . .]s not being. . . .

XE-80: . . . Aten [being] content in the course of every day, being the one who causes his Person to rejoice in . . . , that he might [. . .] the favors of his father, who created his beauty, the Lord of the Two Lands, [NEFERKHEPRURE-WAENRE]. . . .

KHES 170: . . . all (things) that you have said, they come to pass; your name. . . .

KHES 171: . . . toward people and gods, there not being one who knows it. As for their. . . . All the gods. . . .

KHES 180: . . . you while seeing your beauty. You say to me, "(My) heart [is glad with what you have done for me (?)]. . . . How prosperous is a son who does effective things for his father, who begat him . . . your limbs. I give to you my office and my position . . . , . . . beloved of . . . (and) favored [by . . .] . . ." . . . [the King of Upper and Lower Egypt, NEFERKHEPRURE-WAENRE, the Son of Re, AMENHOTEP IV, long in] his lifetime. He says: "[. . . , I am one] who hastens (?) to do effective things in the presence of. . . ."

NR C: . . . HOR-ATEN . . . every [thing (?)]. He says: "I adore Horakhty, pure, pure, upon . . . of heaven at dawn in order to create him(self) every day, as you appear in . . . adoration because of your rising, when you shine . . . [your (?)] temple, that [your (?)] Person might rest in [it]. . . ."

NR J: [Regnal year . . . , month . . . of] the Inundation season, day 10 under the Person of Re-Horakhty, [mighty] bull . . . ; [Two Ladies . . . ; [Horus of Gold], "Who Elevated the Crowns in Upper Egyptian Heliopolis"; King of Upper and Lower Egypt, NEFERKHEPRURE-[WAENRE] . . . the youth, the child (?) . . . .

A block from the bottom of a doorway, built into the Tenth Pylon, comes from The Gateway (called) "NEFERKHEPRURE-WAENRE [is . . .]."

9. An Offering List from Karnak[4]

[His Person decreed the endowing of sacrifices anew for his father], Hor-Aten, [upo]n the offering-tables of Re, starting from Hikuptah and ending at Sambehdet. [Divine offerings] dedicated by the King of Upper and Lower Egypt, NEFERKHEPRURE-WAENRE, to his father Re, as the daily offering in Hikuptah:

Bit-loaves:	baking ratio 60:	240 (loaves)
Pesen-loaves:	" " 40:	87 "
White bread:	" " 5:	12 "
Offering loaves:	" " 20:	12 "
Neferhat-bread:	" " 16:	12 "
White fruit bread:	" " 80:	14 "
Beer, jugs:	brewing ratio 12:	12 (jugs)
Beer, jugs:	" " 20:	22 "
Shayt-bit cakes:	baking ratio 20:	4 (loaves)

Total assorted bread offerings: 379 (*sic!*)

Beer, jugs:	34
Incense (in) cups:	12
Milk (in) half-(jugs):	2 *hin*
Fruit (in) cups:	12
Vegetables, bundles:	4

Vegetables, baskets:	1
Many kinds of fowl:	2
Offering stands:	12
Bronze bowl:	1
Bronze basin:	1
Bronze stand:	1
Bronze censer:	1
Bronze nemset-jar:	1

Sacrifice which the lord dedicated in the new year: 2 offering stands. What is on them:

White bread, a basket: baking ratio 2½: 2 (baskets), which makes white bread, 10 (loaves)

Offering loaves, 2 baskets: baking ratio 25: 10 offering loaves

Neferhat-bread:	baking ratio 10:	2 (loaves)
White fruit bread:	" " 20:	2 "
Beer, large jar:	brewing ratio 5:	2 (jars)
Incense:		2 baskets
Fruit:		2 "
Wine:		2 amphoras
Many kinds of fowl:		2

Divine offerings which his Person dedicated to his father Hor-Aten as the daily offering in the [sunshade of Re which is in Hikuptah]:

Bit-bread:	baking ratio 60:	240 (loaves)
Pesen-loaves:	" " 40:	87 "
Beer, jugs:	brewing ratio 20:	30 (jugs)

White fruit [bread]: [. . .] (*Four lines missing*)
Many kinds of fowl: [. . .]
Wine: [. . .] (*The rest is lost*)

10. Scenes and Inscriptions from the Aten Temples at Karnak

10-A. Fragment Built into Temple of Amenhotep II between Pylons IX and X at Karnak

Long live the King of Upper and Lower Egypt, NEFERKHEPRURE WAENRE, beloved of Horakhty who rejoices in the horizon.

Long live the Son of Re, AMENHOTEP IV, LONG <IN> HIS LIFETIME (sic), given life like Re forever.

10-B. Fragment Found in Luxor Temple

HOR-ATEN, great living Aten who is in jubilee, lord of heaven and earth, residing in the "Mansion of the Benben" in "The Aten is Discovered."

The King's Chief Wife NEFERTITI. . . .

10-C. Another Fragment Found at Luxor Temple

HOR-ATEN, great living Aten who is in jubilee, lord of heaven and earth, residing in "The Aten is Discovered" in the House of Aten.

Lord of the Two Lands, NEFERKHEPRURE-WAENRE; Lord of Crowns, AMENHOTEP IV, long in his lifetime.

10-D. List of Donations to the Aten Temples at Thebes[5]

[. . .] cloth: [. . .]
Good narrow-weave cloth, shirt(s): 5
Good narrow-weave cloth: [. . .]
[. . .] cloth: 2
Tchut-cloth, shirt(s): 2 [+ x]

Following another gap:

[Reckoning of . . . who are subordinates of the House of Aten in Karnak]: 3,622 people . . . the first ones of [their] names (?):

[Upper Egyptians]: 1,049 men
Lower Egyptians: [2,573 men]

What they need for [their] support . . . which is delivered to the House of Aten [in Karnak]: Silver, ...

10-E. A Register of Property and Responsible Officials

The overseer of herds of sheep [belonging to] the House of Aten which is in the southern district:

. . . his [. . . of] small cattle . . . .
[. . .] [. . .]
[. . .] for honey [. . .]: 7,900 (+ x)
Large white loaves: 26,600
Sermet-ale: 290 jars
[. . .] [. . .]
[Fowl]: 500

Sef-geese: [. . .]
Kheto-geese: 21
Deliveries of wheat: 20 [+ x] sacks . . .

The inspector [who] is subordinate to him:

The first ones. . . .
[. . .] 2,850 current ones (?)
Vegetables: 82,729
Assorted vessels and jars: 93,910 (+ x)
[. . .]
[. . .] [. . .] kite
Silver: 5 [. . .]
Bronze: 260 [. . .]

10-F

What follows is a selection of the most distinctive titles borne by officials who appear in the Aten temples.

10-F.1. Religious Titles

Greatest of Seers of HOR-ATEN in the House of Aten in Upper Egyptian Heliopolis. *Variant:* Greatest of Seers of [Aten] in the House of Aten [in Karnak (?)].

Chamberlain and first god's servant of NEFERKHEPRURE-WAENRE.

First God's Father of HOR-ATEN in the House of Aten [in Upper Egyptian Heliopolis].

God's Fathers and lay priests of HOR-ATEN in the House of Aten [in Upper Egyptian Heliopolis].

10-F.2. Administrative Titles

Overseers of the King's Private Apartments who are following [his Person].

Overseer of the Treasury of the [House] of Aten in [Upper Egyptian Heliopolis]. *Variant:* Overseer of the Treasury of the House of Aten in Karnak.

Scribe of the storehouse of divine offerings of [the House of] Aten in Upper Egyptian Heliopolis.

[Overseer of] the herds of sheep of the [western] river [in the House of] Aten in Karnak.

Overseer of herds of small cattle of the House of Aten which is in the Southern District.

Chief Beekeeper of the Southern District.

Chief Beekeeper of the Eastern Water.

10-F.3. Provincial Titles

The Administrator of Sais.

[The Mayor of Per]-Heby (who is) over the House [of] . . .

The Mayor of Nefrusy (who is) over the House [of] . . .

The Mayor of Assiut (who is) over the [House of] . . .

[The Mayor of] Thinis (who is) over the House [of] . . .

The Mayor of Hut-sekhem [(who is) over the House] of THE WORSHIPER.[6]

10-G. Temple or Shrine Names

The House of Aten (*Per-Aten*).

"Discovering the Aten" (*Gemet-pa-Aten*) in the House of Aten.

The Mansion of the Benben (*Hut-benben*) in "Discovering the Aten."

The Booth of Aten in "Discovering the Aten."

"Enduring are the Monuments (*Ruwed-menu*) of Aten continually."

"Distinguished are the Monuments (*Teni-menu*) of Aten continually."

[*Divinity*] residing in "Effective is . . ." (=*Akh* . . .)

10-H. Members of the Royal Family

[. . . AKHENATEN, long] in his lifetime, first officer (?) of [the Aten (?)].

Heiress of great favor, possessor of charm, sweet [of love, . . .], mistress of Upper and Lower Egypt, King's Chief Wife, his beloved, Lady of the Two Lands, NEFERTITI, may she live forever continually.

King's bodily daughter, his beloved, Meretaten, born to the King's Chief Wife NEFERTITI.

King's bodily daughter of the King's Wife (?),[7] [Meritaten (?)], born to the King's Chief Wife [NEFERTITI].

[King's bodily daughter, his beloved], Meretaten, born to [the King's Chief Wife NEFERNEFRUATEN-NEFERTITI], may she live forever continually.

[King's bodily daughter, his beloved], Meketaten, born to [the King's Chief Wife NEFERNEFRUATEN-NEFERTITI], may she live forever continually.

[King's] bodily [daughter], his beloved, Ankhesenpaaten, born [to the King's Chief Wife] NEFERNEFRUATEN-NEFERTITI, may she live forever continually.

10-I. Varia

10-I.1. A Hymn to Akhenaten

[Words spoken by the king's] children . . . :

"Hail to you], (O) Re every day!
Hail to you, (O) Horus every day!
Hail to you, our father [every] day!
[. . .]
Hail to you, (O) King NEFERKHEPRURE-WAENRE—live, prosper, be healthy—his [. . .]s,
Sole one who takes possession of the magic of Horus while your jubilee writings [. . .],
[. . .] himself, like his writings.
Lifetime (?) [. . .] secrets (?), uncovering it more than those who came into being through it.
The jubilee song . . . , [while you are] in jubilee like Re, preeminent among the gods!"

10-I.2. From Tribute Scenes

[Giving] adoration to the Good God by the chiefs of [every] foreign country.

[Presenting] tribute to the victorious king by the chiefs [of] Naharin (and) the chiefs of Kush.

[The] chiefs of every remote foreign country [have come, bearing] every sort of good thing so that they may live.

10-I.3. Speech of Offering Bearers

"[. . .] make healthy this Only One of Re (=Waenre), O living Aten, who begat for yourself Pharaoh, l.p.h., this [beautiful child of yours], the RULER [who makes monuments for] his father. May NEFERKHEPRURE-WAENRE repeat it! Cause him [(to be) continual, being pure in your presence, O living Aten! NEFERKHEPRURE-WAENRE [is] of your Ka, O Aten! Cause [him to be continual!]"

10-I.4. The King in His Chariot

Above the scene: [A beautiful appearance, mounted, by his Person, like Aten in the House of Aten, when he rises.] The Two Lands are illuminated when he traverses [the sky in peace. (O)] great [living Aten, you] are [far away, but your rays are on the faces of] everybody!

Above horse team: Its beautiful name, "Which HOR-ATEN made."

10-I.5. Refrain of Priests

By each group of priests who carry chests of cloth into the temple: "It (=the consecrated cloth) has arrived in peace, that it might favor NEFERKHEPRURE-WAENRE."

10-I.6. Jubilee Inscription

. . . bringing in (for audience) the officials and companions, the standard bearers and chief men of the army, to cause them to stand in the presence of the king at the first jubilee of his Person, which [. . .] made for him . . . the living Aten, every land being beneath his sandals.

10-I.7. An Offering Inscription

This reconstructed text was probably situated above a scene which showed the king taking part in one of the processions at his jubilee. The restorations derive from similarly formulaic language in other contemporary inscriptions.

The Good God, embryo of Aten, AKHENATEN,[8] he says: "[You] shine [beautifully in the horizon of heaven, O living Aten], whose name is great, whose titulary is holy, as [your] rays shine [upon your son, whom you set] on the throne. O Aten who built [himself . . . , may you grant him] valor and victory, all his limbs [being rejuvenated by favor of the god (?)], who shines for him, embraces him and envelopes [him in his light (?), as is done for a son (?)] of the living Aten who grants [. . . to] everybody, while people are not sated with seeing him."

[His Person] has arisen, mounted like a shooting star, [like his father], great living Aten who is in [jubilee]. A very abundant sacrifice [is presented, consisting of] long-and short-horned cattle, oxen, fowl and incense, as well as small cattle [and . . . without] their limit. The king himself [is pure of hands] and respectful, in order to present it to the [Aten].

11. Amenhotep IV performs Jubilee Rites ("Gayer Anderson Relief")

While this small block is comparable in size and subject to the many sandstone fragments from the Theban temples, its material (limestone) precludes any certainty in determining its provenance. The nomen, originally naming the king as Amenhotep IV, was later recut to read "Akhenaten."

On the left stands the king, wearing the jubilee robe, adoring at an altar beneath [Great Living Aten] who is in jubilee, lord of heaven, lord of earth, residing in "Rejoicing in the Horizon of Aten."

To the right, the king (again dressed in the jubilee robe) marches in procession. Above the scene: HOR-ATEN in [the House of Re (?)] in Upper Egyptian Heliopolis.

By the king: [King of Upper and Lower Egypt, Lord of] the Two Lands, NEFERKHEPRURE-WAENRE; [Son of Re, Lord of] Crowns, AMENHOTEP IV.

Attendant in front of king: the chief lector-priest.

Attendant behind the king: the first prophet of NEFERKHEPRURE-WAENRE.

12. Statues from Karnak

A. Fragment of a Baboon Statue

First prophet of Hor-Aten, the King of Upper and Lower Egypt, NEFERKHEPRURE-[WAENRE].

B. Statue of a Soul of Pe Adoring Horakhty

Words spoken by the Souls of Pe: "Adoration of Hor-Aten as he sets in the western horizon of heaven, upon the august and pure mound of Re [. . .]."

13. Graffito from Aswan

Located to the right of the more famous, and later, graffito of Men and Bak (see 66 below), this memorial showed the king (his figure now worn away) presenting four braziers to a hawk-headed figure of HOR-ATEN. Between the figures is an offering stand and four columns of text: Censing to HOR-ATEN [by the King of Upper and Lower Egypt, who lives on Maat, Lord of the Two Lands], NEFERKHEPRURE-WAENRE, the Son of Re [who lives on Maat, Lord of Crowns], AMENHOTEP IV, long in his lifetime.

14. Scarab Found at Sedeinga in Nubia

Long live the Good God whose renown is great; possessor of the great name, whose titulary is holy; [possessor of] jubilee(s)[9] like Tatenen, master of lifetime [like] Aten in heaven, established on the Ished-tree which is in Heliopolis—namely (?),[10] the King of Upper and Lower Egypt, NEFERKHEPRURE-WAENRE, given [life], son of Re, his beloved, AMENHOTEP IV, long [in his lifetime]; and King's Chief Wife NEFERTITI, [may she] live.

15. Relief with Titles of Queen Nefertiti from Temple of Sesebi in Nubia

The scene, which showed Akhenaten and Nefertiti offering to the Aten, was erased and usurped by Sety I. Traces of the queen's inscription, in six columns, are preserved behind the king:

Hereditary princess, greatly favored, sweet of love, lady of Upper and Lower Egypt, [. . . in the] palace, who bears witness to the horizon and ascends (?) to [. . .], the King's Chief Wife, his beloved, [NEFERNEFRUATEN-NEFERTITI, may she] live continually.

16. Scarab Bought in Luxor

Great living Aten who is in jubilee, [lord of heaven and earth], HOR-[ATEN].

Long live Horus, [mighty bull], "Tall-Plumed"; [Two] Ladies, ["Great of] Kingship in Karnak"; Horus of Gold, "Who Elevates the Crowns in [Upper Egyptian Heliopolis]"; King of Upper and Lower Egypt who lives on Maat, Lord of the Two Lands, NEFERKHEPRURE-WAENRE; [Son of Re], who lives on Maat, Lord of Crowns, AMENHOTEP IV, long in his lifetime; (and) the King's Chief Wife NEFERTITI, may she live.

17. Docket on One of the "Amarna Letters"

A few of the cuneiform tablets from Western Asia found at Akhenaten's capital were inscribed with dated annotations in Egyptian. One group of letters was written by King Tushratta of Mitanni to the queen mother, Tiyi, and to Amenhotep IV shortly after the latter became king. The following Egyptian docket is handwritten in ink on the side of the tablet: Regnal [year] 2 (?),[11] first month of the Growing season, day 5 (?), when One (=the king) was in the Southern City (=Thebes) in the estate of "Rejoicing in the Horizon." Copy of the Naharin letter which the messenger Pirizzi (and) the messenger [Tulubri] brought.

18. Small Objects of Amenhotep IV

This selection includes only pieces which use the king's earlier nomen or which describe him as the beloved of a god other than the Aten. Items A through F below are scarabs or seals: multiple examples which are inscribed identically are included under a single entry. G is an inscribed whip handle.

18-A. Two cartouches: NEFERKHEPRURE-WAENRE *and* AMENHOTEP IV.

18-B. Side A: NEFERKHEPRURE-WAENRE, beloved of Thoth (*or* Khonsu).[12]
Side B: AMENHOTEP IV.

18-C. Beloved of Ptah, NEFERKHEPRURE-WAENRE.

18-D. NEFERKHEPRURE-WAENRE, whom Amun has chosen.

18-E. Side A: Neferkheprure, beloved of Maat,
Side B: the beautiful image of Atum (?).[13]

18-F. NEFERKHEPRURE, whom Amun has chosen, who appears for million(s of years).

18-G. The Good God, Lord of the Two Lands, NEFERKHEPRURE-WAENRE, beloved of Weret-hekau, Lady of Heaven.

Part II: Private Documents

19. Contracts from Illahun ("Kahun Letters")

These papyrus documents record a number of business dealings between the chief herdsman Mesuy and his fellow citizens, dated in years 27 and 33 of Amenhotep III and years 2 through 4 of his successor, Amenhotep IV. They have been used as evidence of a long coregency for these kings because the recurrence of the same individuals throughout could suggest that these transactions might not be as far apart as the datelines imply.

19-A. Pap. Berlin 9784

Regnal year 27, third month of Harvest, day 20, under the Person of the King of Upper and Lower Egypt NEBMAATRE, l.p.h., SON OF RE AMENHOTEP III, living forever continually like his father Re every day.

On this day Nebmehy—he was a herdsman of the House of AMENHOTEP—approached the chief herdsman Mesuy, saying, "I am naked. Let there be given <to me> the price of two days (of service) from the slave-woman Kharet." So the chief herdsman Mesuy gave him a skirt, worth three and a half pieces, and a loincloth, worth half a piece. Again he approached, saying, "Give me the price of four days from the slave-woman Henut." So the [herdsman] Mesuy gave him eight sextuple-sacks of grain, worth four pieces; six goats, worth three pieces; and silver, one piece. Total, twelve pieces.

Then the two days from the slave-woman Henut were becoming subject to litigation,[14] and he gave me two days (of service) from Meriremetchef and two days from the slave Sety, in the presence of many witnesses. The roster thereof:

in front of the herdsman Aper;
" " " the herdsman Nan;
" " " (the woman) Kafy;
" " " (the woman) [. . .]y;
" " " (the woman) [. . .]y;
" " " Iotefat;
" " " (the women) Pna, Metet, Tuya and Kaya;

" " " the Nubian woman Markashti;
" " " [. . .];
[" " " A]nkh-Sety.

Done by the scribe Tchutchu on this day.

[Regnal] year 2, month [. . .] of the Growing season, day 27 under the Person of this [good] god, [King of Upper] and Lower Egypt NEFERKHEPRURE-WAENRE, l.p.h., SON OF RE AMENHOTEP IV, may he live forever continually like his father Re every day.

On this day, Nebmehy again approached the herdsman Mesuy [saying], "Let me be given a cow to compensate for three arouras of agricultural land." Mesuy [gave] him a cow worth half a deben in the presence of many witnesses:

in front of Ahmose and his son Nebamun;
" " " Itchutchu " " " Efankh;
" " <"> Hay;
" " " Nyn.

Made by the scribe Tchutchu on this day.

Regnal year 3, Birthday of Isis under the Person of the King of Upper and Lower Egypt NEFERKHEPRURE-WAENRE, l.p.h., the son of Re AMENHOTEP IV, l.p.h., may he live forever continually like his father Re every day.

On this day At, the son of the soldier Menkheper, approached the chief herdsman Mesuy, saying: "Buy for yourself two days (of service) from the slave-woman Henut. Let [me (?)] be given [the thing]s of our lords afterwards on account of the petition." So the herdsman Mesuy gave him the price thereof—a bronze bowl (?), worth two and a half pieces; clothing, [. . .], worth one piece; a kilt (?), worth half a piece: total, four pieces—and he said, in front of many witnesses: "I am fully satisfied with the price of my [slave]-woman. As Amun endures, and as THE RULER endures, if the two days which I am selling you from the slave woman Henut are subject to litigation, let (it) be made up, piece for piece."

in front of the soldier Nebmehy
" <"> " (the woman) Aper;
" " " Nefu and Sety;
" <"> " Maya;
" <"> " (the woman) Satia, daughter of the sem-priest M[. . .]y;
" <"> " Nan;
" " " (the woman) Tia;
" " " (" ") Pna;
" <"> " (" ") Pih(y);

" " " (" ") Itchut;
" <"> " the lay priest Iruru;
" <"> " his wife, Nefru;
" <"> " his daughter, Tuy;
" <"> " (the woman) Ptahmay.
Done by the scribe Tchutchu, son of Inan, on this day.

Verso: The witnesses to the price which Nebmehy's slave Iihersa fetched:
in front <of> (the woman) May;
in " <"> (" ") Ti[. . .]a.

19-B. Gurob Pap. II.1

Regnal year 33, first month of Inundation, day 7 under the Person of the King of Upper and Lower Egypt NEBMAATRE, the Son of Re AMENHOTEP III, living forever continually.

On this day, the purchase which the herdsman Mesuy made from the citizeness Pihy and her son, the lay priest Min: seventeen days (of service) from the slave woman Kharet and four days from the slave-woman Henut. What was given to them to be the price thereof:
a skirt, worth six pieces;
a [. . .]-garment, worth four pieces;
a bull, worth eight pieces;
eight goats, worth four pieces;
[. . . , worth] fifteen pieces.

Then they said: "As the RULER endures, as the RULER endures! If the days are under litigation, let (it) be made up, day for day; for I am satisfied with the price thereof." She (*sic*) pronounced this oath in the presence of the council of assessors of the House of Osiris. The roster thereof:
the god's servant Tchay;
the god's servant Khay;
the lay priest Khaut;
" " " Pawah;
" " " Ra.

The people of this town who heard the matter:
Iuwy;
[. . .];
(the woman) Ra;
(" ") Dy.
Done by the accounting scribe and lay priest Wenennefer.

19-C. Gurob Pap. II.2

Regnal year 33, first month of Inundation, day 10 [+ x] under the Person of this Good God, l.p.h. On this day, purchase which the herdsman [Mesuy of] the Faiyum made from the citizeness Pihy: six days from the slave-woman Kharet. What was given to her to be the payment thereof:

a [. . .] of skirts, worth six pieces;
a [. . .]-garment, worth [four] and a half pieces;
eight goats, worth four pieces.

Then <she> said: "As the RULER endures, as the RULER endures! If the six days which (I) have given to the herdsman Mesuy are under litigation from any people, let (it) be made up, day for day, for I am satisfied with the price thereof."

She pronounced this oath in the presence of the council of assessors of the House of Osiris. Roster thereof:

the god's servant Tchay;
the god's servant Khay;
the lay priest Pawah;
the lay priest Nameh;
the army quartermaster Geregmenu.

Done by the scribe Wenennefer on this day.

19-D. Pap. Berlin 9785

Regnal year 4, second month of Inundation, day 7. Long live the Person of the King of Upper and Lower Egypt NEFERKHEPRURE-WAENRE, the Son of Re, AMENHOTEP IV, long in his lifetime, living forever continually.

On this day the herdsman Mesuy, of [the Faiyum (?) came to lay charges against Hat, born of (the woman) . . .] of the Faiyum. What he said: "As for me, I was sitting in my stable when Hat came up to me with some people behind him, [and he said to me, 'Let cattle be given to me and I will give you] the price, consisting of the female slave belonging to me, [Maatnofret (by name) . . . .' So I gave him] two cows, worth sixteen pieces, and [two] calves, [worth one deben: total, two deben], four (?) pieces."

What Hat said by his own mouth: "Yes, [. . .] exacted by the hand of Pharaoh, l.p.h., from the [. . .] of cattle through me, so I went, pinioned, and came up to the herdsman Mesuy, and [I said to him], 'Let cattle be given to me and I will give you a payment consisting of the slave-woman belonging to me, Maatnofret (by name).' [So he gave me] two cows, worth sixteen pieces, and two calves, worth one deben: total, two deben and four (?) pieces. I swear to having paid in full my payment, consisting of Maatnofret, the slave-woman belonging to me. By [the . . . of] my father and mother, I have paid the price of his cattle.'" Then he declared it to him with an oath by the Lord, l.p.h., saying: "As the RULER, l.p.h., [endures], as the RULER, l.p.h., [endures]! As for the payment of mine, Maatnofret (by name), which I have given to be the price [of] the four head of cattle of the herdsman Mesuy: if it (=the payment) is subject to litigation in times to come or [. . .], (and) if it shall be disputed by any people, let (it) be made up, payment for payment."

[What the council of] assessors said: "Mesuy is right and Hat is wrong." The council of this day:

the priest I[. . .];
" " Irure;
the chief of police Ipaya.

Done by the accounting scribe Tcha . . . .

Citizen witnesses:

the scribe of the House of Re, Hateye;
the herdsman Aperti;
the herdsman [. . .];
[. . .] Maya.

20. Statues of a Husband and Wife found at Balansura

These two funerary statues belonged to Yuny, mayor of the town of Nefrusy in Middle Egypt (see map), and his wife, Mutnofret. They were made by their son Mahu when the latter had succeeded his father in office. Since the mother's monument is the more conventional (as well as the better made) of the two, it seems likely that it had been prepared before the death of her husband early in Amenhotep IV's reign. It was probably at this time, while his father's statue was being readied, that Mahu probably took the opportunity to emphasize his filial piety to both parents by inscribing his mother's statue as well. Some of the uncertainties in the following translation (particularly on the man's statue) may be due to the poor editing of these texts before they were carved, if not to the sculptor's incomprehension of the copy on which he based his work.

20-A. Statue of the Man

On the socle: Adoration of the Ka of Khnum, Lord of Herwer: "May you give me l.p.h. and alertness in your following" for the Ka of one whom his lord praised, the mayor of Nefrusy, Yuny, the true.[15] Made by his son, who causes his name to live, the "child"[16] in the land, the mayor of Nefrusy, Mahu—may he live again!

On the skirt: Adoration of the Ka of Khnum, Lord of Herwer, who gives l.p.h. and who gives a good burial after old age <to> the mayor Yuny. Made by his son, who causes his name to live, the mayor (*sic*).

Left side of the seat: Adoration of the Ka of the lord of continuity, the maker of eternity: "may you grant me a good burial after old age, (attaining) to the state of reverence by means of what you command for yourself, O great god, lord of the West, who makes a place for the one he loves: the mayor of Nefrusy, Yuny, the true. Made by his son, who causes his name to live, the "child" in <Her>wer, namely, the mayor Mahu, the true.

Left edge of the dorsal pillar: [. . .] of adoration in all that you have brought into being (?), a light for every eye, the great Ka of every land: one fragrant in his city, the mayor Mahu—may he live again!

Dorsal pillar: [Adoration of . . . , who . . .] the land, beloved of Re, this great Ka who fills hearts and replicates (?) his beauty in every body. [May you promote me in the] presence of the (royal) entourage, not being poor, but one who is praised, the (true) teaching being in [my] body. [Let me be] among the chiefs of your officials. May my property be more abundant than water, and let there be made a desirable place of [. . .]. Let <me> come to Waenre, as my heart desires. Let me cause all people's hearts to speak with [. . .]. [*Let the king appear*] as good ruler, that he may act for us as well. Made by (his) "child," the overseer of priest(s), the [chief] stablemaster [of his Ka]; by his son, whom his city, Nefrusy, loves: the mayor Mahu—may he live again, and be true.

Right side of the seat: Adoration of the Ka of the good ruler, valiant in victory when he creates life: O great Re of every land, let me be at the head of your officials, my property being more abundant than water, and may you promote me in the presence of the (royal) entourage *at the day when the beauty of your beauties is manifested,*[17] forever! <Made for> (his) "child", the overseer of priests, the chief stablemaster of his Ka, the true beloved king's scribe, the "child" in <Her>wer, great in his city (where) the love of him is good.[18] Made by his son, who causes his name to live, the mayor of Nefrusy, Mahu—may he live again!

Right edge of the dorsal pillar: . . . true [king's] scribe, a mayor praised in his city, Yuny, the true. Made by his son, who causes his name to live, the mayor of Nefr<usy> Mahu.

20-B. Statue of the Woman

On the socle: For the Ka of the chantress of Khnum, Lord of Herwer, Mutnofret.

On the dress: Made by her son, who causes her name to live, the mayor Mahu of Nefrusy. *(The left side of the seat front has virtually the same inscription.)*

Front of the seat, right side: Her "brother," the mayor Yuny of Nefrusy.

Right side of the seat:[19] A boon of Osiris, the great god, ruler of eternity, that he may give bread, water and breath, wine and milk; justification in the land of those with weary limbs *(=the underworld)*; safety upon going out; being fixed on his foundation; going out as Re sees him, and adoring him when he (=*Re*) hears his cry at [dawn]. A "boon which the king gives" of the Lord of eternity for the Ka of the Osiris Mutnofret—may she live again!

Back of the statue, central inscription: [A boon of Osiris, the great god], the ruler of eternity, that he may grant the delivery of bread and [beer], a libation of wine, milk [and . . .]. May you enter so that Re may see you each time he rises and sets, that he may desire and [. . .] your (?) face, whether entering or going out, like one whom he favors:[20] for the Ka of Mutnofret.

Back of the statue, left side: A "boon which the king gives" of Khnum, lord of Herwer, the great god, lord as far as heaven, as he gives (the means of) entering favored and departing beloved, (as) one whose praises are established <in> the house of the king: for the Ka of her son who causes her name to live, the mayor Mahu of Nefrusy.

Back of the statue, right side: A "boon which the king gives" of Thoth, Lord of the Eight, master of the divine word, preeminent in Hesret, that he may give (the means of) entering and departing from his mansion, my (*sic*) mouth (filled with) the provisions of his giving, and <your> body endowed with praises every day: for the Ka of the mayor Mahu of Nefrusy.

21. Statue of Amenemopet

The owner is shown kneeling and holding a stela in front of him. On the base: The king's scribe, overseer of field-workers, Amenemopet, born to the housewife [. . .].

On the stela: [. . .] fashioned [in] gold, establishing [. . . *for the Aten who inspires*] adoration in [*all*] hearts [when he appears at] dawn in the course of every day, at Aten-rise [. . .] to [. . .] in order to illuminate the Two Lands for the beloved son, the Lord of the Two Lands [NEFERKHEPRURE-WAENRE]: may you protect the Son of Re, AMEN<HOTEP> IV, long in his lifetime, forever, forever!

22. Letter from the Steward of Memphis Apy to the King

This document was found in duplicate (thus never delivered?) at Gurob, near the Faiyum. Written less than a month before the "earlier proclamation" of the new capital at Akhet-Aten, it conveys a deceptive impression of calm before the storm which would break out so soon afterward.

The estate servant Apy addresses the Horus, [Mighty] Bull, "Tall-Plumed"; Two Ladies, "Great of Kingship in Karnak"; Horus of Gold, "Who Elevates the Crowns in Upper Egyptian Heliopolis"; the King of Upper and Lower Egypt, who lives on Maat, [the Lord of the Two Lands], NEFERKHEPRURE; the Son of Re who lives on Maat, AMENHOTEP IV, long in his lifetime, may he live forever continually:

"May [Ptah of] the benign countenance, act for you—the one who created your beauty; your true father, from whom you issued to be ruler of the Aten's circuit. May [he] stretch out his [arms] and bring back [for] you the [southerners], prostrate [before] you, while the lands [are filled with] terror. May he place them beneath your sandals, for you are the sole lord, the likeness of Re. [So long] as he shines in heaven, you shall possess continuity and eternity with life and peaceful years."

"[This is] a communication [to my lord], l.p.h., to let One (=*the king*) know that the temple of your father Ptah, South-of-his-Wall, the lord of Ankh-towy, is prosperous and flourishing; that the house of Pharaoh, l.p.h., is in good order; that the palace complex of Pharaoh, l.p.h., is in good order; and that the quarter of Pharaoh, l.p.h., is in good order and security. The offerings of all the gods and goddesses who are on the soil of Memphis [have been issued] in full, and nothing therein has been held back, but is offered—pure, acceptable, approved and selected—on behalf of the life, prosperity and health of the King of Upper and Lower Egypt, who lives on Maat, the

Lord of the Two Lands, NEFERKHEPRURE-WAENRE; the Son of Re who lives on Maat, AMENHOTEP IV, [long] in his lifetime, living forever continually." This is a communication concerning it on regnal year 5, third month of the Growing season, day 19.

Address on the verso: (To) Pharaoh, l.p.h., the lord, from the steward of Memphis Apy.

23. Tomb of the God's Father Hatiay

On a lintel from Hatiay's tomb we see on the panel's left side the dedicator and his two sons, presenting offerings to an enthroned Osiris, Foremost of the West, Lord of Eternity, Ruler of Eternity. *His wife,* Isis the Great, the God's Mother, *stands beside his throne. Above the worshipers:* "Hail to you, [O Osiris, justified] in the divine assembly. You are manifest like Re in the two horizons, his disk being your disk (=*Aten*), his image your image, his awesomeness your awesomeness. For the Ka of the God's Father Hatiay, justified in peace.

Behind the owner: His son, the God's Father Ty, justified *and* his son, the lay priest Mose, justified.

The right side of the panel, in much worse condition than the other, showed a similar row of devotees (of which only the first figure survives) presenting offerings to Sokar, the Great God, Lord of Ro-Setchau, residing in the *Shetchyt*-shrine [. . .], *and* Hathor, mistress of the temple.

Between the two parts of the panel is a column of text: An "offering which the king gives" of Sokar-Osiris, Lord of Ro-Setchau, that he may grant (the power) to come forth as a living Ba in order to see Aten on earth.

Below the panels are two horizontal texts. On the left: An "offering which the king gives" of Osiris, Foremost of the West, Wenen-nefer, Lord of Abydos [. . .]. *On the right:* An "offering which the king gives" of Sokar who resides in the *Shetchyt*-shrine, the Great God, Lord of Ro-Setchau [. . .].

24. Funerary Stela of the Mercantile Agent Huy, from Saqqara

Left: A "boon which the king gives" of the Aten who lives on Maat, by the mercantile agent of the Mansion of the Aten, Huy.

Right: A "boon which the king gives" of Re, ruler of the double horizon, the unique god who lives on Maat, by the chief mercantile agent of the Mansion of the Aten, Huy.

Above the offering scene on the lower part of the stela: Making a "boon which the king gives" for the Ka of the Osiris Huy, consisting of all good things, by his son Iiren (and) by the housewife Nedjem-Mennefer.

25. Small Private Stelae Related to the Royal Cult

25-A. Stela of Menu

In the upper register a king wearing the Blue Crown, [. . . , given] life (?) like Re forever, *is shown enthroned before a laden offering table. He is presumably being adored by the kneeling figure of the owner in the lower register, the text in front of whom is as follows:*

Giving adoration to the Good God, kissing the ground to the Lord of the Two Lands: "I adore your handsome face even as I propitiate your Ka every day." Made by the chief brewer of the House of Re-Horakhty in his Name "Light" (=*Shu*),' (namely) Menu. *The establishment in question belonged to the Aten, who is referred to here by an abbreviated version of his early didactic name, HOR-ATEN.*

25-B. Stela of the Official Kia

In the upper part of the tablet, Amenhotep IV (his figure and names mostly erased) stands on the right, offering a table laden with food to the hawk-headed sun-god enthroned on the left. The main text is inscribed in columns below (of which the bottoms are missing), with the owner's figure (now lost) probably shown in the lower right-hand corner.

Adoration of HOR-[ATEN] . . . at [his] rising [in the] western [horizon] of heaven [by the official] Kia. He says: "Hail [to you, . . .]! When you shine, the subjects (?) live, ... [May you grant(?)] contentment as one favored [before] the king [while attaining] burial with the favor [of. . . . Let me partake of (?)] the divine offerings which the King of Upper and Lower Egypt [NEFER-KHEPRURE-WAENRE] dedicated [. . . , being what] HOR-ATEN [decreed] for him, [namely, to the image of the King of Upper and Lower Egypt, NEFERKHEPRURE-WAENRE, the Lord of Crowns, AMENHOTEP IV], long in his lifetime, and to the image of the King of Upper and Lower Egypt

. . . RE,[21] [consisting of] great loaves of *pesen*-bread and of . . . [for the Ka of the official] Kia, called. . . .

26. From Private Tombs at Saqqara

26-A. Family Tomb of the Vizier Aper-El

Discovered in 1989, this battered tomb reveals a vizier with a Semitic name who also claimed the title of First Servant of Aten, *which is known only from the reign of Amenhotep IV/Akhenaten. Objects buried with Aper-El date to the time of Amenhotep III, but a number of jar sealings from the tomb are in the name of* Neferkheprure beloved of (Osiris) Wenennefer *(=Amenhotep IV). Dated dockets written on wine jars from the tomb indicate that Aper-El's son,* the commander of the horse, commander of chariotry, scribe of recruits of the Lord of the Two Lands, Huy, *was buried no earlier than the tenth regnal year of a king who is likely to be Akhenaten. While this evidence suggests that Aper-El's tenure as vizier extended from late in the reign of Amenhotep III into that of Amenhotep IV, any further conclusions (regarding, among other things, the alleged coregency of these two kings) seem premature.*

26-B. Tomb of the Steward of the Estate of Aten, Meritneith

Substantial portions of this tomb in south Saqqara were evidently completed during the first part of Akhenaten's reign. After the break with orthodoxy, Meritneith changed his name to Meritaten: clear but sporadic traces of this alteration are to be seen on the fragments from the tomb. On the best preserved block (A) are two men, evidently attendants of the priest who performs the "opening of the mouth" on the deceased's mummy. The figure in front carries an ostrich plume and a stack of flat objects named in the inscription above: Words spoken by the lector-priest and *sem*-priest: "Be pure, be pure, O steward of the House of Aten Meritneith (*sic*), justified! Receive the four *abet,* that you may tap the mouth and eyes of the steward of <Aten> Meritaten, justified. Yours is the ostrich plume for the two eyes (*of the deceased*), that your face may not be deprived of it"—namely, the ostrich plume.

Behind this figure is another man, carrying two cloths: Words spoken by < . . . for> the steward of the House of Aten, Meritaten, justified upon the beautiful west, the place of rewarding: "Receive to yourself the *menkhet*-cloth, that your mouth may be opened on your (own) account."

Another fragment, apparently the bottom of a doorjamb (B), contained four columns of mortuary wishes for the Ka of the steward of the House of Aten, Meritneith (*sic*). *A third fragment (C) showed relatives of the deceased in a banquet scene: to the right, and formally separate, is the end of a speech from the adjoining scene, now lost:* ". . . while I was following the King of Upper and Lower Egypt [NEFERKHEPRU]RE-[WAENRE], given life: the steward of the House of Aten, [Meritaten]."

27. Stela of Nakhtmin

The entire piece is a false door in miniature: the owner is visualized as kneeling within a recess (with only his head, sculpted in the round, visible) as he holds a round-topped stela in front of him. The façade of the building that the owner thus occupies is represented by an entablature above his head and by the border that frames the entire piece. On the entablature are cartouches of HOR-ATEN, given life forever continually, *and the royal couple:* NEFERNKHEPRURE-WAENRE, given life; AKHENATEN, long in his lifetime, *and* NEFERNEFRUATEN-NEFERTITI, may she live forever and ever.

Left border: Adoration of the king who lives on Maat, the Lord of the Two Lands, [NEFERKHEPRURE]-WAENRE, the Son of Re, [AKHENATEN],[22] who issued from his limbs to be lord of Aten's circuit: "Hail to you, joyful ruler who has subdued all lands," by the scribe Nakhtmin, justified.

Right border: Adoration of HOR-ATEN, given life forever continually, as he gives continuity and eternity in jubilees to his son, the "Only One of Re" (=Waenre): "Hail to you, O mighty king, lord of every foreign country," by [the scribe] Nakhtmin, justified.

On the tablet: Adoration of Re, when he rises until his setting from life occurs, by the scribe Nakhtmin, justified. He says: "Hail to you, Re, lord of Maat, Atum in his setting. Your rising is beautiful as you shine upon the back of your mother,[23] manifest in the eastern horizon. May she make a greeting to your handsome face, and may she satisfy your Person at the time of your crossing the sky, your heart being joyful. The Sea of Knives has become peaceful, and Re shall have a breeze in the action of the Night Bark, which destroys its attacker.

On top of stela are two representations of Anubis: Anubis who is in the embalming-house, lord of the holy land; *and* Anubis, preeminent in the temple.

On the sides of the stela, Nakhtmin and his wife kneel in adoration below the following texts:

(A) Giving adoration to Re-Horakhty, kissing the ground to living Aten by the scribe Nakhtmin, justified, and his "sister," his beloved, the housewife Tuy, justified.

(B) Adoration of Re when he rises in the eastern horizon of the sky by the scribe Nakhtmin, justified, and his "sister," his beloved, the housewife Tuy, justified.

28. Stela of Panehsy

At the top of this false door, now in the Louvre, a man and his wife are shown on the lintel, adoring the disk of the Aten as it streams down upon a table of offerings: two sets of cartouches, with the divine names erased, stand at either side of the disk. The following text is in front of the man: Adoration of Horakhty when he rises in his horizon, who gives his beauty to the whole land: "One lives after he has given his rays, and the land is bright at your birth every day, (which happens) in order to cause all he has created to live." By the favorite of the Lord of the Two Lands, whom his god, the Lord of Heliopolis, loves: the scribe of the offering table of the Lord of the Two Lands, Khay, son of the overseer of the cattle of the House of Re, the lay priest Panehsy.

By the woman: His beloved "sister," the housewife Tuy.

Left Half of Frame around Scene below: An "offering which the king gives" of Horakhty, the great god, lord of eternity, the god who has no other like him: "How prosperous is the favorite [. . .]."

Same, Right Half: An "offering which the king gives" of Atum, Lord of Heliopolis, the august god, beloved [. . .]."

In the scene below, Horakhty, the great god, lord of heaven and earth, the ruler of eternity *is adored by Panehsy and his wife (their figures now destroyed):* Adoration of Re when he rises in the horizon (and) until he sets in life. "[May he give] me breath, [may he knot together] my limbs, that [I may] see [him each time he appears]." By the overseer of cattle [of the House of Re, the lay priest Panehsy], (and) his [beloved] "sister," [the housewife Tuy].

29. Tomb of Ptahmay

A number of blocks from this tomb were found at Giza and are now preserved in the Egyptian Museum in Cairo. In addition to the tomb owner, Ptahmay, and his wife Ty, a second couple (Mehy and his wife, Husu) is occasionally represented: undoubtedly they are relatives, but specific evidence is lacking–although the description of Mehy as "the Osiris," an epithet not associated with Ptahmay, could suggest that the former had died earlier.

Offering all good and pure things on which a god lives to the Ka of the chief maker of gold leaf of the House of Aten Ptahmay, justified, possessor of reverence; and his "sister," the housewife Ty, justified in the necropolis.

Offering all good and pure things and presenting all sorts of fresh plants to the Ka of the chief of the troop of launderers of the harem Mehy, justified; and his beloved "sister," the housewife Husu, justified.

References in the inscriptions to orthodox divinities alongside the Aten suggest that decoration of the tomb took place sometime before Amenhotep IV changed his name to Akhenaten. The following invocations convey the mixture of Atenist and conventional elements:

For your Ka! Spend a nice day of the Aten's through what your beloved "sister," the housewife Ty, justified, gives to you.

"You rise beautifully, O living Aten!" May he give bread, beer, cool water, and offerings in Heliopolis to the Ka of the chief maker of gold leaf of the House of Aten Ptahmay, justified.

The housewife Ty, justified, she says: "O [my (?)] good [lord (?)], living Aten, give the breath which is yours to give, so that <I> may see you every day."

Making a libation <to> Re-Horakhty when he rises in the horizon of heaven; [and making mortuary offerings of bread and beer], oxen and fowl, cool water, wine, incense, milk and every good and pure thing [while presenting] all sorts of fresh plants to the Ka of the chief maker of gold leaf Ptahmay, justified; the Osiris, chief of the troop of launderers Mehy, justified; and the housewife Ty, justified.

"You set beautifully, O Atum, Lord of the Two Lands, Heliopolitan!" May he give all good and pure things, (along with) breathing the fragrant breath of the northwind, to the Ka of the chief of the troop of launderers Mehy, justified.

The housewife Husu, she says: "You set beautifully, O living Aten! Give me a good lifetime, so that I may see you every day."

30. Texts from the Tomb of Kheruef (Theban Tomb 192)

Kheruef, steward of Queen Tiyi's household, lived into the early reign of Amenhotep IV but spent most of his career under Amenhotep III. The latter's jubilees, which are extensively represented on the portico of his tomb, were no doubt the high points of his life. Reliefs which mention Amenhotep IV are confined to the tomb's façade and entrance corridor.

30-A. Lintel of Façade: Amenhotep IV and Queen Tiyi before the Gods

The King: The Good God, NEFERKHEPRURE-WAENRE, the Son of Re, AMENHOTEP IV, LONG IN HIS LIFETIME, given life like Re.

The Queen: The God's Mother and King's Chief Wife, TIYI, may she live and be young.

The Gods: Re-Horakhty, the Great God, Lord of Heaven
Maat, the Daughter of Re.
Atum, Lord of Heliopolis, as he gives all life, all health, all joy, all provisions.
(Hathor), Chieftainess of Thebes.

30-B. Scenes from the South Side of the Entrance Passage

At the right end, Amenhotep IV offers to Amenhotep III and Tiyi: [. . .] NEFERKHEPRURE-WAENRE, [. . .] AMENHOTEP IV, LONG IN HIS LIFETIME, [. . .].

[. . .] NEBMAATRE [. . .].

Despite the damage to this scene, it is clear that Amenhotep III was identified by only one cartouche and that his costume included a panther skin–details that play a major, although inconclusive, part in debates about the alleged coregency of these two kings. The left side of the wall shows Amenhotep IV offering to the sun-god: Offering a great oblation to Re-Horakhty, that he may make "given life" like

Re everlastingly. *The prayer that accompanied this oblation is laid out in a most unusual fashion, the words being placed in a grid that can be read vertically and horizontally, in the manner of a crossword. It was erased by Akhenaten's partisans, most probably because it is substantially a hymn to the proscribed Theban god Amun.*

Above word square: Adoration of Re in the morning [. . .] in the horizon [. . .].

Word square, horizontal lines: Adoration of Amun-[Re], the divine god, beloved one, [. . .] by [the Good God] Neferkheprure, the Son of Re, Amenhotep IV: "Hail to you, (O) Re, great of appearances [. . .], beautiful of forms, preeminent in his sanctuary, soulful one (?), most hidden of those who are hidden when he sets; mighty of countenance, who has made all that exists; (O) Horus the Elder, lord of the two conclaves, who is in the bark, repeating appearances, [. . .]; (O) Re-Khepri, [. . .] as the solar disk (=*Aten*); (O) Atum, who is over the Two Horizons, perfect, King of the Gods, who advances his divine image, [great] in valor, effective, [. . .], who is satisfied with [. . .], great of [. . .] his mother; good spokesman (?), [. . .] watchful of countenance when the land brightens; (O) Amun-Re, [. . .] as sunlight, . . . ruler of Thebes, foremost of [. . .] Manu, most gracious one of the gods (?), [. . .], the greatest who has come into being (?), lord of those who are with him; (O) Kamutef, [. . .], lord of [. . .], unique, beside whom there is none, [. . .], the eldest of those who are glorified (?). It is the one whose power is great who illumines the earth, who traverses the sky, the lord of exultation: Amun-[Re], the unique god who is peerless, abiding (?), [great] in strength, [. . .], King of Upper and Lower Egypt, . . . the god, lord of heaven, rich in manifestations, [. . .] (at?) the entrance (?) of Manu; Lord of the Thrones of the Two Lands, whose form is hidden, who has made grain [. . .], lord of eternity and master of continuity, great one, good [king], pure lord, [. . .] every [. . .], long of reign, the sunlight, dazzling [. . .] Amun-Re [. . .] the Two Lands [. . .] the Son of Re, Amenhotep IV, [. . .] you, Re, image who came forth from Nun; fashioner of forms, [. . .], lord of ruler[s], the Theban, who sustains everyone; mother of mothers and father of fathers, [Amenhotep], Re of (?) [. . .], presiding over his creation, [. . .], who has made [all] who exist, who has no [duplicate] appearing on earth, whose body is the solar disk, [. . .], who joins [. . .], ruler [of Thebes], [. . .], lord [. . .] who has created what exists and advances all beings; unfathomable one, the eldest . . . Aten. [Hail to you], [. . . great] in terror [. . .] all [. . .], whose [body] is Nun, who sustains the Two Lands. Hail to your presence, king of mankind, [. . .] himself when he made (?) [. . .], great of creativity forever."

Vertical lines: Adoration of Re-Horakhty, the good spokesman of the gods

(?), by the Good God, the Son of Re, [Amenhotep IV]: "[Hail to you], (O) Amun-[Re], the eldest, perfect [. . .], whose power is great, lord of heaven, king (?), Amenhotep [. . .], the great god, lord of the two conclaves, King of the Gods, watchful of countenance, the greatest who ever came into being (?), who illumines the earth, rich in manifestations; the pure lord, ruler of Thebes, presiding over his creation, [. . .], [great] in terror, divine in appearances, who is in the bark, who promotes the dawn, lord of those who are with him, who traverses the sky [. . .] you [. . .], lord of [. . .], beloved one, [. . .] repeating appearances, divine of image, Amun-Re Kamutef, lord of exultation (at the) entrance (?) of Manu [. . .] every [. . .], the sun who has made [all] who exist, [. . .], all [. . .] Amun-[Re], Lord of the Thrones of the Two Lands, [. . .] image without duplicate, who has created what exists, whose [body] is Nun: so says the [Good God] Neferkheprure, [great] in valor [. . .], lord of [. . .], the god Amun, long of reign, who came forth from Nun and appeared on earth, who advances all beings and sustains the Two Lands; who is beautiful in manifestations, foremost of his sanctuary—(i.e.), Khepri, effective as sunlight, the sole unique one whose form is sunlight; the fashioner of his own flesh, who is unfathomable. Hail to your presence, (O) Re, soulful one (?), [. . .] beside whom there is none; peerless, who has made grain; dazzling of forms [. . .] the solar disk; eldest one, king of [man]kind; the Son of Re, Amenhotep IV, [. . .], abiding [. . .], lord of rulers [. . .] himself; most hidden of those who are hidden, [. . .], foremost of [. . .], [great] in strength, lord of eternity, Amun-Re, the Theban, who joins [. . .] when he has made (?) [. . .]; gracious when he sets as the solar disk, great of [. . .], master of continuity, [. . .] who sustains everyone; [. . .], great of creativity, ruler of Thebes, mighty of countenance; Atum, [. . .] Manu, the eldest, King of Upper and Lower Egypt, great one, [. . .] the Two Lands, mother of mothers, [. . .]. Hail to you, who have made all that exists, who is far from his mother, most gracious of those who are glorified (?), [. . .], father of fathers, [. . .] the disk forever."

30-C. Hymn to the Rising Sun

"Adoration of Re in the morning [when he rises] in the horizon of heaven by the hereditary prince and count, the favorite of Horus (who is) Lord of the Palace, the steward of the King's Chief Wife, the first royal herald, Kheruef, justified. [He says]: "Hail to you, (O) Re in his rising, Amun in [your beautiful setting]. You shine on your mother's back, appearing [in glory] as king of the Ennead. [Nut makes] a greeting before your face, and Maat embraces you at all times. [You] traverse [the sky], your [heart] being joyful, for the Lake of the Two Knives has become peaceful and the rebel has fallen, his arms bound, knives having severed his [vertebrae]. As to the One with the Evil Disposition, [his] movements have been checked, and your enemies are fallen [at] the place of their massacre. As for the gods, their hearts are glad when they see you in the morning bark. (They say): 'Re has a breeze continually.' As for the evening bark, it has destroyed the one who attacked it. You cross both your heavens in triumph while your Ennead appears in your following. Your mother Nut enfolds you as you are made to flourish in your place of yesterday."

The king's scribe, first king's herald and steward of the King's Chief Wife, Kheruef, justified. [He] says: "I adore you while your beauty is in my sight and your sunshine appears upon my breast."

30-D. Hymn to the Setting Sun

Adoration of Re as he sets in life in the western horizon of heaven by the hereditary prince and count, sole companion who has access to his lord, favorite of Horus (who is) lord of the palace, the first king's [herald], king's scribe and steward, Kheruef, justified. He says: "Hail to you, master of continuity, Atum, chief of eternity! Now that you have joined with the horizon of heaven, you appear in glory on the western side as Atum, who is in the evening, having come in your power and having no opponent. You rule the sky as Re and you reach both your heavens in happiness. You have banished clouds and tempest. As you descend into the womb of your mother Naune, your father Nun [makes] greeting and the gods of the western mountain are jubilating. Those who are in the netherworld are joyous when they see their far-striding lord!"

"(O) Amun-Re, lord of everyone, welcome! <You have> reached the Two Lands (=the earth) and you have joined the arms of the western mountain. Your Person has attained veneration, being moored at your place of yesterday. The arms of your mother are a protection [around] you as the jackals are overthrowing your enemy. The western souls tow you onto the way which is in the holy land, that you may illuminate the faces of the denizens of the netherworld, hear the summons of the one in the sarcophagus, and raise up those who are placed on (their) side.[24] You feed on Maat from the one who bears it (=Re) and you rejuvenate nostrils with the one who has it. You are thus raised to an august position, and you cause those who have become gods to be provided for. When (you) go forth there, their warmth is (re)generated, for you are restored in your former state, having come as the solar disk, the power of the sky, and being united with the ruler of the Realm of Silence (=Osiris). You impart your beauty inside the netherworld, and now you shine for those who are in darkness. Those who are in the caverns are in joy, adoring you as you approach them with this countenance of yours, (you) who awaken uninjured, who spend every night conceived. At dawn [you are] rejuvenated . . . days as this (divine) youth, radiant (?) in his form, who issues from his mother's womb without ceasing and goes to rest in it at [his] time."

. . . [Kher]uef, [justi]fied. [He] says: "Hail to you, being Re when you rise and Atum after [you] set. May you permit me to be among your favored ones, beholding your beauty every day, and let me grasp the tow-rope of the evening bark and the mooring [post of the morning bark]."

31. The Steward Ramose (Theban Tomb 46)

In texts from his tomb, the owner is described as the hereditary prince and count, fanbearer at the king's right hand, true king's scribe, his beloved, overseer of the granary of Upper and Lower Egypt, Ramose, justified, *with the following wish:* For the Ka of the true king's scribe, his beloved, the steward of the Mansion of the Aten, Ramose, justified. *His wife is* the singer of Hathor, chantress of Amun (?), . . . Nofretkha.

32. Texts from Tomb of the Vizier Ramose (Theban Tomb 55)

Ramose was one of two prime ministers who ran the pharaoh's government. Inscriptions in his tomb at Thebes reveal that his family had held high office in the north for at least a generation previously. Ramose's own career, like Kheruef's, spanned the last decade of Amenhotep III and the early "Theban" period of his son.

32-A. Choral Hymn on behalf of Amenhotep III and Ramose

Adoration is in heaven, celebration in the palace and rejoicing within the courtyard! The Two Banks of Horus are exulting, (for) Amun is upon the great seat when he rises as Amun-Re, Lord of Heaven. May he cause NEBMAATRE, given life, to endure. May he make his lifetime to be united with continuity, his years all together in myriads.

(O) city overseer and vizier Ramose, justified! May your lord Amun favor you in your house of the living. All the western gods exult for love of you, for you have been offered a "boon which the king gives"–

of Amun-Re Harakhty,
of Atum, Lord of Heliopolis,
of his eye, of his hand, of his body,

of Osiris, Chief of the Westerners,
of Hathor, chieftainess of the desert,
(of) [Anubis, Lord of the] Holy Ground, (and)
[of] all the gods of the underworld.

32-B. Ramose's Prayer to Osiris

Giving adoration [to Osiris by] the chieftain of the entire land, the city overseer and vizier Ramose, justified. He says: "In peace have I come, having completed a lifetime in the favor of the Good God. I did what people like and what the gods approve. I did what [the king of] my time favored. I did not transgress what he had decreed. I committed no wrong against the people. I did right (=*Maat*) on earth, for I know that you favor the righteous one who does no deeds of wrongdoing."

By Ramose's wife: Giving adoration <to> Osiris, kissing the ground to Wenennefer, the justified: "Hail to you, (O) king, lord to continuity, son of Nut, heir of Geb, . . . every day." By the chantress of Amun, the housewife Meritptah, justified.

32C. Ramose before the King

Four figures of Ramose present the standard of Amun and other ritual objects to Amenhotep IV, enthroned with the goddess Maat. The entirety of this scene is executed in the conventional style, as is most of the tomb.

Words spoken by the city overseer and vizier Ramose, justified: "For your Ka, the bouquet of your father, [Amun-Re, Lord of the Thrones of the Two] Lands, preeminent in Karnak. May he favor you, love you, and cause you to endure. May [he] grant [you . . . on the] great [seat]. May he overthrow your enemies, dead [or living], while you are established on his seat [of] the living. All life and dominion before you, all health before you, like your father Re every day!"

Words spoken by the speaker of Nekhen, the god's servant of Maat, the city overseer and vizier Ramose, justified: "For your Ka, the bouquet of your father Hor-Aten. May he favor you, love you and cause you to endure. May he grant you millions of years (with) your jubilee records, all lands being under your sandals. May he overthrow your enemies, dead or living. [All] joy before you, all health before you, all life before you, while you are established on the throne of Re forever [like Re]."

Between these first two figures: Presenting the bouquet of Horakhty by the city overseer and vizier Ramose, justified.

Third figure: "[For your Ka, the bouquet of Mut (?). May she favor you], love you and place her arms as a protection behind you. By the city overseer and vizier, Ramose, justified"

Fourth figure: "For your Ka, the bouquet of Khonsu-<Nefer>hotep. May he grant you all joy before you." By the Speaker of Nekhen, the god's servant of Maat, the city overseer and vizier, Ramose, justified.

Between these figures: Presenting a bouquet to the king.

32-D. Ramose Is Rewarded at the Royal Window of Appearances

This scene and its continuation (E, below) are executed in the "revolutionary" art style, in contrast to the conventional style found throughout the rest of the tomb. Above Ramose, who kneels before Amenhotep IV and Nefertiti, is the following: Giving adoration to the Good God, kissing the ground to the Lord of the Two Lands by the hereditary prince and sole companion, the city overseer and vizier Ramose. He says: "When you rise, O Neferkheprure-Waenre, you appear like your father, the living Aten. May he grant you continuity as king and eternity as joyful ruler."

By Ramose, as he is laden with gold collars: The hereditary prince and sole companion, the favorite, [beloved of] the Lord of the Two Lands, the city overseer and vizier, Ramose. He says: "Make healthy [Pharaoh, l.p.h.], O [Aten . . .], [. . .] you (=people), for Aten slakes his heart, (namely) the good ruler, valiant in form. Rise for him, O Aten! Make Pharaoh healthy, O Aten!"

32-E. Ramose transmits a Royal Speech to Foreign Emissaries

[Said] by the king who lives on Maat, the Lord [of the Two Lands . . .], given [life] to the hereditary prince [and sole companion], the city overseer and vizier, Ramose:

"[*Listen to the*] words which I set before you, the guidelines [of the Two Lands . . .] conditions, they come to pass for (?) [. . .] I have decreed it. All that is in the entire land [. . .] more than the kings (who existed) since the god's time (on earth): they are wise (?) [. . .]."

The hereditary prince and sole [companion], the city overseer and vizier

Ramose, he says: "May [the] Aten act as you have decreed, as you [. . .]. May your monuments be established like heaven, and your lifetime like Aten in it. May your monuments come into being like those things of heaven which came into being. You are unique, and this [land] is under his directions. For you the mountains reveal what they hid. Your renown has developed in their hearts, just as your renown came to be in the hearts of men, and they listen to you as men listen."

F. Burial Procession of Ramose

First Register

Following the procession of the favorite of the Good God, the city overseer and vizier Ramose, justified:

By the first prophet [of Amun . . .]: "Go to rest, go to rest on the west of Thebes!"

The second prophet [of Amun . . .].

The third prophet of [Amun . . .].

The fourth prophet of [Amun], Simut, justified.

Second Register

Following the procession of the favorite, the beloved of the Lord of the Two Lands, the city overseer and vizier Ramose, justified:

By the viceroy of Kush.

By the first "king's herald."

By the overseer of the great treasury.

By the second "king's herald" of the Lord of the Two Lands.

The great companions of the palace.

The great officials of the city.

33. Texts from the Tomb of the Cupbearer Parennefer (Theban Tomb 188)

Parennefer had substantially decorated his Theban Tomb before he followed his royal master to Akhet-Aten (see No. 78 below). In the reaction that followed Akhenaten's death, the most important protagonists in the scenes in this chamber were vandalized (both the figures and names), including the king, Parennefer himself and, to some extent, the early manifestation of the Aten.

1. *Beside erased figure of the falcon-headed sun-god:* Re-Horakhty, the great god, lord of heaven. . . .

Lintel, left side: Giving adoration to Re-Horakhty and kissing the ground to the royal Ka of the Lord of Crowns, Lord of the Two Lands NEFERKHEPRURE-[WAENRE] by the king's cupbearer, whose hands are pure, the one whom his lord has favored, Parennefer, justified. He says: "May you be allowed to occupy the seat of the justified ones, seeing Aten at dawn in the eastern horizon of the sky."

Lintel, right side: Giving adoration to Re-Horakhty and kissing [the ground] at your setting from life by the unique excellent one who is effective on behalf of the Good God, one whom the Lord of the Two Lands promoted on account of his character, the Osiris Parennefer, justified.

2. *Exterior jambs:*
(A) The hereditary prince and count, god's father and beloved of the god, sealbearer of the king of Lower Egypt, great [of favor], unique one of the king, who can approach the god's flesh, favored since he came forth from the womb; the overseer of all the crafts of the king, the king's cupbearer whose hands are pure, the one whom his lord favored, Parennefer, justified.

(B) The hereditary prince and count, the sole attendant of the king in the private place, one who entered the palace and came out with favor, the overseer of all the king's work projects in the House of Aten; the king's cupbearer, *etc., as in A.*

(C) The hereditary prince and count, important in his office and great in his official dignity, [. . . in] front of the subjects, the king's confidant who made functional his monuments in the House of Aten; the king's cupbearer, *etc., as in A.*

(D) [. . .] moment to moment in [. . .] Upper and Lower Egypt, the overseer of prophets [. . . , Parennefer].

3. *Outer wall thickness, east side:* Adoring Hor-Aten and [the first prophet] of Hor-Aten, King NEFERKHEPRURE-WAENRE, given life; by the king's cupbearer, whose hands are pure, [Parennefer, justified]. He says: "Hail to you as you dawn in the horizon, having illuminated the circuit of Aten. (O) beauty who is upon all lands, all eyes see by you and awaken when you shine, their arms jubilant on account of your Ka. You are the god who created their limbs: they live when your rays are on earth, while they make merry in the same way I make thanksgiving to your beautiful face [at the] terrace of "Rejoicing in the Horizon" [. . .] fresh green plants of the divine offerings which issue from [. . .]. The hereditary prince and count, whom the king promoted on account of [his] character, [. . .].

4. Back wall door, left jamb:

(A) A "boon which the king gives" of Anubis, [who is in] the embalming-house, that he may allow the corpse to be firm in the necropolis while the Ba is at rest in its mansion every day; for the Ka of the hereditary prince and count, the guardian of the Lord of the Two Land's footsteps in every place he has trodden, the king's cupbearer, whose hands are pure, [. . .],[25] Parennefer, justified.

(B) [. . .] unique excellent one, true witness, quelling (dissent) by what issues from his mouth, the king's cupbearer, whose hands are pure, [. . .], Parennefer, justified.

(C) [. . .] the mouth of Horus in his house, greatly favored one of the Lord of the Two Lands, the king's cupbearer [. . .] Parennefer, justified.

5. North wall, east side:

Behind the king's cupbearer, whose hands are pure, [Parennefer]—quick-witted in the presence of the king daily in the course of every day, *a crowd of workmen and scribes measure grain that is to be transferred to the silos shown at the top of the scene. From within his baldachin the king tells Parennefer,* "Take care of the divine offerings of the Aten!" *Parennefer's reply follows:* The king's cupbearer whose hands are pure, one whom the Lord of the Two Lands favors and loves, [Parennefer, justified], he says: "As for Pre, he knows the employee who is taking care of the divine offerings. But as for the employee who is not taking care of the divine offerings of the Aten, he *(=Aten)* shall deliver him into your hand. The revenues of every god are measured in *oipe*, but for the Aten one measures in heaps!"

6. West wall, upper part of left side, by men bringing gifts: Presenting every sort of good and pure plant and all sweet-smelling flowers as [the] offerings of every day—pure, pure—from what your son, King [NEFERKHEPRURE-WAENRE] gives; by one whom the Lord of the Two Lands favors and loves [. . . , Parennefer, justified].

34. Varia from Thebes

The following pieces attest to the continuous use of West Thebes as a royal necropolis in the earlier part of the reign, before the court moved to el-Amarna.

34-A. Chair of the Necropolis Worker Nakhy

The chair that belonged to this individual, formerly in a private collection at Luxor, has since disappeared. It was probably found at Deir el-Medina, for its owner is described as the servant in the Place of Truth on the west of Akhet-en-Aten, Nakhy.

34-B. Funerary Figurines of Setau

Two shabtis belonging to the servant in the Place of Truth Setau *were found in Tomb No. 1325 at Deir el-Medina. Each one bears, in addition to the customary shabti spell, a more personalized inscription down the front:*

Cairo statuette: May you be given wine and milk which issue from upon the offering table in the presence of Aten.

Brooklyn statuette: May you be given a libation consisting of things which issue from upon the offering table in the presence of Aten.

34-C. Coffin of the Housewife Ta'o

This piece, recovered in poor condition from the same tomb as Setau's figurines, is poorly published, and the texts are difficult to make out. A number of the inscriptions seem to have been made for a man–possibly the Neferronpet who is mentioned once (assuming this is a personal name)–and it is possible that Ta'o was the coffin's secondary owner. Several inscriptions that mention Akhet-Aten can be made out:

The housewife Ta'o—revered one of Akhet-Aten, <she> who belongs to Aten on the day when she receives the breath of life.

[May] you [repose (?)] upon your seat, which the king gives, enduring in Akhet-Aten and receiving the peace of the king's giving forever.

[. . .] with the breath [*of life* . . .] in the Mansion of the House [. . .] of Akhet-Aten, a good year (*or* Neferronpet). . . .

The revered one, a possessor of old age, [. . . as] she cleaves to (?) her place of [. . .] as one [*does something pertaining to*] the Mansion of Aten.

34-D.1. Coffin of the Granary Official Hatiay

The texts on a coffin, found in a tomb at Qurna in 1896, are notable for the way they juxtapose the owner's Atenist connections with the utterly conventional formu-

las (some of them drawn from the Pyramid Texts) and the orthodox mortuary deities invoked here. Among the most significant:

Words spoken by the Osiris, the scribe and overseer of the granary in the Mansion of the Aten, Hatiay, justified. He says: "O mother Nut, spread yourself over me and put me among the imperishable stars that are in you, and I will not die."

Words spoken by Nut, the great and effective one: "(O) my beloved son, the Osiris scribe and overseer of the granary in the Mansion of the Aten, Hatiay, justified. (O) offspring of Geb, ruler of the Two Lands, my beloved son, the scribe Hatiay, justified!"

Words spoken by this son (*of Horus*): "(O) Osiris, scribe and overseer of the granary in the Mansion of the Aten, Hatiay, justified! O heir of the ruler of the Westerners, born to Isis, who gave the desert to you, her arms being behind you: may you live everlastingly!"

34-D.2. Staff of Hatiay

This piece, perhaps pilfered from the tomb before its discovery, is inscribed for the scribe of the double granary Hatiay—may he live again!—the possessor of reverence, (belonging to) the House of Aten in Memphis.

35. Graffiti

35-A. From the Wadi Hammamat

These short inscriptions, left at the greywhacke quarry on the road between Coptos and the Red Sea, are notable for demonstrating the continued activity of a high priest of Amun in the year before Amenhotep IV made his first dramatic break with the orthodox cults.

1. Regnal year 4, third month of the Inundation season, day 11 under the Person of the King of Upper and Lower Egypt NEFERKHEPRURE-WAENRE, the Son of Re AMENHOTEP [IV], when a charge was given to the first prophet of Amun May to bring *bekhen*-stone [for] the statue of the Lord, l.p.h.

2. Regnal year 4, third month of Inundation, [day . . . : coming by the steward (?)] of the Estate of Amun with the first prophet of Amun [May, in order to quarry *bekhen*-stone . . . .].

35-B. From the Eastern Desert

Among a number of rock inscriptions discovered in 1982 at the Wadi Abu Qwei in the eastern desert are some that manifestly date to the reign of Amenhotep IV. One of these features the cartouches of [NEFERKHEPRURE-WAENRE], AMENHOTEP IV and [NEFERNEFRUATEN-NEFERTITI], *partly erased but all recognizable, grouped underneath the rays of the solar orb. Another shows the king's two cartouches being adored by a man holding a double-plume fan, with the following words carved beneath:* Made by the deputy Amenmose belonging to the troop "Re of the Rulers" of the House of Life.

36. Two Private Stelae Found at Zernik

These two rock-cut stelae no doubt owe their placement to the presence of an unusually large outcropping of nummulitic limestone on the east bank of the Nile, some four kilometers south of Esna. While both tablets are in wretched condition today, they are plainly attributable to the earlier reign of Amenhotep IV and belong to a type of private memorial that is encountered frequently in the New Kingdom.

The upper part of the first stela (A) is occupied by the following inscription: Giving praise to Amun, kissing the earth to the Bull of His Mother—"I give praise [to the] height of heaven, and I venerate your beauty"—by the quarryman attached to the works [projects of] the [Aten (?)], Neferronpet. He says: "Hail to you, king of the gods, lord of strength, [lord of (?)] lords, god [who is great of] love, mighty [in . . .]."

In the scene at the bottom of the stela, a figure of Amun-Re, King of the Gods, Lord of Heaven *sits in front of a pile of offerings, with the following inscription:* An offering of good and pure things—(namely) bread, beer, oxen and fowl; cool water, wine and milk; linen, alabaster and incense.

The upper part of the second stela (B) is occupied by a false door, in the central panel of which Amenhotep IV offers to the goddess Nekhbet. Running down the left side is the following inscription: The living Horus, mighty bull "Tall Plumed"; Two Ladies "Great of Kingship in Karnak"; Horus of Gold "Who Elevates the Crowns in [Upper Egyptian] Heliopolis"; King of Upper and Lower Egypt, whom Re has preferred, lord of forcefulness at every victory, NEFERKHEPRURE-WAENRE; Son of Re, his beloved, AMENHOTEP IV, long in his lifetime, beloved of Ro-inty, lady of heaven, [mistress of the Two Lands (?)].[26]

The corresponding space on the right side has: The living Horus, mighty bull "Tall Plumed"; Two Ladies "Great of Kingship in Karnak"; Horus of Gold, "Who Elevated the Crowns in Upper Egyptian Heliopolis"; King of Upper and Lower Egypt, ruler of the Nine Bows, Lord of Crowns who took possession of the White Crown, NEFERKHEPRURE-WAENRE; bodily Son of Re, his beloved, AMENHOTEP IV, long in his lifetime, beloved of Nekhbet the White, lady of heaven, [mistress of the Two Lands (?)].

In the lower part of the stela, beside man in an adoring position: Giving adoration to Nekhbet the White, Lady [of Heaven], the god's mother [. . .], mistress of Upper and Lower Egypt, unique eye, effective eye, lady of the carrying-[chair; and to the Lord of the Two] Lands, NEFERKHEPRURE-WAENRE: "I give [praise to the] height (?) of heaven (?), [and I give adoration (?)] to your Ka every day, ..." [Done by] the overseer of public works Aya, son of Ruty . . . [in] regnal year [. . .], . . . [in] the land to [its limit for his father], in his name, 'Light [which is in] Aten,'[27] when [he was assigned to do] public works to [beautify] The City (=*Thebes*), as he made the . . . [for] rowing the White One [to] the Southern City (=*Thebes*).

Notes

1. N.B., an abbreviated form of the earlier didactic name of the god.

2. Recut from the original AMENHOTEP IV.

3. The gods' bodies, i.e., their statues.

4. For fragments from two other contemporary lists, see Helck 1955–58: 1991–93; 1961: 347–48.

5. This fragment, along with the next (*E*) may belong to the great inscription (6 above) which details the taxes assessed for the Aten Temple at Thebes.

6. This term, written in a cartouche, probably denotes the king.

7. Or, if the titles are read separately, "king's wife, king's bodily daughter." If so, the queen's title here might best be treated as honorific since it is attached to the figure of a child.

8. Recut from "AMENHOTEP IV."

9. Alternative restorations include "[who celebrates] jubilees" and "[plentiful of] jubilees."

10. Literally, "he says," but this could be an overly concise writing of "he is called," assuming it was not miscarved for *ḏt*, "forever."

11. The debate over the reading of this dateline ("regnal [year] 2" or "[regnal year] 12") has generated a vast literature: see Fritz 1991; Murnane 1994.

12. Since the divine name is written with the baboon hieroglyph, "Khonsu" is also possible.

13. The hieroglyphs are not arranged in any customary order. The sign which we translate "image" is a recumbent sphinx.

14. Literally, "getting hot": see Navailles and Neveu 1989.

15. Instead of the customary epithet "true of voice" (*m3'-ḫrw*) normally used for the deceased, the texts on this statue regularly use only "true" (*m3'*). It is hard to tell whether this variant is meaningful, as opposed to merely graphic, since there are other anomalies that are clearly mistakes (e.g., the word "name" is regularly misspelled).

16. Or (since the spelling is identical) possibly "vizier," meaning perhaps his father's deputy? See Schenkel 1985.

17. Or perhaps emend all this to "in order to see your beauty"?

18. Or "in his beloved city, Nefr<usy>"?

19. This text, adapted from a spell written for a man, retains all its masculine endings in this copy.

20. Referring to the deceased's ability to move in and out of the tomb.

21. Most probably either [NEBMAAT]RE (=Amenhotep III) or [NEFERKHEPRU]RE (=Amenhotep IV).

22. Both cartouches have been erased as indicated. While the later nomen, "Akhenaten," can be restored from traces on the entablature, the orthodox cast of these incriptions suggests that they were prepared before the king changed his name.

23. Nut, the sky goddess.

24. A shorter version has: "May you illumine the faces of those in the netherworld and raise up the inert ones" (see Epigraphic Survey 1980: 40, n. *b*).

25. Here and in what follows, the remainder was evidently so stereotypical that Davies did not copy it.

26. Restore this or "mistress of the gods": both are common epithets of Nekhbet.

27. This last is the second part of the early "didactic name" of the Aten, here written with no cartouche as is customary in the early years of Amenhotep IV's reign.

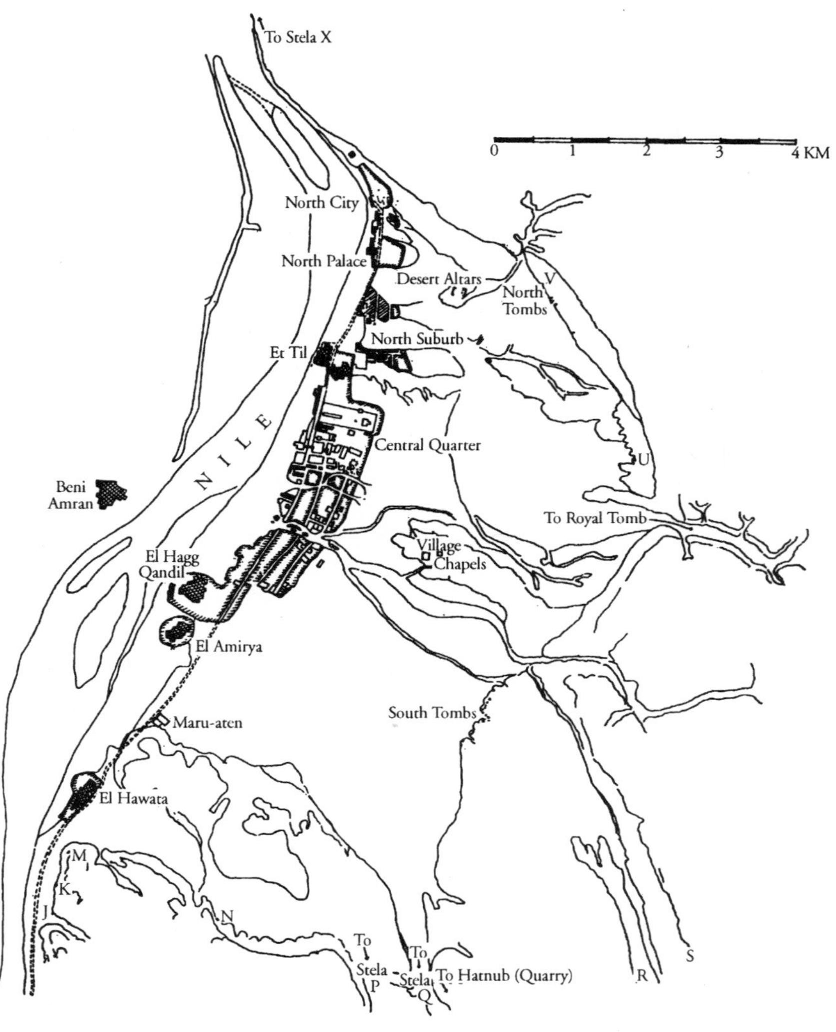

Figure 2: Map of the el-Amarna area

3

The Reign of Akhenaten: Official Inscriptions and Miscellaneous Royal Records

37. The "Earlier Proclamation" on the Boundary Stelae at El-Amarna

The actual foundation decree for the city of Akhet-Aten was initially carved on two stelae located at the northern and southern tips of the city's territory on the east bank (stelae X and M). The sudden deterioration of M, the southern monument, led to the making of another copy some distance farther south (stela K). Only the initial third of the text is substantially preserved, the rest being full of lacunae before it disappears altogether. This is a pity, for in this "earlier proclamation" the king not only set guidelines for the development of his city and its regular activities, but he also provided insights into his own motivation and the events which led to his revolution.

1. Introduction

Regnal year 5, fourth month of the Growing season, day 13: long live the Good God who rejoices [in Maat], Lord of heaven, lord of earth; [great living] Aten [who illumi]nates the Two Banks; the Father, HOR-ATEN—great living Aten who is in jubilee within the [House] of Aten in Akhet-Aten; and the Horus, "Beloved [of Aten]"; Two Ladies, "[Great of Kingship] in Akhet-Aten"; Horus of Gold "Who Raises Up the Name of Aten"; the King of Upper and Lower Egypt who lives on Maat, Lord of the Two Lands, NEFERKHEPRURE-WAENRE; the Son of Re who lives on Maat, Lord of Crowns, AKHENATEN, [long in his lifetime], who is on [the seat of his father HOR]-ATEN, manifest on Re's throne of the living like his father Aten every day. The Good God [. . .] the Aten [. . .] when he rises; a possessor of [provisions], rich in food, [. . .] everything [. . .] who does useful things for the one who fashioned him, the living Aten, lord of the sky—may he cause him to rise [as] master of [. . .] for as far as Aten encircles; may he cause him (to exist) forever, [. . .] seeing his rays while he is on earth [every] day: the King [of Upper and Lower Egypt] who lives on Maat, the Lord of the Two Lands, [NEFERKHEPRURE-WAENRE]; the Son of [Re] who lives on Maat, Lord of Crowns, AKHENATEN, long in his lifetime, living forever.

And the princess, great in the palace, fair of face, beautiful in the double plumes—the mistress of joy, at the hearing of whose voice one rejoices; possessor of graciousness, great of love, whose arrangements please the Lord of the Two Lands; chieftainess [of] the Aten's female entourage, who satisfies him when he rises in the horizon; for whom is done what she has said about any [thing]: the King's Chief Wife, his beloved, Lady of the Two Lands, NEFERTITI, may she live forever.

2. *Initial Appearance and Speech by the King*

On this day, when One was in Akhet-[Aten], his Person [appeared] on the great chariot of electrum—just like Aten, when he rises in his horizon and fills the land with the love and [the pleasantness (?) of] the Aten. He set off on a good road [toward] Akhet-Aten, his place of the primeval event, which he made for himself to set within it daily, and which his son Waenre made for him—(being) his great monument which he founded for himself; his horizon, [in which his] circuit comes into being, where he is beheld with joy while the land rejoices and all hearts exult when they see him.

A great oblation was presented to the Father, HOR-ATEN, consisting of bread, beer, long- and short-horned cattle, calves, fowl, wine, fruits, incense, all sorts of fresh green plants and everything good in front of the mountain of Akhet-Aten; [and also the] offering of a good [and pure] libation on behalf of the life, prosperity and health of the Lord of the Two Lands, NEFERKHEPRURE-WAENRE. After this, One performed the rites of the Aten, who was pleased with what was done for him. One rejoiced, and the heart [of this god] was joyful [concerning] Akhet-Aten with exultation as he hovered over [his] place, so that he could be glad concerning it and about the elevating of his beauty [in it daily in the course of every day]. His Person [stood] in the presence of his father, HOR-ATEN, as Aten's rays were upon him, with life, stability, [dominion, health, and joy] forever and ever.

Then said his Person, "Bring me the king's companions and the great ones of the palace, the supervisors of the guard, the [overseer]s of works projects, the officials and all the [court] in its entirety." So <they> were led in to him at once, and they lay on their bellies in his Person's presence, kissing [the ground before the Good God]. Then said his Person to them: "Behold Aten! The Aten wishes to have [*something*] made for him as a monument with an eternal and everlasting name. Now it is the Aten, my father, who advised me concerning it, (namely) Akhet-Aten. No official had ever advised me concerning it, nor had any people in the entire land ever advised me concerning it, to tell me [a plan] for making Akhet-Aten in this distant place. It was the Aten, my father, [who advised me] concerning it, so that it could be made for him as Akhet-Aten. Behold, I did not find it provided with shrines or plastered with tombs or porticoes (?) . . . or covered with . . . (or) with the remnant of anything which had happened to it, so that it was not [. . . ing] me . . . Akhet-Aten for the Aten, my father. Behold, it is pharaoh, l.p.h., who found it, when it did not belong to a god, nor to a goddess; when it did not belong to a male ruler, nor to a female ruler; when it did not belong to any people to do their business with it. [Its . . .] is not known, (but) I found it *widowed*. . . . It is the Aten, my [father], who advised me concerning it, (saying), 'Behold, [fill] Akhet-Aten with provisions—a storehouse for everything!' while my father, HOR-ATEN, proclaimed to me, 'It is to belong to my Person, to be Akhet-Aten continually forever.'"

"Behold, I am making an oath about it, saying: 'I shall make it [as] the horizon [*for the*] Aten, my [father, . . . them], for they are desired [. . .] for Aten to arise out of them daily, filling them with his fair and loving rays, at the seeing of which every land lives, and shedding them on NEFERKHEPRURE-WAENRE [while he] ordains [for] him [all happiness (?)] in life and dominion continually forever. So make Akhet-Aten as an estate of [the] Aten, my father, in its entirety—for I have made [it as a memorial (?), whether belonging to my name] or belonging to [her] name—namely, the King's Chief Wife, NEFERNEFRUATEN-NEFERTITI—or belonging to his name forever and ever."

3. *The Courtiers' Reply*

Then said the companions, as they replied [to] the Good God: "May your father, HOR-ATEN, act as your father, whose names are (*constantly*) invoked, has decreed, and you will be continually king, enduring forever on the boundary-marker of the Aten. There is no king of [your time who has done the like in providing benefits for his father, consisting of] every [. . .], every [. . .], (and) every [. . .] with every [. . .], monument [upon] monument for the Aten. [He has provided] guidance [for] love of you, so that you might act in accordance with all he has decreed. You are the ruler who [marshals] effective things, one who knows the limits of eternity, while he is the one who sets (things) in your heart at any place he wishes. He did not raise up any other king except for your Person; he did not ordain all that he gives for another, but [he acted for you because you made] for him the House of Aten [in] Akhet-Aten—a great [. . .] that had not known anything functional of Egypt, being perfect (?) like the horizon of heaven—Aten's palace, filled [with] all [sorts of] provisions—for the sake of making a monument for the Aten, at [the seeing of whom] everything that breathes lives, since he is the one who guides the living forever."

"May his lordship govern from Akhet-Aten. May you conduct every land to him. May you tax the towns and islands for him. Every city [down] to every [. . .], its [entirety belongs to] Aten, acting in accordance with what he himself ordains. All flat lands, all hill countries and the islands of the sea are bearing their tribute, their products on their backs, to the maker of their life, at the seeing of whose rays one lives. The breath of his love is caused to be breathed eternally, while his rays are seen, and while his lordship does [as] he pleases and [gives] commands [for you . . . while you] are in Akhet-Aten, rejuvenated like the Aten in the sky forever and ever!"

4. The Decree

Then his Person lifted his arm up to heaven, to the one who fashioned him, HOR-ATEN, declaring: "As lives my father, HOR-ATEN—

The beautiful living Aten who began life and ordains life,

My Father who is with me among [. . .] in his journey,

My rampart of millions of cubits,

My reminder of continuity,

My witness to eternal things,

The one who constructed himself with his own two hands, no craft knowing him;

The one who makes guidance by rising and setting every day without cease, in the sky or on earth, while (all) eyes behold him;

Who has no [equal] when he has filled the land with his rays, causing every face to live;

The one at whom my eyes are sated, seeing him risen daily when he rises in this house of Aten in Akhet-Aten, having filled it utterly with himself, with his fair and loving rays.

"Since he casts them on me, in life and dominion continually forever, I shall make Akhet-Aten for the Aten, my father, in this place. I shall not make Akhet-Aten for him south of it, north of it, west of it (or) east of it. I shall not go past the southern stela of Akhet-Aten toward the south, nor shall I go past the northern stela of Akhet-Aten downstream, in order to make Akhet-Aten for him there. Nor shall I make <it> for him on the western side of Akhet-Aten; but I shall make Akhet-Aten for the Aten, my father, on the orient (side) of Akhet-Aten—the place which he himself made to be enclosed for him by the mountain, on which he may achieve happiness and on which I shall offer to him. This is it!"[1]

"Nor shall the King's Chief Wife say to me, 'Look, there's a nice place for Akhet-Aten someplace else,' nor shall I listen to her. Nor shall any officials in my presence—be they officials of favor or officials of the outside, or the chamberlains, or any people in the entire land—say to me, 'Look, there's a nice place for Akhet-Aten someplace else,' nor shall I listen to them—whether it (=*that other place*) be downstream, whether it be in the south, in the west or in the orient. I will not say, 'I shall abandon Akhet-Aten so that I may hasten and make Akhet-Aten in this other nice place [. . .] together with it forever'; but [I will remain] in this Akhet-Aten, with which he himself has wished to be satisfied forever and ever!"

"At Akhet-Aten in this place shall I make the House of Aten[2] for the Aten, my father."

"At Akhet-Aten in this place shall I make the Mansion of Aten[3] for the Aten, my father."

"At Akhet-Aten in this place shall I make the sunshade[4] of the [King's Chief] Wife [NEFERNEFRUATEN-NEFERTITI] for the Aten, my father."

"In the 'Island of Aten, whose jubilees are distinguished'[5] at Akhet-Aten in this place shall I make the 'House of Rejoicing' for the Aten, my father."

"In the 'Island of Aten, whose jubilees are distinguished' at Akhet-Aten in this place shall I make the 'House of Rejoicing in [Akhet]-Aten'[6] for the Aten, my father."

"At Akhet-Aten in this place shall I make all revenues that [are] in [the entire land] to belong to the Aten, my father."

"At Akhet-Aten in this place shall I make oblations oveflowing for the Aten, my father."

"(And) at Akhet-Aten in this place shall I make for myself the residence of Pharaoh, l.p.h., (and) I shall make the residence of the King's Chief Wife."[7]

"Let a tomb be made for me in the orient mountain [of Akhet-Aten], and let my burial be made in it, in the millions of jubilees which the Aten, my father, decreed for me. Let the burial of the King's Chief Wife NEFERTITI be made in it, in the millions of years [which the Aten, my father, decreed for her. (And) let the burial of] the King's Daughter MERITATEN [be made] in it, in these millions of years.[8] If I should die in any town of the downstream, the south, the west, or the orient in these millions of years, let me be brought (back) so that I may be buried in Akhet-Aten. If the King's Chief Wife NEFERTITI—may she live!—should die in any town of the downstream, the south, the west, or the orient, in these millions [of years, let her be brought (back) so that] she [may be buried in Akhet-Aten. (And) if the King's Daughter MERITATEN dies] in any town of the downstream, the south, the west, or the orient in these millions of years, let her be brought (back) so that [she] may be buried in Akhet-Aten."

"And let a cemetery [be made] for the Mnevis Bull in the orient mountain of Akhet-Aten, so that he may [be buried] in it. Let there be made tomb chapels for the Greatest of Seers, for the God's Fathers of the Aten [and the . . .]s [of the] Aten in the orient mountain of Akhet-Aten, so that they may be buried in it."

"Now, as my father HOR-ATEN lives! As for the [. . .] in Akhet-Aten,

it was worse than those which I heard in regnal year 4;
it was worse than [those] which I heard in regnal year 3;
it was worse than those which I heard [in regnal year 2;
it was] worse [than those which I heard in regnal year 1];
it was worse [than] those which (King) [NEBMAAT]RE heard;
[it was worse than those which] (King) [OKHEPRURE (?) heard];
it was worse [than] those which (King) MENKHEPERRE heard;
[(and) it was] worse [than] those heard by any kings who had (ever) assumed the White Crown.

If I heard a report in the mouth of an official, in the mouth of [. . .], in the mouth of [. . .], in the mouth of a Nubian, in the mouth(s) of any people [. . .] against [my] fath[er] to [. . .], [they] were offensive [. . .]. [I] did not leave (?) [. . . saying], 'it was offensive,' until it would not be offensive. As for the offensive things [. . .] in every mouth, saying, 'I will commit an offense' [against the lord of Akhet]-Aten, my father, HOR-ATEN [. . .] arisen (?) [. . .] any [. . .], nor shall I hear the [. . .] from it either."

"It is the Aten, my father, who [has] desired (?) the House of Re [. . .] taken like [. . .] any [. . .]. I shall [. . .] sealed for Akhet-Aten . . . inasmuch as [*this*] land prospers [. . .] before (?) them in Akhet-Aten; similarly Kharu [. . .]

of [Akhet]-Aten [for the Aten], my [father], [. . .] continually [forever. As for the . . .]s of Kush, as far as [. . .], [. . .] the [. . .] hasten [. . .] Aten [. . .] therein [. . .] which are fixed at the [. . .]ern borders because it . . . in [. . .]. And one shall not say to me, 'The [. . .] ordains (?) . . . seasonally (?) . . . mansion (?) . . . my (?) every . . . in [the House of Aten in Akhet]-Aten (?).' [. . .] there [. . .] my [. . .] the festival (?) of the Aten, my father [. . .] my [. . . for (?)] my father, the [Aten]."

"Now as my father, HOR-ATEN, lives [. . .] on [*earth*] and similarly in [*heaven*], . . . oryxes and ostriches for [the House of] Aten, . . . cattle in [their] running . . . for the Aten [in the House of Aten in Akhet-Aten] continually forever. [Similarly the feast of the] Aten on New Year's Day [. . .] Aten being in festival eternally, . . . festival similarly . . . oblations; (and) similarly all feasts at every season, festivals . . . effectively, long ago (?) . . . me to . . . the King's Chief Wife NEFERTITI, may she live—they belong [to] the Aten, . . . his . . . in [Akhet]-Aten. . . . her . . . with which he is happy in order to offer therewith. Let me not make the royal . . . in the *harbor area* . . . , the . . . of the . . . ; and I shall [not] make it for him in . . . the crag of the . . . with the [north]ern stela of Akhet-Aten; and [I] shall not make [it for him at the crag of the southern stela of] Akhet-Aten; (but) I shall [make] it (?) . . . offerings (?) . . . within them, with fresh lands within them, with new lands within them [. . . in Akhet]-Aten, his [favorite] place [daily, in the course of] every [day]."

"Now make the stelae [for the] offerings (?) which I dedicate to the Aten, my father, in Akhet-[Aten. I myself am the one who should make offerings to the Aten, my father, in the House of Aten in Akhet-Aten. Offerings are not to be made to him there . . . when I am in any (other) city (or) in any (other) town . . . his horizon, the mountain of the Aten, my father, in the House of Aten in Akhet-Aten, being [happy] daily (?) continually . . . festive forever. . . . Similarly the feast of Aten with oblations on the river, [*something*] being . . . offerings of the queen.

If I detect (?) a man of the household;
if I hear a man [. . . of] the officials;
if I hear [. . .] in the mountain of the Aten;
if I detect . . . name (?) [. . .] anything in the House of Aten in Akhet-Aten,
[if . . . *some sort of*] *bovine* which the [. . .]-man has gathered,
it is its foreleg . . . kissing the ground at . . . [for the] Aten in the House of Aten in Akhet-Aten. I am . . . on which (?) my heart is set, offering these [. . .]s of mine which are on [the . . . of] the temple, . . . at every place wherein it is my wish to journey (while) the House [of Aten celebrates] the festivals of [the Aten which are established with every] thing I [provided] for the Aten, my father, in Akhet-Aten."

"Now as for [*the thing*]*s* which [. . .] make [as a] monument . . . , my father receives them . . . on the day when [the] Aten, my [father], . . . [for (?) the] Aten in [Akhet]-Aten, this place which he himself found for himself [continually] forever."

"Now if (?) . . . going about downstream, [or in the west, in] the south, (or) in the orient, in order to make domains [for] the [Aten], great of [. . .], (which) the Aten, my father, has given to me . . . land (?) . . . , I shall make [. . . for the Aten], my father, in the House of Aten in Akhet-Aten. Let there be [. . . for the queen (?)] in her house . . . , with everything in Akhet-Aten to cause him to cross, (whether) crossing downstream (or) to the south, to the west (or) to the orient. Make the [. . . of the] Aten, my father, . . . for the Aten, my father, in the House of Aten in Akhet-Aten continually forever."

"As lives the father HOR-ATEN! Regarding the [millions] of jubilees which [the Aten, my father], decreed for me, . . . utterance (?) [of] the . . . the southeastern stela of [Akhet]-Aten, I shall [not] celebrate a jubilee upriver from them in [the millions of years which the Aten decreed for me (?) . . . , [but I shall celebrate the jubilee at Akhet]-Aten [in this place], eternally and forever, [in the House of] Aten [in Akhet-Aten . . .]. I shall celebrate it in . . . , [. . . the] Aten, my [father], for my [lord] in [Akhet-Aten] continually forever."

"Further, [I] shall [make] . . . , the double-plumed shade of the Aten . . . in the northern road which is at the crag of the [. . . ern] stela, . . . [. . .]s upon [them] . . . [at (?)] the great [mountain] of the Aten, my father, which he himself desired for himself [. . .] continually [forever]."

"[*Something about monuments for the*] Aten, [*probably temples built out of*] stone, [and with], every precious stone in [. . . by (?)] a craftsman (or) a controller [. . .] that the rites may be celebrated in them . . . their (?) city, . . . to say every day [when he] crosses [the sky and sheds light] with his rays, which make [humanity] to live . . . in its entirety . . . it in [. . . and he] fills the House of Aten [with his] graciousness (?) [and as he rejoices over his] monuments, [exulting over] his [. . .]s on earth. I will make the circuit [of Aten] to be administered [for him] . . . , (and) the city (?) similarly, stopping [*something which will produce*] a great [*offense by*] any god (or) any goddess against Akhet-Aten, in a document of any god (or) any goddess . . . [*but it will be in the care of*] the King's Chief Wife, NEFERNEFRUATEN-NEFERTITI in . . . [for the] Aten [continually forever]."

"Now as [for] any [. . .]-people, any adherent of yours, any deputy (or) any other people who shall make [*some sort of observance regarding the*] boundary stelae of Akhet-Aten, from the western mountain to the [eastern] mountain . . . , [*it amounts to so many*] river-miles of sailing, (both) water (and) mountain [of] Akhet-Aten, being water [and mountain belonging to] the Aten, their lord, the lord of Akhet-Aten, (namely) [the father, HOR]-ATEN continually [forever (?), . . . going downstream (or) to the south], to the west, to the orient, to the mountain, to the water, in the river, by ship (?) which . . . in fields . . . , (with) every [. . .] (and) every [. . .], they belong [to my father, the Aten], . . . [consisting of] servants (?), consisting of groves, consisting of all things that exist in the entire land: they belong to my father, [the Aten, in the] House of Aten [in] Akhet-Aten continually forever."[9]

"[Now as for the . . .] which are in [Akhet-Aten . . . , they shall remain] in Akhet-Aten [under] the authority of the great steward of Akhet-Aten, while his scribal palette is in the [. . . of] Akhet-Aten while he [causes] his [subjects] to breathe, making themselves prostrate on their bellies before pharaoh, l.p.h., their lord, and to the queen . . . , ... HOR-[ATEN as far as the downstream, the south, the west], the orient, the mountain . . . in Akhet-Aten, . . . with rejoicing . . . in the . . . of mine [*while someone*] takes possession [*of the property of*] Aten, [so that] I may prevent their being taken from me to another place. And let not . . . to do [it . . .]. I am the one who does. . . ."

From this point, for the next twenty lines, the text becomes too fragmentary for any attempt at restoration, resuming only for the last four lines of Stela K:

[. . .] continually forever. . . . the father, [HOR-ATEN], . . . and effecting the expulsion [*of some group of*] *people*, (with) the army in its entirety. [. . .]s (and) [. . .]s being arranged at the beginning of . . . with exuberant [rejoicing . . .] in Akhet-Aten, on behalf of everyone and upon [the king, the Aten's rays being] upon him, consisting of life and dominion, (namely for) NEFER-KHEPRURE-WAENRE. Then the entire land rejoiced, (being) on holiday [and making oblation] to the Aten, for one has allowed to make an end[10] there, in Akhet-Aten, continually forever.

38. The "Later Proclamation" from the Boundary Stelae at El-Amarna

Exactly one year after the ceremonial foundation of his new city, Akhenaten visited the southeastern corner of Akhet-Aten and issued a second decree. This ordinance (which defined the boundaries with, apparently, more precision than before), was carved on eight stelae in the hills to the east of the city and at least three–all that have been discovered–on the west. Not all these monuments had been finished, however, when the oath embodied in the decree was renewed two years later. The substance of the decree was then confirmed by a supplement (the "colophon") later in the same year, found only on two stelae on the west bank (the last in the series) and probably commemorating their completion at the end of year 8.

Unlike the earliest boundary monuments, the tablets inscribed with the "later proclamation" are regularly accompanied by statues of Akhenaten, Nefertiti and their two eldest daughters (who were alive when the decree was issued). A third child, the king's daughter Ankhesenaten (*sic*),[11] *had come on the scene by the time the later stelae were being finished: emplacements for the statue of a third princess are found at three sites on the east bank, while at least two of the west bank sites were updated when the figures of three daughters were added to the sides of the statues there.*

1. Introduction

Regnal year 6, fourth month of the Growing season, day 13. Long live the Good God who is content with Maat; the lord of heaven, lord of earth, great living Aten who illuminates the Two Banks—(*i.e.*) long live the father, HOR-ATEN, given life forever continually: great living Aten who is in jubilee within the House of Aten in Akhet-Aten. (And) long live the Horus, mighty bull "Beloved of Aten"; Two Ladies "Great of Kingship in Akhet-Aten"; Horus of Gold "Who lifts up the name of Aten"; the King of Upper and Lower Egypt, who lives on Maat, Lord of the Two Lands, NEFERKHEP-RURE-WAENRE, given life everlastingly; Son of Re, who lives on Maat, Lord of Crowns. AKHENATEN, long in his lifetime, given life everlastingly forever.

The Good God, only one of Re (=*Waenre*) whose beauty Aten created,
Truly effective on behalf of the one who made him, who satisfies him with what pleases his Ka,
Who does effective things for the one who fashioned him,
Who administers the land for the one who placed him on his throne and provisions his house forever with countless hundreds of thousands of things,
Who lifts up Aten and and magnifies his name, causing the land to belong to the one who made it,
The King of Upper and Lower Egypt, who lives on Maat, the Lord of the Two Lands NEFERKHEPRURE-WAENRE; the Son of Re who lives on Maat, Lord of Crowns, AKHENATEN, long in his lifetime, given life forever continually.

(And) the princess, great in the palace, fair of face, beautiful in the double plumes; the mistress of joy who attracts favor, at the hearing of whose voice one exults; the King's Chief Wife, his beloved, the mistress of Upper and Lower Egypt, Lady of the Two Lands, NEFERNEFRUATEN-NEFERTITI—may she live and be healthy, youthful, and enduring everlastingly forever!

2. Royal Progress to Akhet-Aten and Rites Held There

On this day one was in Akhet-Aten, in the pavilion of matting that his Person made in Akhet-Aten, the name of which is "Aten is Content." His Person, l.p.h., appeared mounted on the great chariot of electrum, like Aten when he rises in the horizon, having filled the Two Lands with his love. He set off on a good road toward Akhet-Aten[12] on the first anniversary[13] of its discovery, which his Person, l.p.h., did in order to found it as a monument for the Aten, just as the father, HOR-ATEN—given life forever continually—commanded in order to make a memorial for himself in it.

A great offering was caused to be presented—consisting of bread, beer, long- and short-horned cattle, (assorted) animals, fowl, wine, fruit, incense and all sorts of good plants—on the day of founding Akhet-Aten for the living Aten; praise and love were received on behalf of the life, prosperity, and health of the King of Upper and Lower Egypt, who lives on Maat, the Lord of the Two Lands, NEFERKHEPRURE-WAENRE, given life forever continually; the Son of Re who lives on Maat, Lord of Crowns, AKHENATEN, long in his lifetime, given life forever continually.

3. Journey to the Southeastern Corner of Akhet-Aten and Preamble to the Decree

(Then) he went upstream. His Person, l.p.h., took a position on his chariot in the presence of his father, HOR-ATEN, given life forever continually, on the southeastern mountain of Akhet-Aten—the rays of Aten being upon him, consisting of life and dominion, rejuvenating his limbs every day.

Oath spoken by the King of Upper and Lower Egypt, who lives on Maat, the Lord of the Two Lands, NEFERKHEPRURE-WAENRE; the Son of Re who lives on Maat, the Lord of Crowns, AKHENATEN, long in his lifetime, given life forever continually:

"As lives my father, HOR-ATEN, given life forever continually! (And as) my heart is gratified with the king's wife and her children, which will cause the king's chief wife, NEFERNEFRUATEN-NEFERTITI—may she live forever continually—to reach old age in these millions of years, being under the authority of pharaoh, l.p.h.; (and which) will cause the king's daughter Meritaten and the king's daughter Meketaten, her children, to reach old age, being under the authority of the king's wife, their mother, continually forever: here is this genuine oath of mine, which it is my wish to say and which I shall not say falsely continually forever!"

4. The Decree[14]

"As for the southern stela which is on the eastern mountain of Akhet-Aten, *it* is the stela of Akhet-Aten on the basis of which I will make my stand. I shall not go past it to the south continually forever. Make the south-western stela across from it on the western mountain of Akhet-Aten exactly."

"As for the intermediate stela which is on the eastern mountain of Akhet-Aten, *it* is the stela of Akhet-Aten on the basis of which I will make my stand on the mountain of the orient (side) of Akhet-Aten. I shall not go past it to the orient continually forever. Make the intermediate stela which is on the western mountain of Akhet-Aten across from it exactly. I shall not go past it to the west continually forever."

"As for the northeastern stela of Akhet-Aten on the basis of which I make my stand, *it* is the northern stela of Akhet-Aten. I shall not go past it down-stream continually forever. Make the northwestern stela which is on the western mountain of Akhet-Aten across from it exactly."

"Now as for Akhet-Aten, starting from the southern stela of Akhet-Aten as far as the northern stela, measured between stela to stela on the eastern (*var.* western) mountain of Akhet-Aten: it amounts to six river-measures, one and three-quarter rods and four cubits. Similarly, starting from the southwestern stela of Akhet-Aten to the northwestern stela upon the western mountain of Akhet-Aten, it amounts to six river-measures, one and three-quarter rods and four cubits, the same exactly!"

"As to what is inside these four stelae, starting with the eastern (*var.* western) mountain of Akhet-Aten as far as the western (*var.* eastern) mountain, it is Akhet-Aten in its entirety. It belongs to my father, HOR-ATEN—given life forever continually—consisting of hills, uplands, marshes, new lands, basin lands, fresh lands, fields, waters, towns, banks, people, herds, groves and everything that the Aten, my father, causes to come into existence continually forever."

"I shall not ignore this oath which I am making for the Aten, my father, continully forever; but it shall remain upon a stone tablet at the southeastern border of Akhet-Aten."

"Similarly upon the intermediate stela that is on the eastern border of Akhet-Aten."

"Similarly upon the northeastern border of Akhet-Aten."

"Similarly upon the southwestern border of Akhet-Aten."

"Similarly upon the intermediate stela which is on the western mountain of Akhet-Aten."

"Similarly, it shall remain upon a stone tablet at the southwestern border of Akhet-Aten."

"Similarly on the northwestern border of Akhet-Aten."

"It (=*the inscription*) shall not be obliterated. It shall not be washed out, it shall not be hacked out, it shall not be (white)washed with plaster. It shall not go missing. If it does go missing, if it disappears, or if the tablet on which it is falls down, I shall renew it again as a new thing in this place where it is."

5. *Renewal of the Oath*

This oath was repeated in regnal year 8, first month of the Growing season, day 8, when One was in Akhet-Aten, as pharaoh, l.p.h., arose and appeared on the great chariot of electrum and beheld the stelae of the Aten which are on the mountain on the southeastern border of Akhet-Aten, they being established continually forever for the living Aten.

6. *The Colophon*

Regnal year 8, fourth month of Inundation, last day. Another oath spoken by the King of Upper and Lower Egypt, who lives on Maat, the Lord of the Two Lands, NEFERKHEPRURE-WAENRE; the Son of Re who lives on Maat, Lord of Crowns, AKHENATEN, long in his lifetime, at the establishing of the stelae that are on the borders of Akhet-Aten:

"As lives my father, HOR-ATEN, given life forever continually! Regarding the six stelae that I have established at the borders of Akhet-Aten—(namely) the three stelae which are on the orient mountain of Akhet-Aten, together with the three stelae across from them which are on the western mountain of Akhet-Aten":

"Let the southern stela that is on the orient mountain be opposite the southern stela that is across from it on the western mountain of Akhet-Aten, that it may be the southern boundary of Akhet-Aten; while the northern stela that is on the orient mountain of Akhet-Aten is opposite the northern stela that is across from it on the western mountain of Akhet-Aten, that it may be the northern border of Akhet-Aten. Similarly (for) the intermediate stela which is on the orient mountain of Akhet-Aten, opposite the intermediate stela that is across from it on the western mountain of Akhet-Aten."

"Now as for the extent[15] of Akhet-Aten, mountain to mountain, starting from the eastern horizon of heaven to the western horizon of [heaven], it shall belong to my father, HOR-ATEN, given life forever continually—

consisting of its mountains and desert lands,

consisting of [its marshes and new lands as] well [as] (?) its sustenance (?);

consisting of its birds, consisting of all its people,

consisting of all its herds,

consisting of everything which the Aten brings into being and on which his rays shine;

consisting of everything [that is] in the [district (?)] of Akhet-Aten.

[They] belong to my father, the living Aten, to be the House of Aten continually forever. Their entirety is offered to his Ka, and his brilliant rays receive them."

39. Boundary Stela L

This small tablet, quite unlike any of the other boundary stelae at el-Amarna, was carved a few feet to the south of Stela M on the southeastern crag of Akhet-Aten. Although it is too badly weathered for consecutive translation, the traces that remain prove beyond any doubt that it was a royal monument. Further certainty is elusive. If Stela L was not a stopgap, made before the tablets for the Later Proclamation were carved, it may have announced the "disestablishment" of Stela M, which had suffered so badly from wind erosion that it was replaced (as the king promised in the later proclamation) by Stela K some distance to the south.

. . . his Person upon . . . , [his Person's] appearing [upon] his chariot [. . . as he fills the land with] his beauty [. . .]. . . . Akhet-Aten . . . [which (?)] my Person establishes as (?) [a monument for (?)] my father, [the Aten], [. . . *something which*] I did at (?) Akhet-Aten . . . . Now . . . .

40. Private Cult Stelae Dedicated to the Royal Family

These two pieces, along with the one that follows (41-A), served as icons for the cult of the royal family in the homes of officials at Akhet-Aten. Although the protag-

onists appear in poses that are relaxed, and even intimate, they do not exactly descend to their subjects' level in these reliefs. Rather, by emphasizing the affection between the king, the queen and their children, these icons call attention to the life-giving power of the Aten as exemplified by his manifestations on earth, the holy family.

(A) The protagonists are named on the border around the scene: Long live the father, HOR-ATEN, given life forever continually; (and) the King of Upper and Lower Egypt who lives on Maat, the Lord of the Two lands, NEFER-KHEPRURE-WAENRE; the Son of Re who lives on Maat, Lord of Crowns, AKHENATEN, great in his lifetime; (and) the King's Chief Wife, NEFER-NEFRUATEN-NEFERTITI, may she live forever continually.

The scene on the tablet shows the king and queen giving jewelry to their daughters. Above the figures, flanking the solar disk: HOR-ATEN, given life forever continually; great living Aten who is in jubilee, lord of everything Aten encircles, lord of heaven, lord of earth in the House of Aten in Akhet-Aten.

Princess receiving bracelet: King's bodily daughter, his beloved, Meretaten, born [to the King's Chief Wife, his beloved, Mistress of the Two Lands], NEFERNEFRUATEN-NEFERTITI, may she live forever continually.

Princess sitting on Queen's knee: King's bodily daughter, his beloved, Meketaten, born to the King's Chief Wife, [his] beloved, [Mistress of the Two Lands], NEFERNEFRUATEN-NEFERTITI, living forever continually.

Princess standing on Queen's knee: King's bodily daughter, his beloved, Ankhesenpaaten, born to the [King's Chief Wife, his beloved, the Mistress of the Two Lands], NEFERNEFRUATEN-NEFERTITI, may she live forever continually.

(B) Akhenaten (on the left) sits facing Nefertiti and lifts his young daughter, the princess Meritaten, to kiss her, while two other princesses watch from their mother's lap: Meketaten turns to her mother as she points at the scene opposite, while Ankhesenpaaten caresses Nefertiti's cheek. The texts of the Aten and the royal family are entirely conventional, except for the following variant for the queen: The King's Chief Wife, NEFERNEFRUATEN-NEFERTITI, may she live and be made young forever continually.

41. Monuments from El-Amarna Naming Amenhotep III

(A) A small tablet, found in the house of the "chief servitor of the Aten" Panehsy at Akhet-Aten, was apparently used in the cult of the extended royal family at el-

Amarna: Amenhotep III and Queen Tiyi are enthroned before a laden offering table beneath the Aten's streaming rays. This piece, with its unusually lifelike depiction of the old king, has been adduced as evidence for his survival into his son's reign (at least into the eleventh year, after the later didactic name had come into use), and thus for the alleged long coregency of Amenhotep III and Akhenaten.

Flanking the solar disk: HEKA-ATEN, given life forever continually; great living Aten, lord of jubilees, lord of everything Aten encircles, lord of heaven, lord of earth in Akhet-Aten.

Beside the figures: Lord of the Two Lands, NEBMAATRE, Lord of Diadems, NEBMAATRE,[16] *and* Mistress of the Two Lands, TIYI.

(B) Four Fragments of a Granite Bowl from El-Amarna
The interest of these fragments lies in the occurrence of the praenomen of Amenhotep III (spelled phonetically) along with the later didactic name of the Aten–whether in a commemorative dedication or (as has been argued) a survival from the period of the old king's alleged coregency with his son.

King of Upper and Lower Egypt .... [Live] the father, HEKA-[ATEN] ... NEBMAATRE ... (*end of a royal name-ring*) in Akhet-Aten....

(C) Offering Table
The sides are inscribed with two matching texts, of which the one is preserved almost completely: This land is given to you [by (?)] Geb, that [your heart (?)] may be slaked with his beauty. [...] for your Ka, (O) AMENHOTEP III, the breath [of life (?)]. *Of the corresponding formula on the other side there is only* ... in the horizon like Re, (O) Horakhty NEBMAATRE: the breath [of life]. *The principal text is carved on the top of the piece, below the four basins provided for the liquids to be offered:*

Left: [The incense comes, the incense comes–the perfume of] Nekhbet which issues from Elkab: it washes you, it adorns you, it makes its place on top of your two arms. Hail to you, O incense! Take unto yourself the eye of Horus: its perfume is (delivered) to you.

Right: "[These libations of yours], these [libations of yours], they flow forth from Horus, they flow forth from your son. I have come just so that I might bring [to you the eye of] Horus, that you may be refreshed therewith. Take the efflux which issued from you: your heart will not be wearied possessing it. Your enemy (?) is under your sandals. Accept what comes and issues forth to you (at) the voice," three times.

42. Statues of the Royal Family from Akhet-Aten

(A) Base of a Statue Group from the Sunshade of Princess Meretaten: (Upper line) Long live the father, HOR-ATEN, given life forever continually; (and) the King of Upper and Lower Egypt who lives on Maat, Lord of the Two Lands, NEFERKHEPRURE-WAENRE, given life, [Son of Re who lives on Maat, Lord of Crowns], AKHENATEN, great in his lifetime; (and) the bodily king's daughter, his beloved, Meretaten, born to the King's Chief Wife, NEFERNEFRUATEN-NEFERTITI, may she live forever continually. *(Lower line)* Great living Aten who is in jubilee, lord of everything Aten encircles, lord of heaven, lord of earth in the sunshade of the king's bodily daughter, his beloved, Meritaten, born to the King's Chief Wife, his beloved, the mistress of the Two Lands, NEFERNEFRUATEN-NEFERTITI, may she live and be healthy forever continually in the "House of Rejoicing" of the Aten in the House of Aten in Akhet-Aten.

(B) Statuette of Nefertiti from El-Amarna: Long live the father, HEKA-ATEN, given life forever continually, and The [King's] Chief Wife, the lady of the palace, great of love in the House of Aten, the Lady of the Two Lands, NEFERNEFRUATEN-NEFERTITI, [may she] live [forever continually].

(C) Statue Base from Akhet-Aten, removed to Hermopolis: On each side, the names of the Aten and the king appear in the upper line. The lower lines each mention a different princess: [The king's] bodily [daughter], his beloved, Ankhesenpaaten, born to the King's Chief Wife NEFERNEFRUATEN-NEFERTITI, may she live; *and* The King's bodily [daughter], his beloved, Nefernefruaten [junior].

43. Relief Fragment from a Chapel devoted to the Ancestor Cult at El-Amarna

Beside the solar disk: HOR-ATEN, great living Aten who is in jubilee, lord of heaven, lord of earth, residing in the House of MENKHEPRURE (*=Thutmose IV*) in the House of Aten in Akhet-Aten.

By the King, as he elevates offerings to the sun: . . . NEFERKHEPRURE-WAENRE. . . .

44. Reliefs Removed from Akhet-Aten to Hermopolis

(A) This stela, brought from Akhet-Aten to Hermopolis, is inscribed on two sides. On the obverse, the king salutes the Aten while Nefertiti and Princess Meritaten

stand behind him, rattling sistra. On the reverse, the king and queen both raise batons to dedicate offerings, while their daughter shakes a sistrum in honor of the Aten. The texts, virtually identical on both sides, are quite conventional.

Beside solar disk: HOR-ATEN, given life forever continually, great living Aten who is in jubilee, lord of heaven, lord of earth, residing in the "House of Rejoicing" of the House of Aten in Akhet-Aten.

By King: Lord of the Two Lands, NEFERKHEPRURE-WAENRE, given life; Lord of Crowns, AKHENATEN, great in his lifetime.

By Queen: The King's Chief Wife NEFERNEFRUATEN-NEFERTITI, may she live forever continually.

By Princess: Bodily daughter of the king, his beloved, Meretaten, born to the King's Chief Wife NEFERNEFRUATEN-NEFERTITI, may she live forever continually.

(B) Another slab from El-Amarna, found in Hermopolis:
Titulary of Queen: . . . mistress of charm, sweet of love, the King's Chief Wife. . . .

Daughter: Bodily [king's daughter, his] beloved, Ankhesenpaaten, born to [the King's Chief Wife, NEFERNEFRUATEN-NEFERTITI, may she live].

45. Monuments made for Akhenaten's "Other Wife" Kiya

(A) Two calcite vases now owned by the Metropolitan Museum of Art, New York (MMA 20.2.11) and the British Museum, London (B.M. 65901) bear nearly identical inscriptions. The names of Akhenaten appear on both vases, but only on the better preserved of the two, in New York, are the Aten's cartouches preserved: the early didactic name, HOR-ATEN, *is used here. To the right of the king's cartouches (i.e., figuratively behind them) is the following inscription:* The wife and great beloved of the King of Upper and Lower Egypt, who lives on Maat,[17] NEFERKHEPRURE-WAENRE, the beautiful child[18] of the living Aten who shall live forever continually: Kiya.

(B) A narrow strip of wood, probably from a pencase, which is now in the Petrie Museum at University College London (UC 24382), bears the remains of the following text: [The wife and great beloved] of [. . .] NEFERKHEPRURE-WAENRE, Kiya.

A number of small buildings were dedicated to Kiya at Akhet-Aten, evidently in the latter part of Akhenaten's reign (since the Aten's later didactic name was used in them). Invariably, however, both Kiya and her daughter had their names and titles usurped by various of Nefertiti's daughters.[19] *The following selections illustrate both the range of buildings involved and the nature of the alterations made in them.*

(C) A stela fragment from the Maru-Aten complex is inscribed on both sides. On the front, the king offers a libation jar to the Aten, while a royal lady shakes a sistrum behind him.

Beside solar disk: HEKA-ATEN, given life forever continually; great living Aten, lord of jubilee(s), lord of everything Aten encircles, lord of heaven, lord of earth in the sunshade of the king's daughter Meretaten[20] in the Maru of the Aten in Akhet-Aten.

By king: The Lord of the Two Lands, NEFERKHEPRURE-WAENRE, given life, Lord of Crowns, AKHENATEN, great in his lifetime.

Above the lady: The Good ruler Waenre, the King of Upper and Lower Egypt, who lives on Maat, Lord of the Two Lands, NEFERKHEPRURE-WAENRE, given life [. . .] the king's daughter Meretaten [. . .] NEFERKHEPRURE-WAENRE, given life [. . .].[21]

The inscriptions on the back, where the king is shown elevating a censer to the disk, are virtually identical to those on the front face of the stela.

(D) Block from Hermopolis
Beside the disk of the Aten: [Great living Aten], Lord of jubilee(s), lord of all Aten encircles, [lord of heaven, lord of earth in the] house of the king's daughter Meretaten,[22] [in the House of Rejoicing of the] Aten in Akhet-Aten.

(E) Block from the Maru-Aten
This fragment shows a king followed by a queen and a princess, with a fragment of the latter's titles: [King's bodily daughter, his beloved, Meretaten] Junior, (who belongs) to the King of Upper and Lower Egypt, who lives [on Maat, Lord of the Two Lands, NEFERKHEPRURE-WAENRE, born to the king's bodily daughter, his] beloved (?), Meretaten, may she live.[23]

(F) A Block from Hermopolis
Following the Aten's epithets: . . . in the sunshade [of the king's bodily

daughter, his beloved], Ankhesenpaaten, [in the House of Rejoicing of] the Aten [in the House of Aten in Akhet-Aten].[24]

(G) Another Block from Hermopolis
King's bodily daughter, [his beloved], Ankhesenpaaten junior, [may she live].[25]

46. Inscriptions from the Royal Tomb at El-Amarna and Vicinity

The decoration in the royal tomb (most of which is badly damaged today) dwelt largely on the worship of the Aten. Isolated examples of the earlier didactic name of the Aten occur, but the god is most commonly referred to with the later name, HEKA-ATEN, *which is also consistent with the tomb's period of greatest use in the second decade of Akhenaten's reign. While the architecture is suggestive of the arrangements Akhenaten promised to make for his family in the "earlier proclamation" (see above), few of the preserved texts go beyond stereotyped descriptions of the Aten, the king or members of the royal family, such as the following:*

(A) Stela Found in the Royal Tomb at El-Amarna
Akhenaten, Nefertiti and their two eldest daughters offer flowers to the Aten. The texts are entirely conventional, with the exception of the following variant for the queen: The King's Chief Wife, his beloved, Lady of Upper and Lower Egypt and Mistress of the Two Lands, NEFERNEFRUATEN-NEFERTITI, may she live everlastingly and forever.

(B) From the Walls of the Royal Tomb
Most of the scenes in the royal tomb (while abounding in striking details) are generally lacking in exceptional historical or religious interest. Exceptions to this overall pattern are found, however, in chambers at the side of the main axis which were devoted to two of the women in the royal family. Room Alpha is too badly damaged to yield the identity of its occupant. One of the scenes appears to depict the tomb owner's death following the birth of a royal son, however, and on this admittedly slender basis a plausible case has been made for identifying this chamber as the resting place of the child's mother, perhaps Akhenaten's "other wife" Kiya."[26] *An adjoining scene, showing members of the royal family adoring the Aten at sunrise, was originally laid out with only the two eldest daughters, "Meretaten" and "Meketaten", in attendance, but was later adapted to include two of their younger sisters,* Ankhesenpaaten *and* Nefernefruaten Junior.[27] *The date of this change and its relation to either of the burials in this annexe cannot be fixed precisely.*

Room Gamma, on the other hand, was definitely the resting place of Meketaten, the second daughter of Akhenaten and Nefertiti. Two of the scenes are of particular interest:

Wall A: Akhenaten and Nefertiti stand mourning in the bedchamber of the deceased, identified by an inscription above the bed as the king's bodily daughter, his beloved, Meketaten, born of [the King's] Chief [Wife, NEFERNEFRUATEN-NEFERTITI], may she live forever continually. *Outside the room, a wet-nurse carries away the child, who is attended by female fanbearers and identified as* [. . . , born to the king's bodily daughter, his beloved], Meketaten, [born to the King's Chief Wife, his beloved], NEFERNEFRUATEN-NEFERTITI, may she live forever continually.

Walls B-C: Akhenaten and Nefertiti stand in mourning before the sunshade (?) of the king's bodily daughter, his beloved, Meketaten, born to the King's Chief Wife, NEFERNEFRUATEN-NEFERTITI, may she live forever continually. *A figure of the deceased stands within, a cone of ointment on her head. Behind the royal couple, also in attitudes of mourning, stand three of the deceased's sisters, identified as:*

King's bodily daughter, his beloved, Meretaten, born to the King's Chief Wife, his beloved, the Lady of the Two Lands, NEFERNEFRUATEN-[NEFERTITI], may she live forever continually.

The identical inscription, but naming Ankhesenpaaten.

The same, but naming Nefernefruaten Junior.

(C) Inscriptions on the Granite Sarcophagus of Akhenaten, from the Royal Tomb

Fragments from Akhenaten's sarcophagus have been integrated into a restoration which can now be seen outside the Cairo Museum. The decoration is dominated by disks of the Aten (identified as HOR-ATEN *on the ends and* HEKA-ATEN *on the sides) and at each corner by figures of Nefertiti, who stands with arms outstretched to protect the corpse within. Among her fragmentary utterances are the following:*

"Fragrant breeze to your nose [every] day! [May] you appear like Aten at each rising."

"You will be continual, living like Aten [every] day. He is the one who begat [you] so that you might make. . . ."

On Side B, under the Aten's rays: [. . .] for the Aten when [he] rises [. . .] every [. . . of (?)] your father, the living Aten, for his son: "Come, my son, [that] you [may become] a spirit through me. . . ."

On Side D: [Words] spoken [by . . .] Aten . . . : " . . . all . . . continually, as you [. . . your] goodly father, the [Aten, as he] protects (?) the living king, . . . , the only one of [Re, NEFERKHEPRURE]-WAENRE, give life."

(D) Inscriptions on the Granite Sarcophagus of Princess Meketaten from the Royal Tomb

Only fragments survive, with extended speeches being few–e.g., Words spoken by the living Aten: "My rays are upon her [. . .]." *By contrast to Akhenaten's sarcophagus, the later didactic name of the Aten is found throughout; and in addition to Meketaten's parents, the inscriptions also mention her sister Ankhesenpaaten, as well as her paternal grandparents, Amenhotep III,* NEBMAATRE, *and* the King's Chief Wife *and* King's Mother TIYI. *Avoidance of spellings that employ the gods' images proscribed in the second half of the reign provides a terminus post quem for the decoration of Meketaten's sarcophagus.*

(E) Other Objects from the Royal Tomb(s)

All of the following items came from burials of the royal family, whether in the royal tomb or another nearby:

1. Alabaster Bowl

On side panels: The king's daughter and king's wife NEBMAATRE *(sic)*;[28] <daughter of> the Good God NEBMAATRE, given life like Re; (and) born to the King's Chief Wife TIYI, may she live forever.

2. "Heirlooms"

Limestone bowls which originally belonged to the King of Upper and Lower Egypt . . . Khafre *(Fourth Dynasty) and to Thutmose III (mid-Eighteenth Dynasty):* Long live the Horus, [. . .] like [. . .] in heaven, . . . , lord who performs the ritual, MENKHEPERRE, bodily [son] of Re, his beloved, THUTMOSE III, [beloved of] Hathor, lady of An[. . .], [as she gives life], stability and dominion, his heart being joyful as he leads [the Kas of (?)] all [the living] like Re everlastingly.

3. Votive Shabti of Nefertiti

This calcite figurine, deposited in the royal tomb, is reconstructed from two fragments that were acquired by the Brooklyn Museum and the Louvre (Paris).

Hereditary princess, great one in the palace, favored of [the King of Upper and Lower Egypt NEFERKHEPRURE-WAENRE, the Son of Re AKHENATEN, long in] his lifetime; the King's Chief Wife NEFERNEFRUATEN-NEFERTITI, may she live forever [continually].

4. Fragment of Amphora from Tomb No. 29 in the Royal Wadi

Below the handle is an oval stamp with the text, identifying this item as belonging to the inner (burial) chamber of Nefernefrure.

47. Jar Dockets and Sealings from El-Amarna

(A). Dockets on Supply Jars from the Maru-Aten, East Village and North Suburb

1. [Regnal year . . .]. Wine of the House of NEBMAATRE. . . .
2. Genuine good wine of the Mansion of the ATEN.
3. Regnal year (*blank*). Wine of the Mansion of NEFERKHEPRURE in [Akhet]-Aten. [The chief] vintners of the island. . . .
4. Regnal year 2. Wine of the House of the Greatest of Seers of [the Aten (?)] . . . .
5. Regnal year 8. Wine of the House of ATEN, [of] the western river. The chief vintner Hati[a . . .].
6. Regnal year 9. Potted meat of the children [of ATEN], of the rendering-room (?) of (the institution named) "Ka of ANKH-RE."[29]
7. Regnal year 10. Wine of the House of NEFERNEFRUATEN, may [she] live, of the western river; the chief of the garden (=*master vintner*) Nefer [. . .].
8. Regnal year 11. Wine of the house (of) LIVE ATEN, l.p.h.,[30] of the western river. The chief of the garden (called) [. . .]ka[. . .].
9. [Regnal] year [X +] 2. Wine of the House of ATEN, l.p.h., of the Mansion of Aten. [The chief] of the garden Simarmi.
10. Regnal year 13. Wine of the House "Satisfying ATEN."
11. [Regnal year] 17. Wine [of] the House of the KING'S WIFE, may she live, [of] the southern oasis. . . .

(B) Ostracon from el-Amarna

Given to the palace, l.p.h., by the hand of the servitor Hornakht: twice-good wine, in a container of four jars, valued at [. . .] jars, together with 1 basket of *tchai*-containers along with 1 basket [of . . .].

(C) Dockets on Supply Jars from el-Amarna

1. Regnal year 1: wine of the Estate of ATEN . . . . The chief of the garden (=*master vintner*) Rufy.
2. Regnal year 4: wine of the Estate of Horakhty, [of] the western river. The chief of the garden Pa[. . .].
3. Regnal year 7: wine, twice-good, of the Estate of LIVE ATEN, of the western river. The gardener Perb[. . .].
4. Regnal year 7, first month of the Inundation season, day 3: Festival of Everlastingness. Potted meat of the rendering-room (?) [of] the Estate of ATEN , l.p.h. The chamberlain Tutu and the servant Hesuefemiunu.
5. Regnal year 8: wine of the Shade [of LIVE RE (?)] which is in Akhet-Aten, l.p.h.

6. Regnal year 9: twice-good wine of the [. . .] river, [of] the Estate of "ATEN Gleams." The chief of the garden Pashed.

7. Regnal year 9, first month of the Inundation season: the rendering-room (?) under the authority of the god's father [Ay (?)]. Potted [meat] for the festival (called) "Joyous (?) [is . . .]."

8. [Regnal year] 10: wine of the Estate of NEBMAATRE-in-the-Bark [of the] western [river]. The chief [vintner . . .].

9. [Wine of the Estate of] NEBMAATRE, [of the] oasis which is in the western river.

10. Regnal year 12: wine of the house of the Greatest of Seers, of the western river. The chief of the garden Pa-Atenemnekhu.

11. Regnal [year] 13: wine of the Estate of the King's Daughter Meketaten [of the western river], of the chief of the garden Sakaia.

12. Regnal year 14: wine of the Estate of ATEN [of] the western river, of the chief of the basin (=*master vintner*) Mek.

13. Regnal year 14: wine of the Estate of LIVE RE of the western river. The chief of the basin Neferronpet.

14. Regnal year 14: wine of the Estate of AKHENATEN, l.p.h., long in his lifetime, of the western river, of the gardener Iny.

15. Regnal year 14: wine of the estate of the King of Upper and Lower Egypt . . . , king . . . .

16. Regnal year 14: potted meat of the KING'S WIFE, may she live, which [the] butcher (?) Pa[. . . made].

17. Regnal year 15 . . . , rendering-room (?) of the KING'S WIFE, may she live, ...

18. Regnal year 16: potted (meat) of the children of ATEN, l.p.h., [of] the rendering-room(?) . . . the KING'S WIFE. . . .

19. First month of Inundation, day 11. Good potted (meat) of the 2 cattle of Kush, made in the processing establishment of the Great House (*or* Pharaoh), l.p.h.

20. Regnal year 17: wine of the Estate of NEBMAATRE . . . . The chief of the basin [. . .]nakkht.

(D) Unprovenanced, from El-Amarna

[Regnal year . . .]. Wine of the House of Aten which is in the . . . . [The chief] vintner Amenemhat, belonging to the Mansion. . . .

(E) Jar Sealings from el-Amarna

1. Wine of Perwer [. . .].
2. Wine, twice-good, of the House of Aten.
3. Wine of the House "Satisfying Re."
4. Wine of the House "Satisfying Aten."
5. The House of Aten in Re's (?) Heliopolis.

6. Good wine of the house "Effective is living Aten."
7. Good wine of Men[. . .].
8. Wine of the Mansion of Aten.

48. Stela from Heliopolis, Showing the Royal Family Kneeling and Making Obeisance to the Aten

This piece is divided into three registers. At the top, the king (followed by his queen and one of their daughters) kneels in adoration of the sun.

Beside disk: HOR-ATEN, given life forever continually; great living Aten who is in jubilee, lord of heaven, lord of earth, residing in (the temple) "Elevating Re in Heliopolis."

No text apart from the epithets beside the disk survives in the middle register, in which Akhenaten and the queen prostrate themselves before the Aten. In the lowest register two of the daughters are seen doing the same. Below them, and to the left, was their elder sister, the king's bodily daughter, his beloved, Meketaten, born to the King's Chief Wife, his beloved, mistress of the Two Lands, NEFERNEFRUATEN-NEFERTITI, [may she live forever continually].

49. Fragment Found at Matariah, near Heliopolis

Beside disk: [. . .] like [Re] forever [. . .], great living [Aten] who is in jubilee, lord of everything Aten encircles, lord of heaven, lord of earth, lord of (the foundation called) "Wall of Re" in Re's Heliopolis.

By princess: The king's bodily daughter, his beloved, Meretaten.

50. Slab found at Memphis

This block, a small part of a typical offering scene of the king before the Aten, shows a libation vessel inscribed with cartouches of the king and queen, as well as with this unusual epithet attached to the god's early name: HOR-ATEN, residing in the House of Akhenaten.

51. Statuary in Northern Egypt

(A) Pedestal in the Cairo Museum:

Of this grey granite statue group only part of the pedestal's two longer sides remain. The titulary of the Aten occupied both lines on one side: the later didactic name, HEKA ATEN, *is used here, and the god is described as being* in the House of Aten in the [. . .]. *Although the temple's name cannot be further identified, the traces do not fit any of the known sanctuaries from Akhet-Aten. On the other side, following Akhenaten's cartouches in the upper line, there is room in the lower line for the following:* [The king's bodily daughter, his beloved, Ankhesenpaaten Junior, born to the king's daughter] Ankhesenpaaten, born to the King's Chief Wife NEFERNEFRUATEN-NEFERTITI, [may she live]. *No other texts survive, nor is there any further indication of the remaining princesses whose names are assumed to have stood here.*

(B) Statue Base from the Faiyum:

This piece was reused twice–first in a post-Amarna pharaonic building (of which part of a secondary inscription survives on the top of the pedestal) and then in a modern house, where it was found in 1953. Its likeliest origin is the nearby site of Kom Medinet Gurob, where many objects from the Amarna Period were found; but (in view of this piece's stated provenience in Akhet-Aten) it may well have been brought to the Faiyum from its original home in the "Mansion of the Aten" south of the king's house at El-Amarna.

One of the longer sides is devoted exclusively to the Aten's earlier titulary: [Live] the father, HOR-ATEN, given life forever continually–great living Aten who is in jubilee, lord of everything Aten encircles, lord of heaven and lord of earth in the Mansion of the Aten in Akhet-Aten.

On the remaining three sides, the upper line is devoted to the king and queen, with the lower line belonging to their daughters:

The King of Upper and Lower Egypt, who lives on Maat, the Lord of the Two Lands, NEFERKHEPRURE-WAENRE, given life; the Son of Re who lives on Maat, Lord of Diadems, [AKHENATEN], long in his lifetime, continually in the favor of Aten.

The Chief King's Wife, his beloved, the Lady of the Two Lands, NEFERNEFRUATEN-NEFERTITI, may she [live forever continually].

The king's bodily daughter, his beloved, Meretaten, born to the King's Chief Wife, NEFERNEFRUATEN-NEFERTITI, may she live forever continually.

The king's [bodily] daughter, [his beloved, Meketaten, born to the King's] Chief Wife, [NEFERNEFRUATEN-NEFERTITI], may she live [forever continually].

The king's bodily daughter, his beloved, Ankhesenpaaten, born to the King's Chief Wife, NEFERNEFRUATEN-NEFERTITI, may she live.

52. Relief Fragments found at Assiut

Among a number of Amarna Period blocks found here (bearing both the earlier and later didactic names of the Aten), is one inscribed with the following: [... great living Aten] who is in jubilee, [lord of] everything Aten encircles, lord of heaven, lord of earth, residing in (the temple) "Firm is the Life of Aten."

53. Ritual Objects found at Karnak

(1) Five Altars from Karnak:

All five of these pieces are rounded shafts of granite that taper up from the base and served as stands for the public presentation of offerings. A-D were discovered reused inside the Karnak Temple. Altar E, which was discovered earlier, was once believed to come from Armant but was found, like the others, at Karnak. The inscriptions, which are broadly similar on all of these pieces, are notable in that they appear to describe the offerings each altar was intended to carry.

Altar A: HOR-ATEN residing in (the temple) "Rejoicing in the Horizon of Re" in his house in Upper Egyptian Heliopolis, the great and first (place) of Re. What is presented to him at his rising in the eastern horizon of [heaven] as the normal offering of every day:[31]

Pesen-bread: 2 (loaves)
Bit-cakes: 2 (loaves)
Beer: 2 jars
Vegetables: 5 bunches

(as well as) fresh flowers, (assorted) offerings and incense which [the king] gives (?).

The same text, in far worse condition, is found also on Altars B and E.

Front and Back:[32] *an inscription of* HOR-ATEN residing in "Rejoicing in the Horizon of Aten" in Upper Egyptian Heliopolis, the great and first (place) of Aten *faces a band of hieroglyphs which names* The Horus, Mighty Bull "Tall-Plumed," King of Upper and Lower Egypt, Lord of the Two lands, Master of Ritual, NEFERKHEPRURE-WAENRE, the bodily son of Re, his beloved, AKHENATEN, long in his lifetime.

The text of Altar C is completed to some extent by that of Altar D. Front: Long live the High Priest of Hor-Aten, King of Upper and Lower Egypt NEFERKHEPRURE-WAENRE—may he achieve (the state of) "given life."

Three remaining sides: [King of Upper and Lower Egypt] NEFERKHEPRURE-WAENRE, long in his lifetime, beloved of Hor-Aten. *The second line of Altar D has, however:* Long live Hor-Aten: what is presented to him [every] day. . . . *There is no room for the full remainder of the formula as it is written on Altars A, B and E.*

(2) Libation Bowl from Karnak

Inscription around the rim: Making a libation to Aten [*sic*],[33] HOR-ATEN, at his rising in the eastern horizon of heaven by the king who lives on Maat, NEFERKHEPRURE-WAENRE, the Son of Re AKHENATEN, long in his lifetime and great[34] in victory; (and) as he makes libation at his (=*Aten's*) setting in the western horizon of heaven.

54. Gilded Wooden Shrine Made for Queen Tiyi by Akhenaten

The sides of the shrine meant to enclose the sarcophagus of Queen Tiyi were found dismantled in the entrance passage to Tomb 55 at the Valley of the Kings where they had been abandoned, probably after the more portable elements of the queen's burial had been removed to accommodate the tomb's mysterious final occupant (see chapter 5 below). The shrine was clearly manufactured in the later years of Akhenaten's reign, for the later didactic name of the Aten is used throughout and the composition of the text favors phonetic spellings in place of conventional hieroglyphs that might be interpreted as allusions to the old gods (such as the seated goddess "Maat" in Amenhotep III's praenomen, or the vulture associated with the goddess Mut in the term "mother"). Since the names and figures of the dedicator, Akhenaten, were vandalized, however, it is possible that the initial burial took place after his death: a half-hearted attempt to insert Amenhotep III's name in place of Akhenaten's was apparently made at this same time.

Door Posts: Left. [Long live] the father, HEKA-ATEN, given life forever continually; (and) the King of Upper and Lower Egypt, who lives on Maat. NEFERKHEPRURE-WAENRE;[35] (and) the king's mother, TIYI, may she live forever. *Right.* King of Upper and Lower Egypt, who lives on Maat, Lord of the Two Lands, NEBMAATRE; King's Chief Wife, his beloved, king's mother of Waenre, the Mistress of the Two Lands,[TIYI], may she [live] forever.

Upper Traverse: Left. Long live the King of Upper and Lower Egypt, Lord of the Two Lands, NEBMAATRE; (and) the king's mother, King's Chief Wife, TIYI, [may she] live.

Right. Long live the King of Upper and Lower Egypt who lives on Maat, NEFERKHEPRURE-WAENRE;[36] what he made for the king's mother,[37] the King's Chief Wife, TIYI.

Door leaves: HEKA-ATEN, given life forever continually; great living Aten, lord of jubilees, lord of everything [Aten] encircles, lord of heaven, lord of earth in the House of Aten in Akhet-Aten. *And on the other side,* . . . NEBMAATRE, given life forever; [King of Upper and Lower Egypt] AMENHOTEP III, long in [his] lifetime;[38] [King's] mother, TIYI, living forever continually.

On one of the side panels of the canopy, Akhenaten offers to the Aten, followed by Queen Tiyi, with the following invocation addressed to her: When the Aten appears in his horizon, his rays lift you up at dawn in order to see him every [day]. May you live on the Ka of the living Aten, may [you] breathe the air with finest incense (?).

Lateral panels: [Long live HEKA]-ATEN, given life forever continually; (and) the King of Upper and Lower Egypt who lives on Maat, the Lord of the Two Lands, NEFERKHEPRURE-WAENRE,[39] the Son of Re, who lives on Maat, AKHENATEN, great in his lifetime: what he made for the king's mother, the King's Chief Wife TIYI, may she live forever.

55. Buhen Stela Describing a War in Nubia

[Regnal year 1]2 (?), third (?) month of Inundation, day 20 (of) HEKA-[ATEN] . . . , (and of) the King of Upper and Lower Egypt, who lives on Maat, Lord of [the Two Lands], WAENRE [*sic*], [the Son of Re who lives on Maat, Lord of Crowns, AKHENATEN, long in his lifetime], . . . , having appeared on [the throne of] his father, the Aten. . . . [Now his Person, l.p.h., was in Akhet-Aten when one came to tell his Person that] the enemies of the foreign country Ikayta [were plotting rebellion and had (even) invaded the land of] the Nilotic Nubians, while taking all sustenance away from them [as they roamed the desert in order to *escape from him (?)*].

Thereupon his Person charged the King's Son [of Kush and overseer of the southern countries with assembling an army in order to defeat the] enemies of the foreign country of Ikayta, males [as well as females. These enemies were found on the eastern side of] the river, to the north of the cistern(s) of the mining region . . . upon the highland, and the fugitive was smitten . . . , [while the] cry of victory was in their heart(s)—"a [*fierce*] lion, slaying [*myriads throughout*] the land (?) [in] valor and victory!"

List [of the plunder which his Person carried off from the country] Ikayta:

Living Nilotic Nubians:	82 [+ x]
[Young warriors]:	. . .
[Nilotic Nubian women]:	. . .
Their children:	12
Total of living "head(s)":	145
Those who were impaled:	[. . .]
[Slain]:	[. . .]
[Hands]:	[. . .]
Total:	225
Total sum:	361 [*sic*]

The King's Son of Kush, the overseer of the [southern] countries [Thutmose, said]: " . . . ." *After a gap of uncertain length:* "[Fear of you is in the]ir [hearts]. There are no rebels in your time, for they have achieved nonexistence! The chiefs [of . . . *have fallen*] to your might. Your battle cries are like a fiery flame (following) after every foreign country. [. . .], (and) every foreign country is united with one wish, (namely) that they might despoil their land(s) daily [. . .] in order that breath may be sent to their nose(s) by your Ka. (O) [Lord of] the Two Lands WAENRE, may your Ka act in order to reach [*all your enemies*]."

56. A Stela from Amada Describing War in Nubia

Except for the date and a few internal variations, this text appears to be identical to that of the better preserved war stela at Buhen.

[Regnal year . . .], first [month] of Inundation, day 16 (of) THE LIVING RULER,[40] (and of him) whose sword is victorious, beloved of Aten in the land [of . . .], [King of Upper and Lower Egypt who lives] on Maat, Lord of the Two Lands, NEFERKHEPRURE, Son of Re who lives on Maat, Lord of Crowns, [AKHENATEN, long in his lifetime, who has appeared upon] the seat of his father the Aten like Re in the sky and on earth every day.

Now his Person, [l.p.h., was in Akhet-Aten when one came to tell his Person that] enemies of the foreign country Ikayta were plotting [rebellion and had (even) invaded the lands of the Nilotic Nubians] while taking all sustenance away from them [as they] roamed (?) the desert (?) in order to [fill their bellies (?)]. *The rest is lost.*

57. Minor Epigraphs on Statues, Scarabs, Seals, and Other Objects

In addition to items that are unambiguously inscribed for Akhenaten, we include here others that might belong to either part of the reign–objects inscribed with the earlier name of the Aten, or with the king's praenomen, followed by an epithet that is either Atenist or generically royal.

(A) Many objects are inscribed with one or both cartouches of the earlier didactic name: HOR-ATEN.

(B) Excavations at Tell el-Quesar, a site located north of Assiut in Middle Egypt, yielded a number of limestone blocks dating to the Amarna period. The published report of the find[41] *prints two cartouches as the representative form of the Aten's names found on these fragments:* The Living Ruler of the Horizon who Exults in the Horizon, in his Name of "Light which is in Aten."

This, however, is a curious hybrid, hitherto unparalled, which combines the later didactic name in the first cartouche with the earlier one in the second. While the report's author may have combined the best preserved exemplars of each cartouche from different blocks, without realizing that they belonged to different stages of the Aten's titulary, the possibility remains that this is an accurately described variant which might have been made (perhaps due to a draftsman's oversight) during the period of transition between these two styles.

(C) More frequently objects are found inscribed with one or both cartouches of the later didactic name of the Aten: HEKA-ATEN.

(D) Double cartouches: NEFERKHEPRURE-WAENRE AKHENATEN.

(E) Single cartouches: NEFERKHEPRURE-WAENRE.[42]

(F) NEFERKHEPRURE-WAENRE, ruler of Thebes.

(G) NEFERKHEPRURE-WAENRE, image of Re.

(H) Neferkheprure-Waenre, whose provisions in the House of Aten are great.

(I) NEFERKHEPRURE-WAENRE, who celebrates jubilee(s) like living A<t>en.

(J) Neferkheprure, <beloved of> Aten <in> Re's Heliopolis.

(K) NEFERKHEPRURE-WAENRE, who appears like Re.

(L) Maat of NEFERKHEPRURE-WAENRE (*or* NEFERKHEPRURE-WAENRE, the true).

(M) NEFERKHEPRURE-WAENRE, master of strength.

(N) NEFERKHEPRURE-WAEN<RE>, rich in possessions.

(O) NEFERKHEPRURE-WAENRE, beloved of Aten.

(P) Neferkheprure-Waenre, beloved of Aten.

(Q) NEFERKHEPRURE-WAENRE, possessor of fragrant breeze.

(R) NEFERKHEPRURE-WAENRE, beloved of Horakhty.

(S) NEFERKHEPRURE-WAENRE, who satisfies Aten.

(T) The Good God, Lord of the Two Lands, NEFERKHEPRURE-WAENRE, manifest (in) foreign lands.

(U) King of Upper and Lower Egypt who lives on Maat, NEFERKHEPRURE-WAENRE.

(V) Neferkhepr<u>re, *protected by a winged serpent.*

(W) Neferkheprure, who appears like Re.

(X) Neferkheprure, Re of all the subjects. *The entire formula is also found inside a cartouche.*

(Y) King of Upper and Lower Egypt, Neferkheprure.[43]

(Z) Akhenaten.

(AA) NEFERNEFRUATEN-NEFERTITI.

(BB) King's Wife NEFERNEFRUATEN-NEFERTITI.

(CC) King's Chief Wife, NEFERNEFRUATEN-NEFERTITI.

Notes

1. The burden of this passage is that the king will not relocate the Aten's cult center elsewhere in Egypt. He does not promise (as is often assumed) never again to leave the site.

2. I.e., the god's estate, which (as will be seen in the "later proclamation") was virtually coterminous with the territory of Akhet-Aten.

3. Referring to the great temple of the Aten, at the north end of the central city.

4. I.e., a mortuary chapel. Its location is unknown, but similar buildings are attested for the king's mother, some of his daughters, and his other wife, Kiya.

5. Probably meaning the area of the central city at el-Amarna.

6. These two "Houses of Rejoicing" were located respectively within the great temple of the Aten and the great palace which lay across the road from it, but it is impossible to tell which was which.

7. These were probably the "great river palace" at the north end of the site and the smaller "north palace" that lay between this complex and the central city.

8. Arrangements of this sort appear, in fact, to have been made in the tomb built for Akhenaten in the desert hills, some 13 km. east of the city.

9. The provisions in this paragraph appear to anticipate the more detailed instructions regarding the dimensions of Akhet-Aten in the "later proclamation."

10. Literally, "to moor" or "tie up" like a boat.

11. Named thus on Stela A, instead of the more usual "Ankhesenpaaten."

12. Probably to the central city, as opposed to the more general reference to the territory of Akhet-Aten above.

13. Literally, "first occasion."

14. Most of the geographical variants of the stelae on the west bank are omitted in the translation of the following provisions.

15. Literally, "breadth."

16. The praenomen has been deliberately substituted for the nomen here, thus avoiding the hated name of Amun.

17. The British Museum text adds "Lord of the Two Lands" here.

18. This refers to the king.

19. This usurpation by the princesses, long believed to have been directed toward their mother, Queen Nefertiti, is now recognized as an attack on Kiya: see Hanke 1978: passim.

20. Usurped from "the wife and [great beloved], Kiya."

21. Carved over "the wife [and great beloved of] the King of Upper and Lower Egypt," etc., "[the beautiful child] of [living] Aten who lives continually forever, Kiya; the king's bodily daughter, his beloved, . . . , born to the wife and great beloved of the King of Upper and Lower Egypt, who lives on Maat, NEFERKHEPRURE-WAENRE, [the beautiful child of living Aten who lives continually forever, Kiya]."

22. Usurped from "of the king's wife [*sic*] Kiya."

23. Usurped from Kiya's daughter: see (C) above for the full wording of the formula.

24. Usurped from "the wife and great beloved, Kiya."

25. Usurped from "[. . .], born to the king's wife, the greatly beloved Kiya."

26. See Martin 1989a: 37-40.

27. The latter two were Akhenaten's third and fourth daughters.

28. Erroneously substituted in antiquity for the princess's name, perhaps Sitamun.

29. An abbreviation of the Aten's didactic name.

30. Another abbreviated form of the Aten's name.

31. In Egyptian *imenyt*, here spelled in a peculiar way that avoids the punning reference to Amun that is implicit in the more normal spelling.

32. The two texts are slightly different: the fuller variants are given in this translation.

33. A mistake, surely, for "the father."

34. The same word, with different nuances, is used to qualify both prepositional phrases here.

35. Akhenaten's praenomen was later erased and that of his father (spelled conventionally, with the figure of the goddess Maat) was substituted in red ink.

36. Erased, except for sundisk hieroglyphs.

37. In the published hand copy this title is followed by "the king's daughter," but since these signs do not appear on the facsimile drawing (Davis 1910: 22, cf. pl. xxxv right), they were probably published by mistake—particularly since Queen Tiyi never claimed the blood royal elsewhere.

38. The epithet, which is associated with no one but Akhenaten, suggests that his names originally stood inside the cartouches, and that they were subsequently reworked in the name of his father—an assumption that is further supported by the pre-Amarna spelling of Amenhotep III's praenomen with the Maat-goddess here (see n. 35 above).

39. Erased, except for sundisk hieroglyphs.

40. Probably an abbreviation of HEKA-ATEN, as suggested by Schulman 1982: 302.

41. Kamal 1911: 3.

42. In a few exceptional cases, the seated sun-god hieroglyph is substituted for the initial sundisk of "Neferkheprure."

43. The otiose "Re" at the end of the name may have been added for balance (so that the name might be read from both directions) or to refer to the element "Waenre" that is not included here.

4

Inscriptions of Private Individuals in the Reign of Akhenaten

58. The God's Father Ay

58-A. Wooden Box from the Funerary Equipment of Ay and his Wife

Lid
The king's true scribe, his beloved, the God's Father, Ay.
The troop leader and master of the horse, the God's Father, Ay.

She who was greatly favored of Waenre, the housewife Tiyi.
She whom the King's Chief Wife favored, the housewife Tiyi.

Side A
Over the Mummy of the Deceased and a mourning Woman:
[The troop leader and master] of the horse, the God's Father Ay.
His "sister," the housewife Tiyi.

By a Man offering Water and Incense to Ay's Mummy:
"Incense, fragrant and sweet-smelling . . . when [he] appears. . . ."

Side B
Over the Mummy of the Deceased and a mourning Woman:
The troop leader and master of the horse, the God's Father Ay.
His "sister," the housewife Tiyi.

Over Offerings and Ritualist:
"For your Ka, so that your Ka may become cool. It is the Unique One of Re (=*Waenre*) who has ordained them for you: they belong to you continually forever, (O) God's Father Ay."

Side C: She who was greatly favored of Waenre and one whom the King's Chief Wife favored: the king's ornament, Tiyi.

Side D: The troop leader and master of horse, the fanbearer at the right hand of the king, the king's true scribe, his beloved, Ay—may he live again!

B. Tomb of Ay at El-Amarna (Nr. 25)

58-B.1. Outer Door, Jambs

Left Jamb
(A) Titulary of HOR-ATEN

(B) Titularies of King and Queen

(C) . . . their [. . .], elevating praise (?) . . . [on behalf of] the Lord of the Two Lands, [King of Upper and Lower Egypt], NEFERKHEPRURE-WAENRE: may you allow (me) to see you in the eastern horizon until your setting from life comes to pass. For the Ka of the favorite of the Good God, the fanbearer at the right hand of the king, the true king's scribe, his beloved, the God's Father Ay—may he live again.

(D) . . . lasting continually, ... So long as you exist, his Person shall exist—(namely), the Son of Re, AKHENATEN, long in his lifetime: May you grant that (I) follow you like your favorite. For the Ka of the favorite of the Good God, the fanbearer at the king's right hand, the commander of all horses of his Person, the true king's scribe, his beloved, the God's Father, Ay, justified.

(E) . . . upon you . . . (and) a lengthy lifetime for the king and for the King's Chief Wife, NEFERNEFRUATEN-NEFERTITI, may she live forever continually. May you allow me to receive continually (the power of) his Ka. I am a servant whom his Person brought into being. For the Ka of the favorite of the Good God, the fanbearer at the right hand of the king, the confidant throughout the entire land, the true king's scribe, his beloved, the God's Father Ay—may he live again.

(F) Welcome, O living Aten, . . . , [who has benefited the ruler more than any] king (?) who (ever) came forth, while there is [not] another who knows you except your son, the King of Upper and and Lower Egypt, NEFERKHEPRURE-WAENRE. May you grant me[1] a good lifetime while seeing your beauty every day without ceasing. For the Ka of the favorite of the Good God, the nurse of the King's Chief Wife, NEFERNEFRUATEN-NEFERTITI, may she live forever continually, Tiyi, justified.

Right Jamb
(G) Titulary of HOR-ATEN

(H) Titularies of King and Queen

(I) [Welcome!] How [beautiful is] your rising when you have filled [the Two Lands with your] beauty, being fair and great and manifest [on earth on behalf of (?)] your son, the [King of Upper] and Lower Egypt, [NEFERKHEPRURE-WAENRE]. May you give to me the offering loaves that come forth in your presence until the old age which is yours to give comes to pass. For the Ka of the favorite of the Good God, the fanbearer at the right hand of the king, the true king's scribe, his beloved, the God's Father Ay—may he live again.

(J) Welcome when you rise, (O) Aten, . . . who administers [. . . all that the] Aten [encircles], all this <for> his son when he . . . , the Son of Re, AKHENATEN, long in his lifetime: may you grant that I be sated with seeing you without cease. For the Ka of the favorite of the Good God, the fanbearer at the right hand of the king, the commander of all the horse of his Person, the true king's scribe, his beloved, the God's Father Ay, justified.

(K) Welcome, O living Aten, who begets himself by himself every day! Every land is in festival [when you] appear, [and all rejoice in] your rays which are in [their faces (?)] when you set in . . .upon . . . your [. . .], on behalf of the King's Chief Wife, NEFERNEFRUATEN-NEFERTITI, may she live forever continually. May you grant contentment and joy [every] day [in the favor] of Waenre. For the Ka of the favorite of the Good God, the fanbearer at the right hand of the king, the confidant throughout the entire land, the true king's scribe, his beloved, the God's Father Ay—may he live again.

(L) . . . who illuminates (?) . . . : [may you follow] what your [lord] says . . . , . . . your life when you rise to give him eternity; who administers the land for the one who placed him on his seat and causes the land to exist for the one who made him; the King of Upper [and Lower] Egypt. NEFERKHEPRURE-WAENRE: May you grant that my Ka be lasting, enduring and well at rest in Akhet-Aten. For the Ka of the favorite of the Good God, the great nurse who nourished the goddess,[2] the king's ornament, Tiyi, justified.

58-B.2. Entrance, Ceiling Inscriptions

West: Adoration to you, O living Aten, who made heaven and has concealed himself within it: even while he is in our face(s) we do not know his body, *but he is revealed* (?) to his beloved son; and he has endowed him with a million jubilees, while the King's Chief Wife, his beloved, the Lady of the

Two Lands, NEFERNEFRUATEN-NEFERTITI—may she live forever continually—is beside Waenre. May you grant me a good funeral, like (only) you can do, in the great mountain of Akhet-Aten. For the Ka of the favorite of the Good [God, the fanbearer at the right hand of the king], the king's true scribe, [his] beloved, [the God's Father] Ay, may he live again.

Middle: Adoration to you, O living Aten, who rises and brings to life what he encircles; who made the land and created its[3] grasses in order to bring to life what he has made; master of rays (?), Aten (?), lord of (?) [humankind, who makes] them . . . at seeing his rays while his son is on . . . when he rises in the horizon: may you grant that he endures continually, just like you, . . . his Person . . . . [For the Ka of . . . , the king's] scribe, his beloved, the God's Father Ay, [may he live again].

East: Adoration to you, O living Aten, the god who made all these things. You are in heaven, but your rays are [on earth . . .], your [son] Waenre: may you love him, the lord of life and lifetime, your [child] who issued from your rays, the Son of Re AKHENATEN, [long in] his [lifetime], the beloved lord (?) . . . for (?) . . . his lord for . . . , without an instance [of . . .].

58-B.3. East Thickness

In the upper register, the royal family sacrifices to the Aten. Akhenaten and Nefertiti are followed by their three eldest daughters and by the sister of the King's Chief Wife [NEFERNEFRUATEN-NEFERTITI]—may she live forever continually—Mutnodjmet. *Following this lady are her attendants, including two dwarves:* The dwarf (named) Hemetnisweterneheh *and* The dwarf Mutef-Pre.[4] *The register underneath this scene is mostly devoted to the texts translated below, accompanied by the kneeling figures of the tomb owner and his wife—the latter described as* The favorite of the Good God, the nurse who nourished the goddess (=*the queen*), the king's ornament, Tiyi, justified.

Adoration of HOR-ATEN, given life forever continually; (and of) the King of Upper and Lower Egypt NEFERKHEPRURE-WAENRE, the Son of Re AKHENATEN, long in his lifetime; (and of) the King's Chief Wife, NEFERNEFRUATEN-NEFERTITI, may she live forever continually: "Adoration to you when you rise in the horizon, O living Aten, lord of continuity, (and) kissing the ground when you rise in heaven in order to illuminate every land with your beauty. Your rays be upon your beloved son, and may your two hands bear millions of jubilees for the King of Upper and Lower Egypt NEFERKHEPRURE-WAENRE, your child, who issued from your rays. May you bequeath to him your lifetime and your years. May you hearken, on his behalf, to what is in his heart. May you love him and make him be like Aten.

May you rise to give him continuity and set (only) after you have given him eternity. May you fashion him at dawn like (you do) your aspects of being. May you construct him in your image like Aten, the ruler of Maat who issued from continuity—the Son of Re, who lifts up his beauty and administers the dues of his rays for him: the King of Upper and Lower Egypt, who lives on Maat, the Lord of the Two Lands, NEFERKHEPRURE-WAENRE, (and) the King's Chief Wife, NEFERNEFRUATEN-NEFERTITI, <may she> live forever continually."

The God's Father, the favorite of the Good God, the fanbearer at the right hand of the king, the commander of all the horse of his Person, the true royal scribe, his beloved, Ay. He says: "Hail to you, O living Aten who rises in heaven as he floods hearts (*with light*), every land being in festival at his appearance, their hearts being content with rejoicing when their lord, who made himself, is risen over them. Your son presents Maat[5] to your benign countenance while you exult when you see him. He has issued from you—a continual son, who issued from Aten, effective for the one who is effective for him, who slakes the heart of Aten when he rises in heaven. He is joyful on account of his son as he embraces him with his rays and gives him continuity as king like the Aten—(namely) NEFERKHEPRURE-WAENRE, my god who made me and brought my Ka into being! May you cause me to be sated with seeing you without cease. Your nature is like Aten's, abounding in property, a high Nile flowing every day, who revives Egypt, (with) silver and gold like the sands of the sandbank, while the land awakens to jubilate, being rich through his Ka. (O) one whom the Aten has begotten, you will be eternal, (O) NEFERKHEPRURE-WAENRE, living and healthy inasmuch as he (=*the Aten*) begot you!"

The God's Father, fanbearer at the right hand of the king, commander of all the horse of his Person, true king's scribe, his <beloved>, Ay. He says: "I am one who is true to the king, one whom he fostered, who is straightforward to the Lord of the Two Lands, and effective for his lord. As his favorite, who sees his beauty when he appears in his palace, I follow the Ka of his Person, while I am in front of the officials and the king's companions, the first of all the followers of his Person. He has placed Maat in my innermost being. My abomination is falsehood, for I know that Waenre, my lord, rejoices in Maat, he who is knowledgeable like Aten and truly perceptive. He doubled for me my rewards in silver and gold while I was the first of the officials in front of the subjects, for my nature and my character were good, and he made my position there. My lord instructed me just so that I might practice his teaching. I live by adoring his Ka and I am fulfilled by following him—(the one who is) my breath, by whom I live, my northwind, my millions of Niles flowing daily, NEFERKHEPRURE-WAENRE: may you grant me a lengthy lifetime in your favor."

"How prosperous is the one you favor, O son of the Aten. All he does shall be lasting and enduring, while the Ka of the Lord of the Two Lands is with him continually, and he shall be sated with living when he reaches old age—(even) my lord, who constructs people, brings lifetime into being and makes a good fate for his favorite, (whose) heart is satisfied with Maat, whose abomination is falsehood. How prosperous is he who hears your teaching of life, for he will be fulfilled by seeing you without cease while his eyes behold the Aten daily. May you grant me a good old age like a favorite of yours. May you give me a good funeral by the decree of your Ka, in my tomb[6] within which you ordained for me to rest in the mountain of Akhet-Aten, the place of the favored ones. Let me hear your sweet voice in the Mansion of the Benben when you do what your father, the living Aten, favors. May he make you exist continually! May he reward you with jubilees like the number (of grains) of the sandbank, being measured in *oipe*; like the totality of the sea, being measured in *dja*. The totaling and reckoning of the mountains, weighed upon scales, and of the feathers of birds and the leaves of trees—(such) are the jubilees of the king, the only one of Re (=*Waenre*), verily unto eternity as continual king, and of the King's Chief Wife, his beloved, who is at one with her beauty, she who satisfies the Aten with a sweeet voice and with her lovely hands bearing the sistra, the lady of the Two Lands, NEFERNEFRUATEN-NEFERTITI—may <she> live forever continually, while she is beside Waenre continually, continually, just as heaven shall be lasting, bearing the one that is in it, while your father, the Aten, is rising in heaven to protect you every day, just as he has fashioned you. May you give me the pure offering bread that is issued in your presence as the unused offerings of your father Aten, which are what your Ka has to give. May you grant that my Ka may belong to me, lasting and enduring <in the fashion> of when I was on earth following your Ka and introduced to it by name at the place of the favored ones after you have caused me to rest in it. My mouth is full of righteousness: may my name be pronounced because of it, as you have ordained, since I am like any favorite of yours who follows your Ka. May I depart, laden with your favor, following old age." For the Ka of the fanbearer at the right hand of the king, the true king's scribe, his beloved, the God's Father Ay—may he live again.

58-B.4. West Thickness

On this wall, the upper register that is usually devoted to a representation of the royal family (as on the east thickness in this tomb and comparable places in others) is filled instead with the Great Hymn to the Aten, inscribed with large hieroglyphs in thirteen vertical columns. Below, and formally separate, are the kneeling figures of The fanbearer at the right hand of the king, the commander of all the horse of his Person, the confidant thoughout the entire land, the favorite of the Good God, the God's Father Ay, *and his wife,* The favorite of the Good God, the great nurse of the King's Chief Wife NEFERNEFRUATEN-NEFERTITI—may she live forever continually—the king's ornament, Tiyi.

Adoration of HOR-ATEN, [living] forever [continually—Great living Aten] who is in jubilee, Lord of all that Aten encircles, Lord of Heaven, Lord of Earth, Lord of the House of Aten in Akhet-Aten; and the King of Upper and Lower Egypt, who lives on Maat, the Lord of the Two Lands, NEFER-KHEPRURE-WAENRE, the Son of Re who lives on Maat, Lord of Crowns, AKHENATEN, long [in his lifetime]; and the King's Chief Wife, his beloved, the Lady of the Two Lands, NEFERNEFRUATEN-NEFERTITI, may she live, be healthy and youthful everlastingly forever. He says:[7]

"Beautifully you appear from the horizon of heaven, O living Aten who initiates life—
For you are risen from the eastern horizon and have filled every land with your beauty;
For you are fair, great, dazzling and high over every land,
And your rays enclose the lands to the limit of all you have made;
For you are Re, having reached their limit and subdued them <for> your beloved son;
For although you are far away, your rays are upon the earth and you are perceived."

"When your movements vanish and you set in the western horizon,
The land is in darkness, in the manner of death.
(People), they lie in bedchambers, heads covered up, and one eye does not see its fellow.
All their property is robbed, although it is under their heads, and they do not realize it.
Every lion is out of its den, all creeping things bite.
Darkness gathers, the land is silent.
The one who made them is set in his horizon."

"(But) the land grows bright when you are risen from the horizon,
Shining in the orb (=*Aten*) in the daytime, you push back the darkness and give forth your rays.
The Two Lands are in a festival of light—
Awake and standing on legs, for you have lifted them up:
Their limbs are cleansed and wearing clothes,
Their arms are in adoration at your appearing.
The whole land, they do their work:

All flocks are content with their pasturage,
Trees and grasses flourish,
Birds are flown from their nests, their wings adoring your Ka;
All small cattle prance upon their legs.
All that fly up and alight, they live when you rise for them.
Ships go downstream, and upstream as well, every road being open at your appearance.
Fish upon the river leap up in front of you, and your rays are within the Great Green (sea)."

"(O you) who brings into being foetuses in women,
Who makes fluid in people,
Who gives life to the son in his mother's womb, and calms him by stopping his tears;
Nurse in the womb, who gives breath to animate all he makes
When it descends from the womb to breathe on the day it is born –
You open his mouth completely and make what he needs.
When the chick is in the egg, speaking in the shell,
You give him breath within it to cause him to live;
And when you have made his appointed time for him, so that he may break himself out of the egg,
He comes out of the egg to speak at his appointed time and goes on his two legs when he comes out of it."

"How manifold it is, what you have made, although mysterious in the face (of humanity),
O sole god, without another beside him!
You create the earth according to your wish,[8] being alone–
People, all large and small animals,
All things which are on earth, which go on legs, which rise up and fly by means of their wings,
The foreign countries of Kharu and Kush, (and) the land of Egypt.
You set every man in his place, you make their requirements, each one having his food and the reckoning of his lifetime. Their tongues differ in speech, their natures likewise. Their skins are distinct, for you have made foreigners to be distinct.
You make the inundation from the underworld,
And you bring it to (the place) you wish in order to cause the subjects to live,
Inasmuch as you made them for yourself, their lord entirely,[9] who is wearied with them,[10]
the lord of every land, who rises for them,
The orb (=*Aten*) of the daytime, whose awesomeness is great!

(As for) all distant countries, you make their life:
You have granted an inundation in heaven, that it might come down for them
And make torrents upon the mountains, like the Great Green, to soak their fields in their locale(s)."

"How functional are your plans, O lord of continuity!
An inundation in heaven, which is for[11] the foreigners (and) for all foreign flocks which go on legs;
(And) an inundation when it comes from the underworld for the Tilled Land (=*Egypt*),
While your rays nurse every field:
When you rise, they live and flourish for you.
You make the seasons in order to develop all you make:
The Growing season to cool them, and heat so that they might feel[12] you."

"You made heaven far away just to rise in it, to see all you make,
Being unique and risen in your aspects of being as 'living Aten'—manifest, shining, far (yet) near.
You make millions of developments from yourself, (you who are) a oneness: cities, towns, fields, the path of the river.
Every eye observes you in relation to them, for you are Aten of the daytime above the earth (?).
You have traveled just so that everybody might exist.
You create their faces so that you might not see [your]self [as] the only (thing) which you made."

"You are in my heart, and there is none who knows you except your son, NEFERKHEPRURE-WAENRE,
For you make him aware of your plans and your strength.
The land develops through your action, just as you made them (=*people*):
When you have risen they live, (but) when you set they die. You are lifetime in your (very) limbs, and one lives by means of you.
Until you set, (all) eyes are upon your beauty (but) all work is put aside when you set on the western side.
(You) who rise and make [*all creation*] grow for the king, (as for) everyone who hurries about on foot since you founded the land,
You raise them up for your son, who issued from your limbs, the King of Upper and Lower Egypt, who lives on Maat,
The Lord of the Two Lands, NEFERKHEPRURE-[WAENRE],
Son of Re, who lives on Maat, Lord of Crowns, AKHENATEN, long in his lifetime;
(And) the King's Chief Wife, his beloved, the Lady of the Two Lands,

NEFERNEFRUATEN-NEFERTITI—may she live and be young forever continually."

58-B.5. North Wall, East Side

Ay and Tiyi, standing before the royal window of appearances, are rewarded with collars and vessels of precious metal by Akhenaten, accompanied by the queen and the three eldest daughters. Nefertiti's sister Mutnodjmet was shown with the younger daughters inside the palace at the left, but her figure is lost and can only be surmised by the presence of her two customary attendants–the dwarf Hemetniswetrneheh *and* the dwarf Mutef-Pre. *To the right, laden with honors, the tomb owner is greeted by his friends. Bystanders' reactions are captured in the exchanges between sentries and street boys along the top (from left to right):*

First Sentry: "For whom is this shouting being made, my child?"

First Boy: "The shouting is made for Ay, the God's Father, and Tiyi: they are become people of gold!"

First Sentry: "May you look at these (things)—they're the beauties of a lifetime!"

Second Sentry: "Run and see for whom this great shouting is, and return quickly!"

Second Boy: "I'll do (it): look at me!"

Visitor: "For whom is the shouting being made?"

Third Sentry: "Stand up, so you can see benevolences—(namely) those which Pharaoh, l.p.h., has made for Ay, the God's Father, and Tiyi, to whom Pharaoh, l.p.h., gave millions of portable treasures, as well as every sort of thing."

Third Boy: "Look at that stool and that bag![13] Let's see what is done for Ay, the God's Father."

Fourth Boy: "Don't delay, for I must go and bring them <to> my boss."

58-B.6. Inner Door, Lintel

At either end of the lintel, kneeling figures of Ay and his wife salute the solar disk, shown in the center with the names of the HOR-ATEN, the king and the queen below.

Left: Giving adoration to the Aten and kissing the ground to his beloved son, the Lord of the Two Lands, NEFERKHEPRURE-WAENRE: "Lifetime is at your hand, and you grant it to whomever you wish. The land lives only on what you assign. How prosperous is the one who places you in his heart, for then he will achieve old age in good fortune." For the Ka of the favorite of the Good God, the fanbearer at the right hand of the king, the true king's scribe, his beloved, the God's Father Ay; (and) the great nurse who nourished the goddess, the king's ornament, Tiyi.

Right: Giving adoration to the Aten and kissing the ground to the Lord of continuity: "Adoration be given to you when you rise in the horizon (and) until your setting from life comes to pass; and may my favor be lasting every day in [the presence of] Waenre, until the old age which is his to give comes about, in favor and tranquillity." For the Ka of the favorite, etc. (*as above*).

58-B.7. Inner Door, Jambs

Left Jamb

A. Long live the Good God, who is pleased with Maat, lord of all that Aten encircles, lord of heaven, lord of earth, great living Aten who illuminates the Two Banks. Long live the Father, HOR-ATEN, given life forever continually—great [living Aten] who is in jubilee in the House of Aten in Akhet-Aten.

B. Long live the Horus. the Mighty Bull, "Beloved of Aten"; Two Ladies, "Great of Kingship in Akhet-Aten"; Horus of Gold, "Who Elevates the Name of Aten"; the King of Upper and Lower Egypt, who lives on Maat, Lord of the Two Lands, NEFERKHEPRURE-WAENRE; the Son of Re who lives on Maat, Lord of Crowns, [AKHENATEN], long in his lifetime; (and) the King's Chief Wife, his beloved, NEFERNEFRUATEN-NEFERTITI, may she live forever continually.

C. The fanbearer at the right hand of the King, commander of all the horses of his Person, true king's scribe, his beloved, the God's Father Ay, may he live again. He says: "I was one favored of his lord in the course of every day. My favor increased from year to year because (I) was very effective in his opinion, and he doubled rewards for me like the number of sands while I was first of the officials in front of the subjects."

D. The fanbearer at the right hand of the king, the great companion who is near to his lord; true royal scribe, his beloved, the God's Father Ay, justified. He says: "I was straightforward and true, devoid of rapacity. My name reached the palace only because of being effective for the king, because of hearkening to his teaching and executing his laws, (and) not confusing words or neglecting conduct. My greatness was in being close-mouthed, being prosperous, one who requested for himself a good old age and who loved life."

E. The fanbearer at the right hand of the king, the king's confidant throughout the entire land; the king's true scribe, his beloved, the God's Father Ay—may he live again. He says: "O each one who lives on earth, all generations who come into being, let me tell you the way of living and testify to you concerning (my) rewards, and then you shall read aloud my name and what I did. I was righteous on earth. Make adoration to living Aten and you shall endure in life. Say to him, 'Make the ruler healthy!,' and he will double rewards for you."

Right Jamb
F. Same as A.

G. Same as B.

H. The fanbearer at the right hand of the king, the commander of all the horse of the Lord of the Two Lands; true king's scribe, his beloved, the God's Father Ay, justified. He says: "I was excellent, a possessor of character, fortunate, blithe, patient, desiring authoritative direction when (the time of) following his Person's Ka came about, just as he has ordained. I listened to his voice without cease, and the result of this is the reward of an old age in peace."

I. The fanbearer at the right hand of the king, the great companion to be confided in; the true king's scribe, his beloved, the God's Father Ay, may he live again. He says: "I was one true to the king, one whom he fostered;[14] straightforward to the Lord of the Two Lands, serviceable <to> his lord; one who saw his beauty when he appeared in his palace, while I was in front of the officials and companions of the king, (being) the first of his lord's followers. He has set Maat in my inner being, and my abomination is lying. I live only by worshiping his Ka, and I am fulfilled only by seeing him."

J. The fanbearer at the right hand of the king; whom the Lord of the Two Lands loves on account of his character; true king's scribe, his beloved, the God's Father Ay, justified. He says: "O each one who loves life and desires a good lifetime: worship the king, unique like Aten, without another who is great except for him, and he will grant you a lifetime in tranquillity, (with) food and provisions which are his to give."

58-B.8. Hall Ceiling

West: "Be adored at (?) the appearance of your beauty, O living Aten who ordains life. May you[15] see Re's sunbeams after he has risen and when he makes illumination at the door of your tomb. May you inhale the breezes of the north wind, and may he strengthen your limbs with life, the favored one who has reached old age, the righteous one who has done what his lord says. You are the first among the king's companions, while similarly you are in front of the illuminated spirits. May you develop as a living Ba in the august mountain of Akhet-Aten. May you exit and enter according to the inclination of your heart. May your rank be invoked on earth while you consume food beside your god. Follow your heart at the season of your desiring, your tomb being festive every day, (with) a worthy state of reveredness in peace. The result of this is interment, which comes to pass from the two arms of the king, Waenre."

"I[16] am a servant whom his lord developed and whom he buried, for my mouth was full of righteousness. How prosperous is one who carries out his teaching, for he shall reach the district of the favored ones." For the Ka of the favorite of the Good God, true-hearted to the one who confided in him, one who abandoned falsehood in order to do Maat, the favorite who reached these (conditions) in favor: the fanbearer at the right hand of the king, the commander of all the horse of his Person, the true king's scribe, his beloved, the God's Father Ay, justified.

East: "May you adore Re each time he appears, and when you see him may he hearken to what you say. May he give you breath, may he knot up your limbs. May you exit and enter like his favorite. May your corpse be firm, may your name last, may [. . .] be delightful for your Ka. May you inhale the breezes of the north wind. May you be given offerings and provisions, and may you receive sacrificial food which is the king's to give, (with) bread, beer, and food at every place of yours. May your name be firm on your tomb, and may every generation invoke you when it comes into being. May you occupy your place which is the king's to give in the necropolis of Akhet-Aten. May there be made for you a 'boon-which-the-king gives' offering of bread and beer which is satisfying to your Ka. May you be united with your place of eternity, and may your mansion of eternity receive you, (with) ox(en) dragging you and a lector priest in front of you, purifying the catafalque with milk, their numbers being as the king, Waenre, decrees for a favorite whom he developed. May he send you up to the place of the favored ones (as) one who completed his lifetime in well-being, your tomb being festive every day just as when you were alive. It is your god who has decreed it for you, the living Aten, lord of continuity, and they[17] are lasting continually forever for the righteous one who is devoid of doing wrong." For the Ka of the favorite of the Good God, the fanbearer at the right hand of the king, the true king's scribe, his beloved, the God's Father Ay, justified.

Middle: "Be adored when you rise in the horizon, O Aten! You[18] shall not cease from seeing Re. Open your [eyes] to see him. When you pray to him, may he listen to what you say. The breath of life, may it enter your nose. Raise yourself up on your right side, so that you may place yourself on your left side. May your Ba be glad on the highland. May the children of your house libate for you (with) bread, beer, water, and breath for your Ka. May you stride through the gates of the underworld. May you see Re at dawn at his appearance in the eastern horizon; and may you see Aten at his setting in the western horizon of heaven. May you be given offerings and provisions from the offering-trough of the House of Aten. May you be given incense and libation from the 'staircase of the living one,' Aten. It is the king, the Aten's son, who decrees it to you continually. May you receive all that comes forth in his presence every day, without ceasing. May you receive all gifts in the necropolis when your Ba rests in your tomb. May your Ba not be opposed in what it wants, but be content with the daily offerings–(with) the intelligence lasting and the heart in its proper position beside the lord of continuity. May your name be pronounced every day continually forever, as is done for an excellent favorite like you!" For the Ka of the one whose favors are enduring in the presence of the Lord of the Two Lands, the God's Father Ay, justified.

59. The "First Servant of Akhenaten" Ahmose

The following inscriptions are found in Ahmose's tomb (Nr. 3) at el-Amarna.

59.1. Lintel of Outer Door

Virtually the identical text is inscribed on the outer lintel of Pentu's tomb. The chief variants from the copy in Ahmose's tomb are given in the notes below.

Left side: Tendering adoration to the living Aten and kissing the ground [to] the Good God by the sealbearer of the King of Lower Egypt, the sole companion, the attendant of the Lord of the Two Lands, the favorite of the Good God, one beloved of his lord every day, the true king's scribe, his beloved, the steward of the House of AKHENATEN, overseer of the front hall of the Lord of the Two Lands, Ahmose, justified, possessor of reveredness.[19]

Right side: Tendering adoration [to] the living Aten and kissing the ground to the good king by the sealbearer of the King of Lower Egypt, one who can approach the god's flesh, the chiefest of chiefs, most [knowledgeable of those who know] <in> the Two Lands, the first companion of the companions, the king's true scribe, his beloved, the overseer of the front hall of the Lord of the Two Lands, the steward of the House of AKHENATEN, Ahmose, justified, possessor of reveredness.

59.2. Jambs of Outer Door

Left side:

A. [A "boon which the king gives" of HOR-ATEN (and)] NEFERKHEPRURE-WAENRE: may he grant entry and exit in the king's house, limbs being filled with joy every day. For the Ka of the true king's scribe, overseer of the front hall and steward of the House of AKHENATEN, long in his lifetime, Ahmose, [justified].

B. A "boon which the king gives" [of HOR-ATEN (and)] AKHENATEN: may he [grant] favor and the receiving of offering loaves from his offerings. For the Ka of the true king's scribe, his beloved, the overseer of the front hall and steward in the House of AKHENATEN, long in his lifetime, Ahmose, [justified].

C. A "boon which the king gives" [of HOR-ATEN] (and) NEFERKHEPRURE-WAENRE: [may he give] l.p.h., happiness, joy, and exultation to the Ka of the king's true scribe, his beloved, the fanbearer at the right hand of the king, Ahmose, [justified].

D. [A "boon] which the king gives" [of HOR-ATEN] (and) AKHENATEN: [may he give] rejoicing daily and the seeing of his handsome face every day. For the Ka of the true king's scribe, the fanbarer at the king's right hand, [Ahmose, justified].

Right Side:

E. A "boon which the king gives" of HOR-ATEN (and) NEFERKHEPRURE-[WAENRE]: may he permit [me to] follow his footsteps in every place he treads. For the Ka of the king's true scribe, [his] beloved, [the overseer of] the front hall, the steward [of the House of AKHENATEN, long in his lifetime, Ahmose, justified].

F. A "boon which the king gives" of HOR-ATEN (and) AKHENATEN: may he permit the seeing of Aten from his appearance until his setting as Aten comes to pass. For the Ka of the king's true scribe, his beloved, overseer of the front hall and steward of the House of AKHENATEN, [long in his lifetime, Ahmose, justified].

G. A "boon which the king gives" [of HOR-ATEN (and) NEFERKHEPRURE]-WAENRE: may he give a good lifetime seeing his beauty, and a good funeral after old age. For the Ka of the king's true scribe, his beloved, the fanbearer at the right hand of the king, [Ahmose, justified].

H. A "boon which the king gives" [of HOR-ATEN (and) AKHENATEN]: may he grant a station within the palace in order to see the king, Waenre. For the Ka of the true king's scribe, his beloved, the fanbearer at the right hand of the king, [Ahmose, justified].

59.3. Thickness of East Wall: Hymn to the Setting Sun

The king's true scribe, his beloved, the fanbearer at the right hand of the king, the overseer of the front hall and steward of the House of AKHENATEN, long in his lifetime, Ahmose, justified. He says: "You set beautifully, O living Aten, lord of lords, ruler of the Two Banks, when [you have] crossed the sky in peace, the entire world being jubilant to your face, tendering adoration to the one who constructed them and kissing the ground to [the one who brought] them [into being]. Your beloved son, the King of Upper and Lower Egypt who lives on Maat, NEFERKHEPRURE-WAENRE, has guided the entire land and every foreign country in all that you encompass at your appearance, just so that celebration be made at your rising and your setting also."

"O god who lives on Maat in front of people's eyes, it is you who made when there was no one who had made any of this, it was from your mouth that they issued forth! May you give me favor in the king's presence every day without cease, and a good funeral after old age upon the highland of Akhet-Aten. I have completed a lifetime in happiness, being in the following of the Good God everywhere he went, being loved when I was his attendant. From when I was a youth until I reached the state of reveredness in peace, he developed me. How joyful is one who follows the ruler: he is in festival every day!"

59.4. Thickness of West Wall: Hymn to the Rising Sun

By the figure of Ahmose in an adoring posture: The true king's scribe, his beloved, the fanbearer at the right hand of the king, the overseer of the front hall, the steward of the House of AKHENATEN, long in his lifetime, Ahmose, justified. He says: *The text of the hymn follows: see the tomb of Meryre I (70.7) below.*

60. The King's Scribe and Steward, Any

The following inscriptions all come from Any's tomb at El-Amarna (No. 23).

60-A.1. Entrance Passage

A label attached to the tomb owner's adoring figure introduces the shorter hymn to the Aten as follows: The king's acqaintance, whom his lord loves, the favorite whom the Lord of the Two Lands made with his Ka, who has reached the revered state in the favor of the king; the true king's scribe, his beloved, scribe of the offering table of the Lord of the Two Lands, scribe of the Aten's offering table on behalf of the Aten in the House of Aten in Akhet-Aten, the steward of the House of AAKHEPRURE, Any, justified in a good funeral. [He] says: *see below, in the tomb of Meryre I (70.8), for a translation of the hymn in all its versions.*

60-A.2. Shrine, Left Wall

Any is shown seated in front of a laden offering table while he is addressed by the servant who stands in front of him. Variants of this text, some of them quite close to this version, are found in the tomb of Huya (66.12) below.

"May you receive offerings [of the king's giving]—bread, [beer, and food—at] every place of yours, that your name might be enduring [on] your tomb (?), so that any generations which may come into being shall invoke [you] without having to search for your name [in your tomb], and you will be a Ba [for whom] is performed the 'boon which the king gives' ritual, consisting of your bread, beer, your [. . .] and the [offerings] which come forth from the presence [of the king] in the door of [the tomb] which you [made]." (Said by) Meryre, the servitor and agent of the king's scribe Any, justified.

Titles of Any: The king's scribe, beloved of [his] lord, [the . . . of] the Aten, the scribe of the food-laden table of the Lord of the Two Lands in Akhet-Aten, [steward of the House of] AAKHEPRURE, given life, Any, justified [. . .] in peace.

60-A.3. Shrine, Right Wall

Any, shown seated with a lady behind him, receives a libation from the servant standing in front of him.

By Any: [True] king's [scribe, whom his] lord [loves, steward of] the Lord of the [Two] Lands, the scribe of the offering table of the House of AAKHEPRURE, . . . , Any.

By the lady: [His wife], the housewife Awy[. . .], she says: "(O) Any (?), . . . as a son (?) . . . . May you attain eternity (?) [. . .] (and) may he decree for you your place of continuity."

By the servant: "[(O) . . . of the] Lord [of the Two Lands] . . . Any (?), [may he grant] a thousand [of] bread, . . . , (and) every [. . .], that you may go forth [as] heir [of . . .], may you be one of . . . . [May] the king ordain for you a good funeral <on> the mountain of Akhet-Aten, [the place of] continuity: you will exist inside it, your place belonging to your Ka! I am one <who acts> as you say (?), the servant and agent (?) of the king's scribe Any, justified, (called) Meryre.

60-A.4. Jambs of Outer Door

Bottom Left: "Adoration to you, O living Aten, possessor of sunbeams, who makes brightness—at whose rising everyone lives! May he grant a good lifetime while one beholds his beauty, and a good funeral in Akhet-Aten." For the Ka of the King's scribe and steward, Any, justified.

Bottom Right: "Adoration to you, O living Aten, lord of lifetime who grants repetition (of life), master of fate who brings fortune into being. May he grant that Aten be seen at his every appearance. May you adore him, that he may hear what you say and give you breath unto your nose." For the Ka of the King's scribe, the scribe of the table of the Lord of the Two Lands, the steward Any, justified.

60-B. Votive Stelae

These six small stelae were found inside Any's tomb. While similar ex-votos are known for other close contemporaries, these are the only objects of this nature which survive from Akhet-Aten.

1. Stela of Pakha
Any, shown seated in front of a laden offering table, is offered a bouquet by the dedicant.

Above Pakha: "<For> your Ka, the bouquet of the Aten, that he may grant me [*sic*] breath and knit up your limbs so that you may see Re each time he appears. Adore him, that he may listen when you speak."

Above Any: The king's true scribe, his beloved, the scribe of the table of the Lord of the Two Lands, the steward Any, justified in a good funeral.

Below the scene: Made by the overseer of works projects Pakha, justified.

2. Stela of Nebwawi
In the upper register, Any (with titles as in A above) stands on the right, addressed by a standing figure of the scribe Nebwawi; he says: "Behold the bull, (of which) it was said, 'Bring it.'"

In the lower register, Nebwawi leads a garlanded ox, with the following text inscribed above: The scribe Nebwawi, he says, "Let us behold the good things which the ruler does for his table scribe, for whom he has decreed a good funeral in Akhet-Aten."

3. Stela of Anymen
The dedicant stands, holding a libation jar, before the tomb owner, who is seated with a laden offering table in front of him.

By Anymen: "A libation of wine is made to you." Done by the servant of the king's scribe Any, Anymen.

By Any: For the Ka of the king's true scribe, his beloved, the scribe of the table of the Lord of the Two Lands, the steward Any, justified.

4. Stela of Tchay
The dedicant, identified as Charioteer of the king's scribe Any, (called) Tchay, *is shown driving his master's chariot, while behind him stands* the king's true scribe, his beloved, the scribe of the table of the Lord of the Two Lands, the steward Any, justified: "I have come in peace by favor of the king, that he may decree for me a good funeral and permit that I attain the revered state in peace."

5. Stela of Ptahmay
The king's scribe, the steward Any, justified in a good funeral, *is shown seated to the left of a laden offering table. In front of him, his arm upraised in greeting, stands another official, with the following text inscribed above his head:* By his brother, Ptahmay. "May there be made for you a 'boon which the king gives' consisting of bread, beer, oxen, fowl, wine and milk."

6. Stela of Iay.
The dedicant is shown presenting a bouquet to the seated figure of his master: "<For> your Ka, the bouquet of the Aten, that he may favor you, that he may love you." By the servant Iay.

61. The Chief Steward, Apy

This man, one of the few individuals known both from Thebes and El-Amarna (cf. 22 above), came from a prominent Memphite family, being related to the vizier Ramose (32 above).

61-A. Doorjamb from the House of the Steward Apy

The owner is shown kneeling and adoring the names of the god, HOR-ATEN, *and of the king, while uttering the following words:*

Giving adoration to the Good God, kissing the ground to the victorious king by the king's scribe, the steward of Memphis Apy, justified. He says: "I give you adoration while my heart rejoices and my eyes see your beauty. O ruler who lives on Maat and causes the land to grow by means of his Ka, may you give good a life every day to the Ka of the king's scribe, the overseer of the large inner palace of pharaoh, l.p.h., in Akhet-Aten, the steward Apy, justified."

61-B. Tomb of Apy at El-Amarna (No. 10)

61-B.1. Entrance Passage
The "shorter Hymn to the Aten" appears on both sides of the entrance passage. The version on the left side was laid out only in ink and is virtually all gone today. For the text carved on the right, which is also extant in a number of other tombs, see Meryre I (70.1.8 below). On the right side, below the hymn, Apy is shown kneeling, with the personal ending as follows: For the Ka of the king's scribe, the steward Apy—may he live again!

61-B.2. Entrance, Left Side (Top)
Above another copy of the shorter hymn to the Aten (see above, B.1), Akhenaten and Nefertiti are shown offering boxes to the Aten: these caskets are in the shape of double cartouches, with adjoining figures of Shu (king) and Tefnut (queen). The first three daughters, shaking sistra, stand behind their parents. Apart from the early titulary of the Aten, the names of the king and the standard inscriptions which identify the daughters, the only text worth noting refers to the queen:

The hereditary princess, great of favor, lady of charm, endowed with joy—to give favor to whom the Aten rises, and to double the love of whom it sets; the King's Chief Wife, his beloved, the mistress of Upper and Lower Egypt, Lady of the Two Lands, NEFERNEFRUATEN-NEFERTITI, may she live forever continually.

Figure 3:
Akhenaten and Nefertiti each offer to the Aten boxes decorated with the emblems of their divine counterparts, Shu and Tefnut

61-B.3. Ceiling Inscriptions

A "boon which the king gives" of the living one, Re-Harakhty, the august god, beloved one who lives on Maat every day: may he grant the smelling of incense, receiving of ointment and drinking of the river's stream without my Ba's being hindered from what it has desired. For the Ka of the king's scribe, the steward Apy.

61-B.4. Entrance, Right Jamb

A. Standard titularies of the Aten, the king and queen.

B. "[Adoration to you, O living] Aten . . . , rising in (?) it. May you grant a lifetime as Aten in heaven to the King of Upper and Lower Egypt who lives on Maat, the Lord of the Two Lands NEFERKHEPRURE-WAENRE, given life forever continually. May he grant a good name in Akhet-Aten to the Ka of the steward Apy."

C. "[Adoration] to you, the living [Aten] . . . of (?) your rays (?) while they embrace your son, the Son of Re who lives on Maat, the Lord of Crowns, AKHENATEN, long in his lifetime–may he grant the receiving of offering loaves in the House of Aten to the Ka of the steward Apy.

D. [Adoration to you, . . . festival (?) of . . . at every [. . .] of theirs [. . .]. May you give her continuity in her life–(namely) to the King's Chief [Wife], his beloved, the Lady of the Two Lands, NEFERNEFRUATEN-NEFERTITI, may she live forever continually–causing Aten to be seen daily at Akhet-Aten on behalf of the Ka of the steward Apy.

62. The Chief Workman (?) Apy

Scarab

A "boon which the king gives" of the living Aten who illuminates every land with his beauty: may he give the fragrant breezes of the north wind, (along with) consumption of offerings and endowing with provisions. May I receive the pouring of water for me, (and) a libation of wine and milk on the offering table of my tomb. May rejuvenating water be sprinkled for me at each new year's day. For the Ka of the chief workman[20] of the House of Gold, Apy.

63. The Chief Sculptor Bak and His Father Men

63-A. Relief in the Granite Quarry at Aswan

On the right, the chief sculptor Men appears before a seated colossal statue of Amenhotep III, while on the left his son, the chief sculptor Bak, offers at an altar while Akhenaten (erased) performs his usual oblation to the Aten.

Above Men: Offering every good and pure thing, consisting of bread, beer, long-horned oxen, [short-horned cattle], fowl, and all sorts of fine vegetables by the overseer of works projects in the Red Mountain, the chief sculptor in the big and important monuments of the king, Men, son of Baimyu.

Over statue: Re-Harakhty, mighty bull who appears in Maat, King of Upper and Lower Egypt, Lord of the Two Lands, NEBMAATRE; bodily Son of Re, NEBMAATRE,[21] ruler of rulers,[22] master of strength, whom Re has preferred, achieving (the state of) "given life" with his heart joyful along with his Ka like Re forever continually.

On both sides of the Aten's disk: [HOR-ATEN], given life forever continually; great living Aten who celebrates the jubilee, lord of heaven, lord of earth, lord of everything Aten encircles, lord of the House of Aten in Akhet-Aten.

Above Bak: Giving adoration to the Lord of the Two Lands and kissing the ground to Waenre by the overseer of works projects in the Red Mountain, a disciple whom his Person himself instructed, chief of sculptors in the big and important monuments of the king in the House of Aten in Akhet-Aten, Bak, the son of the chief of sculptors Men and born to the housewife Ry of Heliopolis.

63-B. Fragment of Men, from Luxor

Right side: . . . [who made the "Ruler of] Rulers," Men, justified.

Left Side: . . . the chief workman . . . .

63-C. Naos of Bak

A "boon which the king gives" of the living Aten who illuminates the land with his beauty: may he give a good life endowed with favor, the heart's ease, and a good old age for the Ka of the disciple of his Person, the chief sculptor of the Lord of the Two Lands, the favorite of the Good God, Bak, justified.

A "boon which the king gives" of the living Horakhty, the living Aten who illuminates the Two Banks: may he allow the receiving of offering loaves that come from the (divine) presence on the offering table of the living Aten, for the Ka of the chief sculptor Bak and his "sister,"[23] the housewife Tahere.

Breathing incense and receiving ointment be allowed for the Ka of the disciple of his Person, the chief sculptor Bak, justified.

Breathing breezes of fresh myrrh be allowed for the Ka of the chief of the works projects of the Lord of the Two Lands Bak, justified.

Your Ba's going out into the world, your corpse's being alive and striding among the possessors of continuity–let this be permitted for the Ka of the disciple of his Person, the chief sculptor Bak, justified.

May wine and milk be poured for you, and the receiving of offering loaves which come forth into the presence–let this be permitted for the Ka of the housewife Tahere.

64. The Deputy Hat

Shawabti Figurine
A "boon which the king gives" of the living Aten who illuminates every land with his beauty: may he give the fragrant breeze of the north wind, an extensive lifetime upon the beautiful west, (and) libation(s) of wine and milk on the offering table of his tomb. For the Ka of the deputy, Hat–may he live again!

65. The Builder Hatiay

Front Hall Door Lintel from the House of Hatiay at El-Amarna
*At the center, stereotyped names and titles of the god (*HOR-ATEN*), the king and the queen are adored by kneeling figures of the owner at the left and right ends.*

Left side: A "boon which the king gives" of the living Aten who illuminates the land: may he give a good lifetime while receiving his Ka, for the Ka of the overseer of works projects and confidant of the Lord of the Two Lands, Hatiay–may he live again!

Right side: A "boon which the king gives" of the living Aten, lord of heaven: may he grant a good old age while seeing his beauty, and a good funeral in Akhet-Aten; for the Ka of one whom the Good God favored, the overseer of works projects and confidant of the Lord of the Two Lands, Hatiay–may he live again!

66. The Chief Steward of Queen Tiyi, Huya

The following reliefs and inscriptions are found in the tomb of Huya at El-Amarna (No. 1)

66.1. Thickness of Outer Wall, East: Hymn to the Rising Sun[24]

Adoration of HEKA-ATEN,[25] given life forever continually: "[Hail to] you, who rises in the sky and shines at dawn in the horizon of heaven. [Welcome in peace, lord of peace!] The entire land is assembled at your appearing, their arms [in] adoration at your rising while they kiss the ground. When you shine for them, [they] clamor [to the height of heaven and receive] joy and exultation. It is when they see your Person that they rejoice, as you give your rays to all who position themselves [outside when you join] the sky, after you have made a good start.[26] May you cause me to be continually in the place of favor, in my tomb of justification; (and as for) my Ba, may it come forth to see your rays and receive nourishment from its offerings. May one be summoned by name and come at the voice.[27] May I partake of the things which issue [from the presence, that I might eat *shenes*-loaves, *bit*-pastry, offering loaves, jugs <of beer>], roasted meat, hot food, cool water, wine, milk, everything which issues [from the Mansion of the Aten in Akhet-Aten]." For the Ka of[28] the favorite of the Lord of the Two Lands, the overseer of the royal quarters, treasurer, steward in the house of the King's [Chief Wife TIYI, Huya, justified].

66.2. Thickness of Outer Wall, West Side

The figure of Huya appears on the west side of the outer thickness, adoring the sun: For the Ka of one praised by Waenre, the overseer of the royal quarters, the treasurer, steward of the King's Chief Wife [TIYI, Huya, justified].

For the hymn to the rising sun inscribed above this figure see Meryre I (70.7) below.

66.3. South Wall, East Side

The royal family are seen banqueting inside the palace: Akhenaten and Nefertiti are seated on the left, along with smaller figures of Meritaten and Meketaten. Queen Tiyi and her daughter Baketaten feast on the right. Between these two groups, Huya receives a roast fowl from the hands of a servant of the king.

Over Queen: The King's Mother,[29] King's Chief Wife, TIYI, may she live forever continually.

Beside her daughter: The King's bodily daughter, his beloved, Baketaten.

By Huya: The overseer of the royal quarters of the King's Wife [TIYI], Huya.

Below this scene are two subregisters which show servants and musicians in attendance on the royal banquet above. Huya is shown either tasting or receiving a

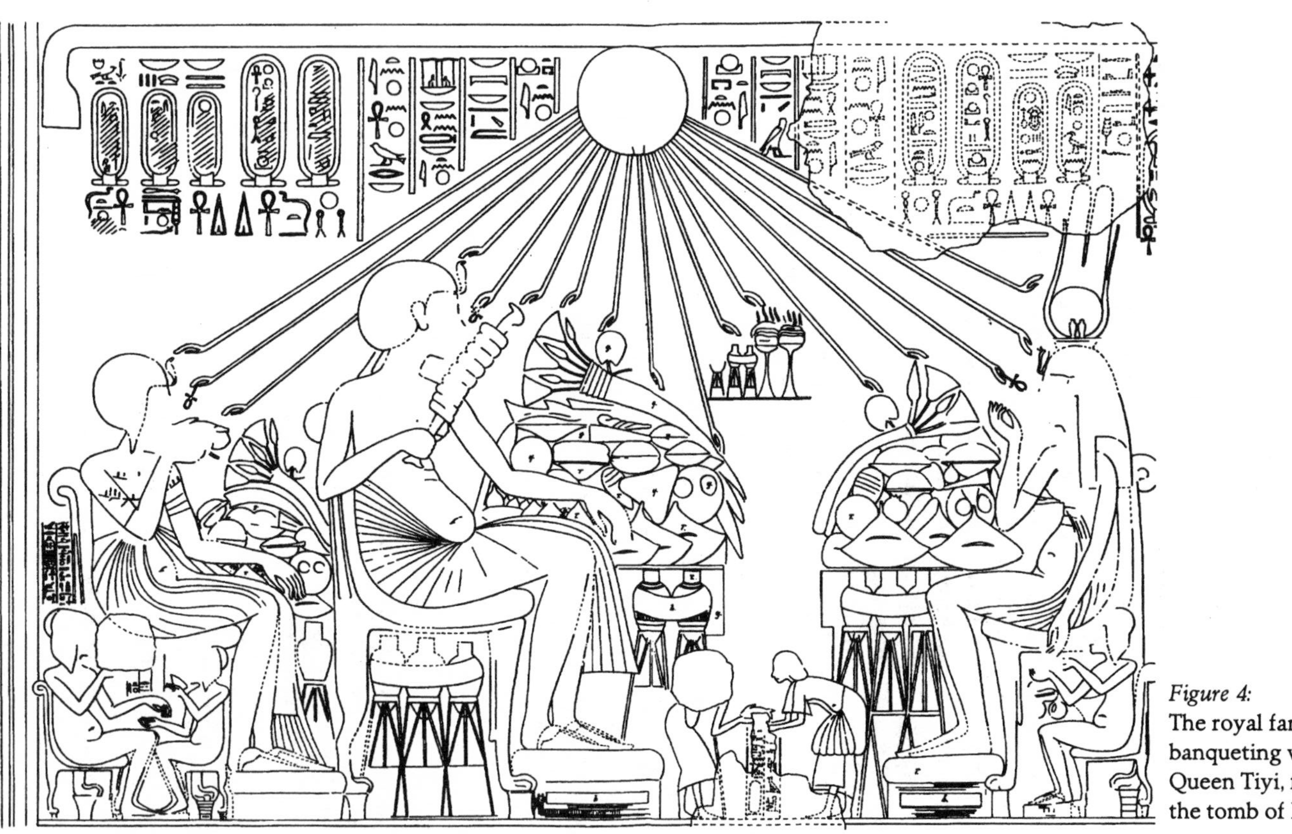

Figure 4: The royal family banqueting with Queen Tiyi, from the tomb of Huya

portion of food: The favorite of Waenre, the attendant of the Lord of the Two Lands in every place he wishes, overseer of the royal quarters, treasurer, steward of the King's Mother, the King's Chief Wife TIYI—may she live—Huya, justified.

66.4. South Wall, West Side

The scene matches its companion on the east side of the wall (1.3 above) and shows the royal family drinking and eating sweets. Queen Tiyi sits on the left, her daughter Baketaten standing beside her. Akhenaten and Nefertiti are seated on the right. Princess Ankhesenpaaten stands on her mother's footstool, while another sister (name lost) stands beside her mother's chair and helps herself to fruit from a dish in front of her. Servants offer ointment cones (?) and napkins to the royal family, directed from the middle of the scene by Huya. Attendants and musicians occupy the subregisters below. The texts are all standard except for those above Nefertiti: The hereditary princess, great of favor, lady of charm, sweet of love, mistress of Upper and Lower Egypt, King's Chief Wife, his beloved, the mistress of the Two Lands, [NEFERNEFRUATEN-NEFERTITI], may she live forever continually.

66.5. East Wall

Akhenaten is shown leading his mother, Queen Tiyi, into her mortuary chapel, called a "sunshade." Between the columns of the portico which surrounds the open altar court are statues of Amenhotep III and Tiyi, apparently alternating with statues of Akhenaten and Nefertiti.

The texts which accompany the scene are mostly short and standard. Akhenaten is shown leading his mother by the hand: Leading the King's Wife (and) King's Mother TIYI, in order to cause her to see her sunshade. *Her daughter,* the king's bodily daughter, his beloved, Baketaten, *leads the row of attendants behind the queen mother, while preceding the royal couple into the sunshade is* the overseer of the royal quarters and steward of the Great King's Wife TIYI, Huya.

Above Akhenaten and Tiyi, beside sundisk: Great living Aten, lord of jubilees, lord of everything Aten encircles, lord of heaven and lord of earth in Akhet-Aten.

Beside the sundisk above the building: Great living Aten, lord of jubilees, lord of everything Aten encircles, lord of heaven and lord of earth in the sunshade of the King's Mother, King's Chief Wife [TIYI], may she live.

In a subregister beneath the main scene, Huya was shown leading groups of subordinates in eight vignettes.

First scene: Appointing the overseer of the royal quarters of the Great King's Wife [TIYI], (named) Huya.

Second and Third Groups: mostly destroyed.

Fourth scene: Appointing . . . .

Speech of fourth group of servants, several with upraised hands: "(Long) live (?) the ruler, the Aten,[30] while he is continual [and eternal], as he raises up generations upon generations."

Fifth Scene: [Appointing . . . the steward of] the King's Chief Wife [TIYI, Huya, to be] . . . . *Above the head of this fifth group, the leaders of which carry standards surmounted by broad fans, is another label, apparently the troop's name:* "Arisen in the beauty of Maat."

Sixth scene, showing Huya followed by a company whose leaders carry standards surmounted by plumes: Appointing [the overseer of] the royal [quarters, Huya, to be] standard-bearer of the troop of "Aten Appears for Him."

Seventh scene, in which Huya brandishes a staff as he leads a company of young men whose leaders carry plumed standards: Appointing the overseer of the royal quarters Huya to be standard-bearer of the troop of young fighters (called) "Aten Appears for Him."

Above seventh group: [The troop] of "Aten is Manifest [for Him]."

The eighth scene, in which Huya leads a mixed company of men and boys: The people of the overseer of the royal quarters, the treasurer Huya, (namely), the company of porters of the House of Aten in Akhet-Aten."

66.6. West Wall

*Akhenaten and Nefertiti, followed on foot by their two eldest daughters with their attendants, are borne from the palace in a carrying chair in the direction of a kiosk with adjoining altars. Asiatic captives are led in from the right, while officials and Nubian tribute-bearers parade in the subregisters below. The titularies of the god (*HEKA-ATEN*) and the royal family are standard. The action of the scene is described as follows:*

Regnal year 12, second month of the Seed season, day 8. Long live the (twice royal) father, HEKA-ATEN, given life forever continually. Appearance of the King of Upper and Lower Egypt NEFERKHEPRURE-WAENRE and the King's Chief Wife NEFERNEFRUATEN-NEFERTITI—may she live forever continually—on the great carrying chair of electrum, in order to receive the products of Kharu and Kush, the west and the east. All foreign countries gathered as one, and the islands in the midst of the sea are presenting products to the king upon Akhet-Aten's great throne of receiving the dues of every foreign country, while the granting of the breath of life is made to them.

One of the officials in the uppermost subregister is singled out for identification as the favorite of the Lord of the Two Lands, the overseer of the royal quarters, treasurer and steward of the king's wife [TIYI], Huya.

66.7. North Wall, West Side

The tomb owner, described as the overseer of the royal quarters, overseer of the double treasury, steward of the king's mother and king's chief wife [TIYI], Huya, *is appointed to office at the royal window of appearances. The king and queen stand within the balcony, while the scene is witnessed by two princesses in the palace behind. The action of the scene is described as follows (above an official outside the building, followed by two scribes):*
Appointing Huya <as> overseer of the royal quarters, treasurer and steward in the house of the king's mother.

Speech of Huya: "Adoration to your Ka, O Waenre, good ruler who makes officialdom, O great Nile of the entire land, O Ka of everybody when you raise up generations from generations in order to [. . .] for (?) the Aten, you being continual, O shade of [everybody (?)], being continual [forever]."

Huya's triumphant return to his house is shown below, but no texts survive.

66.8. North Wall, East Side

The king and queen stand within the royal window of appearances and toss gold collars down to Huya. The two eldest daughters witness the scene from the right side of the building, while Huya's colleagues are ranged respectfully in front of it on the left. Huya's speech of gratitude to the king is as follows: "O good ruler, energetic in bringing things about, for whom the Aten rises! [Many are the things] which the Aten is able to give at his own satisfaction, O pharaoh, l.p.h., the child [of] Aten, at the seeing of whom I live!"

In the subregister below, workmen on Huya's staff are shown at their tasks, under the watchful eye of Huya, followed by a scribe and an attendant. The action

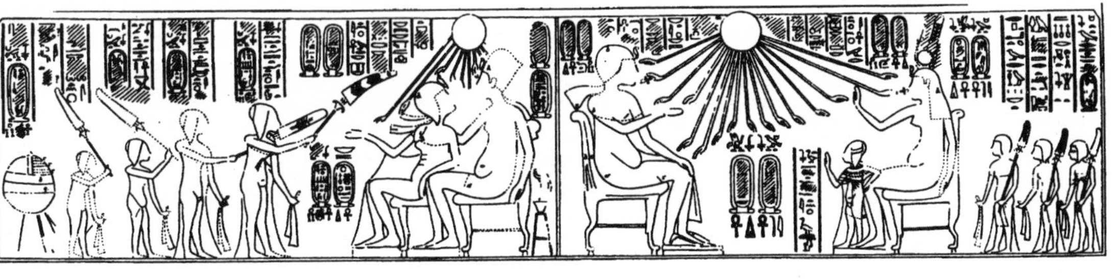

Figure 5:
(A) Lintel from the tomb of Huya, showing Akhenaten and Nefertiti with their family (left) and Amenhotep III with Queen Tiyi and their daughter (right); (B) The sculptor's workshop, also from the tomb of Huya

of the scene is described as being the appointment of craftsmen belonging to the favorite of the Lord of the Two Lands, the overseer of the royal quarters, [treasurer], steward of [the King's] Chief [Wife TIYI], Huya.

Behind Huya: [The ...] of the king's wife [TIYI], the scribe of the House of Charm (?),[31] Nakhtiu.

At the upper right-hand corner of the subscene is a sculptor's workshop. The master craftsman is surrounded by subordinates, each labeled sculptor, *at work at carving various parts of furniture or wooden statuary. The master himself, labeled* the overseer of sculptor(s) of the King's Chief Wife TIYI, (named) Iuti-Iuti, *is painting a completed statue of the princess* Baketaten.

66.9. North Wall, Lintel of Door

On the left side Akhenaten and Nefertiti, seated on chairs beneath the Aten's rays at the right end of the scene, are greeted with fans by their four eldest daughters. The names and titles of the god, king, and queen are standard. The four daughters are also described in the following conventional fashion: the king's bodily daughter, his beloved, Meret-Aten, [born to] the King's Chief Wife NEFERNEFRU-ATEN-NEFERTITI, may she live forever. *Titularies of the other three princesses–*Meketaten, Ankhesenpaaten *and* Nefernefruaten "Junior"*–follow the same pattern.*

On the right panel we see Amenhotep III, described as King of Upper and Lower Egypt, NEBMAATRE, given life, *sitting alone at the left side of the scene. Facing him is* the King's Chief Wife TIYI, may she live, *seated, with* the king's bodily daughter, Baketaten, *standing on the footstool in front of her. The queen's titles are given more fully above three attendants who stand behind her:* The hereditary princess, great of favor, lady of charm, sweet of love, who fills the palace with her beauty, mistress of Upper and Lower Egypt, the King's Chief Wife, his beloved, Lady of the Two Lands, TIYI. *Mother and daughter both salute the king with an upraised right arm, under the all-encompassing rays of the sun, with the conventional later titulary:* [HEKA-ATEN], given life forever continually; great living Aten, lord of jubilee(s), lord of everything Aten encircles, lord of heaven and lord of earth in Akhet-[Aten].

This piece figures significantly, if inconclusively, in the debate regarding the alleged coregency of Amenhotep III with Akhenaten.

66.10. Doorway of Shrine

Left outer jamb: [Adoration to] your Ka, (O) [NEFERKHEPRURE-WAENRE, given life], the good ruler who creates officialdom and fills the

Two Lands with his beauty. Millions and myriads of all sorts of things are offered to your Ka—food and catch at every place, O my lord who brought me into being, the one who decrees (?) for [*me all good things, and benefits*] me (?) by favor [of . . .]. For the Ka of the overseer of the royal quarters, the treasurer and steward in the house of the King's Mother and King's Chief Wife TIYI, Huya [justified].

Right outer jamb: "Adoration to your Ka, O lady of the Two Lands, who illuminates the Two Lands with her beauty, King's Mother, King's Chief Wife TIYI, the possessor of abundant food—may they be decreed for [my] Ka [. . . as what endows] me with a good life in union with joy, as one who seeks all that is given in [. . .] of his." For the Ka of the overseer [of the royal quarters, the treasurer and steward in the house of the King's Mother, the King's Chief Wife TIYI, Huya, justified].

Left inner jamb:
A. "Adoration to your Ka, O NEFERKHEPRURE-WAENRE: may I adore you every day, O sun, appearing as Aten, who fills the Two Lands with his beauty. O my lord, . . . continually, every land [is . . . at] seeing (?) your beauty and following you every day." For the Ka of the overseer of the royal quarters of the King's Chief Wife, Huya, justified.

B. "Adoration to your Ka, O NEFERKHEPRURE-WAENRE! Your Ka is welcome in peace, O [great] Nile [of the] entire [land], [. . .] life . . . . May he give continuity and eternity while I am following you in the jubilee courtyard." For the Ka of the overseer of the double treasury of the King's Chief Wife, Huya, justified.

Right inner jamb:
A. "Adoration to your Ka, O NEFERKHEPRURE-WAENRE, my lord. [May you] grant favor to me, O one beloved like Aten, the one who decrees to [*his son the lifetime of*] Re without making cease . . . ." [For the Ka of the overseer of the royal quarters of the King's Chief Wife, Huya, justified].

B. "Adoration to your Ka, O NEFERKHEPRURE-WAENRE, O light, at the seeing of whom one [lives], O Ka of the entire land, ... their [. . .] belong to you continually as [. . .]." [For the Ka of the treasurer of the King's Chief Wife, Huya, justified].

Upper Lintel:
Left: "Adoration [to] your Ka, O living Aten, lord of continuity, lord of fate and fosterer of fortune, who illuminates the Two Lands with his beauty."

Right: "Adoration to your Ka, O sun, Ruler of the Double Horizon, when you are manifest—dazzling, fair and radiant continually forever."

Lower Lintel:

Left: A "boon which the king gives" of the "Only One of Re" (*or* Waenre), the good ruler who makes officialdom and fills the Two Lands with his Ka, the King of Upper and Lower Egypt NEFERKHEPRURE-WAENRE.

Right: A "boon which the king gives" of the one who is long in his lifetime (=*king*): "I give adoration to your handsome face, and I propitiate your Ka every day, O good ruler AKHENATEN, long in his lifetime.

66.11. Shrine, West Thickness

[. . . the overseer of the royal quarters, the treasurer and steward in the house of] the King's Mother, King's Chief Wife [TIYI], Huya . . . (as?) the waters of the Nile surge against the sands of the sandbank, the [light] of Aten, [it] is . . . when he rises among millions . . . . may my father (?) protect you . . . , you being continual after (having achieved) victoriousness.

66.12. Texts on the East Thickness of Shrine and the Ceiling of the Entrance Hall

In addition to the three variant copies of this text in the tomb of Huya, yet another variant occurs in the tomb of Any (see 60.A.2 above). In the translation that follows the most extensive variants used by Huya are employed without comment, except where there is a notable difference between the versions.

Receiving offerings of the king's giving, consisting of bread and beer,[32] and food at every place of yours, that your [name] may endure upon your tomb, and that each (future) generation, when it comes into being, may invoke you, and that your Ba (?) may live in your tomb, without your name having to be sought in your tomb, (but) may every mouth [make *or* say] for you a "boon which the king gives," consisting of [. . .], the bread of [your house] and the beer of your house. For the Ka of the favorite of Waenre, one beloved of his lord, the overseer of the royal quarters, the overseer [of the double treasury], the steward of the King's Chief Wife TIYI, Huya.[33]

66.13. Doorway in South Wall of Shrine

Beneath piles of bread and flowers a woman is shown kneeling on each side of the door: His 'sister', the housewife Wenher, justified *(right side); and* His mother, the housewife Tuy, justified *(left).*

66.14. Shrine, East Wall

At the funeral rites of the tomb owner, mourners stand behind a priest who libates the offerings piled in front of the mummy while uttering the following prayer: "May

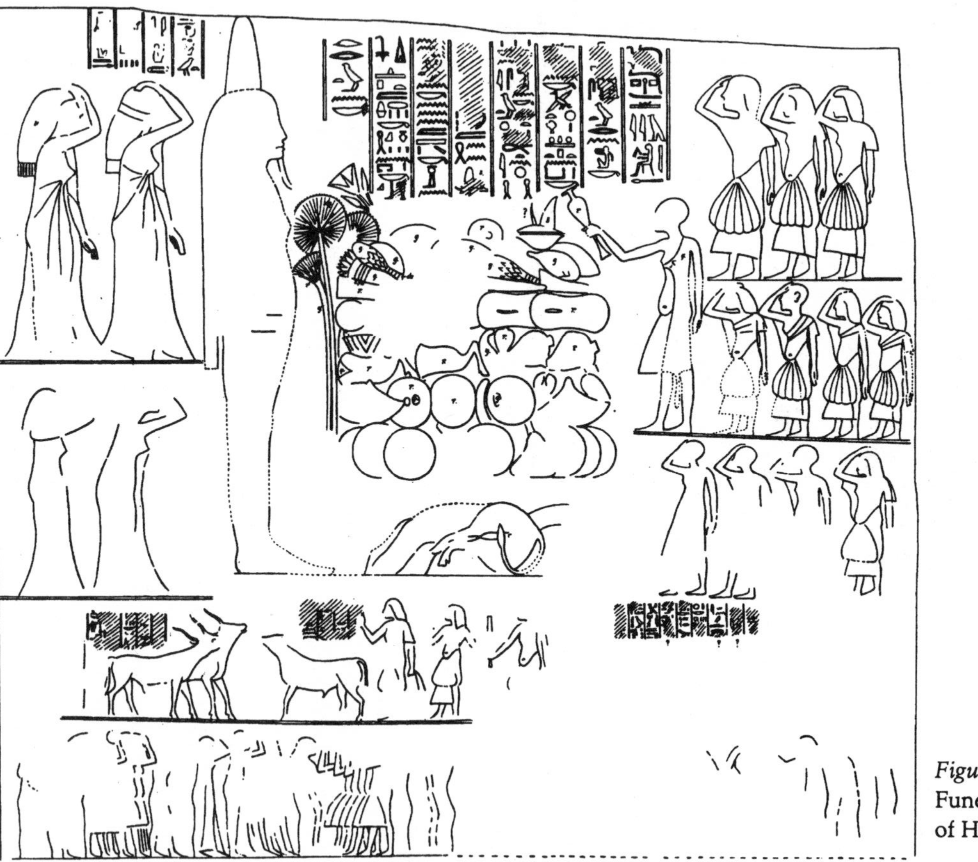

Figure 6:
Funeral ceremonies before the mummy of Huya

a 'boon which the king gives' offering be made for you, consisting of your bread and the beer of your house. May libation be made to you of water from your pool, and may there [be] brought [to you fruit (?)] from your trees. May invocation be made for you [with the] ritual (?) of Aten. May you be offered *pat*-cakes upon the offering table on behalf of your Ka [every day], and may your name be remembered: the overseer of the royal [quarters], the overseer of the double treasury, Huya, justified.

Behind the mummy stand four wailing women. The two on top are described as His mother Tuy, justified *and* [. . .], justified.

In the subregisters below, men with cattle are shown on top, while mourners appear below. Texts to the upper subregister (badly damaged) are as follows:

Right: . . . [on] the west, shouting . . . , a high [. . .] in the great chapel (?), . . . your [. . .] is there exceedingly . . . every day . . . .

Left, above cattle at left: . . . water [from] the river . . . ; and at right: . . . (when) your rays go forth (?) . . . ; may you come mourning (?) . . . .

66.15. Shrine, West Wall

The funeral procession is shown in four registers, each mourner following the men who bring offerings to the tomb. Only a few of the inscriptions survive, beside women in the third register: His sister (?) Nebet (?), *and* His sister Kherpu(t).

66.16. North Wall, Foot of Right Door Jamb

Adoration to your Ka, O Waenre. When you appear [everyone] lives. (O) ruler of the entire land, may you grant l.p.h. and good lifetime doing [. . . on behalf of] your son for goodness' sake. [For] the Ka of the favorite of Waenre, [the overseer of the royal quarters, the treasurer and steward of] the King's Mother, Great King's Wife TIYI, Huya.

67. The Chief Builder Maanakhtef

Door frame from Maanakhtef's House at el-Amarna
Right door post:
A. A "boon which the king gives" of the living Aten, lord of continuity, who makes destiny and brings fortune into being, who causes everything

he has created to live: May he permit that one enter favored and depart beloved, (with) speech prospering without misadventure; for the Ka of one who was effective for the king and not given to neglectfulness, the overseer of successful building projects in Akhet-Aten, Maanakhtef—may he live again!

B. A "boon which the king gives" of the Son of Re who lives on Maat, Lord of Crowns, AKHENATEN, long in his lifetime, lord of lifetime, who gives success to the one he has preferred and prospers the funeral of the one who has placed him in his heart: may he give a good lifetime while seeing his beauty, without ceasing from hearing his voice; for the Ka of one who was excellent and favored with respect to the Good God, a leader among the (royal) entourage, a disciple whom his Person instructed, the overseer of successful building projects, Maanakhtef—may he live again!

Left Door Post:

A. A "boon which the king gives" of [THE ATEN],[34] given life forever continually; the godly god who is content with Maat, at whose rising everyone lives: may he give a good lifetime, [. . .], health and [. . . in] Akhet-Aten. For the Ka of one whom the Good God favored, one beloved of the Lord of the Two Lands on account of his character, a disciple whom his Person instructed, the overseer of successful building projects for the Lord of the Two Lands, Maanakhtef—may he live again!

B. A "boon which the king gives" of the King's Ka who lives on Maat, the Lord of the Two Lands, [NEFERKHEPRURE-WAENRE], the son of the Aten, greatly beloved one, at the seeing of whom one lives and is healthy: may he cause my eyes to be sated with his handsome face, and (me to) kiss the ground [in his presence] every day. I am his slave, the servant of the Lord [of . . .]. For the Ka of one who is effective and true of heart, with the teaching of his Person in his heart, the overseer of successful building projects in all the monuments of his Person, Maanakhtef—may he live again!

On the door lintel the owner is shown four times adoring names of the Aten, the king and the queen. While all of the cartouches are defaced by malicious hacking, they are to all appearances conventional in their composition. The labels attached to Maanakhtef's figures are as follows:

Right: Giving worship to the Aten and kissing the ground to the lord of continuity by the favorite of Waenre; . . . (of) every [. . .] who made [. . .] in every monument which his Person made: the overseer of successful building projects . . . , a disciple whom his Person instructed,[35] Maanakhtef. "(I) come before you adoring your beauty, (O) Aten who illuminates the two shores." May he give l.p.h. to the Ka [of] the follower of the Good God, the overseer of successful building projects, Maanakhtef, justified.

Left: Giving worship to the Aten and kissing the ground to Waenre by the favorite of "Long in his Lifetime," . . . ,[36] . . . his offices; the overseer of successful building projects for the Lord of the Two Lands, the chief spokesman,[37] Maanakhtef. He says to the Aten . . . of all that is said [on] the throne of Re . . .[38] the [Aten]. May he grant a good lifetime, just as his [ray]s (?) make [illumination] for the Ka of the overseer of successful building projects [in] Akhet-Aten, Maanakhtef, justified.

68. The Fanbearer on the King's Right Hand, May

The following inscriptions come from the tomb of May at El-Amarna (No. 14).

68.1. North Thickness

Adoration of HOR-ATEN, given life forever continually; (and) the King of Upper and Lower Egypt who lives on Maat, Lord of the Two Lands, NEFERKHEPRURE-WAENRE, the Son of Re who lives on Maat, Lord of Crowns, AKHENATEN, long in his lifetime; (and) the King's Chief Wife, his beloved, Lady of the Two Lands, great of love, NEFERNEFRUATEN-NEFERTITI, may she live forever continually.

"You appear beautifully from the horizon of heaven, the living Aten that determines life—

For you are risen from the eastern horizon and have filled the Two Lands with your beauty;

For you are bright, great, shining and high above every land, and your rays encompass lands to the limit of all you have made;

For you are in the sun, reaching their limit and subduing them for your beloved son.

Your rays are upon your effective image, the ruler of Maat who issued from continuity: may you give to him your lifetime and your years; may you hearken for him to what is in his heart; and may you love him and cause him to be like Aten, your child who issued from your rays, the King of Upper and Lower Egypt, NEFERKHEPRURE-WAENRE.

For you he has made Akhet-Aten the great, the big, the beloved—the mistress of favor, rich in possessions, within which is the sustenance of Re. One rejoices at seeing its beauty, fair and lovely. One sees it as if looking at the sky—its limit unreachable—with the Aten rising in it to fill it with his rays, and embracing his beloved son—the son of continuity—who issued from Aten and governs the land for the one who placed him on his throne and causes the land to exist for the one who made it.

Every land is festive at his appearance. Their totality is offering to his Ka on behalf of Aten who rises in the horizon at the start of every dawn. His son is presenting Maat to your handsome face, (O Aten), while you exult when you see him. He has issued from you alone: may you grant him <eternity> as king like the Aten. O NEFERKHEPRURE-WAENRE, may you live and be healthy like the Aten!"

The hereditary prince and count, the sealbearer of the King of Lower Egypt, the sole companion, [. . .] , genuine [king's scribe], his beloved; general of the Lord of the Two Lands, the steward of the House of "Pacifying Aten," [May]. He says: "I am a servant of his creating, one who was straightforward on behalf of the Lord of the Two Lands and effective for his lord who placed Maat in my body and detestation of falsehood, for I know that the son of the Aten, NEFERKHEPRURE-WAENRE, rejoices at it. He has doubled my favors for me like grains of sand, for I was the first of officials in front of the subjects, and my lord advanced me so that I might execute his teachings as I listened to his voice without cease. My eyes are seeing your beauty in the course of every day—O my lord, knowledgeable like Aten, content with Maat! How fortunate is the one who listens to your teaching of life—for he shall be sated with seeing you and he shall reach old age!"

"May you grant me the good funeral which is your Ka's to give, in the tomb in which you decreed for me to rest—the mountain of Akhet-Aten, the place of the favored ones. O my millions of Niles flooding daily, NEFERKHEPRURE-WAENRE, my god who made me, by whose Ka one lives, cause me to be sated with following you without cease. O one whom the Aten fashioned: you are continual! O my millionfold prayer, Waenre: how fortunate is he who follows you, for you cause all he has made to go on existing, being firm continually; for his lord shall bury him, with his mouth full of righteousness.

68.2. South Thickness

Adoration of HOR-[ATEN, given life everlastingly forever; (and) the King of Upper and Lower Egypt who lives on Maat, the Lord of the Two Lands], NEFERKHEPRURE-WAENRE, the son of Re who lives on Maat, Lord of Crowns, [AKHENATEN], long in his lifetime; (and) the hereditary princess, she who is great in the palace, fair of face and beautiful in the Two Plumes, she whom the living Aten loves, the King's Chief Wife, his beloved, the

Lady of the Lands [*sic*], NEFERNEFRUATEN-NEFERTITI, may she live forever continually.

The fanbearer at [the right hand of the king], . . . , whom the king of Upper Egypt advanced and the King [of Lower Egypt promoted], whose Ka the sovereign made, one beloved of his lord every day, who reached old age as his well-being came and spent lifetime with his limbs healthy; one great of praise and goodly of stride; one who followed his lord, his attendant for a lifetime while the love of him was enduring—the king's scribe, scribe of recruits, steward of "Pacifying Aten," steward of Waenre in Heliopolis, overseer of the cattle of the House of Re in Heliopolis, [overseer of] all [the works projects] of the king, the general of the Lord of the Two Lands, May. [He] says:

"Hear what I say, everybody, great and small, that I may tell you the good things which the ruler did for me, so you will say, 'How great (?) are these things done for this poor man.' Beseech (?) for him continuity in jubilees and eternity as Lord of the Two Lands, and he will do for you [just] as [he] did for me—the god who gives life!"

"I was a poor man on both my father's and my mother's side—but the ruler built me up, he caused me to develop, he fed me by means of his Ka when I was without property. He caused me to acquire people in numbers. He caused my brothers and sisters to be many, he caused all my people to assemble for me when I became master of my town, and he caused me to mingle with officials and courtiers when I was the least of underlings. He gave me sustenance and food every day when I was begging for the bread which he gives."

68.3. Ceiling Inscriptions at Entrance

Only the middle band is substantially preserved: "Be adored when you rise in the horizon, O Aten, Horus of the double horizon, <you> shall not cease from seeing Re! Open your[39] eyes to see him, that your corpse may be enduring and your name lasting, while the mortuary priests [. . .] you."

Of the northern band, only the following fragments are intelligible: . . . , that your beauty (?) be caused to [endure] (?), O Aten, . . . his [. . .] when he makes illumination; who makes [. . .] every tomb with the breath of life when he comes to . . . ; . . . every day. For the Ka of the overseer of [. . .] of the entire land, the overseer of works projects of the Lord of the Two Lands (?), May.

68.4. Entrance Jambs

Left Side
A. Standard titularies of HOR-ATEN, king and queen.

B. [A "boon which the king gives" of the] great living [Aten] who is in jubilee, lord of heaven and earth who illuminates the Two Banks: "May he cause me to see his beauty in the course of every day, his rays streaming down upon my breast." For the Ka of the great confidant of his lord, to whom all matters are said in order to raise them up before the Lord of the Two Lands: the fanbearer at the right hand of the king, true [king's] scribe, his beloved, May, justified.

C. [A "boon which the king gives" of the King's Ka which lives on Maat], the Lord of the Two Lands, NEFERKHEPRURE-WAENRE, given life forever: may he grant a good funeral of his Ka's commanding in the district of Akhet-Aten to the Ka of the one who was excellent in the presence of the Lord of the Two Lands, who filled the ears of Horus with Maat, the general of the Lord of the Two Lands, the true king's scribe, his beloved, May, justified.

D. [A "boon which the king gives" of the King's Ka which lives on Maat, the Lord of Crowns, AKHENATEN], long in his lifetime: may he grant entry and exit in the king's house in the favor of the Good God until the goodly revered state comes to pass. For the Ka of one whom the king made great because of his good character, whose position his (own) excellence made, the steward of "Aten is Propitiated," the true [king's scribe, his] beloved, May, [justified].

E. [A "boon which the king gives" of the King's Chief Wife], his beloved, the Lady of the Two Lands, [NEFERNEFRUATEN]-NEFERTITI, may she live forever continually: may she give her favors, established and lasting, and limbs united with the joy which is hers to give, for the Ka of the king's follower in his august falcon-ship, the master of the protocols following after the Lord of the Two Lands, overseer of all the works projects of the king, true king's scribe, his beloved, [May, justified].

Right Side
F. Same as A

G. [A "boon which the king gives" of the great living Aten], lord of heaven and earth, who illuminates the Two Lands with his beauty: may he give a sluiceful of water, a bellyful of breeze, and the reception of favors in the presence of the Lord of the Two Lands. For the Ka of the Good God's favorite, one whose place in the king's house was exalted, the fanbearer at the right hand of the king, [the true king's scribe, his beloved, May, justified].

H. A "boon [which the king gives of the] living [King's] Ka which lives on Maat, the Lord of the Two Lands, NEFERKHEPRURE-WAENRE, given life forever: may he grant life, prosperity, health, and alertness in the presence of the Lord of the Two Lands, and a good lifetime while seeing the beauty of every day without ceasing. For the Ka of one important in his office and great in his dignity, an official worthy of trust, the army commander of the Lord of the Two Lands, [the true king's scribe, his beloved], May, [justified].

I. A "boon which the king gives" [of the king's Ka which lives on Maat], the Lord of Crowns, AKHENATEN, long in his lifetime: may he grant a good remembrance in the king's house and permanence in the mouth(s) of his entourage. For the Ka of the one who was effective upon the heart of his lord, who recognized him as one who did effective things–the steward of the House of Waenre in Heliopolis, [the king's true scribe, his beloved May, justified].

J. A "boon which the king gives" of the King's [Chief Wife, his beloved, the Lady of the Two Lands, NEFERNEFRUATEN]-NEFERTITI, may she live forever continually: may she grant an entry favored, a departure beloved, and contentment in Akhet-Aten. For the Ka of one whom the king favored both when he was a youth and when he had reached the goodly revered state–the fanbearer at the right hand [of] the king, [true king's scribe, his beloved, May, justified].

68.5. Entrance, Lintel North End

Only fanbearers and bowing attendants are preserved behind the personages named below:

Bodily [king's daughter], his beloved, Meketaten.

[Bodily king's daughter], his [beloved], Ankhesenpaaten, [born to] the King's Chief Wife NEFERNEFRUATEN-NEFERTITI, may she live.

Sister of the King's Chief Wife, Mutnodjmet.

The king's attendants in all their multitudes, those who accompany their lord [. . . and who listen to] the voice of his Person.

69. The Chief of Police, Mahu

The reliefs and inscriptions that follow all come from Mahu's tomb at El-Amarna (No. 9).

69.1. Jambs of Outer Door

Left Jamb:

A. [Adoration of] HOR-ATEN, given life forever continually, and the King of Upper and Lower Egypt, Lord of the Two Lands NEFERKHEPRURE-WAENRE, the Son of Re, Lord of Crowns, AKHENATEN, long in his lifetime, and the King's Chief Wife NEFERNEFRUATEN-NEFERTITI, living forever continually.

B. "[Adoration to] you, O living [Aten]! When you rise to give life to what you have created, they live at seeing your rays while you give your lifetime in years to the King of Upper and Lower Egypt who lives on Maat, the Lord of the Two Lands, NEFERKHEPRURE-WAENRE, given life forever." By <Ma>hu, justified.

C. "[Adoration to] you, O living Aten, august god, beloved one, who created himself and gave birth to himself by himself. May you <give> south and north to your son,[40] who issued from your limbs, the Son of Re who lives on Maat, Lord of Crowns, AKHENATEN, long in his lifetime." By <Ma>hu, justified.

Right Jamb:

D. Identical with A.

E. "[Adoration to you], O living Aten, and kissing the ground to Waenre, the god who constructs people and causes the Two Lands to live. May you grant me a good funeral after old age." For the Ka of the chief of the Medjay of Akhet-<Aten>, Mahu, justified.

F. "[Adoration] to [you], O living Aten, lord of continuity—for[41] you are dazzling, fair, powerful, <your> love being great [and extensive]." [For the Ka of the Chief of the Medjay of Akhet-Aten, Mahu, justified].

69.2. Jambs of Inner Doorway

Left Jamb:

A. Long live the twice royal? father HEKA-ATEN, given life forever continually; (and) the King of Upper and Lower Egypt, Lord of the Two Lands, NEFERKHEPRURE-WAENRE, the Son of Re, Lord of Crowns, AKHEN-ATEN, long in his lifetime; (and) the King's Chief Wife NEFERNEFRU-ATEN-NEFERTITI, may she live forever continually.

B. "Adoration to your Ka, O living Aten, lord of sunbeams, who illuminates the Two Lands with your rays on behalf of every land; and when you set in the western horizon, they lie down." For the Ka of the Chief of the Medjay of Akhet-Aten, Mahu, justified.

C. "Adoration to your Ka, [O King of Upper and Lower Egypt] who lives [on Maat, Lord of the Two Lands], NEFERKHEPRURE-WAENRE! O my god, may I hear the king's voice as he does what is favored for his divine father, the Aten." For the Ka of the Chief of the Medjay of Akhet-Aten, Mahu, justified.

D. "Adoration to your Ka and to your rays when you rise in the eastern horizon of heaven, their arms being in adoration of your Ka, their hearts living therefrom." For the Ka of the Chief of the Medjay of Akhet-Aten, Mahu, justified.

Right Jamb:
E. Identical to A.

F. "Adoration to your Ka when you appear beautifully, O living Aten, lord of continuity. May you grant me a good funeral after old age." For the Ka of the Chief of the Medjay of Akhet-Aten, Mahu, justified.

G. "Adoration [to] your Ka, O Aten . . . , living Aten, lord of continuity—for you are dazzling, fair and powerful. May you[42] grant love <to> the Chief of the Medjay of Akhet-Aten, Mahu, justified.

H. "Adoration to your Ka, [(O) King of Upper and Lower Egypt] who lives on Maat, Lord of the Two Lands, NEFERKHEPRURE-WAENRE, given life." May he grant favor given (?) to the Ka of the Chief of the Medjay of Akhet-Aten, Mahu, justified and revered.

69.3. Front Wall, South Side

Mahu is shown exercising his office in a number of vignettes on this wall. At one end he is shown inspecting a storeroom and then reporting to [The . . . and] vizier of Akhet-Aten, [. . .], *who is followed by another official,* [The . . . of] the Lord of the Two Lands, his favorite, Heqanefer. *Other episodes show* the chief of the Medjay of Akhet-Aten, Mahu *traveling in a chariot, inspecting a squad of Medjay police, and escorting three bearded prisoners into the vizier's presence.* The Chief of the Medjay of Akhet-Aten, Mahu, he says: "Let those officials hear the people who would join those of the desert hills." *Receiving the chief of police in front of the portico of an official building,* The vizier, he says: "As the Aten endures, so may the ruler endure!"[43] *Behind the vizier are* The great officials of pharaoh, l.p.h., and the leaders of the army who stand in the presence of his Person.

69.4. Back Wall, South Side

At one end, the royal couple are seen leaving the temple beneath the streaming rays of HEKA-ATEN, given life forever continually; great living Aten, lord of the jubilee, master of all Aten encircles, lord of heaven, lord of earth in the House of Aten in Akhet-Aten. *The king and queen ride in the same chariot, while between them is a small figure of* The king's bodily daughter, his beloved, Meretaten, born to the King's Chief Wife NEFERNEFRUATEN-[NEFERTITI], may she [live] forever [continually]. *The royal escort whose members run in front of the royal chariot includes the vizier and* The Chief of the Medjay of Akhet-Aten, Mahu, justified.

At the other end of the wall, the royal chariot is arriving in the vicinity of a number of portals which have been identified as the boundary stelae.[44] *The titles of the Aten, king, queen, and the princess Meretaten are the same as they appear at the other end of this wall. Mahu appears several times, bowing to the king and once making a brief speech:* "O Waenre, you are forever, O builder of Akhet-Aten, whom Re himself made!" *Above a row of running Medjay policemen in front of the royal chariot:* The Medjay of Akhet-Aten.

69.5. Back Wall, North Side

The scene is divided into several subsections. Mahu's reward in front of the palace, on top, is mostly destroyed, but he is shown, followed by his men, greeting with upraised arms a standard-bearer who comes out to meet him from the palace. The Chief of the Medjay of Akhet-Aten, Mahu, he says: "May you raise up generations to generations! O ruler <like> Aten, [you are] continual!"

In the register below, Mahu and his men are shown visiting the temple. The party is shown approaching the precinct on top. [The Chief of the] Medjay [of Akhet-Aten, Mahu], justified, he says: . . . . *Following their chief is a row of* [The] Medjay of Akhet-Aten, the joyful refrain which they utter: "He has raised up [generations to] generations, [the good ruler who rises, the] Aten: he is continual." *A row of women bring up the rear, but their texts are almost totally destroyed.*

In the lower subregister Mahu kneels before the temple while uttering the following short speech: "May the pharaoh, l.p.h., be healthy! O Aten, make him continual, this Waenre who builds with [his] Ka." *Behind Mahu his men extol* "The good ruler who has made monuments for his father—may he repeatedly do it continually forever, O my good lord!"—so say the Medjay of Akhet-Aten. *Behind the Medjay a charioteer and two attendants declare:* "May he bring into being the million(s) of generations, being continual like Aten!"

69.6. Hymn to the Sun
(North and South End Walls, North Thickness)

For all that this hymn was inscribed no fewer than four times in this tomb, Mahu's text is the shortest of the five preserved versions (see 70.8). Here it ends as follows: For the Ka of the chief of the Medjay of (*var.* in) Akhet-Aten, Mahu, justified (*var.* may he live again).

70. The "Greatest of Seers" of the Aten, Meryre (I)

The following reliefs and inscriptions are found in Meryre I's tomb at El-Amarna (No. 4).

70.1. South Wall, West Side: Meryre's Appointment to Office

*Meryre is carried on the shoulders of his friends into the presence of Akhenaten, who stands in the royal window of appearances with Nefertiti and one daughter–presumably Meritaten–all under the rays of the Aten. The texts of the god (*HEKA-ATEN*) and the royal family are conventional. In front of the royal building is the following speech:* Said the king who lives on Maat, the Lord of the Two Lands, NEFERKHEPRURE-WAENRE to the Greatest of Seers of the Aten, Meryre: "Behold, I am attaching you to myself, to be the Greatest of Seers of the Aten in the House of Aten in Akhet-Aten. I do this for love of you, specifically because you are my servant, who listens to the instruction. As for every mission which you undertake, my heart is content with it. I give you the office specifically so that you may eat the provisions of pharaoh, l.p.h., your lord, in the House of Aten."

Exclamation of the crowd: "He has brought into being generations upon generations, the good ruler! So long as the Aten rises, he is continual!"

Exclamation of Meryre: By the Greatest of Seers of the Aten in the House of Aten, Meryre, justified. He says: "Many are the things which the Aten is able to give at his (own) satisfaction!"

In the subregisters below Meryre is presumably escorted by a jubilating crowd, with a number of women bringing up the rear. The label attached to one of these

Figure 7:
Meryre I carried on the shoulders of his colleagues into the presence of the royal family

ladies is preserved. She says: "Twice great is your reward! It is the Only One of Re (=*Waenre*) who is giving it!"

70.2. North Wall, West Side: Royal Visit to the Temple

*The king, queen and four of their daughters, followed by their retinue, are all shown in chariots as they proceed from their residence to the temple. The texts which describe the god (*HEKA-ATEN*) and the royal couple are all conventional, as are most of the princesses' labels:*

King's bodily daughter, his beloved, Meretaten, born to the King's Chief Wife, his beloved, the Lady of the Two Lands, [NEFERNEFRUATEN-NEFERTITI].

Virtually identical formulas follow for the next two princesses, Meketaten *and* Ankhesenpaaten, *except that their mother's cartouche is followed by the words* may she live forever continually. *The text that describes the fourth princess is somewhat different:* King's wife and bodily King's Daughter,[45] his beloved, Nefernefruaten "Junior," born to the King's Chief Wife, his beloved, the Lady of the Two Lands, NEFERNEFRUATEN-NEFERTITI, may she live forever continually.

Standing before the Great Temple of the Aten to receive the royal family are groups of female musicians, priests, and officials. In front of one such group are the words: "Welcome in [peace], O [lord of peace], beautiful with . . . [for the] king (?) . . . . He has appointed you [. . . of (?) the Lord] of the Two Lands." *Behind these men is another group described as* The first servitors of Aten in the House of Aten in Akhet-Aten.

70.3. Northeast Corner, Lower Register: Meryre Rewarded

The king and queen, accompanied by two of their daughters, watch as servants decorate Meryre with gold collars. Behind the royal persons is a large granary which adjoins a magazine of equal size. An ample villa with a garden, probably Meryre's house, stands to the left. Behind Meryre himself, next to the public area where his reward takes place, is a harbor area and adjoining cattle sheds.

Speech by the king: What the King of Upper and Lower Egypt who lives on Maat, the Lord of the Two Lands, NEFERKHEPRURE-WAENRE says: "O Overseer of the House of Silver and Gold, reward the Greatest of Seers of the Aten in Akhet-Aten, Meryre! Place gold at his neck, at his rear, and gold at his feet, on account of his heeding the instruction of pharaoh, l.p.h., and doing all that is said on account of this. The beautiful places which pharaoh, l.p.h., has made, in the Mansion of the Benben in the House of Aten, for the Aten in Akhet-Aten, are filled with all sorts of good things—namely, wheat and barley: abundant is Aten's offering table for the Aten."

Reply of Meryre: The Greatest of Seers of the Aten in the House of Aten in Akhet-Aten, the fanbearer at the king's right hand, one praised by the Lord of the Two Lands, Meryre. He says: "Health [to Waenre],[46] the beautiful child of the Aten. Cause him to achieve your (?) lifetime, cause him to be continual and eternal."

Said by someone inside Meryre's house: "Welcome [in peace (?)], now that you have received [your] reward, (O) [Greatest of] Seers of the Aten [in the House of] Aten in Akhet-Aten, Meryre . . . forever."

Above another person nearby: "Servant . . . of Aten . . . of the [great living (?)] Aten, [lord of] heaven . . . ."

70.4. Pillared Hall, North Doorway

The right-hand side of the lintel is mostly destroyed. On the left: "Adoration to you, O living Aten, lord of continuity who made eternity, King's Ka, Lord of the Two Lands, [NEFERKHEPRURE-WAENRE], long in his lifetime[47]—the ruler who makes officials and builds up the commons; the fate which gives life, lord of what is decreed! May you grant me a good funeral [in the mountain of Akhet-Aten]." By the Greatest of Seers of the Aten in the House of Aten [in Akhet-Aten, Meryre, justified].

Left Jamb:

A. "Adoration to you,[48] O [HEKA]-ATEN, given life forever continually. May he cause the seeing of Aten each time he appears. Adore him so that he may listen to what you say." For the Ka of the Greatest of Seers of the Aten in Akhet-Aten, Meryre,[49] justified.

B. "[Adoration to you], (O) HEKA-ATEN, given life forever continually. May he give a tomb chapel for the one who prepared it, that the Ba may rest upon its corpse <in> the place of continuity. For the Ka of the favorite of the Lord of the Two Lands, the fanbearer at the king's right hand, Meryre, justified."

C. "Adoration [to you], (O) HEKA-ATEN, given life forever continually. May he allow entering and departing from within the tomb, and seeing the rays of Aten when he rises." For the Ka [of] the Greatest of Seers of the Aten in Akhet-Aten, Meryre, justified.

D. "Adoration to [you], O HEKA-[ATEN], given life forever continually. May he permit the flesh to live and the limbs (?) [. . .], breathing the sweet breeze [of the] north wind." For the Ka [of] one praised of the Lord of the Two Lands, the fanbearer at the right hand of the king, Meryre, justified.

Right Jamb:

A. "[Adoration to you], HEKA-ATEN, given life forever continually. May he permit the receiving of offering loaves that come from the presence of the Aten." For the Ka of the Greatest of Seers of the Aten in Akhet-Aten, Meryre, justified.

B. "[Adoration to you], HEKA-ATEN, given life forever continually. May he grant a good funeral <in> the mountain of Akhet-Aten." For the Ka [of] the sealbearer of the king of Lower Egypt, the sole companion and fanbearer at the right hand of the king, Meryre, [justified].

C. "[Adoration to you], HEKA-ATEN, given life forever continually. May he give power on earth, effectiveness in the underworld, and the Ba's coming out and refreshing itself in the tomb." For the Ka [of] the Greatest of Seers of the Aten in Akhet-Aten, Meryre, [justified].

D. "[Adoration to you], [HEKA]-ATEN, given life forever continually. May he grant [. . .] at this land of the living, possessing the favor of the Good God." For the Ka of the sealbearer of the King of Lower Egypt, the sole companion and fanbearer at the right hand of the king, Meryre, [justified].

70.5. Pillared Hall, South Doorway

Lintel, left side: "Adoration to your Ka, O one who lives on Maat, Lord of the Two Lands, [NEFERKHEPRURE-WAENRE]—O Nile, upon whose command one becomes rich, my Ka of every day! The one who heeds your designs and causes it [*sic*] to be repeated in his heart does not grow poor. How fortunate is the one who stands in your presence and turns his heart to <your> instructions—for you then grant him the old age that is yours to give, and a goodly period by means of your governance."[50] By the Greatest of Seers of the [Aten] in the House of Aten, the fanbearer at the right hand of the king, Meryre.

Lintel, right side: "Adoration to your Ka, O living Aten who illuminates the [Two] Lands with his beauty; King's Ka which lives on Maat, Lord of

Crowns, [AKHENATEN], long in his lifetime. You are the ruler, successful in fate, who brings into existence and makes to flourish the limbs [of everybody]. My heart rejoices at seeing your beauty, and I live at hearing what you say. May you grant to <me> an old age that is not far from you, and a good funeral in [Akhet-Aten]." By the Greatest of Seers of the Aten in the [House of] Aten in Akhet-Aten, the fanbearer [at the right hand of the king], Meryre.

Foot of left jamb: "[Adoration to you, O living Aten who illuminates the Two] Lands with his beauty; King's Ka who lives on Maat, Lord [of Crowns, AKHENATEN, long in his lifetime (?)]. May he grant a good funeral <in> the mountain of Akhet-Aten, and a place of favor in which you will be continually." For the Ka of one praised of the Lord of the Two Lands, the Greatest of Seers of the Aten in Akhet-Aten, Meryre.

Foot of right jamb: "Adoration to you, O living Aten who illuminates the land in his rising; King's Ka who lives on Maat, NEFERKHEPRURE-WAENRE. May he give an extensive span in life until the old age that is his to give comes to pass." For the Ka of one praised of the Lord of the Two Lands, the Greatest of Seers of the Aten in the House of Aten in Akhet-Aten, Meryre, justified.

70.6. Inscriptions Framing the Entrance to the Tomb

Foot of left jamb: "Adoration to your Ka, O one who lives [on] Maat, Lord of the Two Lands, NEFERKHEPRURE-WAENRE; good ruler who sets [his] Ba . . . against [the one who attacks] him, the one who makes all plans; the one who [. . .] among the living (?), . . . which shall exist . . . [to] travel. May he grant the receiving of a good old age [and a departure possessing the favor of the king." For the Ka of the Greatest of Seers of the Aten] in the House of Aten in Akhet-Aten, . . . [. . .]s which exist every day, [Meryre], justified.

Foot of right jamb: "Adoration [to] your Ka, O one who lives on Maat, Lord of Crowns, AKHENATEN, long in [his] lifetime; the good ruler who loves humankind [and changes ill-disposed] people into peaceful ones; the good ruler [who governs] the living and sets [rejoicing in] my limbs each time I make. . . . May you grant to me a good old age and an important. . . . For the Ka of the Greatest of Seers of the Aten in the House of Aten [in Akhet]-Aten, the fan]-bearer [at the right hand of] the king, Meryre, [justified].

70.7. Hymn to the Rising Sun

All three versions of this text are found on thicknesses of doorways leading in and out of the tomb, on which the tomb owner or his wife appears adoring the rising sun.

The prayer is uttered here by the wife of Meryre (I) in an abbreviated form; but this translation includes the entire composition, with major variants recorded in the notes.

Your rising is perfected, O HEKA-[ATEN],[51] given life forever continually. O living Aten, without another except for him, who makes eyes healthy with his rays, the one who makes all that exists! You appear from the eastern horizon of the sky just to bring life to all you have made—namely, people,[52] cattle, creatures that fly up and alight, and every sort of crawling creature [which is] in the earth. It is when they see you that they live, and when you set they go to sleep.

You cause your beloved son, who lives on Maat—the Lord of the Two Lands, NEFERKHEPRURE-WAENRE, as he lives with you continually, with the King's Chief Wife, his beloved, the Lady of the Two Lands, NEFERNEFRUATEN-NEFERTITI (may she live forever continually), beside him,[53]—to be doing what pleases your heart and to be seeing what you do every day: it is at seeing your beauty that he rejoices. Give him life, [stability and dominion], joy,[54] and [all] you have encircled [under his supervision]. Let them be governed on behalf of your Ka. As for your child, whom you yourself begat, one knowledgeable like . . . : the south as well as the north, the west, the east and the islands in the midst of the Great Green sea are in acclamation of his Ka. His southern border extends as far as the wind, and the northern one to what Aten illuminates. All their chiefs are in submission, weakened because of his divine power.

O good Ka who makes the Two Lands festive and creates the requirements of the entire land! Keep him with you continually, inasmuch as he desires to see you. Give him very many Sed Festivals with peaceful years. Give to him with the love of your heart—like the multitudes of sand of the shore, like the scales of fish upon the river, and the hairs of cattle. Keep him here until the swan turns black, until the crow turns white, until the mountains stand up to go, and until the flood flows backwards, while I am in the following of the Good God[55] until he decrees the funeral which is his to give.

By Meryre's wife, as she adores: The great favorite of the Lady of the Two Lands, Tenro, justified. She says: "Adoration to you, O one who makes the years and creates the months, who makes the days and reckons the hours. O master of lifetime, by [whom] one reckons time, may you [grant] your lifetime as Aten to your son Waenre!"[56]

70.8. Hymn to the Sun

This composition, along with the preceding hymn, is addressed by the tomb owner to the sun. A popular composition at El-Amarna, it is also found in a number of other tombs: Any (60), Apy (61), Mahu (69) and Tutu (89). While differences exist among all these copies (particularly between Any and Meryre I on one side, and Apy and Mahu on the other), the version in Tutu's tomb differs markedly from all the rest. This translation is a composite of all the texts, based for the most part on the version in this tomb: trivial mistakes and omissions from one copy to the next are ignored, but the more important variants are given in the notes.

The king's acquaintance, whom his lord loves, the favorite [of] the Lord [of the Two Lands], the Greatest [of Seers of the Aten in the House of Aten in Akhet-Aten], Meryre, [justified, he] says:[57]

Adoration of HEKA-ATEN,[58] given life forever continually, by the king who lives on Maat, the Lord of the Two Lands, NEFERKHEPRURE-WAENRE; the Son of Re who lives on Maat, the Lord of Crowns, AKHEN-ATEN, long in his lifetime, given life forever continually: "You appear beautifully, O living Aten, lord of eternity[59] dazzling, fair, powerful.[60] The love of you is great and extensive. Your rays reach the eyes of all you created,[61] and your bright hue revives all hearts[62] when you have filled the Two Lands with love of you, O august god[63] who constructed himself by himself—maker of every land, creator of what is on it: namely, people, all sorts of long- and short-horned cattle,[64] all trees and what grows on the ground—they live when you rise for them."[65]

"You are the mother and father of all you make. When you rise, their eyes see by means of you.[66] When your rays have illuminated[67] the entire land, all heart(s) rejoice at seeing you[68] manifest as their lord. When you set in the western horizon of heaven, they repose in the fashion of those who are dead, heads covered, noses obstructed, until the occurrence of your rising at dawn from the eastern horizon of heaven. Their arms are in adoration of your Ka: when you have revived all hearts with your beauty, one lives; and when you give forth your rays, every land is in festival.[69] Singing, chanting, and joyful shouting are in the courtyard of the Mansion of the Benben and (in) every temple[70] in Akhet-Aten, the place of truth in which you have become content.[71] Food and provisions lie within it, while your son is pure in doing what you praise."

"O Aten, who lives in his appearances! All that you make is dancing in front of you, and as for your august son,[72] his heart exults with joy. O living Aten, who is born in the sky daily,[73] that he might give birth to his august son, Waenre, just like himself,[74] without ceasing—the son of Re who raises up his beauty, NEFERKHEPRURE-WAENRE."[75]

"I am your son, who is effective for you[76] and raises up your name. Your might and your power are established[77] in my heart. You are the living Aten:

continuity is your image, for you made the distant sky in order to rise in it and see all you make—while you are one, but with millions of lives in you, in order to make them live. The breath of life penetrates into noses when your rays are seen.[78] All sorts of flowers are continually alive, growing on the ground and made to flourish, because of your rising: they grow drunk at the sight of you,[79] while all sorts of cattle are prancing[80] on their legs. Birds which were in the nest are aloft in joy, their wings which were folded are spread out in adoration to the living Aten, the one who makes them . . . all. . . ."

70.9. Texts on South Wall of Antechamber

East Side: "Adoration to you, O Waenre! I give adoration to the height of heaven and I propitiate the one who lives on Maat, the Lord of Crowns AKHENATEN, long in his lifetime. O Nile, at whose command one grows rich, food and provisions for Egypt; O good ruler, my builder, who made me, brought me up and caused me to mingle with officialdom; O Light (=*Shu*), at the seeing of whom I live; my Ka of every day!" By one uniquely favored by the Lord of the Two Lands, whom the King of Upper Egypt promoted and the King of Lower Egypt advanced; whom the Lord of the Two Lands made by means of his Ka: the Greatest of Seers of the Aten in the House of Aten in Akhet-Aten, the fanbearer at the right hand of the king, Meryre, justified. He says: "I give you adoration, I adore your beauty, [I] extol your good regulations. O my lord, may <you> give me old age not far from [you], [without] my eyes having to search for your beauty, until the state of reveredness occurs in peace in the august highland of Akhet-Aten."

West side: "Adoration to you, O one who lives on Maat, lord of all that is, Lord of the Two Lands, NEFERKHEPRURE-[WAENRE], given life, the beautiful child of the living Aten! So long as heaven exists, so will you exist! You shall achieve many years and myriads of jubilees, being here continually forever. All the world is calling out to your Ka, for they belong to you, their ruler, adoring your course *in the sky* in order to achieve power like the living Aten. You are born like the Aten is born: your lifetime is eternity, the lifetime of Re as king of the Two Lands, the years of Aten in heaven, while you dwell in Akhet-Aten, the beautiful place which you made for Re, to which all come." By one uniquely excellent and beloved of his lord, one whom the Lord of the Two Lands favored on account of his character, the Greatest of Seers of the Aten in the House of Aten in Akhet-Aten, Meryre.

By a figure of Meryre, arms extended in adoration: The sealbearer of the King of Lower Egypt, the sole companion, one whom the Lord of the Two Lands favored, the Greatest of Seers of the Aten in the House of Aten in Akhet-Aten, Meryre, justified.

70.10. Antechamber, Framing of North Door Jambs

Another version is found at virtually the same place in the tomb of Panehsy. The most important variants, along with the personal endings for Panehsy, are given in the notes.

A. "Adoration to you, O living Aten, King's Ka who lives on Maat, the Lord of the Two Lands, NEFERKHEPRURE-WAENRE, given life."[81] May he grant a good old age and a departing with favor to the mountain of Akhet-Aten,[82] for the Ka of the Greatest of Seers of the Aten in Akhet-Aten, Meryre, justified.[83]

B. "Adoration to you, O living Aten, King's Ka who lives on Maat, AKHENATEN, long in his lifetime."[84] May he grant a good funeral after old age and interment at the favored ones' cemetery. For the Ka of the sealbearer of the King of Lower Egypt, the sole companion, the fanbearer at the right hand of the king, Meryre, justified.[85]

C. "Adoration to you, O living Aten, (and) the King's Chief Wife, his beloved, NEFERNEFRUATEN-[NEFERTITI], may she live continually forever.[86] May he grant a lengthy lifetime while seeing your beauty, without ceasing from beholding you every day." For the Ka of the Greatest of Seers of the Aten in Akhet-Aten, Meryre, justified.[87]

D. "Adoration to you, O living Aten, King's Ka who lives on Maat, Lord of the Two Lands, NEFERKHEPURE-WAENRE, given life." May he grant[88] the receiving offering loaves that are issued in the (divine) presence, and of libations and offerings in the House of Aten.[89] For the Ka of the sealbearer of the King of Lower Egypt, one whom his Lord loves, the great favorite of the Lord of the Two Lands, Meryre, [justified].[90]

E. "Adoration to you, O living Aten, King's Ka who lives on Maat, Lord of the Two Lands, NEFERKHEPRURE-WAENRE, given life.[91] May he give an entry favored, a departure beloved, and the receiving of the favors of the Lord of the Two Lands.[92] [For the Ka of the Greatest of Seers of the Aten] in Akhet-Aten, Meryre, justified.[93]

F. "Adoration to you, O living Aten, King's Ka who lives on Maat, Lord of Crowns, AKHENATEN,[94] long in his lifetime. May he grant being in your mansion of continuity and your place of everlastingness, without it happening that your name is forgotten forever." For the Ka of the hereditary prince and count, sealbearer of the King of Lower Egypt, one whom his lord loves, Meryre, justified.[95]

G. "Adoration to you, O living Aten, and the King's Chief Wife, his beloved, Lady of the Two Lands, NEFERNEFRUATEN-[NEFERTITI, may she] live forever continually.[96] May he grant the permanence of your resting in your tomb, and that one may pronounce your name continually forever." For [the Ka of the Greatest of Seers of] the Aten in Akhet-Aten, Meryre, justified.[97]

H. "Adoration to you, O living Aten, King's Ka who lives on Maat, the Lord of the Two Lands, NEFERKHEPRURE-WAENRE, given life. May he grant[98] that the children of your house offer libation to you at the door of your tomb." For [the Ka of the] sealbearer [of the King of Lower Egypt], the sole companion, [the fanbearer at the right hand of the king, Meryre, justified].[99]

70.11. Thicknesses of Outer Walls

East side: The sealbearer of the King of Lower Egypt, the king's acquaintance, the favorite of his lord; straightforward to the King of Upper Egypt and [effective (?)] for the King of Lower Egypt; the Greatest of Seers of the Aten in the House of Aten in Akhet-Aten, Meryre, [he] says: "Adoration of Aten in [his setting in the western horizon of] heaven. You set beautifully, O HEKA-[ATEN], given life continually forever! When you cross the sky in peace, the entire world calls out to [your face and gives] adoration at your rising over [them . . . your] beloved [son] likewise, alone except for you, as king continually. Dazzling in your hues [you] appear, you who make the eyes of all that he has created, *in order that [they] might experience* (?) [. . .] when he has [caused] all small cattle to live. It is through seeing [your] rays that one becomes healthy, and it is through seeing you that their hearts [become alive]. [Your beloved] son, the King of Upper and Lower Egypt who lives on Maat, the Lord of the Two Lands, NEFERKHEPRURE-WAENRE, will continue to [. . .] forever."

West side: The sealbearer of the King of Lower Egypt, whom his lord loves, the favorite whom the Lord of the Two Lands fostered, the Greatest of Seers [of] the Aten [in the House of] Aten in Akhet-Aten, the fanbearer at the right hand of the king, Meryre, [he] says: "Adoration of Aten in his rising from the eastern horizon of heaven. How beautiful is your rising, O [HEKA-ATEN], given life forever continually. With your beauty you have illuminated the Two Lands, and as a solar globe (=*Aten*) you have encircled the

Two Banks. [As for] all [those] upon whom [you shine], you make them flourish for your beloved son, for whom you have ordained the lands so that he might satisfy his zeal and do what pleases your Ka. It is with a [loving] heart that he governs them for you, and the land is under him as it was under you. The Nine Bows are [in] his Person's presence, and their chiefs are gathered under his sandals. May you permit him to spend your time as king, being here with you continually, seeing your rays every day. May you give [him] jubilees and many years, all that you encircle being under his supervision—namely, your child, who issued from your limbs, the Lord of the Two Lands, [NEFERKHEPRURE-WAENRE], given [life forever continually]."

71. The "Overseer of the Royal Quarters," Meryre (II)

The following reliefs and inscriptions come from Meryre II's tomb at El-Amarna (No. 2).

71.1. East Wall of Main Chamber

Akhenaten and the queen are shown enthroned, with their six daughters behind, inside a kiosk, receiving the tribute of foreign lands, which is depicted in numerous subregisters below and on both sides of the kiosk. The occasion is described as follows:

Regnal year 12, second month [of the Seed season, day] 8. The King of Upper and Lower Egypt [who lives] on Maat, Lord of the Two Lands, NEFERKHEPRURE-WAENRE, the Son of Re who lives on Maat, Lord of Crowns, AKHENATEN, long in [his] lifetime; (and) the King's Great Wife, his beloved, NEFERNEFRUATEN-NEFERTITI, may she live forever [continually].

Appearance [of his Person] on the throne of his (divine and royal) father, the Aten, who lives on Maat, while the chieftains of every foreign land are presenting [products to the king and] begging peace from him, so that [they might be] allowed to breathe the breath [of] life.

The six princesses behind the throne all bear the identical title, King's bodily daughter, his beloved. *They are:*

(1) [Meret-Aten].
(2) [Meket]-Aten.
(3) Ankhesenpaaten.
(4) Nefernefruaten Junior.

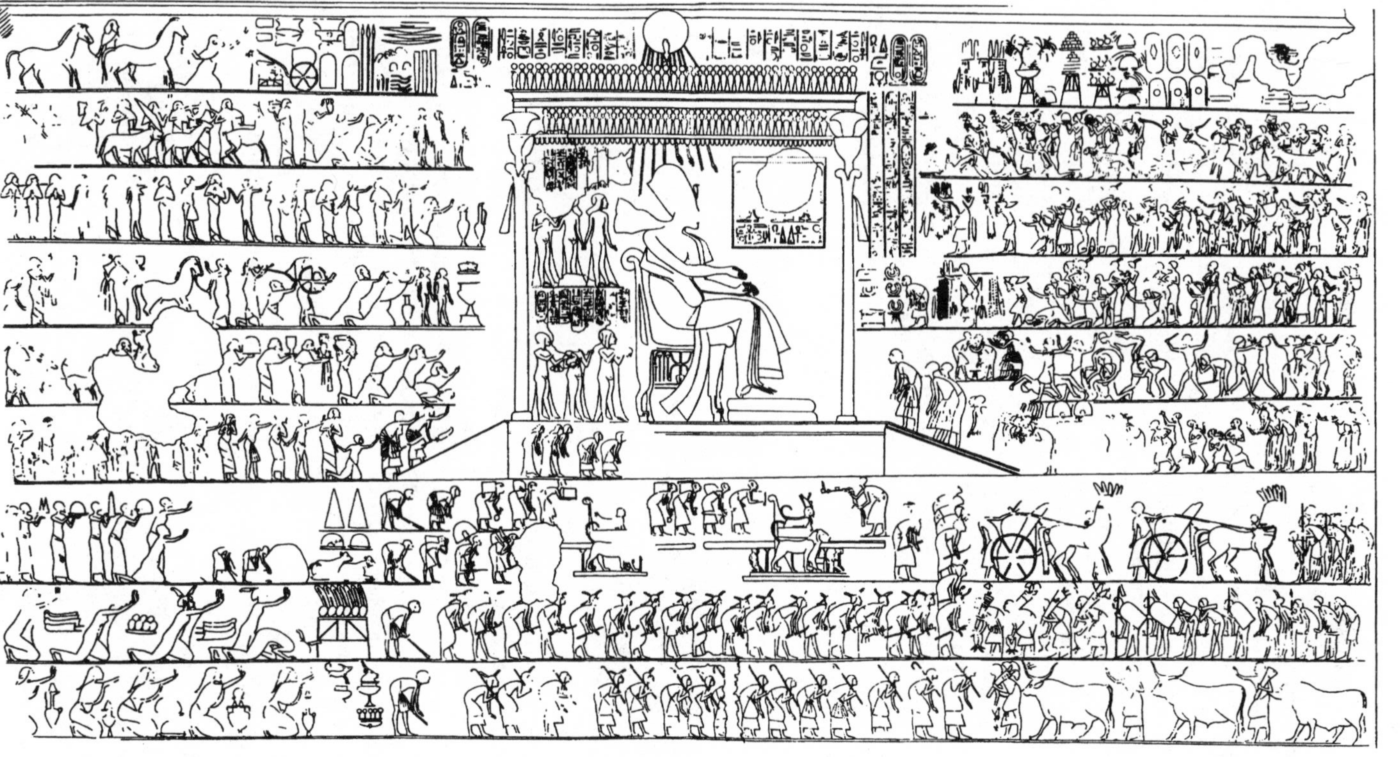

Figure 8:
The royal family receives foreign tribute in year 12, from the tomb of Meryre II

(5) Nefernefrure.
(6) Setepenre.

All six are described as born to (Queen) NEFERNEFRUATEN-NEFERTITI, may she live forever continually, *but while the titularies of the first four describe their mother as* King's Wife, *the last two daughters' titles refer to her as* King's Great Wife. *The other inscriptions in this scene (names and titles of the Aten, king and queen) are all conventional.*

71.2. Outer Jamb, West Side

. . . Giving praise to the ruler when he sets in the western horizon of heaven. . . . . May he give fragrant breeze to the Ka of the king's [true] scribe, [his beloved, the steward], the overseer of the royal quarters and the apartments of the King's Great Wife NEFERNEFRUATEN-NEFERTITI, may she live forever continually. [For the Ka of . . .] Meryre, [justified, possessor of] reveredness in Akhet-Aten.

71.3. Thickness of Outer Wall

East Side: "When you set in life, [the land] is worshiping you, the east and the west are giving you adoration, (O) HEKA-ATEN, given life forever continually, as you set, alive, from the sight [of . . .]. (As for) . . . , they raise an outcry [to] the height of heaven at seeing Akhet-Aten, which Re made to be given to his son, who lives on Maat, while he (=*Aten*) causes him (=*king*) to plunder every foreign country on which he shines, and he bequeaths the whole circuit to him in order to slake his heart with them [and to do what pleases his Ka], for they are under the feet of Waenre, the one beloved like the [Aten], [until] the sea [gets up] on legs, until the mountains stand up to go, until water flows backwards. O beautiful ruler of the Aten, you are . . . the Aten. May he cause your southern borders [to extend as far as the] wind, and your northern one to what Aten illuminates. It is your strength which protects the Two Lands, and your might which makes the subjects live, (O) Waenre, beloved like Aten, long [in his lifetime]." The king's scribe, overseer of the houses of the royal quarters, the steward Meryre, justified.

West Side: "[Adoration of HEKA-ATEN, . . .], living [Aten], lord of love, who gave birth to himself by himself . . . . [May he give] peaceful years, jubilees . . . [to the king . . .], given life forever. May you grant . . . , his lifetime (being) like your lifetime in . . . . [*Receive this from your father,* (O)] Waenre, who gives you continuity and eternity in the House [of Aten in Akhet-Aten. *When creation sees* (?)] the lovely [rays (?)] of the living Aten . . . , . . . their . . . , all herds, consisting of all sorts of small cattle that go on foot, which are dedicated to the House of Aten. The Aten ordains them just for the one who is long in his lifetime, the great and good Nile [of the entire land]. May you appoint his lifetime among the living [until] I reach the revered state in peace. May you ordain for [him] his [tomb] on the face of the great mountain of Akhet-[Aten], as for a favorite of the king." For the Ka of the steward, the treasurer, the overseer of the royal quarters of [the King's Chief Wife], NEFERNEFRUATEN-NEFERTITI—may <she> live forever continually—the king's scribe Meryre, justified.

71.4. Architraves

West: A "boon which the king gives" of the living Aten who illuminates the Two Lands with his beauty when he rises to give life to everything Aten encircles, one beautiful of manifestations and dazzling of colors, at seeing whose beauty eyes live, at whose shining for them hearts are healthy. May he grant the fragrant breeze of the north wind, milk coming forth on the offering table, and all sorts of offerings—all kinds of vegetables, bread, beer and foodstuffs at every place of yours, all good and sweet things—for the Ka of the overseer of the royal quarters, the king's scribe, the steward Meryre, justified in Akhet-Aten.

East: "Adoration to your Ka, O NEFERKHEPRURE-WAENRE, good ruler, beloved of Aten, the great Nile of the entire land, at seeing whom they live, O 'Only One of Re' (=*Waenre*), beloved like Aten. May Re give to you myriads of jubilees at each rising of his, to protect the one whom the Aten bore—(for) you are his son, who lives on Maat, and he bequeaths to you all the things he encircles that you might slake your heart with them. May you grant that my lifetime be a good one, while <I> behold your beauty, until reaching the tomb which I have made on the great mountain of Akhet-Aten." For the Ka of the king's scribe Meryre.

1.5. North Wall, East Side
See chapter 5, 97-A.

72. The Cupbearer Meryre

This pyramidion was once attached to the mortuary chapel of Meryre and his family.

Side A: The owner and his wife are seated before a table, receiving incense and libation from a man who stands in front of them and is identified as His bodily son, the (ritual) dancer (?) of Neferkheprure [*sic*], Huy—justified, alive. *The main text is as follows:* A "boon which the king gives" of the living Aten, lord of sunbeams, who illuminates the Two Banks, (and) the King's Ka: consisting of a good old age from the Aten—the living one, handsome of face, the shining one, <for> the cupbearer of Neferkheprure [*sic*] Meryre, may he live again; (and) the housewife Nubnefer.

Side B: The owner, followed by his wife, daughter, and younger son, stand with their arms outstretched in adoration. The text above them is as follows:

A "boon which the king gives" of the living Aten, lord of all Aten encircles, who illuminates the Two Banks, lord of sunbeams, the Aten, <for> the cupbearer of the House of Aten in Akhet-Aten, Meryre, may he live again.

The housewife, favorite of the Aten, Nubnefer, justified.

His daughter, Hetepty, justified.

His son, Yuny.

Side C is is laid out identically to Side B, but the texts are too badly eroded for consecutive translation: only the beginning of a "boon which the king gives" *formula and the name of one of the sons,* Huy, *are preserved.*

Side D is laid out identically to Side A. The badly eroded texts are as follows: A "boon which the king gives" of the living Aten, lord of [heaven and earth (?)], Aten, lord of [sunbeams (?)], Aten [. . .] who establishes . . . Aten . . . in the (?) . . . , [the cupbearer of the House of Aten in Akhet-Aten, Meryre], may he live again.

The housewife Nubnefret, [justified].

[His] son (?) Huy.

[His daughter], Itiat (?).

73. The Vizier Nakht-(pa-Aten)

73-A. Inscriptions from the House of the Vizier Nakht at El-Amarna

Front door, left jamb: . . . in favor; the Lord of the Two Lands, who builds up everybody, may he cause . . . the favorite of his lord, who performs the instruction of the Lord of the Two Lands . . . . writings on stone, the overseer of the city and vizier Nakht, justified.

West loggia, south niche, left side: . . . , overseer of [. . .] in the House "Satisfaction of Re," overseer of works projects in [Akhet]-Aten, overseer of the city and vizier, [Nakht, justified].

Same, north niche, right side: . . . [in Akhet]-Aten, the vizier Nakht, justified.

Fragment: . . . AKHENATEN, great in his lifetime, the god who makes humanity . . . .

73-B. Tomb of Vizier Nakht-pa-Aten at El-Amarna (No. 12)

Remains of the outer doorjambs (now destroyed) identified the owner as the hereditary prince, count, sealbearer and the vizier Nakht-pa-Aten.

74. The Mayor of Akhet-Aten, Neferkheperu-her-sekheper

While the cutting of this individual's tomb at El-Amarna (No. 13) was nearly completed, the inscriptions were never carved, although texts on the façade (roughed out in paint) could be discerned: only those on the left jamb of entrance are intelligible.

A. Standard titulary of the king and queen.

B. . . . in the jubilee . . . , whom the Lord of the Two Lands loves on account of his character; possessor of favor in the presence of the Lord of the Two Lands; the may<or of> Akhet-Aten, Neferkheper-her-sekheper, justified.

C. [A "boon which the king gives" of . . . AKHENATEN], long in his lifetime—may you give . . . [the] right ways (?) for him, that he may be invoked at the forefront of the officials: the mayor of Akhet-Aten, Neferkheper-her-sekheper, justified.

D. [A "boon which the king gives of] the King's Chief Wife, [his] beloved, the Lady of the Two Lands, NEFERNEFRUATEN-NEFERTITI, may she live forever continually—may [you] give [. . .] in Akhet-[Aten, for the one who had (?)] entry into the presence in the privacy of the palace: the mayor of Akhet-Aten, Neferkhepru-her-sekheper, justified.

75. The Chief Bowman Nekhu-em-pa-Aten

A. A lintel from Nekhu-em-pa-Aten's house at El-Amarna shows the tomb owner at each end, adoring the cartouches of HEKA-ATEN, the king and queen in the center.

Left end: "I adore your beauty like the Aten's, (O) NEFERKHEPRURE-WAENRE, the ruler, the love of whom is bright, as you are continually! May you celebrate jubilees and conduct generations of people like the Aten, while I follow you continually like one whom you favor." For the Ka of the chief bowman, master of the horse, (and) royal cupbearer, Nekhu-em-[pa]-Aten—may he live again.

Right side: "Adoration to your Ka, O living Aten, lord of the circuit of living Aten, who is present, being alive every day [without] ceasing. May you cause me to see the king every day, following him continually—the reward (?) [of] an official who knows his instruction. May you give me life according to [my] desire [because of] my well-disposedness, and burial because of [*sic*] [a good (?)] old age." [For the Ka of the chief bowman, master of the horse (and) royal cup-bearer, Nekhu-em-pa-Aten, justified].

B. Another fragment which names this individual (from his house or his tomb?) preserves one foot of the kneeling owner, with the final words of a longer inscription above: . . . good [. . .] of the Only One of Re. For the Ka of the royal cup-bearer Nekhu-em-pa-Aten.

76. The Commander, Pa-Aten-emheb

Only the entrance of this man's tomb at El-Amarna (No. 24) was carved, from which come the following fragments:

A. . . . forever and ever.

B. . . . . [For the Ka of the king's scribe], general of the Lord of the Two Lands Pa-Aten-emheb.

C. . . . . [For the Ka of] the king's scribe and steward of the Lord of the Two Lands, Pa-Aten-emheb.

D. . . . , which is yours (*=feminine*) to give. For the Ka of the king's scribe and general in Akhet-Aten, Pa-Aten-emheb.

77. The First Servant of the Aten, Panehsy

A. Altar in the Form of a Sanctuary from the Official Residence of Panehsy at El-Amarna

Left jamb: Long live the (divine and royal) father, HEKA-ATEN, given life forever continually; (and) the Lord of the Two Lands, NEFERKHEPRURE-WAENRE....

Right jamb: identical, except for Lord of Crowns AKHENATEN. *Above a scene, which shows the king, queen, and eldest daughter adoring the Aten:*

HEKA-ATEN, given life forever continually; great living Aten, lord of jubilees, lord of everything Aten encircles, lord of heaven, lord of earth in the House of Aten in Akhet-Aten.

Lord of the Two Lands, NEFERKHEPRURE-WAENRE, given life; Lord of Crowns, AKHENATEN, long in his lifetime.

Lady of the Two Lands, NEFERNEFRUATEN-NEFERTITI, may she live forever continually.

King's bodily daughter, his beloved, Meretaten, born to the King's Chief Wife, NEFERNEFRUATEN-NEFERTITI, may she live forever continually.

B. Tomb of Panehsy at El-Amarna (No. 6)

77-B.1. Thickness of Outer Wall, West Side

The king and queen are shown adoring the Aten, elevating dedicatory scepters under the sun's rays. Three daughters, rattling sistra, stand behind their parents. Beside the disk of the sun is the earlier form of the Aten's extended titulary: [HOR-ATEN], given life forever continually; great living Aten who is in jubilee, lord of everything Aten encircles, lord of heaven, lord of earth in the House of Aten in Akhet-Aten (and) in the mountain of Akhet-Aten.

Like that of the Aten, the cartouches of the king and queen were erased, but the rest of their titularies are intact. The king's titles are brief and standard, but the queen has a longer variant of her usual titulary: The hereditary princess, whose favor is great, Mistress of Upper and Lower Egypt, fair of face, beauteous in the double plumed crown, who cleanses the heart of the king in his house, at whose every utterance one is content, the King's Chief Wife, <his> beloved, Lady of the Two Lands, [NEFERNEFRUATEN-NEFERTITI], may she live forever continually.

Each of the daughters is described as King's bodily daughter, his beloved,

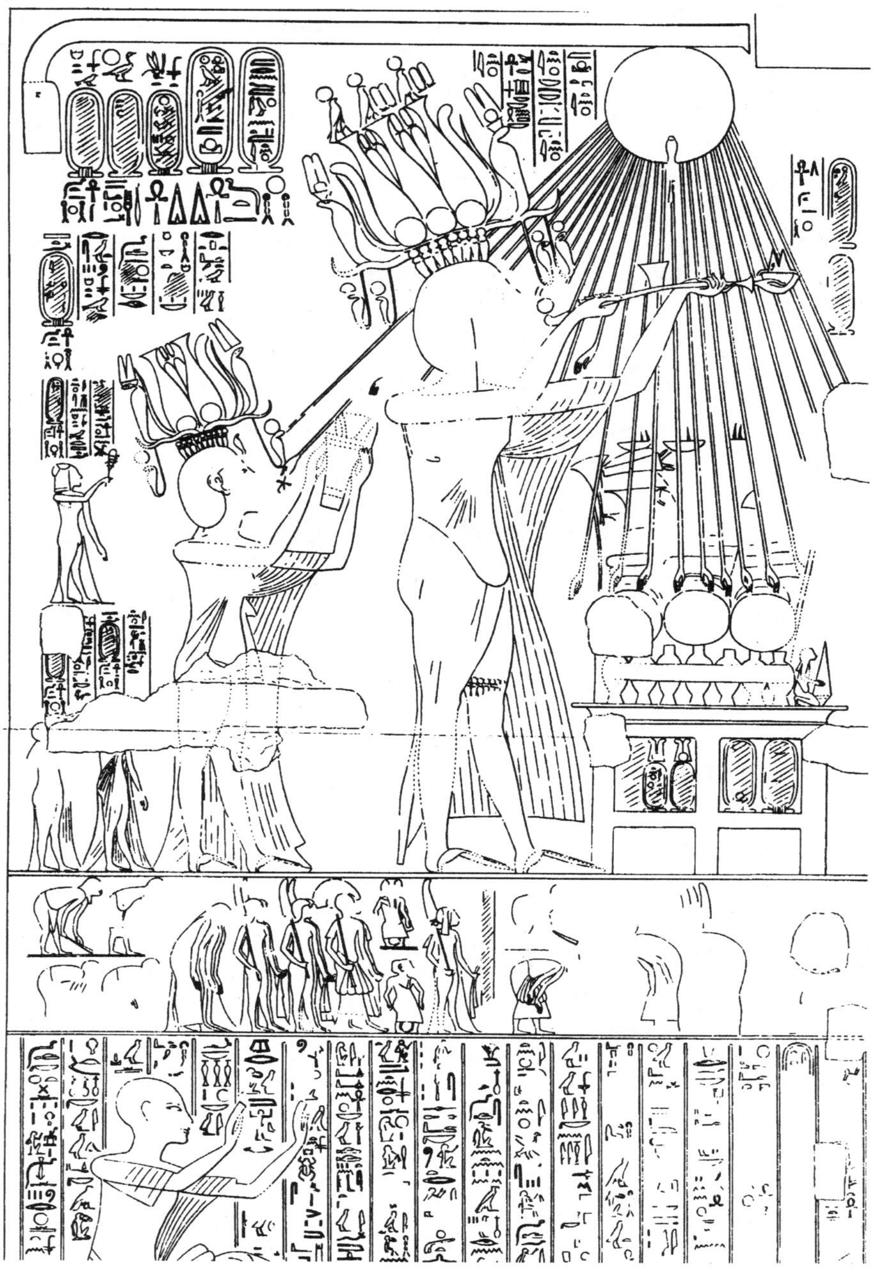

Figure 9:
On a thickness at the entrance to the tomb of Panehsy, the royal family (top) and the tomb owner (bottom) adore the sun

and born to the King's Chief Wife, his beloved, the lady of the Two Lands, NEFERNEFRUATEN-[NEFERTITI], may she live forever continually. *From top to bottom, we see* Meretaten, Meket-Aten, *and* Ankhesenpaaten.

Beneath the scene is a short subregister in which The sister of the King's Chief Wife, NEFERNEFRUATEN-[NEFERTITI, may she live forever continually], Mutnodjmet *is shown with a retinue of attendants.*

In the lowest register the tomb owner is shown kneeling, his arms outstretched in adoration as he utters the following prayer: Adoration of [HOR-ATEN], given life forever continually, in his rising from the eastern horizon, and propitiating him in his setting in the western horizon.

"Hail to you as you rise in the sky and as you shine at dawn in the horizon of the sky. Welcome in peace, lord of peace! All people live at seeing you. The entire land is assembled at your appearance, their arms being in adoration at your rising." By the first servant of Aten in the House of Aten in Akhet Aten, Panehsy, justified. He says:

"Adoration to you, my god who built me, the one who fated good things for me; the one who brought me into being, who gave me bread, who made my property by means of his Ka; the ruler who made me from among humankind, who caused me to mingle with his favorites, who caused every eye to know me when you distinguished me from the hindermost, who caused me to be powerful when I had been poor. All my kindred [acquire] property, now that I have become a favorite of the one who makes it. My town comes to me at every season now that I am promoted on account of it, through what the lord of Maat [has] ordained. Let me give adoration to the height of heaven as I adore the Lord of the Two Lands, Akhenaten,[100] the fate which gives life, master of what is ordained, the light (=*Shu*) of every land, by the seeing of whom one lives; the Nile of the entire world, [through] whose Ka one is satisfied; the god who makes officialdom and builds up the commons, the breeze of every nose, through whom it is allowed to breathe."

For the Ka of the first servant of Aten in the House of Aten, Panehsy.

77-B.2. Thickness of the Outer Wall, East Side

The scene is laid out on lines virtually identical to that on the western side (77-B.1), although the king and queen wear different crowns; and the king censes the Aten, while the queen elevates a bouquet. The texts of the Aten, the king, the three daughters (within the scene) are standard. The queen's sister is shown below the scene, as in the parallel, but her texts are destroyed. The titulary of the queen (car-

touches erased) can be read as follows: The hereditary princess, great of favor, Mistress of all women, for whom, when she says anything, it is done, the King's Chief Wife, his beloved, NEFERNEFRUATEN-NEFERTITI, may she live forever continually.

Below the scene is the main text: Adoration [of the great living Aten] (and) the King of Upper [and Lower Egypt] who lives on Maat, [the Lord of the Two Lands, NEFERKHEPRURE-WAENRE], the Son of Re who lives on Maat, Lord of Crowns, AKHENATEN, [long in his lifetime; (and) the King's Chief Wife, his beloved, the Lady of the Two Lands, NEFERNEFRUATEN-NEFERTITI, may she live forever] continually.

"Adoration to you, O Pre, sole one, god . . . living [. . . in/of] the entire [land], lord of food. All arms are adoring <you>: they live when they see [you] . . . . O Shu who gives life, and causes the land to live in exultation (?). O Lord of the Two Lands, sovereign [*who benefits*] his children; Nile [of the] orphan who is impoverished (?), life [of] everyone . . . [who say]: 'How [*fortunate* (?)] is he, your favorite.'" By the great favorite of [the Good God, the first servant of the] Aten in the House of Aten in Akhet-Aten, Panehsy. He says: "O everyone [who is in] Akhet-Aten who desires a good [lifetime], I will recite to you the good deeds which [the] ruler did for me, when he caused me to mingle with the officials and courtiers, so that I was promoted and respected, so that my opinions mingled with those of the officials and I am now found to be[101] a king's acquaintance—Re in his Person, the one who [*relieves* (?)] the poverty of the one he favors, who makes officialdom by means of his Ka; the Fate who gives life, lord of what is ordained. One is healthy when he is satisfied, and every land is laden with joy while acclamation is done in the king's house and power comes to pass in the palace."

[I am (?) a possessor of] reveredness, one who desists from loudness in his instructing, a possessor of favor every day, his limbs being healthy at seeing your beauty, while . . . ; then others after me shall say: "How fortunate was the king's acquaintance, the first [servant] of the Aten, Panehsy!"

77-B.3. South Door, Jambs

A. A "boon which the king gives" of HEKA-ATEN, [given life] forever continually. May he grant entry, while possessing Maat, to the Lord of the Two Lands, being one whom his lord promoted on account of well-counseled offices. For the Ka of the favorite of the Good God, the first servant of At[en] in the House of At<en> in Akhet-<Aten>, Panehsy.

B. A "boon which the king gives" of the King's Ka which lives on Maat, the Lord of the Two Lands NEFERKHEPRURE-[WAENRE], given life. May he give lifetime and old age, limbs being firm while old age is ordained for your time. For the Ka of the first servant of Aten in the House of Aten in Akhet-Aten, Panehsy.

C. A "boon which the king gives" of the King's Ka which lives on Maat, Lord of Crowns, AKHENATEN, long in his lifetime. May he permit the receiving [of offering loaves] which issue from the presence, his arms being pure, and the kissing of the ground in the broad court. For the Ka of the first servant of Aten in the House of Aten in Akhet-Aten, Panehsy.

D. A "boon which the king gives" of the King's Chief Wife, his beloved, NEFERNEFRUATEN-NEFERTITI, may she live forever continually. May adoration of the king in his house be granted—namely, my lord who built me, made me, and fostered me. For the Ka of the first servant of Aten in the House of Aten in Akhet-Aten, Panehsy.

E. A "boon which the king gives" of [HOR-ATEN], given life forever continually. May he give entry and exit in the king's house, speech prospering without the cessation of its success until the revered state comes to pass in peace, under the favor of the Lord of the Two Lands. For the Ka <of> the first servant of Aten in the House of Aten in Akhet-Aten, Panehsy, justified.

F. A "boon which the king gives" of the King's Ka which lives on Maat, the Lord of the Two Lands, NEFERKHEPRURE-[WAENRE], given life. May he give sight of the living Aten in his appearing. Worship him, that he may hear when you speak, like his favorites. For the Ka of the second prophet of the Lord of the Two Lands, NEFERKHEPRURE-[WAENRE], given life, Panehsy justified.

G. A "boon which the king gives" of the King's Ka which lives on Maat, the Lord of Crowns, AKHENATEN, long in his lifetime. May he grant the receiving of offering loaves which issue from the presence in every festival of the living Aten in the Mansion of the Benben. For the Ka of the first servant of Aten in the House of Aten in Akhet-Aten, Panehsy, justified.

H. A "boon which the king gives" of the King's Chief Wife, Lady of the Two Lands, [NEFERNEFRUATEN-NEFERTITI], may she live forever continually. May she give a favored entry, a loving departure and a good remembrance in the presence of the king, your name being good in the mouth(s) of the courtiers. For the Ka of the second prophet of the Lord of the Two Lands, NEFERKHEPRURE-WAENRE, given life, Panehsy, justified.

77-B.4. South Wall, West Side

The king and queen are in the royal window of appearances, accompanied by their eldest daughter, Meritaten. *Three other princesses*–Meket-Aten, Ankhesenpaaten, *and* Nefernefruaten "Junior"—*stand to the left of the building. To its right, Panehsy is shown being rewarded by the king before a crowd of officials, including scribes and Asiatic delegates. No texts specific to this occasion are preserved here, and the epigraphs belonging to the Aten and the royal family are conventional. In one of the subregisters below, however, Panehsy is shown being greeted by his subordinates, with the following text:* The great favorite of the Lord of the Two Lands, the first servant of [the] Aten in the House of Aten in Akhet-Aten, Panehsy. "Let [Pharaoh], l.p.h., be healthy. O Aten, cause him to be continual!"

77-B.5. South Wall, East Side

Panehsy, followed by several subregisters of offering bearers, presents a bouquet to Akhenaten who, along with the queen, offers flowers to the Aten. Behind the royal couple stand their first four daughters, also holding bouquets. The texts are all conventional; but (doubtless for reasons of space) the texts given to Meritaten and Meketaten only refer to their mother as King's Wife [NEFERNEFRUATEN-NEFERTITI], may she live; *while the longer columns of their two sisters above permit fuller writings. In both cases the queen is* King's Chief Wife, *and the tags which follow her cartouche are also adjusted for the available space:* may she live forever continually *(Ankhesenpaaten); and* may she live and be healthy forever continually *(Nefernefruaten Junior).*

77-B.6. North Wall, West Side

Panehsy is shown in attendance on the king and queen as they elevate food offerings to the Aten. The epigraphs, so far as they are preserved, contain nothing out of the ordinary. The tomb owner is shown with subordinates in the subregister below, uttering a prayer, now badly damaged, on behalf of the king: The king's acquaintance, one beloved of his lord, the great favorite of the Lord of the Two Lands, the first servant of Aten in the House of Aten in Akhet-Aten, [the . . .] for the lord [of the Two Lands (?)], [the . . . of] Re, Panehsy: "[The entire land is assembled at your rising, that you may make healthy] this Waenre, your [beautiful] child. [May] you [give] to [him] millions of jubilees (?), [and dominion over (?)] all lands (?)."

77-B.7. North Door, Lintel

The tomb owner is shown worshiping the cartouches of the Aten, king and queen from both ends.

Left: "Adoration to you, O living Aten, lord of what is and creator of what exists. When you rise, everybody lives and their arms tender adoration to you. The entire land is assembled at your appearance. May you <make>

healthy this Waenre, your beautiful child. May you give him millions of jubilees." By the first servant of Aten in Akhet-Aten, Panehsy, [justified].

Right: "Adoration to you, O Aten, [lord of] continuity and maker of eternity; King's Ka which lives on Maat, Lord of the Two Lands, NEFERKHEPRURE-WAENRE, given life—my lord, who constructed me, who fostered me, who gave a long life, following his Ka." By the sealbearer of the King of Lower Egypt, beloved of the Lord of the Two Lands, the favorite of his lord every day, the first servant of Aten in the House of Aten, Panehsy, justified.

77-B.8. North Door, Jambs

These texts, which occur in several tombs at El-Amarna, are translated at 70.10 (tomb of Meryre I), with the variants for Panehsy's tomb given in the notes.

77-B.9. Ceiling Inscriptions

A. [A "boon which the king gives" of the Aten (?) for] the [great] favorite of the Lord of the Two Lands, [his beloved (?)], the first [servant] of Aten in the House of Aten in Akhet-[Aten, Panehsy, justified]. [May he be granted] a good burial on the desert [of Akhet-Aten] . . . .

B. "Adoration to your Ka, O ruler, clothed with love like the Aten, who makes the eyes of the land, by means of whom they see; their Nile, which makes them live; breath of life, whose voice is heard . . . Aten . . . , NEFERKHEPRURE-WAENRE. Let my eyes see you daily, O my lord, without ceasing, while love [of me] is firm—for one lives by following the lord; one does not live from property." For the Ka <of> the first servant of Aten in the House of Aten in Akhet-Aten, Panehsy.

C. The great favorite of the Good God, the first servant of Aten in the House of Aten in Akhet-Aten, Panehsy, justified. He says: "O everybody in Akhet-Aten who desires [a good] lifetime, [I will] recite to you the good things which the ruler, my lord, did for me—namely, his giving me gold with praise on the day of doing a great thing for his lady, the king's daughter; the one whom the Lord of the Two Lands rewarded, whom his lord promoted on account of his office, the one whom the King of Upper Egypt made and the King of Lower Egypt fostered, whom the Lord of the Two Lands made by means of his Ka."

77-B.10. Abaci of Columns

The favorite of the Lord of the Two Lands, the overseer of the storehouse of the Aten in Akhet-[Aten, Panehsy, justified].

The favorite [of] the Lord of the Two Lands, the overseer of the cattle of the Aten [in Akhet-Aten], Panehsy, [justified].

The favorite of his lord, the servant of the Lord of the Two Lands NEFER-KHEPRURE-WAENRE, [Panehsy].

77-B.11. Tablets on Columns

Spoken by the tomb owner, who is shown twice while adoring cartouches of the Aten, king and queen.

North Column, left side: "Adoration to you, O living Aten, lord of continuity who made eternity. Let me give adoration to Waenre, let me propitiate the good ruler." By the first servant of Aten, Panehsy.

Right side: "Adoration to you, O living Aten who illuminates the Two lands with his beauty, King's Ka, you being (?) 'The Only One of Re' (=*Waenre*), son of the Aten, l.p.h., daily in the course of every day." By the first servant of Aten, Panehsy, [justified].

The tablet on the south column is destroyed.

77-B.12. Lintel of South Door

Spoken by the tomb owner, who appears at both ends, adoring the cartouches of the Aten, king and queen at the center of the lintel.

Left side: "Adoration [to you, O living Aten] . . . people adore . . . people, they live at your rising, being hale and strong at having seen you, as he (=*king?*) is magnified in the palace." By the first servant of Aten in the House of Aten in Akhet-Aten, Panehsy, [justified].

Right side: "Adoration to you, O living Aten, who illuminates heaven and earth in his rising; lord of continuity who made eternity. When he appears, every land is in joy, and his rays are on the eyes of all he has created: one says 'life' when he is seen, but one dies from not seeing him." The first servant of Aten in the House of Aten in Akhet-Aten, Panehsy, justified.

77-B.13. East Architrave

Long live the Good God who is contented with Maat, lord of everything Aten encircles, lord of heaven, lord of earth, great living Aten who illuminates the Two Banks; long live the divine and royal father, HOR-ATEN, given life everlastingly forever—great living Aten who is in jubilee, lord of heaven, lord of earth in the House of Aten in Akhet-Aten; and the King of Upper and Lower Egypt who lives on Maat, the Lord of the Two Lands, NEFERKHEPRURE-WAENRE; Son of Re who lives on Maat, Lord of Crowns, AKHENATEN, [long] in his lifetime; (and) the King's Chief Wife, his beloved, Lady of the Two Lands, NEFERNEFRUATEN-NEFERTITI, may she live forever continually.

77-B.14. Shrine, East Wall

Panehsy and his family are shown seated before a table, probably a funerary meal. Panehsy's son is sitting on a stool beside his father's chair, while two small daughters stand beside their mother. A servant who stands before the family group extends a bouquet toward them.

Over Panehsy: By the great favorite of Waenre, the first servant of Aten in the House of Aten in Akhet-Aten, Panehsy, justified.

Over his wife: His "sister," his beloved, the housewife Iabka, justified.

Over priest: "May he (=*king*) give praise to the Aten, that he (=*god*) may give you a good old age like a favored one."

78. The Cupbearer, Parennefer

The following reliefs and inscriptions all come from the tomb of Parennefer at El-Amarna (No. 7).

78.1. Outer Doorway

Only the bottom of the south jamb survives, bearing the remains of an invocation for the Ka of the pure-handed cupbearer of the king's Person, [Parennefer].

78.2. Thicknesses

On the south Parennefer stands, laden with gold collars and his arms outstretched in adoration, with the following text:

Giving adoration <to> the living [Aten] who illuminates every land by means of his beauty and who rises so that everyone might live; the king's Ka which lives on Maat, the Lord of the Two Lands, NEFERKHEPRURE-

WAENRE, given life, who makes fate and brings fortune into being—master of burial, who grants old age; master of lifetime, on the day of whose prospering one waxes. It is at seeing you that one lives and is healthy, and at awakening one [adores] your handsome face.

May he grant a good lifetime in the king's following, contentment and joyfulness every day, and the attainment of these in a good funeral by means of the favor of the Good [God]; coming [and going] from the king's house with limbs enhanced by the favor that is his to give; for the Ka of one whom the Good God favored, the king's server when he (=*the king*) was a youth, the king's cupbearer, pure-handed one [of his Person], Parennefer—may he live again! He says: "May you grant your lifetime to your beloved son, the Lord of the Two Lands [NEFERKHEPRU]RE-[WAENRE]. May you direct him in . . . jubilee; your rays, consisting of life and dominion, rejuvenating his limbs every day . . . continually in Akhet-Aten while propitiating your Ka daily. May you grant me a [good] old age [in] the favor of the king, following his Ka every day, and a good lifetime while seeing the Lord of the Two Lands in his beauty without ceasing." [For] the Ka of the king's pure-handed cupbearer, Parennefer, [justified].

On the north the royal couple, attended by servants and fanbearers and accompanied by their three eldest daughters, proceed on foot beneath the streaming sunbeams of the Aten. The remaining texts are all conventional.

78.3 East Wall

The royal family (only the king and one of the princesses remain) are enthroned within a kiosk, which is bathed in the rays of the solar disk. In front stands Parennefer, accompanied by a kneeling servant, tendering ointment to the king. Assorted courtiers and musicians are shown standing behind numerous tables laden with food and drink. Apart from the remains of standard titularies for the Aten and the king, only the speech of the assembled courtiers survives:

[Words] spoken (?): "[O Pharaoh] (?) who is established for millions of years and myriads [of jubilees (?)], O brilliant child of the Aten, may you be young for us . . . while you shine with the brilliance of the living Aten and see his beauteous rays . . . to double for you the reckoning (?) of jubilees which he has decreed for you. As for each land, it gives to you . . . , to do as you desire . . . causing to live the heart . . . [for] the only one of Re (=*Waenre*) because the Aten loves him."

78.4. West Wall

Parennefer is shown being rewarded by the king and then proceeding amid a jubilating crowd to his house. Akhenaten and Nefertiti are shown inside the royal window of appearances, while beside it stand the couple's three eldest daughters (the youngest, Ankhesenpaaten, attended by two female servants) followed by the sister of the King's Chief Wife NEFERNEFRUATEN-NEFERTITI—may she live forever continually—named Mutnodjmet. *The inscriptions of the royal family and the Aten (=early didactic name) are for the most part quite conventional, although the queen's titulary is less standard:* King's Chief Wife, his beloved, mistress of Upper and Lower Egypt, Lady of the Two Lands, *etc. A continuation of the scene, only roughed out in paint, shows Parennefer in his chariot being received at the entrance of his home by his wife. The short labels and speeches which accompany the figures are very fragmentary, and the best preserved is the legend attached to Parennefer's wife, as follows:* The housewife, favorite of the King's Chief Wife, called [. . .]—[she] says: " . . . . Give him [. . .] . . . [by favor of (?) the King's Chief Wife NEFERNEFRUATEN]-NEFERTITI—may she live forever continually."

79. The High Priest of Re Pawah

Doorpost from the House of Pawah at El-Amarna

A. [Long live (?)] . . . the Lord of the Two Lands, NEFERKHEPRURE-WAENRE, given life; and the King's Chief Wife, his beloved, Mistress of Upper and Lower Egypt, Lady of the Two Lands, NEFERNEFRUATEN-NEFERTITI, may she live forever continually.

B. ". . . the great radiance (?) which issues from your rays: may you cause me to see him in his first jubilee—(this is) my prayer which is in my heart." For the Ka of the Greatest of Seers of the Aten in the House of Re, Pawah.

C. ". . . sands of the sandbank: may you cause me to be sated with them—namely, what you have made. Seeing you daily is the prayer of my heart." For the Ka of the Greatest of Seers of the Aten in the House of Re, Pawah.

D. ". . . , their . . . in them, their Nile upon them in front of him. You are the light (=*Shu*): I live from seeing you, and I flourish at hearing your voice." For the Ka of the Greatest of Seers of the Aten in the House of Re, Pawah.

80. The Chief Physician, Pentu

The following reliefs and inscriptions come from Pentu's tomb (No. 7) at El-Amarna.

80.1. Outer Door

On the lintel (similar to that on the façade of Ahmose's tomb, 59.1 above) Pentu is shown standing at each end, arms outstretched in adoration at the divine and royal names inscribed in the center.

Left side: Giving adoration to the living Aten and kissing the ground to the Good God by the sealbearer of the King of Lower Egypt, the sole companion, the attendant of the Lord of the Two Lands, the favorite of the Good God, one whom [his] lord loves every [day], king's scribe, king's subordinate, first servant of Aten in the Mansion of the Aten in Akhet-Aten, the chief of physicians, the chamberlain, Pentu, justified.

Right side: Giving adoration to the living Aten, kissing the ground to the good king by the sealbearer of the King of Lower Egypt, one who approaches the god's flesh, chief of chiefs, acquaintance of [Waenre] (?), first companion among the companions, king's scribe, king's subordinate, first servant of Aten in the Mansion of the Aten in Akhet-Aten, the chief of physicians, the chamberlain, Pentu, justified.

Left Jamb:
A. A "boon [which the king gives" of HOR]-ATEN: may he grant [the receiving] of offering loaves . . . . For [the Ka of] the king's scribe [Pentu], justified.

B. A "boon [which the king gives"] of HOR-ATEN: may he grant entry (?) as a notable . . . , . . . the House of Aten. For [the Ka] of the [king's] subordinate, Pentu, justified.

C. A "boon which the king gives" of [HOR-ATEN]: may he [grant] dignity (?) . . . , . . . Pentu, justified.

D. A "boon which the king gives" of HOR-[ATEN]: [may he grant . . .], . . . without making cease, that his name might remain on earth. For the Ka of the chief physician Pentu, justified.

Right Jamb:
E. A "boon which the king gives" of HOR-ATEN: may he give mortuary offerings—bread, beer, oxen, fowl, cool water, wine and milk, offered . . . . [For] the Ka of the king's scribe [Pentu, justified].

F. [A "boon which the king gives" of] HOR-ATEN: may he grant the power of coming forth at the voice . . . in order to receive libation (?) . . . , ... [For] the Ka of the king's [subordinate], Pentu, [justified].

G. [A "boon which the king gives" of] HOR-[ATEN]: may he give . . . in the high ground . . . . [For] the Ka of [the . . . , Pentu, justified].

H. [A "boon which the king gives"] of HOR-ATEN: may [he] grant [. . .] as he plans (?) to listen (?) . . . . [For the Ka of the Chief of] physicians [Pentu, justified].

80.2. North Thickness

The tomb owner stands with arms outstretched in adoration of the sun outside the doorway. For the text see the duplicate in the tomb of Huya (=66.1 in this volume).

80.3. South Thickness

The tomb owner stands as above, adoring the sun: [The king's] scribe, king's [subordinate], the first servant of Aten in the Mansion of [the] Aten in Akhet-Aten, the chamberlain and chief physician, Pentu, justified. He says, in giving adoration to HOR-ATEN, given life forever continually, who comes [every] day [forever]: "Adoration to you, O Re, lord of the horizon! When you cross heaven, every face is upon you without cease, by night and day, risen in the eastern horizon and setting in the western horizon. When you set from life and joy, all eyes are wailing: they are benighted (?) after you have set[102] and become enfolded in [the sky. One eye does not see another. All snakes[103] that crawl lie down; but they are illuminated when your shining comes to pass. It is to see your beauty that they awake: when [you] appear they can see, and they become aware of themselves when you give them your rays.

May you grant that I rest in my place of continuity, that I be enclosed in the cavern of eternity; that I may go forth and enter into my tomb without my Ba's being restrained from what it wishes; that I might stride to the place of my heart's determining, in the groves which I made on earth; that I might drink water at the edge of my pool every day without cease."

80.4. North Wall, Upper Part

Akhenaten and Nefertiti, followed by the first three of their daughters, enter the forecourt of the Aten Temple, where they watch as Pentu is decorated with gold collars. The texts are mostly conventional, but the rewarding of Pentu is described as follows: Rewarding [the king's scribe], the king's subordinate, the first servant of Aten [in] the [Mansion of the Aten in Akhet-Aten, the chamberlain and chief physician Pentu, justified]. *Only the beginning of Pentu's address to the king survives:* "Many are the things which the [Aten] is able to give [at his own satisfaction]. . . ."

80.5. North Wall, Lower Part

Akhenaten and Nefertiti watch as Pentu is decorated with gold collars. The king's speech is too badly damaged for consecutive translation; but Pentu's speech is as follows: "Make healthy the pharaoh, l.p.h., your beautiful child, O Aten! Let him achieve your lifetime, let him be continual!"

80.6. South Wall, Lower Part

Akhenaten, seated inside the palace, witnesses yet another public decoration of Pentu: The king's scribe, king's subordinate, first servant of Aten in the Mansion of the Aten in [Akhet]-Aten, [chief of] physicians, Pentu. *Farther back, the crowd which escorts Pentu to his reward is described as:* People of the outer hall, all the subordinates of the House of [. . .].

81. The Court Lady Py

Shabti Figurine

May you breathe the fragrant breezes of north wind,
May you go forth into the sky on the arm of the living Aten,
  Your limbs protected,
  Your heart content,
  Without anything evil happening to your limbs,
  Being whole, without putrefrying.
May you follow Aten when he rises at dawn, until his setting from life occurs,
  (With) water for your heart,
  Bread to your belly,
  Clothing to cover your limbs.

O shabti: if you are detailed for work, if you are summoned, if you are assessed for work, "I will do it, here I am!"—so will you say. The true favorite of Waenre, she whom the king adorned, Py, may she live, may she be healthy!

82. The Housewife Qedet

On a fragment of relief now in Zurich, from the tomb of the lady's unknown husband: A "boon which the king gives" of the living Aten who illuminates every land with his beauty: may he give the fragrant breezes of the north-wind, libation(s) of wine and milk, and offerings of all sorts of vegetables for the Ka of his "sister," the housewife Qedet.

83. The Military Standard-Bearer Ramose

Inscription on a Bronze Vase found at El-Amarna

Six similar vases were found at El-Amarna in 1926-27. They are variously decorated with cartouches of the king, the queen and the Aten (using both early and late forms of the didactic name). This example bears large cartouches of HEKA-ATEN *along with the following legend:*

Made (*i.e.*, dedicated) by the standard-bearer of the company called "Aten is Caused to be Satisfied," Ramose.

84. The Commander and Steward, Ramose

A. Doorpost from the House of Ramose at El-Amarna

A. [*Adoration of the Aten . . . , who loves*] Maat, who causes unrighteousness to be an abomination: may he give a lifetime with . . . [to Ramose].

B. [Adoration of the Aten . . . , may he give . . . to the scribe of (?)] recruits, the general of the Lord of the Two Lands, Ramose, possessor of reveredness in Akhet-Aten.

B. Tomb of Ramose at El-Amarna (No. 11)

Although a fine double statue of the deceased and his wife is preserved in the shrine at the back of this tomb, the only inscriptions are on thicknesses of the entrance passage. On the left thickness is a conventional scene which shows Akhenaten and Nefertiti, accompanied by their daughter Meritaten, offering incense and ointment to the Aten. The right thickness has a kneeling figure of the tomb owner, his arms extended in adoration of the sun, as he says:

"Welcome, O One who lives on Maat, Lord of the Two Lands, NEFERKHEPRURE-WAENRE. O living sun for everybody, by whose beauty one becomes healthy, the seeing of you means rejuvenation (?) . . . when he rises. There is no poverty for the one who places you in his heart: He does not say, 'Would that I had something' but he is continually on a good path until he reaches the state of reveredness. Let me give you adoration millions of times, let me adore you when you appear! I am an official of the ruler's making: may he grant me a good funeral and interment in the desert cemetery of the favorites through the Ka of every day, namely that which the 'Only One of Re' (=*Waenre*), the light (=*Shu*) of everybody, makes. O living Aten, give him myriads of jubilees, [with enjoyment of (?)] your rays (?) on earth, being beauteous and possessing continuity just like you. [*As for any dissidents*], fear of him is in their hearts, as is that of the son who is effective for the one who fashioned [him]. [*As for this servant of yours, let him be given* (?)] food (?) as you have commanded, [*providing the* . . .]s of your Ka's giving, making (?) a poor man of . . . , [the . . . of] all people, the one who builds my [. . .]. May he let me [come to] be in . . . of his making [every day (?)]. [May he grant] me interment, and may [he] grant me . . . within Akhet-Aten. For the Ka of the king's scribe, the general of the Lord of the [Two] Lands, the steward of the House of NEBMAATRE (=*Amenhotep III*), Ramose.

85. The Chief Charioteer Ranofer

Fragments from the House of Ranofer at El-Amarna

A. From a Niche in the North Loggia

Left side:

1. . . . twice over. I am [*beloved (?) of*] the lord [of . . .]. For the Ka of the first charioteer of his Person, the master of the horse of the entire stable, Ranofer, justified.

2. . . . the lifetime of everyone whom you favor. For the Ka of the first charioteer, etc.

Right side:

1. . . . your [*lifetime* (?)] everlastingly. For the Ka of the great favorite, the first charioteer of his Person, the master of the horse of the [entire] stable, [Ranofer, justified].

2. . . . , [*king or god, who confers a benefit*] at the seeing of him. For the Ka of the great favorite, etc.

B. Posts of Door between Anteroom and Loggia

From the Left Side:

. . . everything that the Aten [encircles], King's Ka, ruler of the Nine Bows . . . which live through his Ka, my Ka of every day. May he grant . . . NEFERKHEPRURE [*sic*], the . . . of his giving . . . . For the Ka of the first charioteer of his Person, the master of the horse of the entire stable, Ranofer, justified.

From the Right Side:

Adoration of the Ka . . . . May he grant the receiving of offering-loaves [that come forth] from the presence . . . of Re in the Mansion of the Benben . . . like the . . . appears . . . . For the Ka of the first charioteer of his Person, the master of the horse of the entire stable, Ranofer, justified.

86. Rudu

The interior of this man's tomb (No. 1A at El-Amarna) was never completed. Not even the titles of the tomb owner are preserved in the only remaining inscriptions on the outer lintel, which showed the man kneeling at both ends with the following prayer: "[. . . . May he grant . . .] in the presence of the Lord of the Two Lands and a good burial which is [the king's] to give on the great mountain of Akhet-Aten, like every favorite of Waenre." For the Ka of Rudu.

87. The Standard-Bearer, Suty

The tomb of Suty at El-Amarna (No. 15) is unfinished and was not inscribed, with the exception of the jambs on the façade. While the Aten's cartouches are thoroughly destroyed, the earlier form of the didactic name was probably employed because the king is referred to as "Good God," a term that seems to be avoided late in Akhenaten's reign.

Left Jamb
A. Standard names and titles of the Aten, king and queen.

B. [A "boon which the king gives" of the living Aten] who illuminates every land with his Ka: may he grant a good funeral after old age, and repose in the [mountain] of Akhet-Aten, the place of Maat. For the Ka of the standard-bearer of the company of [NEFERKHEPRURE]-WAENRE, Suty, justified, possessor of goodly reveredness.

C. A "boon which the king gives" of the living Aten who illuminates every land with his appearance: may he grant the Ka of the Good God, repose in the presence every day, and going forth at the festival of the sixth day of the lunar month, with fate and fortune (?), and receiving what his Ka gives. For the Ka of the standard-bearer of the company of [NEFERKHEPRURE-WAENRE], Suty, justified and possessor of goodly reveredness.

D. A "boon which the king gives" of the living Aten, lord of life (?) . . . rays (?): may you grant a coming forth at dawn from the burial chamber to see Aten when he appears every day, without ceasing. For the Ka of the standard-bearer of the company of NEFERKHEPRURE-WAENRE, Suty, justified, [possessor of] goodly [reveredness].

Right Jamb:
E. Standard titles of the Aten, king and queen.

F. [A "boon which the king gives" of the living Aten . . . . May he] grant [the reception of offering loaves (?)] which issue from the presence. For the

[Ka] of the standard-bearer of the company of NEFERKHEPRURE-WAENRE, Suty, justified, possessor of goodly reveredness.

G. [A "boon which the king gives" of the living Aten], . . . , the light (=*Shu*), Lord of Ka, of great inundation, from the Ka of whose giving the land lives: may he grant the fragrant breeze of the north wind to the Ka of [the standard-beaerer] of the [company of] NEFERKHEPRURE-WAENRE, Suty, justified, possessor of goodly reveredness.

H. [A "boon which the king gives" of the living Aten], . . . , tall-plumed, brilliant of manifestations, the one who loves the Lord of the Two Lands: may <he> grant the seeing of Aten (and) his rays (?) . . . . For the Ka of the standard-bearer of [the company of] NEFERKHEPRURE-WAENRE, Suty, justified, possessor of goodly reveredness.

88. The Treasurer, Sutau

In the tomb of Sutau at El-Amarna (No. 19) only the north thickness of the outer doorway was sufficiently finished to be inscribed for its owner. Sutau is shown kneeling, his arms raised in adoration, with the following text inscribed in front of him:

"Adoration . . . to lead . . . in his . . . in its entirety (?) . . . , they (?) being . . . , . . . the great . . . two times, healthy . . . . May this [. . .] of yours be [. . .] upon Waenre, [whom you] begot (?), and . . . your [. . .], the one who is effective on behalf of his father. May you permit my eyes to rejoice (?) at seeing you . . . those things which your [son (?)] heard, namely, the King of Upper and Lower Egypt who lives on Maat, the Lord of the Two Lands, NEFERKHEPRURE-WAENRE, the Son of Re, AKHENATEN, [long in his lifetime], and the King's Chief Wife, his beloved, NEFERNEFRUATEN-NEFERTITI, may she live continually forever."

The treasurer Sutau, [he says: "O] my lord, who made me into a respected man, you are the one who brought me up by means of your Ka. I was a poor man [on the side of my father and] my [mother], but the ruler built me up, for you caused me to be in front of the [officials of] the entourage daily, possessing numerous subordinates indeed, while saying to me, 'Do [this!' And you assigned] me to be a servant, to be one of ten who reply on command, O ruler of [. . .] who fosters, as you appointed me treasurer of the Lord of the Two Lands, the servant of the one who is long in his lifetime, the agent of the king for silver and gold, fat, fine oil, gum and [. . .], which are made firm on account of the service of your favorite," the treasurer of the Lord of the Two Lands, Sutau.

89. The Chamberlain Tutu

The following reliefs and inscriptions are found in the tomb of Tutu at El-Amarna (No. 8).

89.1. Outer Doorway

Right Jamb

A. Long live the father, HOR-ATEN, *followed by conventional titularies of the king and queen.*

B. It is adoring your rays that I have come, O unique living Aten! You are continuity, and heaven is your temple, as you appear in [it] each [day] in order to give birth to your son who issued from your limbs, the King of Upper and Lower Egypt NEFERKHEPRURE-[WAENRE], . . . the living Aten! For the Ka of the chamberlain Tutu, justified.

C. With Maat-laden speech, on which you live, have I come to you, O Aten; for I have followed your son, who acted for me from his nature—(namely) Waenre, the righteous ruler, son [of] continuity, the living Aten, King of Upper and Lower Egypt, NEFERKHEPRURE-[WAENRE]; may he give . . . with your Ka in my presence continually forever. For the Ka of the chamberlain Tutu, justified.

D. It is with arms worshiping you and eyes beholding you without cease that I have come to you—for you are the life-giving (?) breeze [*that sustains the king (or similar).* May he grant] a good burial in the mountain of Akhet-Aten, the place of Maat. For the Ka of the chamberlain Tutu, justified.

E. To you have I [come], O Aten, the one who created himself (?) that you might give birth to your son . . . ; [may he grant . . .] for him like the favored ones. For the Ka of the chamberlain Tutu, justified.

Left Jamb

A. Long live the Father, HOR-ATEN, *followed by standard titularies of the king and queen.*

B. To you have I come, O living Aten, for Maat makes her abode in me: I am not rapacious, I do not do evil, [I do] nothing that your son hates . . . . May you grant the moisture and breath that are the Royal Ka's gift. For the Ka of the overseer of all which the Lord of the Two Lands has decreed, Tutu, justified.

C. To you have I come, O Aten, that I might perform a kissing of the ground to your beauteous rays as you place yourself over your son. My arms are in a gesture of "Welcome, welcome," of the beauty [of] your rays (?), [acting] as the lord of [continuity (?)] to cause the Son of Re AKHENATEN, long in his lifetime, to live. May you grant the receiving of offering loaves in the Mansion of the Benben to the Ka of the overseer of all works projects of his Person, Tutu, justified.

D. To you have I come, O Aten! I am a servant whom the Lord of the Two Lands brought up by means of [his Ka (?)]. He is the one who made me to be a [man belonging to (?)] "Living on Maat" (*i.e., Akhenaten*); and I have, from his wealth, the [. . .] like the Aten, whose sustenance is great: the Son of Re, AKHENATEN, [long in his lifetime]. May you grant your Ka to me [in] justification forever continually. For the Ka of the overseer of the gold and silver of the Lord of the Two Lands, [Tutu], justified.

E. To you I have [come], O Aten, that I may adore your beauty. As for [. . .], . . . your (?) [. . .] when he issues from you: the Son of Re AKHENATEN, [long in his lifetime]. May you grant [. . .]s seeing you daily. For the Ka of the chamberlain [Tutu], justified.

F. [To you have I come, O Aten], . . . [*that you may act for*] the Son of Re, AKHENATEN, [long in his lifetime. May you grant . . .] so long as I endure, without ceasing. For the Ka of the chamberlain [Tutu], justified.

G. [To you have I come, O Aten . . . *to benefit*] the Son of Re, AKHENATEN, [long in his lifetime. May you grant . . .] all [. . .]s forever and ever. For the Ka of the chamberlain [Tutu], justified.

Foot of Left Jamb: In front of the tomb owner, kneeling with arms raised in adoration to Akhenaten, [. . .] the beautiful king (?), as he acts in [his] rising like Aten, as he gives himself at dawn (?)—for you are satisfied with Maat. [The . . . of] Aten *belongs* (?) to you; great is [. . .], for you have issued from him, you achieve his lifetime in [peace] and [elevate (?) *his beauty* (?)]. Your [. . .] is [. . .], . . . to [his] place every day. May you (?) grant . . . when Waenre hears it. May you grant that my name be *acclaimed* (?) forever. For [the Ka of the chamberlain Tutu].

89.2. Ceiling Inscriptions in the Entrance

North: May you stand at dawn in your place of continuity in order to see Aten when he rises. May you purify yourself and put on clothing after the fashion of when you were on earth. For the Ka of the Good God's favorite, the chamberlain Tutu.

Middle: When you adore Aten, may he grant you breath and may his rays prosper your limbs. May you raise yourself up and forget weariness, and may he revive your face by the beholding of him. For the Ka of the first servant of "NEFERKHEPRURE-WAENRE in the bark,"[104] the chamberlain Tutu.

South: May you follow Aten like his favorites in the courtyard of the Mansion of the Benben. May you perform a kissing of the ground to his rays when you are in the place of Maat. For the Ka of the chamberlain Tutu.

89.3. Ceiling Inscriptions in the Hall

North: . . . , who appointed you (?) to the house (?) of life. May the Ka which your lord gave you when you acted (?) as the first servant of Aten reach you. May you be exalted . . . asking for . . . *personnel of some sort* who greet you at dawn. For the Ka [of] the beloved chamberlain of the Lord of the Two Lands, the treasurer [of] the Aten in the House of Aten in [Akhet]-Aten, Tutu.

Middle: . . . your [. . .] forever. It shall not come to pass that . . . . [For the Ka] of the chamberlain of the Lord of the Two Lands, the district overseer . . . , [Tutu].

South: . . . , your name enduring continually, without its having to be sought upon what [you have] made . . . , . . . your house in the horizon, while the [. . .] of the king is there. For the Ka of the [chamberlain] of the Lord of the Two Lands, [the . . .] in Akhet-Aten, Tutu.

89.4. Columns

Although the columns in Tutu's tomb were not all finished, a number of them were elaborately decorated. Stereotyped titularies of the Aten (using the later didactic name) were inscribed at the bases of the abaci, while the shafts bore a scene of the royal family at worship. Engaged to the two columns in the back row which flanked the entrance to the shrine were the wings of a small gateway, of which only the left wing is substantially preserved. Below a frieze of the Aten's cartouches are two registers, again showing the royal family adoring the Aten, while on the wall at the bottom is a kneeling figure of the tomb owner with upraised arms and the following text inscribed in front of him: Adoration to your Ka, O living Aten, ... May you ordain for me a good lifetime, as one whom his lord favored. For the Ka of the chamberlain of the Lord of the Two Lands, Tutu, [justified].

89.5. Architraves

Each architrave begins with standard titularies of HOR-ATEN, *the king and the queen. The continuations, however, are more distinctive.*

South: The ruler who is born like the Aten and will last continually just like him, while celebrating the millions of jubilees which the living Aten—given life forever continually—decreed for him.

North: She sees the ruler in splendor, without ceasing, for he is like the Aten, his father, firm and living continually: the Lord of the Two Lands, NEFERKHEPRURE-WAENRE, given life forever continually.

West: Adoration [to you, the] living Aten, from all you make. May they worship you inasmuch as you have made them and they live through you continually—for [*you are lord (?) of*] all you have created—the maker of all waters (?), who shines upon their limbs. May you rise for me, that I may see you and live.

89.6. North Wall Thickness

In the upper register we see the royal family offering sacrifice beneath the streaming sunbeams of the Aten (for whom the earlier didactic name is employed here). Akhenaten presents two libation vessels, while the queen is shown holding a smoke-pot for incense. The three eldest daughters (their figures now removed) stood in the upper subregister behind their parents, while below is [The sister of the King's Chief] Wife [NEFERTITI] – may she live forever continually – [Mutnodjmet]. *All the other labels attached to the figures in this scene are conventional.*

Below this, Tutu is shown kneeling in adoration, with a hymn to the sun inscribed in front of his figure. For a translation of this composition (which in this version is the most eccentric as well as the most complete of the five major copies) see 70.8 in this volume. Behind Tutu's kneeling figure is the following label: The chamberlain Tutu, justified. He says: "Listen to what your son Waenre says, O living Aten, O he who fashioned him. Cause him to be continual."

89.7. South Wall Thickness

Adoration [to] your [Ka], HOR-ATEN, given life everlastingly forever, that you may favor the king who lives on Maat, the Lord of the Two Lands NEFERKHEPRURE-WAENRE, your child, who issued from your rays; that you may establish him in your office of King of Upper and Lower Egypt, as ruler of what Aten encircles; that you may grant him continuity as often as you make yourself, your son and your image, with respect to achieving your lifetime; the Son of Re, AKHENATEN, long in his lifetime; and the King's Chief Wife, NEFERNEFRUATEN-[NEFERTITI], living forever continually.

"When you [rise] you illuminate the Two Lands and your rays are upon your beloved son, your hands bearing life and dominion. Your love is great and abundant, and you are dazzling in your noble hues when you have flooded heaven and earth with your beauty. Your son, who issued from your limbs, adores you, and for him you listen to what is in his heart and do it just as it issues from his mouth. May you love him and cause him to be like Aten when you are in heaven and your rays are upon him, who is effective [for his father] (?), the Lord of the Two Lands, NEFERKHEPRURE-WAENRE. May you give birth to his Person as you give birth to yourself every day without ceasing, for you have constructed him with your very own rays to achieve the lifetime of Aten. When you cross heaven, his eye is on your beauty while he exults in joy at beholding you, the living Aten. May you favor him while what is under heaven to its limit and all who see your rays belong to your son – [the Son of Re who lives on Maat, Lord of Crowns], AKHENATEN – inasmuch as you make them so that he might slake your heart by means of them."

"In adoration of the Aten have I come, the sole living god, master of sunbeams, who makes luminosity, rises in heaven and illuminates the Two Lands; who revives for himself all that he created by dispelling darkness and giving his rays, so that every land is filled with love of him. Grasses and trees sway before you, and the denizens of the waters leap up at your appearance. Every sentient being stands at its place with [limbs] cleansed and putting on clothing. All labor is taken up and their tasks performed. When you have awakened the Two Lands at your rising, in your form of a living sundisk (=*Aten*), their mouths are filled with the nourishment that is yours to give. All cattle [are content with their] grasses, for you dispel evil and you have given health. Everybody is up at your rising so that they may see their lord when he appears. As for your only son, who issued from your body, you embrace him with your beauteous rays, . . . the lord of heaven . . . shining in your form of living Aten. Every land is quivering at your rising, and your rays are upon the million jubilees of your son who lives on Maat, the King of Upper and Lower Egypt, NEFERKHEPRURE-WAENRE – my god, who built me and fostered me. May you grant me my eye seeing him, my arms adoring him, and my ear hearing his voice, with his Ka being in my presence without cease."

"I am a servant whom [his lord] favored. His teaching and his character are in my innermost being without [. . .]ing (?) that with which he has been charged. I shall speak truly to his Person, for I know that he lives on it."

The first servant of NEFEKHEPRURE-WAENRE in the House of Aten in Akhet-Aten, the chamberlain Tutu, he says: "O my lord, who lives on Maat, NEFERKHEPRURE-WAENRE, I am [your] servant, [who does what] you [want]. O [WAENRE], given life like the Aten, your father! May you endure just like him. I do not do what his Person hates: my abomination in my innermost being is wrongfulness, the great abomination of Waenre. Because I know he lives on them, I have elevated righteous things to his Person. You are Re, who begat Maat, for you have granted . . . . My voice is not loud in the king's house. I do not swagger in the palace. I do not receive the reward of wrongdoing in order to repress Maat falsely, but I do what is righteous to the king. I act only according to what he decrees as my charge. By means of Waenre's Ka I wax powerful; and through the rewards which he gave me I grew rich. [I do not . . .] my lord falsely by my knowledge. I do not set wrongdoing in my innermost being when I am before him in the palace, in the [company?] of the favorites – for every day he rises early to instruct me, inasmuch as I execute his teaching, and no instance of any wickedness of mine can be found, . . . the teaching of the Lord of the Two Lands. I am straightforward and true in the knowledge of the king, [and I (?)] prosper . . . my lifetime (?) in adoring his Person, for I am in his following. 'May you cause me to be fulfilled by seeing you' is my heart's prayer. May you ordain for me a [good] burial after old age in the mountain of Akhet-Aten . . . . [May] he [grant (?)] that I be allowed to breathe your sweet breeze of the north wind. May it (=*my nose*) inhale the incense of the service of NEFER-KHEPRURE-WAENRE, this god! How (?) prosperous is a king who does what his father, [the Aten], favors . . . today (?). May you cause my name to be lasting on all I have made, without the name of your favorite having to be sought, but may you make a memorial which is mentioned by name. How prosperous is he whom you favor in every position of his. . . . , [. . .] offerings (?) for the Aten in Akhet-Aten."

"All king's scribes who know their business, whose hearts are skilled in serviceable things, all who get up to promenade past this [tomb], . . . the living Aten, may you say to him: 'Make him be continual, O living Aten who begets himself. Yours is continuity, as it is for your son Waenre. May there come from his limbs fragrant breeze which is the royal Ka's to give, for the Ka of the chamberlain Tutu, [justified]."

89.8. West Wall, North Side

Akhenaten and Nefertiti, enthroned at the door of the palace and accompanied by two of their daughters, Meritaten and Ankhesenpaaten, receive Tutu in audience. Behind the chamberlain the outer courtyards and outbuildings are represented.

Speech of the King: What the King of Upper [and Lower Egypt], who lives on Maat, the Lord of the Two Lands, [NEFERKHEPRURE-WAENRE], said: "[O officials (?)] and chief men of the army who stand in the presence of Pharaoh, l.p.h., my intention is to confer an exceptional reward, equivalent (?) to a thousand [of what is ordinarily done] for people. Such a reward made for another of his officials is unheard of, but <I> do it for the chamberlain Tutu because of his love for Pharaoh, l.p.h., his lord. Now, I am laying [a charge on . . .], . . . [the custodians (?)] of copper [and] genuine [. . .], the commanders of hosts, cavalry commanders, king's scribe<s>, commanders of the army, commanders of all the troops of every foreign country [which are] detailed (?) to the houses of Pharaoh, l.p.h., every servitor of Aten belonging to the Aten in [his] temple . . . , . . . [in (?)] Upper and Lower Egypt: Pharaoh, l.p.h., his good lord, ordains that all the officials and the chief men of the entire land be obliged to give him silver, gold, [cattle], clothing and copper vessels – they being imposed upon you like taxes . . . , . . . the plan which Pharaoh, l.p.h., is making for the great servant of Pharaoh, l.p.h. No official can do it for his own distinction (?),[105] but it is found out through years of service (?) and one hears of it only today. Look: Pharaoh, l.p.h., his good lord, is causing his great officials, and likewise any official in the entire land whom Pharaoh, l.p.h., built up, to give him silver, gold, clothing, copper vessels and cattle every year."

Speech of Tutu: What the first servant [of the King of Upper and Lower Egypt, NEFERKHEPRURE-WAENRE], the chamberlain Tutu said: "O my good lord, O ruler of reputation, abounding in property, long in lifetime, great of monuments! All you decree comes to pass as for Aten the lord, the living Aten, who makes his decrees in heaven every day. You are my life: my health consists of seeing you, O one of a million high Niles, my [lord]! [How prosperous is (?)] he who places him in his heart, O catch of fowl who comes into being at every season, great of reward in silver and gold, more than he can set himself to carry on his shoulder. It is to slake your heart in the course of every day that the living Aten rises for you, O Waenre–beauteous like Aten, enduring and alive [forever] continually."

"[. . . the Aten], your dazzling father, who begat you. May he give you his rising. Those who are on earth (?), who see his rays–people, all cattle, all things that walk on their legs–they see Aten rising every [. . .]. . . . greater (?) for you than the catch (?) from the bank of the river, the number of grains (?) of sand or the hairs (?) of a feather. They belong to you, O beloved of the Aten, . . . [AKHENATEN, long in] his lifetime, while you are lasting in his office continually, O Re whom the Aten begat, NEFERKHEPRURE-WAENRE! May you raise younger generations in myriads. May you achieve . . . [*more than some other sort of beings*]: they do not take possession, they do not return in vigor (?), nor do they give birth for a million generations; but you are rejuvenated like the Aten – may you live forever continually."

In the courtyard before the palace, Tutu addresses the staff: The chamberlain Tutu, he says to the [. . .]s (?) and all the [. . .]s: "The [. . .]s [of] his Person (?), . . . your house continually. Pharaoh, l.p.h., [has ordered (?)] the commanders of hosts, masters of the horse, commanders [of the army] and [every commander of] troops (?) . . . every servant of Aten belonging to the Aten . . . , [. . .]s in the entire land, . . . all [. . .]s belonging to the House of Aten [and all] people: Pharaoh, l.p.h., your [lord, has commanded you to give] great wealth, the rewards of NEFERKHEPRURE-[WAENRE], to his servant who harkens to his goodly teaching of living thereby. The property which he gives to [me] is assessed upon [. . .] the [. . .]s . . . who does them (?) in order to honor me as a favorite more than any favorite of his."

89.9. West Wall, South Side

At a ceremony attended by court dignitaries before the royal window of appearances, Tutu is rewarded with gold collars. He is then shown leaving the palace and returning in triumph to his house.

Speech of the King: [What the King of Upper and Lower Egypt], who lives on Maat, the Lord of the Two Lands, NEFERKHEPRURE-[WAENRE said to] the chamberlain Tutu: "Look, I am appointing you to be the first servant of NEFERKHEPRURE-[WAENRE in the House of] Aten in Akhet-Aten. For love of you <I> do this, because you are my great servant who harkens to my teaching. As for every undertaking which you perform, my heart is content with it. I give you the office so that you may eat the provisions of Pharaoh, l.p.h., your lord, in the House of Aten."

Speech of Tutu: [What] the chamberlain Tutu [said]: "O ruler who makes monuments for [his father] – and he repeats it – may you foster generations from generations . . . . [O] Waenre, [you] are Re. It is the living Aten who begat you, and you will achieve his lengthy lifetime, while he rises in heaven to give birth to you, O my lord, wise like the father – perceptive, precise, searcher of hearts. Your [hands (?)] are like the rays of Aten, so that you can build people according to their various characters. O my lord, may the Aten give you the many jubilees which he decreed for you. You are his child: it is from him that you issued. O Waenre, image of Re continually, who raises up Re and satisfies Aten, who causes the land to understand the one who makes it, may you illuminate his name for the subjects and administer for him the dues owed to his rays. May he acclaim you in heaven joyfully on the day in which you appear. The entire land quivers for you–Kharu, Kush, all lands, their arms being extended to you in adoration to your Ka as they beg for life in wretchedness, and they <say> 'Give us breath!' Terror of you stops up their noses and their prosperity comes to an end. Your divine power is in them as a repellant, after your war cry has annihilated their limbs like the fire which devours them. The rays of the Aten will rise over you continually, and the one who makes your monuments to be like the fixity of heaven is manifest in them forever. So long as the Aten exists, you shall be alive and rejuvenated continually."

Speech of the Foreigners: The servants belonging to every foreign country, they say: "O living Re, NEFEKHEPRURE-WAENRE, <we> are under [your commands (?)] continually forever."

By the Soldiers: The standard-bearers who are in the following of the Personage, the lovely-faced one, at the seeing of whom one lives, NEFERKHEPRURE-WAENRE.

Speech of the Officers: The officials and chief men of the army who are standing in the presence of Pharaoh, l.p.h. What they say: "The ruler is bright on the Aten's behalf and abounding in property, and consequently One (=*Pharaoh*) makes men."

Speech of the Scribes: The scribes of . . . , [they] say: "May you (*plural*) say, 'Make NEFERKHEPRURE-[WAENRE] healthy, O Aten . . . [who makes] people and raises up generations.'"

Speech of the Vizier and Other High Officials: Words spoken by the officials and companions: "How good they are, your plans, O NEFERKHEPRURE-WAENRE! How prosperous is he who is in your following (?), O beautiful child of the Aten! You shall raise up generations and you shall be continual like the Aten!"

Speech of Tutu's Waiting Charioteer: Words spoken by the <cha>rioteer: " . . . beauteous like the Aten, the one who begat him, [NEFERKHEPRURE]-WAENRE, the one who builds people and raises the younger generations while he is lasting like heaven when Aten is in it."

Tutu's Address to His Subordinates: Adoration [of] the King of Upper and Lower Egypt, NEFERKHEPRURE-WAENRE, by the chamberlain Tutu, having been appointed (?) to be First Servant of NEFERKHEPRURE-WAENRE in the palace (?) and in the House of Aten in Akhet-Aten. Said by the chamberlain Tutu to his chief administrators: "Behold how good are the things which Pharaoh, l.p.h., my lord, has done for me, while I was [. . .] with regard to what was good and exact (?) – one who said what was righteous and did not botch any business of my lord on which I was sent. I shall continue to act according to what issues from his mouth."

The Subordinates Reply: "As for the ruler, who makes monuments for his father – and he repeats doing it–may [he] (=*Aten*) make healthy NEFER-KHEPRURE-WAENRE. O Aten, give him a million jubilees: your child, <whose> character is like your character. May you grant that he achieve your lifetime."

Speech of Tutu in his chariot, as he is driven to the temple: The chief Servitor of NEFERKHEPRURE-[WAENRE in the House of Aten in] Akhet-Aten, the chamberlain Tutu says: "O ruler who makes monuments for [his] father – and <he> repeats it – say . . . the Aten . . . is . . . in the temple (?) [which you made] to be [the House of] Aten. . . daily (?), O [Aten]!"

89.10. West Wall: Inscription on Lower Part of North Side

The chamberlain Tutu, he says: "O you leaders of everybody, scribes [who know] their business, and chief lay priests of the House of Aten; you who are serviceable to Aten, excellent (?) officials, and king's acquaintances whose hearts are experienced in life; all who wish to attain old age, interment and a goodly funeral when one is sated with living: hear, you who enter my tomb and behold the great things that were done for me! I was the servitor of Waenre, the ruler who lives on Maat. When I followed him, he rose early to reward me because I did what issued from his mouth. I made no concealment with respect to any case of wrongdoing in any business [of] his Person when I was chief spokesman of the entire land – in expeditions, works projects, crafts, and everything which living persons do; and similarly the affairs (?) of the [army] commanders (?) and the commissions to all foreign countries. I was the one who reported their words to the palace, while I was in [the presence (?)] every day. I went out to them on the king's business, bearing every instruction of [his] Person. [I administered] works projects in his monuments while I was the chief one in the office of chamberlain, being pure on behalf of Waenre [daily in the course of every day (?)]."

89.11. West Wall, Lower Part of South Side

[O Aten], ... , . . . when [he] rises [for] the child of the Aten; living Re, great of love, at whose decree the land lives. When you open your eyes, the land is rich in the property which you proclaim, for you are the mother who begets everyone, one who nourishes millions by means of your Ka. Your awesomeness is a rampart of copper millions of cubits long, for you have enclosed the lands by means of your strength to the very limit of Aten's rays.

O King of Upper [and Lower Egypt], NEFERKHEPRURE-[WAENRE]; O beloved ruler whose prodigies are great, perfect in your beauty, the colors of your limbs being like the rays of your father when he is rising, namely, the living Aten who illuminates what [he has] created: [your nature] is like his nature. [He has] come forth in order that he might [. . .] you as a [. . . of] his limbs, inasmuch as he is beauteous in his flesh. . . . So long as he exists you shall exist continually. As for the Aten, you are his beloved son, for you are just like him. Acclamations belong to you as far as heaven. . . . . lifetime. May he cause you to exist continually, and may eternity belong to you. May you celebrate jubilees, and may the Aten continue to beget you each time he appears, when he rises in heaven to illuminate [the Two Lands] for you. . . . [Kharu (?)] together with Kush are led in to you, bowing, at Akhet-Aten. Southerners as well as northerners kiss the ground to you, and they adore [. . .] . . . . for Pre, lord of fate who makes lifetime, begot you.

O NEFERKHEPRURE-[WAENRE], heaven contains living Aten and the breezes in it. You give them to the nostril(s) of your favorites. . . . [the offering table of the (?)] Aten, having on it cattle and all manner of fowl. There is no end [to the . . . which] is in it. Its plots of land (?) are filled with things abounding in life, being cut off from any reduction, ... [. . .] is seen in them. Aten, when he rises in [heaven, . . .] at your decree. All those you favor see him there rising, while every destructive one is destined to the slaughtering place of . . . , [. . .] since Pre is a nature excellent for everybody.

O [NEFERKHEPRURE-WAENRE], . . . [. . .]s, you construct him so that he travels upon the way (?) with a heart released (?) . . . like (?) [. . .]s.[106] The sixfold torch (?) is measured by the rod-standard; the limbs are clothed in fine fabric, being powerful (?) by means of your Ka. The house is filled [with what] they [. . .], so that he calls to one in a thousand. (As for) the risen one (?), he travels in the bark which is <on> the lake of Maat (?) with a crew equipped with mourners (?) and defenders (?), possessing the decree of the ruler who constructed [his children], the Son of Re AKHENATEN, long in his lifetime, and the King's Chief Wife, his beloved, [NEFERNEFRUATEN-NEFERTITI], may she live forever continually.

The chamberlain Tutu, he says: "Let me relate all . . . , those things which you placed [in] my heart and which you [set] in my innermost being. Let me cause my . . . all [. . .]s . . . . How beneficial is the teaching of Waenre which he has commissioned me to fulfill! As for [. . .], . . . the Aten who begat him. . . . He hearkens to Maat more than to a heap of possessions, more than to quantities of . . . . I hear . . . [. . .]s [in] the eastern horizon [of heaven], . . . millions, the Re who lives on Maat, NEFERKHEPRURE-[WAENRE]."

"All of you who follow him, may you hearken to his teaching—namely, that of the only one of [Re, who practices (?)] Maat, the lord [of (?) . . .] himse[lf (?), who makes to tremble (?) [. . .]. [As for the opponent of] this [god] (?), he descends to the slaughter and fire devours [his] limbs, while the Aten rises [so that] you may see . . . , [. . .] is caused (?) . . . , . . . that which pertains to the body of everybody. Your eyes are raised up [in order to] see the circuit of Aten when he rises [on the] highland [of Akhet]-Aten. The [. . .]s in them say, . . . , they belong [to] us. Silence is kept and the land is distant, but the ruler judges him, [. . .] beholds the rays of Aten. [As for someone about whom one (?)] hears a report . . . while [it] is in the mouth(s) (?) of other [. . .]s so that he sets it here (?), [. . .] the river (?), and he becomes an enemy among you and hides in . . . in order to go . . . while consorting with (?) . . . , . . . property while our names endure on them through the decree of the beauteous ruler . . . , . . . life (?) . . . the mountain at the place [which he] says. As for Kharu [and Kush (?)] . . . , a single offering is established . . . to reach him. As for those who bear witness to him, . . . [on (?)] you to be (?) his genuine (?) . . . Aten like . . . , while [he] is continual, namely, NEFERKHEPRURE-WAENRE."

[The chamberlain] Tutu, he says: "O my lord, only one of Aten, who elevates his name, his son, . . . , . . . [his] Person . . . , . . . [his] Person (?) [to] breathe the breath of life; the one who beholds him daily, the only one of Re (=*Waenre*), my [. . . of] every day: may you [extol (?)] my name and my [reputation (?)] for a lifetime in . . . the king: he is the one who instructed me! Behold, I am telling you: it is good to hearken. As for the ruler, he is the light [of everybody]. [*As for*] . . . , [he shall] have (?) the funeral, the prosperity, the contentment: behold, it all belongs to the ruler. May he give to [you the favor of his] father, [great] living Aten. He is the one who satisfies (?) him for . . . his . . . on the day (?) . . . Aten when he rises to exercise his divine power against the one who knows not his teaching. His favor is for the one who knows him, to the extent that you hearken to the king, to your lord who answers (?) . . . with the rays of the [Aten], the august one (?), the ruler, as he appears. When the Nile comes forth, it waters the Two Lands. The apportioners of festivals . . . birds (?) alone (?). [. . .]s are made (?), . . . upon them while [*benefitting* (?)] me with his property, while they are in joy, but everything displeasing, . . . that he may . . . [his] father, [the] Aten."

90. Varia and Anonymous

90-A. Votive Stela of Two Asiatics

The owners are shown seated, consuming an unidentified substance through a tube or pipe. Only the names are inscribed: the man is Teru-Re, *while the woman is* The housewife Iirburaa.

90-B. Part of a Box Belonging to a Viceroy of Nubia

. . . Horakhty who rejoices in the horizon, as he gives l.p.h., contentment of mind and body in the mansions of youthfulness (?), for the Ka of the hereditary prince and count, the sealbearer of the King of Lower Egypt, the sole companion, the King's Son of Kush, overseer of the southern foreign countries . . . .

90-C. Tomb Nr. 18 at El-Amarna

Only the façade was completed, and what little remains (the left jamb of the outer door) is so poorly preserved that even the name of the tomb owner is lost.

1. Early Titulary of the Aten.

2. "Adoration to your Ka, O living Aten, consisting of what your son, who issued from your body, says to you – (namely) your child, who knows you, who elevates you . . . ."

3. "Adoration to your Ka, O ruler, true continually like Aten, firm, living, who leads (?) generations, whom the living Aten fashioned. . . ."

4. "Adoration to your Ka, O King's Chief Wife of the Only One of Re (=*Waenre*), she whose double plumes are high, she who is dazzling of qualities and sweet of voice in the palace . . . ."

90-D. Heart Scarab

This piece, evidently manufactured in antiquity for sale on the open market, must have remained unused, for its text never included the name of an owner: A "boon which the king gives" of the living Aten, the one who illuminates every land with his beauty: may he give a lengthy lifetime as one whom his Ka favors, and a great (?) and good funeral of the Aten's giving. May he give bread, beer, oxen and fowl, a thousand jars of incense and oil, <every>thing good and pure for the Ka <of> *(blank)*.

90-E. Fragment from El-Amarna

A limestone weight found near the entrance of the Great Temple is inscribed for . . . , the overseer of the front hall, overseer of the courtyard (?) of Aten in the House of Rejoicing of the Aten, User.

Notes

1. Both here and in the other offering formula assigned to Ay's wife (*L*) the pronouns are masculine.

2. The determinative indicates that the queen is meant.

3. Literally, "their."

4. These two names mean "The King's Wife shall exist forever" and "His mother is Pre."

5. Or perhaps "offerings."

6. Literally, "mansion."

7. Although scholarly opinion is divided on this issue, there is no doubt in this translator's mind that the hymn which follows is uttered by the king. In any case, Ay's titulary should not be inserted into the text at this point (as do many translators, following Davies): although the tomb owner's titles are inscribed directly below the hymn's first column, the hieroglyphs used in this label are much smaller than those used for the hymn above, and they are also arranged within their own separate margin lines.

8. Literally, "heart."

9. Alternatively, "just as you make them. You are lord of them all," etc.

10. At the very least this alludes to the god's benevolence in taking trouble over humanity; but it may also have been meant to evoke associations with Osiris, the "weary one" par excellence, who controls the rising of the Nile in the orthodox religion but whose functions were usurped by Akhenaten's god.

11. The text, which makes no sense here, probably should be emended thus to match the following sentence.

12. Literally, "taste."

13. These objects, shown between the two boys, must be part of Ay's reward: presumably they have been laid down in the street by a porter (the fourth boy?) before being carried into the house.

14. Or "to the one who fostered his name."

15. The addressee, initially the god, now becomes the tomb owner.

16. The tomb owner now speaks.

17. I.e., all the preceding promises. The boundary between the collective singular and plural in Egyptian is fluid.

18. As on the west side, the address changes abruptly from the god to the tomb owner.

19. Here and at the end of the text on the right the version in Pentu's tomb is as follows: "king's scribe under the authority of the king, first servant of Aten in the mansion of the Aten in Akhet-Aten, the chief physician and chamberlain, Pentu, justified."

20. See L. Habachi *MDAIK* (1965): 90 (with fig. 12); but perhaps "chief porter"?

21. The praenomen is used a second time to avoid having to mention "Amun" in Amenhotep III's nomen.

22. The name of one of the two quartzite "colossi of Memnon" in front of Amenhotep III's mortuary temple in West Thebes.

23. I.e., his wife. The tall vertical sign which is the main component of this word was misread by the original sculptor, who substituted another that makes no sense as it stands.

24. With restorations from the parallel inscription in the tomb of Pentu (80 below).

25. Pentu has "Adoration [to you], HOR-[ATEN]."

26. This phrase, which is used in the boundary stelae to describe the king's progress into the central city to offer sacrifice (see above, 36, 37), refers here to the sun's progress in his daily course across the sky.

27. This refers obliquely to the ritual invocation which the deceased desires from posterity.

28. This phrase is omitted in Pentu's version, which begins abruptly with the tomb owner's titles: "king's scribe, chamberlain, first servant of Aten in the Mansion of the Aten in Akhet-Aten, the chief of physicians, Pentu, justified. He says [*sic*]."

29. Throughout Huya's tomb this word is spelled phonetically, thus avoiding the normal spelling with the vulture hieroglyph that might be associated with the goddess Mut.

30. Changed from "the ruler belonging to Aten." The final version might also be read as "the ruler, the one belonging to Aten"—but the genitive which is common to both versions may have been carved by mistake.

31. Or emend to "House of Life"?

32. Ceiling B has: ". . . all which comes forth in the [presence] of Waenre, the one beloved like the Aten . . . , all [*foodstuffs*]," etc.

33. Thus, the version in the shrine. Ceiling A has: "For the Ka of the overseer of the royal harem, the overseer of the double treasury and steward of the King's Chief Wife, Huya, justified." Ceiling B is similar, but with the variant "steward in the house of the King's Mother, the King's Chief Wife TIYI, Huya, justified in peace."

34. Although the god's cartouches are thoroughly erased, the earlier form of the didactic name was probably used here (based on references to the Aten as a "god," which seems to be avoided later in Akhenaten's reign (Perepelkin 1978: 143–49).

35. The final version is cut into a thick layer of plaster over an earlier version, which was "who did what [His Person] instructed" here.

36. Here too the final version is cut into a layer of plaster. The underlying version has "as (?) a works project" here.

37. The original version here was "a boon-which-the-king-gives."

38. The text is garbled here: it is unclear whether the signs in the hand copy belong to the original or later version.

39. The tomb owner is now being addressed.

40. The text has, erroneously, "daughter."

41. Preceding this clause the sculptor carved "may he give" in error.

42. "You" is feminine, as if spoken to the queen (if it was not carved thus in error.

43. This text, located between the vizier and Mahu, is oriented as if it is spoken by the latter.

44. See O'Connor 1987-8.

45. Or "King's bodily daughter of the king's wife."

46. Meryre addresses his speech directly to the Aten on behalf of the king.

47. As Sandman points out, these titles should precede the praenomen, but the epithet generally follows the nomen: most probably the original text was compressed here for lack of space.

48. On both jambs the opening formula was recut from "a 'boon which the king gives' of" (the Aten), etc.

49. On both jambs the name "Meryre" has been inscribed over that of another individual, one "Hatiay."

50. Does a pun lurk in the choice of words and spellings in this last clause? Instead of the full spelling, only a single hieroglyph, the adze, was used for the word "period"—perhaps an allusion to one of the ceremonial adzes used in the "opening of the mouth" ritual in the orthodox religion? If so, the subtext of this passage would have the tomb-owner receiving the benefit of this rite through the king's ritual baton, which is the principal sign in the word "governance."

51. Earlier tombs, such as Ahmose's (see 59 above), have "HOR-ATEN."

52. Ahmose version: "all people."

53. Omitted in Ahmose and Huya versions.

54. Or possibly "strength of heart" instead of "joy," as in the tomb of Ahmose (cf. 59.2 above). The version in Meryre I's tomb differs from the other two, for it substitutes "give him eternity as king of the Two Lands" and concludes at this point.

55. Thus Ahmose; the Huya version has "of the Lord of the Two Lands" and ends.

56. For the personal epigraphs of the other two versions, see 59.4 and 66.2 above.

57. For the other personal introductions, see the other tombs.

58. Thus in all versions except for those of Apy and Tutu, where the earlier didactic name of the Aten is used.

59. Tutu substitutes for this clause, "O [my] (divine and royal) father, O living Aten who ordains life."

60. Apy and Meryre I substitute "bright" here.

61. Thus Any and Meryre I. Apy and Mahu substitute, "Your rays are pervasive (?) for everyone." The version in Tutu's tomb is damaged but clearly differs from the rest: "[they] being your bright hue."

62. Tutu probably had "the love [of you fills all lands with] your [life]" (?).

63. Meryre I substitutes "good ruler."

64. Thus Meryre I and Any; the others have "herds and all sorts of short-horned cattle."

65. Tutu substitutes: "They [live] (as) your rays shine for them."

66. All four versions in Mahu's tomb end here, and they diverge both from copies in other tombs and one another. For the variants that are abbreviations and corruptions of the main text, see the notes in Sandman's edition. All four copies in this tomb end with: "For the Ka of the chief of the Medjay of (or in) Akhet-Aten, Mahu, justified (or may he live again)."

67. Tutu's version diverges here ("when your rays have illuminated your [. . .]") and omits the following two and a half clauses.

68. Any has "the entire land is in joy and rejoicing at seeing you," etc.

69. Tutu adds "and provisioned when you illuminate it."

70. Meryre I substitutes "every sunshade."

71. Thus Apy and Tutu; Any and Meryre I substitute "(and) every place in which you are content."

72. Meryre I omits the preceding clause; and Tutu omits "august."

73. Thus Tutu; Meryre omits this clause and the last; Apy and Any have "who is content in the sky."

74. Tutu again omits "august" and substitutes "who issued from his body" for "Waenre."

75. Meryre ends here with "without ceasing forever."

76. In Egyptian, *akh enek*, a pun on the royal name Akhenaten.

77. Any: "firm."

78. Tutu: "Breath enters into noses when you give yourself to them."

79. Any's text ends here.

80. Apy's text ends; Tutu's version continues almost to the end.

81. Panehsy A has "Adoration to your Ka" and omits the epithets before the king's praenomen.

82. Panehsy A adds "your place of eternity."

83. Panehsy A: "For the Ka of the great favorite of the Lord of the Two Lands, the first servant [of] Aten in Akhet-Aten, Panehsy."

84. Panehsy G: "Adoration to your Ka, (O) NEFERKHEPRURE-WAENRE, given life."

85. Panehsy G: "For the Ka of the great favorite of Waenre, the first servant [of the Aten in Akhet-Aten, Panehsy], justified."

86. Panehsy B: "Adoration to your Ka, (O) AKHENATEN, long in his lifetime."

87. Panehsy B: "For the Ka of one whom his Lord favored, the servant of the Lord [of the Two Lands], NEFERKHEPRURE-[WAENRE] in the House of Aten, Panehsy, justified."

88. Panehsy D: "Adoration to your (=*feminine*) Ka, (O) NEFERNEFRUATEN-NEFERTITI, living forever continually. May she grant" etc.

89. Panehsy D: "in the Mansion of the Benben."

90. Panehsy D: "For the Ka of the favorite of his lord, the servant of the Lord of the Two Lands, NEFERKHEPRURE-[WAENRE] in the House of Aten, Panehsy."

91. Panehsy E: "Adoration to your Ka, O NEFERKHEPRURE-[WAENRE], given life."

92. Panehsy E adds "daily in the course of every day."

93. Panehsy E: "For the Ka of the great favorite of the good ruler, the [first] servant of Aten [in] Akhet-Aten, [Panehsy, justified]."

94. Panehsy F: "Adoration to your Ka, O AKHENATEN."

95. Panehsy F: ". . . forever. For the Ka of the favorite . . . [Panehsy], justified."

96. Panehsy C: "Adoration to your Ka, O NEFERKHEPRURE-[WAENRE], given life."

97. Panehsy C: "For the Ka of the great favorite of the good ruler, the first servant of Aten in Akhet-Aten, Panehsy, justified."

98. Panehsy H: "Adoration to your (=*feminine*) Ka, O NEFERNEFRUATEN-

NEFERTITI, may she live forever continually. May she grant a good remembrance in the presence of the king and his favor in every season; and that the children" etc.

99. Panehsy H: "For the Ka [of] the favorite [of his] lord, [the servant of] the Lord of the Two Lands, NEFERKHEPRURE-WAENRE, in the House of Aten, Penehsy, justified."

100. Written with neither a cartouche nor honorific transposition of the term "Aten", thus understood not only as a name but an epithet of the king, "one effective on Aten's behalf" or "the luminous manifestation of Aten."

101. Or "when I was found to be (a mere)" etc.

102. Or "all eyes are wailing in their night; and after you have set" etc.

103. Literally, "every snake," a collective which is referred to by a plural pronoun.

104. Apparently referring to Tutu's role in a traditional cult of the king's statue, which appeared in public within a bark-shaped shrine borne on the shoulders of the cult's priests.

105. Or, emending the order of the signs, "for his fellow."

106. This badly broken section seems to deal with the king's provisions for the Aten's cult.

5

In the Aftermath of the Heresy

I. King Nefernefruaten

91. Private Stela Showing Two Kings Seated Together

This private cult stela, while not unusual for the intimacy shown in the scene it bears, is nonetheless odd because its protagonists appear to be two kings. The solar globe beams its rays down on two seated figures, their feet resting on cushioned footstools, before a table laden with offerings. The figure in front, who wears the Double Crown, has turned to face the figure behind him (shown wearing the Blue Crown) whose chin he caresses. The essential clue to identifying these figures as Akhenaten and Nefertiti lies in the presence of only three cartouches for the names of this couple – an anomaly difficult to explain for two male coregents, but entirely natural for a king and queen.[1] *The royal name-rings, along with the margin lines and cartouches for the Aten, were carved but never filled: perhaps the piece was needed too quickly to receive its final finish, or it might have been bought uncompleted by the owner, who only had the following notice of ownership scratched on the horizontal line below the scene:* Made (*i.e.*, dedicated) by the soldier of the ship "Appearing in Maat", Pa-se.

92. Box Found in the Tomb of Tutankhamun

On the two knobs are the names of MERETATEN *and* ANKHKHEPRURE BELOVED OF NEFERKHEPRURE, *while on the strip of wood between the knobs is the following:*

King of Upper and Lower Egypt who lives on Maat, Lord of the Two Lands, NEFERKHEPRURE-WAENRE; Son of Re, Lord of Crowns, AKHENATEN, long in his lifetime.

King of Upper and Lower Egypt, Lord of the Two Lands, ANKHKHEPRURE BELOVED OF NEFERKHEPERRE [*sic*]; Son of Re, Lord of Crowns, NEFERNEFRUATEN BELOVED OF WAENRE.

King's Chief Wife MERETATEN, may she live forever.

93. Miscellaneous Records from El-Amarna

93-A. Fragmentary Stela from El-Amarna ("Coregency Stela")

Fragments of this monument are preserved in the Cairo Museum and the Petrie Museum of University College London. While the stela is carved on both sides, variations in the workmanship could suggest that each surface was used separately at different times. The "reverse," and perhaps the earlier of the two sides, shows a kneeling official, his arms raised in adoration, at the lower left-hand corner. The focus of this man's worship is not preserved, but a text is inscribed in columns above and in front of him:[2] . . . of mine (?). Then did . . . , . . . to enter and depart from [the necropolis] . . . to live because of (my) hearing under you, . . . the great [. . .] of the Lord of the Two Lands: the doorkeeper (?) [of the] House [of Rejoicing] of the Aten [in Akhet-Aten], ...

On the other side, probably carved later than the first, is a scene which, based on a careful examination of the original,[3] *showed Akhenaten seated on the left, followed by a standing figure and faced by a pair of figures, all beneath the solar globe in the center. It is also apparent that the piece (which was recut in antiquity) bore on the upper right-hand side the names of three individuals at each stage. In its original version it named Akhenaten, Queen Nefertiti and their eldest daughter, Meritaten. The latter two were suppressed in the final version and the names of King Nefernefruaten and (apparently) Princess Ankhesenpaaten carved instead.*[4] *The god's cartouches are missing, but his surviving epithets are characteristic for the Aten's later titulary.*

Original Text:

Lord of the Two Lands, NEFERKHEPRURE-WAENRE; Lord of Crowns, AKHENATEN, given life, long in his lifetime.

Great King's [Wife] NEFERNEFRUATEN-NEFERTITI, may she live forever continually, [born to the King's Chief Wife NEFERNEFRUATEN-NEFERTITI, may she live forever continually].

King's bodily daughter, his beloved, MERETATEN, may she live forever.

Final Version:

Lord of the Two Lands, NEFERKHEPRURE-WAENRE; Lord of Crowns, AKHENATEN, given life, long in his lifetime.

Lord who Performs the Ritual, ANKHKHEPRURE BELOVED-OF-

WAENRE; Unique Lord, NEFERNEFRUATEN BELOVED-OF-AKHENATEN, given life forever continually.

[King's bodily daughter, his beloved], Ankhes[enpaaten].

93-B. Supply Jar from Akhenaten's Last Year, Re-used by One of His Successors

A record of Akhenaten's last year, Regnal year 17, honey . . . , *was erased and the jar re-inscribed for* Regnal year 1, wine . . . *under one of Akhenaten's successors–either Nefernefruaten, Smenkhkare or Tutankhaten.*

93-C. Variant Names of King Nefernefruaten

While it has been generally assumed that Tutankhamun was preceded on the throne by a single king who changed his name during the course of his reign, it now seems likelier that two rulers are involved. The earlier is most probably to be identified with Akhenaten's queen: not only is this individual's personal name identical with the longer variant of Nefertiti's name (Nefernefruaten), but the throne-name is occasionally written with a feminine ending (Ankhetkheprure, in place of the usual Ankhkheprure). Both names, moreover, are marked by a number of epithets which set them off, both from Nefertiti as queen and from her successor, Smenkhkare (who also took the throne-name Ankhkheprure). A selection of the names associated with King Nefernefruaten on small objects is given below:

Praenomen	*Nomen*
ANKHETKHEPRURE BELOVED (fem.) OF WAENRE	NEFERNEFRUATEN BELOVED OF NEFERKHEPRURE-WAENRE
ANKHKHEPRURE BELOVED (fem.) OF NEFERKHEPRURE	NEFERNEFRUATEN THE RULER
ANKHKHEPRURE BELOVED OF NEFERKHEPRURE-WAENRE	NEFERNEFRUATEN BELOVED OF AKHENATEN
ANKHKHEPRURE BELOVED OF ATEN	NEFERNEFRUATEN BELOVED OF WAENRE
ANKHKHEPRURE	

94. Graffito from the Tomb of Pere

This graffito, written in ink on the walls of a private tomb at Thebes, is ostensibly a humble artisan's petition in behalf of a sick relative. Beneath this apparent meaning, however, may lurk a more "political" appeal–for Amun to return to public visi-

bility after his banishment during Akhenaten's reign. In any case, the terms in which this petition is couched reflect the regime's efforts to build bridges between the royal establishment and the orthodox cults which Akhenaten had suppressed. This persecution had been replaced by a policy of renewed state patronage by the time this document was composed, but the capital at El-Amarna still functioned, and conciliation apparently stopped short of repudiating the heretic and his works.

Regnal year 3, third month of Inundation, day 10. The King of Upper and Lower Egypt, Lord of the Two Lands ANKHKHEPRURE BELOVED OF ATEN (?), the Son of Re NEFERNEFRUATEN BELOVED OF WAENRE (?).

Giving worship to AMUN, kissing the ground to WENENNEFER by the lay priest, scribe of the divine offerings of AMUN in the Mansion of ANKHKHEPRURE in Thebes, Pawah, born to Yotefseneb. He says:

"My wish is to see you, (O) lord of persea trees! May your throat take the north wind, that you may give satiety without eating and drunkenness without drinking. My wish is to look at you, that my heart might rejoice, (O) AMUN, protector of the poor man: you are the father of the one who has no mother and the husband of the widow. Pleasant is the utterance of your name: it is like the taste of life; it is like the taste of bread to a child, a loincloth to the naked, like the taste of . . . -plant in the hot season. You are like . . . with one who bears . . . when his father was . . . . You are like the taste of [favor from the] RULER, the breeze to [him] who was in prison, peace [to the troubled man (?) who] invokes a possessor of (good) character when he has returned."

"Come back to us, O lord of continuity. You were here before anything had come into being, and you will be here when they are gone. As you have caused me to see the darkness that is yours to give, make light for me so that I can see you. As your Ka endures and as your handsome, beloved face endures, you shall come from afar and cause this servant, the scribe Pawah, to see you. Grant him the condition of 'Re awaits him!', for indeed, the following of you is good."

"O AMUN, O great lord who can be found by seeking him, may you drive off fear! Set rejoicing in people's heart(s). Joyful is the one who sees you, O AMUN: he is in festival every day!"

For the Ka of the lay priest and scribe of the temple of AMUN in the Mansion of ANKHKHEPRURE, Pawah, born to Yotefseneb: "For your Ka! Spend a nice day amongst your townsmen." His brother, the outline draftsman Batchay [of] the Mansion [of] ANKHKHEPRURE.

II. King Smenkhkare

This ruler's throne-name, Ankhkheprure, resembles his predecessor's so closely that they were once believed to be identical. Missing, however, is the variety of epithets which mark his predecessor's praenomen (see 93.C), not only in the documents translated below but in the small objects from this reign which were found at El-Amarna. Moreover, the same regularity is also seen with the distinctive personal name ("Smenkhkare Holy-of-Manifestations") attached to this figure.

95. Miscellaneous Records from El-Amarna

95-A. Tomb of Meryre II, North Wall, East Side

In a scene that was only roughed out in paint, the tomb owner is shown before Akhenaten's son-in-law, King Smenkhkare, and his consort, Meretaten. Since the cartouches bearing the names of the royal couple had been removed by thieves before Davies copied the tombs at El-Amarna, they are restored on the basis of the earlier nineteenth-century copy.[5]

King: King of Upper and Lower Egypt, ANKHKHEPRURE, Son of Re, SMENKHKARE, HOLY-OF-MANIFESTATIONS, given life forever continually.

Queen: King's Chief Wife, MER<ET>ATEN, may she live forever continually.

The Aten: HEKA-ATEN, given life forever continually; great living Aten, lord of jubilees, lord of everything Aten encircles, lord of heaven and earth in the House of Aten in Akhet-Aten.

95-B. Dated Docket on a Wine Jar

Regnal year 1. Wine of the House of SMENKHKARE HOLY-OF-MANIFESTATIONS [of] the western river. The chief of the basin (=master vintner) Sakaia.

96. Miscellaneous Inscriptions from Thebes

96-A. Inscription in the names of Akhenaten and Smenkhkare

A calcite jar found in the tomb of Tutankhamun in the Valley of the Kings had its inscribed decoration expunged before it was deposited among the dead king's burial goods. The inscription has been reconstructed, on the basis of the extant traces, as two pairs of royal cartouches:

King of Upper and Lower Egypt, NEFERKHEPRURE-WAENRE, given life; the Son of Re, AKHENATEN, long in his lifetime.

King of Upper and Lower Egypt, ANKHKHEPRURE; the Son of Re, SMENKHKARE HOLY-OF-MANIFESTATIONS, given life like Re.

96-B. Gilded Wooden Coffin found in Tomb 55 in the Valley of the Kings

The coffin that contained the remains of the man who was this tomb's final occupant originally belonged to Akhenaten's "other wife," Kiya. When the coffin was adapted for its secondary owner, the sections of gold foil inscribed with Kiya's name and titles were cut out and patches of newly inscribed foil were inserted in their place: the contents of these added elements, wherever preserved, are underlined in the translation that follows. All the names inside the cartouches (both primary and secondary versions) were destroyed before the coffin and its attendant burial goods were deposited in Tomb 55. Although the original text undoubtedly referred to Akhenaten as Kiya's husband, it is still debated whether the usurpation was done on behalf of Akhenaten himself or an ephemeral successor.

Vertical inscriptions:[6]

(A) The good ruler, image of Re,[7] King of Upper and Lower Egypt who lives on Maat, Lord of the Two Lands, [NEFERKHEPRURE-WAENRE], the beautiful child of the living Aten who shall be truly alive continually forever in heaven and on earth.

(B) The good ruler . . . , King of Upper and Lower Egypt who lives on Maat, Lord of the Two Lands, [NEFERKHEPRURE-WAENRE], the beautiful child of the living Aten who shall be alive continually forever, . . . [AKHENATEN], long in his lifetime.

(C) The good ruler who appears in the White Crown, King of Upper and Lower Egypt who lives on Maat, Lord of the Two Lands, [NEFERKHEPRURE-WAENRE], the beautiful child of the living Aten who shall be alive continually forever, Son of Re who lives on Maat, Lord of Crowns, [AKHENATEN], long in his lifetime.

(D) The greatly beloved ruler, King of Upper and Lower Egypt who lives on Maat, Lord of the Two Lands, [NEFERKHEPRURE-WAENRE], the beautiful child of the living Aten, who shall be here continually forever, lord of heaven. You shall be alive, his heart [*sic*][8] on his throne. May you behold [. . .] beloved of Waenre.

(E) The good ruler, greatly beloved, King of Upper and Lower Egypt who lives on Maat, Lord of the Two Lands, [NEFERKHEPRURE-WAENRE], the beautiful child of the living Aten who will be here continually [forever]; the Son of Re who lives on Maat, Lord of [Crowns, AKHENATEN] . . . every day without cease.

(F) *Inscription on the Foot Panel:*

Words spoken by (King) . . . ,[9] justified: "Let me[10] breathe the fragrant wind which issues from your mouth, that I might see your beauty daily. This prayer [of mine] is that [I] might hear your sweet voice of the north wind, that (my)[11] limbs might grow young with life through your desire. May you give to me your two arms bearing your Ka, that I may receive it, that I may live on it. May you summon <me> by my[12] name continually, without its being sought in your mouth. O m<y> father Horakhty, (King) . . . ,[13] you are like Re[14] continually forever, living like Aten—. . .[15] King of Upper and Lower Egypt who lives on Maat, Lord of the Two Lands, (King) . . . ,[16] the beautiful child of the living Aten who shall be here, alive, continually forever—namely, the Son of Re, (King) . . . , justified.[17]

III. King Tutankhamun

97. Stela of King Tutankhaten

A number of monuments (most notably the "golden throne" from Tutankhamun's tomb, on which the king and queen are shown beneath the solar globe) were made during the earlier part of the reign, when the king's legitimacy was still based on his relationship with the Aten. Only the top of this more modest monument from the same period is preserved. The king, who wears the Blue Crown, presents flowers to enthroned figures of Amun-Re, King of the Gods *and* Mut, Lady of Heaven, Mistress of the Gods. *At the time this monument was inscribed, the king was still using his original Atenist personal name (cf.* 98-A*):* Lord of the Two Lands, NEBKHEPRURE, Lord of Crowns, TUTANKHATEN, given life everlastingly.

98. Miscellaneous Records from El-Amarna

Although a number of small objects from El-Amarna are inscribed for Tutankhamun, only a few have more than the king's name(s).

98-A. Block Fragment naming Prince Tutankhaten

The only object that belongs with any certainty to the future Tutankhamun's pre-royal career is inscribed for The King's bodily son, his beloved, Tutankhuaten.

98-B. Dockets on Provisions Jars

This is one of several jar inscriptions that can be attributed to Tutankhamun's early reign: Regnal year 1: wine belonging to the estate of ATEN [in . . . by] the chief of the garden (=master vintner)[18] Rufy.

99. Restoration Inscription of Tutankhamun

The decree carved on this large red granite stela (discovered in the Great Hypostyle Hall at Karnak in 1905, with a fragmentary duplicate found in the foundations of the temple of Montu in 1907) was issued on the occasion of the king's official repudiation of the Atenist legacy (clearly indicated by the royal couple's abandonment of their earlier personal names in favor of forms compounded with "Amun" instead of "Aten"). After a tendentious account of the heresy period, it describes at length the measures Tutankhamun took to restore the orthodox cults to their full primacy and to compensate them for the damage they had suffered under Akhenaten's regime.

In the lunette there is a double scene in which the king presents flowers to Amun-Re, Lord of the Thrones of the Two Lands, Lord of Heaven, King of the Gods, *who is followed by* Mut, Lady of Isheru, Mistress of all the Gods, *while Amun presents life to the king's nose. The figures of Queen Ankhesenamun, which stood behind the king on both sides of the piece, were erased when the stela was taken over by Horemheb.*

[Regnal year . . .],[19] fourth month of Inundation, day 19 under the Person of Horus, the mighty bull "Whose Births are Perfect"; Two Ladies "Whose [Laws] are Good, [Who Pacifies] the Two Lands"; Horus of Gold "Whose Crowns are Exalted, Who Satisfies the Gods"; King of Upper and Lower Egypt [NEBKHEPRURE]; the Son of Re, TUTANKHAMUN RULER-OF-UPPER-EGYPTIAN-HELIOPOLIS,[20] given life like Re forever [continually], and beloved of [Amun-Re], Lord of the Thrones of the Two Lands, Pre-eminent in Karnak, as well as Atum, Lord of the Two Lands, the Heliopolitan, Re-Horakhty, Ptah South-of-his-Wall, Lord of [Ankh]towy (=Memphis), and Thoth, Master of the Divine Words—having appeared [on] the Horus [Throne of] the Living like his father[21] Re every day: the good [god], son of Amun, child of Kamutef, effective seed and holy egg which Amun himself begat—the father of the Two Lands (?), who built the one who built him, who fashioned the one who fashioned him; at whose birth the Ba's of Heliopolis were assembled to make a king of continuity, a Horus enduring forever; the good ruler who performs benefactions for his father and all the gods, having repaired what was ruined as a monument lasting to the length of continuity, and having repelled disorder throughout the Two Lands, so that Maat rests [in her place] as he causes falsehood to be abomination and the land to be like its primeval state.

When his Person appeared as king, the temples and the cities of the gods and goddesses, starting from Elephantine [as far] as the Delta marshes . . . , were fallen into decay and their shrines were fallen into ruin, having become mere mounds overgrown with grass. Their sanctuaries were like something that had not come into being and their buildings were a footpath—for the land was in rack and ruin. The gods were ignoring this land: if an army [was] sent to Djahy to broaden the boundaries of Egypt, no success of theirs came to pass; if one prayed to a god, to ask something from him, he did not come at all; and if one beseeched any goddess in the same way, she did not come at all. Their hearts were weak because of their bodies,[22] and they destroyed what was made.

But after some time had passed over this, [His Person] appeared upon the throne of his father and he ruled over the shores of Horus (=Egypt): Black Land and Red Land were under his supervision, and every land was bowing to his power.

When his Person was in his palace, which is in the Domain of AAKHEPERKARE (=Thutmose I), like Re within heaven, his Person was governing this land and managing the daily affairs of the Two Shores. Then his Person took counsel with his heart, investigating every excellent deed, seeking benefactions for his father Amun and fashioning his noble image out of genuine electrum. He gave more than what had been done previously: he fashioned his father Amun to be upon thirteen carrying-poles, his holy image being of electrum, lapis lazuli, turquoise, and every precious stone—for the Person of this noble god had formerly been upon only eleven carrying-poles; he fashioned Ptah South-of-his-Wall, Lord of Ankhtowy, his holy image being of electrum, [upon] eleven [carrying]-poles, his holy image being likewise of electrum, lapis lazuli, turquoise and every precious stone—for the Person of this noble god had formerly been upon only nine carrying poles. And his Person made monuments for the gods—[fashioning] their statues out of the best genuine electrum from foreign lands; building their shrines anew as monuments for the length of continuity and endowed with possessions forever; instituting divine offerings for them, consisting of regular daily sacrifices; and providing their food offerings on earth.

He gave more than what had existed before, surpassing what had been done since the time of the ancestors: he installed lay priests and higher clergy from among the children of the officials of their cities, each one being the "son-of-a-man" whose name was known; he multiplied their [offering tables], silver, copper and bronze, there being no limit to [anything]; he filled their workrooms with male and female slaves from the tribute of His Person's capturing. All [the possessions] of the temples and cities [were increased] twice, thrice, fourfold, consisting of silver, gold, lapis lazuli, turquoise, every precious stone, as well as royal linen, white linen, fine linen, moringa oil, gum, fat, [. . . . , . . .], incense, aromatics, and myrrh, without a limit to any good thing. Out of fresh pine of the hilltops, the choicest of the Negau-region, did his Person, l.p.h., hew their river barges, worked with the best gold of the highlands so that they would light up the river. His Person, l.p.h., consecrated male and female slaves, as well as female singers and dancers who had been maidservants in the king's house: their service is assessed against the palace and against the [treasury] of the Lord of the Two Lands, and I am causing them to be preserved and protected[23] for my fathers, all the gods, in order that they may be satisfied with the doing of what their Ka(s) desire, so that they will preserve the Tilled Land (=Egypt).

As for the gods and goddesses who are in this land, their hearts are joyful: the lords of shrines are rejoicing, the shores are shouting praise, and exultation pervades the [entire] land now that good [plans] have come to pass. As for the Ennead(s) which are in the temples, their arms are raised in admiration and their hands are filled with jubilees continually forever. Life and dominion proceed from them to the nose of the victorious king, the Horus "repeater of births,"[24] the beloved son [of his father, Amun-Re King] of the Gods, who fashioned him (=the king) to fashion him (=the god)—namely, the King of Upper and Lower Egypt [NEBKHEPRURE], the beloved of Amun, his eldest son, truly the one whom he loves, the one who protects the father who fashioned him, whose kingship is the kingship of his father Osiris; the Son of Re, [TUTANKHAMUN RULER-OF-UPPER-EGYPTIAN-HELIOPOLIS], a son who is effective for the one who fashioned him, rich in monuments, with wonders abundant, who makes monuments in righteousness of heart for his father Amun; a king whose (re)births are perfect, the sovereign [who has refounded] Egypt.

On this day, when One was in the beautiful palace which is in the Domain of AAKHEPERKARE, the justified, [his Person, l.p.h.], was rejuvenated, and vigor coursed through his body, for Khnum had constructed him [to be a mighty king]: strong of arm is he—much larger in valor than a mere strongman, great in valor like the Son of Nut (=Seth), strong-armed like Horus—no equal unto him has come into being among the multitudes of every land united. Knowledgeable is he like Re, [skilled like] Ptah and discerning like Thoth—one who ordains laws, whose decrees are effective . . . , excellent of utterance: namely, the King of Upper and Lower Egypt, Lord of the Two Lands, Lord who Performs the Ritual, Master of Strength, [NEBKHEPRURE], who satisfies the land (?) . . . ; the bodily [Son of Re], his beloved, lord of every foreign land, Lord of Crowns [TUTANKHAMUN RULER-OF-UPPER-EGYPTIAN-HELIOPOLIS], given life, stability, and dominion like Re [forever continually].

100. Miscellaneous Inscriptions of the Reign

100-A. Stela in the Hypostyle Hall at Karnak

Another commemorative inscription from Karnak describes the fashioning of a new processional cult image for Amun–possibly the one that is referred to in the "restoration inscription" above. The substance of the text, given below, is preceded by a full royal titulary and a lengthy eulogy which has not been translated here. Given the poor condition of the text, the longer restorations are offered here as plausible suggestions in context.

Decree of [His] Person, l.p.h., [on this day]: [That there be made a processional] image of his father Amun-Re Lord of the Thrones of the Two Lands in Karnak; that [his august image be] fashioned [of genuine] gold from [the booty] of his Person's prowess, out of the revenues of all the foreign lands [in the workmanship] of eternity; that [its appearance] be like Aten when he crosses the sky every day, at [whose appearance] those who are in [the sky] exult, and at [whose rising] over the land the subjects rejoice as they protect his place for him [so long as they are on] earth. [His servants tax] all lands, millions of things being in them–namely, [long- and] short-horned cattle, birds, wine and incense [without] their [limit], which fill the Two Shores to overflowing, their heaps reaching up to the sky. Now he has [filled] his [treasury] with objects without their limit, [stocking his workrooms with] male [and female slaves] from the children of the [chief]s (?) of Kush. [*The inhabitants of Thebes*] serve as priests [at] the feasts of his father, [Amun-Re, King of the Gods . . .]. *The rest of the inscription is illegible.*

100-B. Royal Charge for the Chancellor Maya

Below the lunette (now mostly destroyed, containing a double scene with the king standing before an enthroned deity), the following text is inscribed in horizontal lines:

Regnal year 8, third month of the Growing Season, day 21 under the Person of the Horus, Mighty Bull "Whose Births are Perfect"; Two Ladies, "Whose Laws are Good, Who Pacifies the Two Lands"; Horus of Gold, "Who Elevates the Crowns and Satisfies the Gods"; King of Upper and Lower Egypt, NEBKHEPRURE; Son of Re, TUTANKHAMUN, given life. On this day, his Person ordained the hereditary prince and count, the fan-bearer at the right-hand of the king, the king's scribe, the overseer of the treasury Maya, to tax the entire land and institute divine offerings for all the gods of the Tilled Land (=Egypt) starting from Elephantine Island and ending at Smanebbehdet (in the Delta).

To the left of a kneeling figure of the deceased in an adoring posture: An offering which the king gives . . . [and also Horus] Protector of his Father: may

[he] give . . . every day, a happy lifetime [and a good burial] after old age until reaching [the necropolis . . . . For the Ka] of the hereditary prince and count, the fan bearer [at the right-hand of the king, . . . of the] sole lord who is among . . . , the true [royal scribe] whom he loves, the overseer of the treasury, [Maya, justified].

100-C. Stela of Merymery

The effects of the restoration are further illustrated in this memorial, which records the providing of a grant of land, made (as a mortuary endowment?) from property of the Memphite god Ptah to one of his priests.

[The King of Upper and Lower Egypt] NEBKHEPRURE, [Son of Re], TUTANKHAMUN RULER-OF-UPPER-EGYPTIAN-HELIOPOLIS, given life forever, beloved of Ptah South-of-his-wall, Lord of Maat.

[Regnal year . . .], third month of the Harvest season, day 16. (Long) live his Person, the King of Upper and Lower Egypt, NEBKHEPRURE; [the Son of Re] TUTANKHAMUN RULER-OF-UPPER-EGYPTIAN-HELIOPOLIS, given life like Re.

On this day his Person was doing what his father Ptah, the lord of Maat, praises, . . . in the horizon of "Ptah of the Handsome Face." His Person decreed the giving of a grant of land to the god's father Meryptah for the [. . .]s of Merymery: a landgrant [of] a field of 40 aruras [in the fields of the domain of Ptah]. [The king's scribe] Merymery came on account of [it].

100-D. Renewal Inscriptions for Amenhotep III from Luxor Temple

Work on the Great Colonnade at Luxor, begun by Amenhotep III, was carried forward by Tutankhamun, who laid out but did not finish the decoration: this was completed by Ay, Horemheb and Sety I. Throughout the building we see the efforts which the later "Amarna pharaohs" made to associate themselves with Amenhotep III, both as a great king and the last orthodox ruler before the heresy. Ritual scenes on the doorjambs and columns, for example, regularly alternate Tutankhamun and Amenhotep III as the celebrants, to convey an impression (no doubt deliberately) that the two were collaborating in the hall's decoration.[25] *The public relationship between the two kings is further specified by texts of Tutankhamun inside the colonnade, of which a few are translated here. It is still in dispute whether Tutankhamun claims Amenhotep III literally as his father or uses the term metaphorically for "ancestor."*

1. Great Colonnade, North Wall, East and West Sides

The following label, attached to Tutankhamun as he issues from the palace, describes him as renewing the monument of his father, the King of Upper and Lower Egypt NEBMAATRE.

2. Great Colonnade, West Face of Eastern Architrave

Although the architrave texts were completed by Sety I, they had already been laid out and partially carved under Tutankhamun. It is thus the latter who claims credit for the following:

He restored Luxor anew, in likeness to the horizon of heaven, as does a son who is effective on behalf of his father, the King of Upper and Lower Egypt, ruler of the Nine Bows, Lord of the Two Lands, NEBMAATRE, beloved of Amun-Re, Lord of Heaven.

He is the one who has made great his house and embellished his temple in the monument which his father made—namely, the Son of Re who elevates his beauty, the Lord of Crowns AMENHOTEP RULER-OF-THEBES, [beloved of] Amun-Re King [of the Gods].

100-E. Lion Statues from Soleb in Nubia

These two red granite lions, now in the British Museum, were originally made by The King of Upper and Lower Egypt NEBMAATRE, given life like Re: the mighty lion, beloved of Amun-[Re forever], *who adds on each one that* he made it as his monument for his living image on earth, 'NEBMAATRE Lord of Nubia' residing in the fortress of Arising in Maat," that he might achieve the condition of "given life." *The following inscription was subsequently added by Tutankhamun:*

May the gods grant peace to the King of Upper and Lower Egypt, the Lord of the Two Lands, Lord who performs the ritual, NEBKHEPRURE, the Son of Re, Lord of Crowns, [TUT]ANKHAMUN [RULER-OF-UPPER-EGYPTIAN-HELIOPOLIS], who renewed the monument of his father, the King of Upper and Lower Egypt, Lord of the Two Lands NEBMAATRE IMAGE-OF-RE, Son of Re, AMENHOTEP RULER OF THEBES: he made it as his monument for his father, Amun-Re Lord of the Thrones of the Two Lands, Atum Lord of Heliopolis, Yah,[26] that he might achieve the condition of "given life like Re" forever continually.

100-F. "Astronomical Instrument" in Chicago

Now in the Oriental Institute Museum (Chicago), this wooden handle of an instrument used in making astronomical sightings is inscribed with texts which specify that the piece, originally made under Thutmose IV, was refurbished by his descendant Tutankhamun. The usefulness of this genealogical information is compromised, however, by the vagueness of the term that expresses the connection.

Face 1

The Good God, who has acted with his two hands on behalf of his father Amun, who set him on his throne, the King of Upper and Lower Egypt,

NEBKHEPRURE; Son of Re, TUTANKHAMUN RULER-OF-UPPER-EGYPTIAN-HELIOPOLIS: renewing the monument of his forefather,[27] the King of Upper and Lower Egypt MENKHEPRURE, Son of Re, THUTMOSE IV, given life like Re forever continually.

Face 2
The Good God, Lord of the Two Lands, Lord who performs the ritual, Lord of Crowns, NEBKHEPRURE; the bodily son of Re, his beloved, Lord of every foreign land, TUTANKHAMUN RULER-OF-UPPER-EGYPTIAN-HELIOPOLIS: renewing the monument of his forefather,[28] the Lord of the Two Lands MENKHEPRURE, the Lord of Crowns THUTMOSE IV, given life, stability and dominion, being joyful together with his Ka like Re forever.

100-G. Chest Lid belonging to the Treasury Scribe Penbuy

While the exact date of this object is unclear, it belongs to a period when the rapprochement with Amun did not yet exclude the continued cult of the Aten. The likeliest environment for this piece would seem to be the reign of Tutankhamun.

A "boon which the king gives" of Amun-Re King of the Gods, Lord of Heaven, Ruler of Thebes, Lord of Continuity and Ruler <of Eternity>: may he grant the receiving of offering loaves which proceed from the presence upon the offering table of the lord of the gods, as well as kissing the ground and receiving the sacred bouquet which comes forth from within the great shrine, my limbs being firm while following his Ka. For the Ka of the treasury scribe of the Domain of Aten, Penbuy.

100-H. Inscriptions of the Viceroy of Nubia Huy

These vignettes illustrate the persistence of the cult of the divine King in Egypt's southern provinces.

1. Scene from Huy's Tomb at Thebes
This episode from Huy's viceregal career shows him being greeted by various functionaries of his administration in Nubia.
[The deputy of Wawat].
[The deputy] of Kush.
The Mayor of "Arising in Maat."
The Overseer of Cattle.
The High Priest of [NEBKHEPRURE] residing in "Satisfying the Gods," Khay, he says: "Praise be to you! May he love you for [ever and ever], and may he grant that you be endowed with the life which is his Ka's to give."

The deputy of the fortress of NEBKHEPRURE, named "Satisfying the Gods," Penne.

The Mayor of "Satisfying the Gods," Huy.

His brother, [the second] prophet of NEBKHEPRURE residing in the fortress, named "Satisfying the Gods," Mermose.

The lay priest of NEBKHEPRURE residing in the fortress, named "Satisfying the Gods" *(No name).*

2. *Blocks from Buildings at Faras in Nubia*

Only the most stereotyped sorts of texts are preserved on the fragments from Tutankhamun's temple in the walled town of the late Eighteenth Dynasty, which was named "(NEBKHEPRURE is) Satisfying the Gods". More substantial remains survive, however, from the chapel which the wife of the viceroy of Kush Amenhotep (nicknamed Huy) dedicated to his memory. On one of these slabs, which were originally designed as facing for the building's mudbrick walls, the viceroy, described as The King's Son of Kush, overseer of the southern foreign lands, and fan-bearer at the right hand of the king, Huy, *adores the two cartouches of Tutankhamun. An inscription above the figure's head informs us that the chapel was commissioned* by his sister who causes his name to live, the chief of the female attendants of Nebkheprure (named) Taemwadjsy. *On other blocks these individuals are named more fully as* [The King's Son of Kush, fan-bearer on the right hand] of the king, overseer of the gold-lands of Amun, overseer of the cattle of Amun in this land of Kush, the "brave" of his Person in the cavalry, the king's scribe Huy, and the chief of the female attendants of Nebkheprure residing in "Who Satisfies the Gods," (named) Taemwadjsy.

100-I. Monuments of Ay from the Reign of Tutankhamun

1. *A cache of assorted fragments dating from the reigns of Tutankhamun and Ay includes a piece of gold foil, probably from the side of a casket, which shows* The Lord of the Two Lands NEBKHEPRURE, given life like Re forever *in the act of smiting a defeated enemy. Behind him stands* The King's Chief Wife, ANKHESENAMUN, *while the royal couple are saluted from the left side of the scene by* The God's Father Ay.

2. *Inscriptions added by King Ay to the architraves of Tutankhamun's "Temple of NEBKHEPRURE in Thebes" allude to the relationship between the two kings in the following tantalizing terms:*

Block 9, side 2: . . . he (=Ay) made, as his monument for his son, the Good God, [Lord of] the Two Lands, [Lord] who performs the ritual, King of Upper and Lower Egypt [NEBKHEPRURE] . . . . *and* . . . divine [image (?)]

who makes [law]s (?) in the house of his father, Amun: King of Upper and Lower Egypt [NEBKHEPRURE] . . . .

Block 26, side 2: . . . he made, as his monument for his son, the Good God, Lord of the Two Lands, [Lord] who performs [the ritual, King of Upper and Lower Egypt, NEBKHEPRURE . . . *and* . . . the Good God, Son of Amun, who makes [good laws] (?). . . .

These fragments, which reverse the stereotyped equation of father:son: :predecessor: successor, could imply that Ay was Tutankhamun's father. The lateness of this claim (in Ay's reign, following Tutankhamun's death) is suspicious, however, and its implications are far from clear: perhaps it was meant to assert nothing more than Ay's seniority and his quondam advisory role vis-a-vis his youthful predecessor.

100-J. Monuments of Horemheb from the Reign of Tutankhamun

1. Tomb at Saqqara
See below, 105-A.

2. Seated Scribal Statue from Karnak
While most of the inscriptions on this piece are designed for the benefit of Horemheb himself, there is on the unrolled papyrus which rests on his lap the following prayer on behalf of King Tutankhamun:

[A prayer (?)] from the beginning of continuity to the end of eternity, for the King of Upper and Lower Egypt, Lord of the Two Lands, NEBKHEPRURE, [the Son of Re] TUTANKHAMUN RULER-OF-UPPER-EGYPTIAN-HELIOPOLIS, given life.

Setting the guidelines for establishing the annals which [belonged (?)] to the writings of the shrine (?) of Thoth by the scribe, discerning in [his] mouth, [skilled in] his [fingers], on whose part there is no [oversight (?)] which he saw (?), one who is clear-sighted: [the prince and count, chancellor of the King of Lower Egypt, sole companion, fan-bearer at] the king's right hand, generalissimo [. . .], Horemheb—one who is discriminating in words, who satisfies *[his superiors with]* his good character; who takes initiative (?) . . . , [he says: "You have set] rules for the Domain of Amun, giving to him . . . , his [. . .], his fields, . . . fashioned . . . in it, while you have founded The City (=Thebes) anew . . . , being prosperous for its lord forever, . . . [making (?)] them to be content, ... Your name is established [on account of] all [your benefactions], for you shall do them [for the ones who have acted] for you, having appeared on the throne of Horus, O NEBKHEPRURE, ruler of Thebes!"

100-K. Varia Attributed to Tutankhamun's Reign

Fragments of gold foil which bear the following titles were apparently found in the Valley of the Kings:

1. Hereditary prince, count, [sealbearer] of the King of Lower Egypt . . . .

2. . . . [God's] father, fan-bearer . . . .

3. . . . vizier, doer of Maat, prophet of Maat, she who unites the god[s] (?) . . . .

4. Great [. . .] of [his] Person . . . .

Another band, though not clearly associated with the preceding pieces, preserves the end of a name, [. . .]y. While these fragments were published with the finds from the pit of goods associated with the royal burials of Tutankhamun and Ay, it is questionable whether they were ever part of this cache. Their attribution to the God's Father Ay, though sometimes proposed, is thus not proved, nor is it commonly accepted.

101. Miscellaneous Inscriptions from the Tomb of Tutankhamun

The inscriptions on most of the following objects, while conventional enough in themselves, are notable for the manner in which the Aten is made to resume its traditional role as a manifestation of the sun-god, and for this deity's thoroughly orthodox coexistence with other members of the Egyptian pantheon.

101-A. Wooden Chest (Cairo Museum No. 738)

Rear: Long live the Good God, the son of Amun and the child of Kamutef, whom Mut, Lady of Heaven, nursed and whom she suckled with her milk; whom the Lord of the Thrones of the Two Lands (=Amun) created to be ruler of the circuit of Aten; to whom he bequeathed the throne of Geb and the effective office of Atum: the King of Upper and Lower Egypt, Lord of the Two Lands, NEBKHEPRURE, given life forever.

Long live the Good God, image of Re, eldest son of Aten in heaven, who makes monuments and they come into being at once: he is Re and Atum as well, one who annihilates evil at the House of Re in Heliopolis, in that he purifies it as if at the primeval occasion and the Ba's of Heliopolis are content—the King of Upper and Lower Egypt, NEBKHEPRURE, <living> forever.

Long live the Good God, whose crowns are dazzling, the King of Upper and Lower Egypt, NEBKHEPRURE, the bodily Son of Re, TUTANKHAMUN RULER-OF-UPPER-EGYPTIAN-HELIOPOLIS, given life forever.

Left Side: Long live the Good God, the son of Atum and protector of Horakhty—the pure seed who came into being as Khepri, the holy egg of the Lord-to-the-Limit, whose beauty the Ba's of Heliopolis created: the King of Upper and Lower Egypt, Lord of the Two Lands, NEBKHEPRURE—a king whose monuments are important and whose divine signs are great—he is Re and Atum: the bodily Son of Re, his beloved, TUTANKHAMUN RULER-OF-UPPER-EGYPTIAN-HELIOPOLIS, given life like Re forever.

The King of Upper and Lower Egypt, image of Amun, good ruler, beloved, who establishes the land under his plans, the Lord of Crowns, Lord of the Two Lands, NEBKHEPRURE; bodily Son of Re, his beloved, TUTANKHAMUN RULER-OF-UPPER-EGYPTIAN-HELIOPOLIS, given life like Re forever.

Long live the Good God in very truth, son of the White Crown whom the Red Crown bore: the King of Upper and Lower Egypt, ruler of joy, Lord of the Two Lands, NEBKHEPRURE; bodily Son of Re, his beloved, Lord of Crowns, TUTANKHAMUN RULER-OF-UPPER-EGYPTIAN-HELIOPOLIS, given life like Re forever.

Right Side: Long live the King of Upper and Lower Egypt, ruler of joy, who takes possession of the White Crown and assumes the Double Crown in life and dominion—the Lord of the Two Lands NEBKHEPRURE, who makes monuments and they come into being at once for his fathers, all the gods—for he has built their mansions anew, fashioned their images out of electrum and provided their food-offerings on earth: the reward for one who performs benefactions is very numerous jubilees—namely, for the Lord of Crowns, TUTANKHAMUN RULER-OF-UPPER-EGYPTIAN-HELIOPOLIS.

Long live the Good God who has arisen in the White Crown, the sovereign who elevates the Double Crown; King of Upper and Lower Egypt, Lord who Performs the Ritual, Lord of the Two Lands, NEBKHEPRURE; bodily son of Re, his beloved, lord of every foreign land, TUTANKHAMUN RULER-OF-UPPER-EGYPTIAN-HELIOPOLIS, given life like Re forever.

Front: Long live the Horus, mighty bull "Whose Births are Perfect"; Two Ladies "Whose Laws are Good and Who Pacifies the Two Lands"; Horus of Gold "Who Elevates the Crowns and Satisfies the Gods"; King of Upper and Lower Egypt, whom Amun chose to be ruler of every land assembled, Lord of the Two Lands, Lord who Performs the Ritual, Lord of Crowns,[29] NEBKHEPRURE; bodily Son of Re, his beloved, lord of every foreign land, TUTANKHAMUN RULER-OF-UPPER-EGYPTIAN-HELIOPOLIS, given life and health like Re forever.

Lower Right: Long live the Good God, image of Re, excellent son of Aten in heaven, the King of Upper and Lower Egypt, Lord of the Two Lands, NEBKHEPRURE; bodily Son of Re, his beloved, rich in monuments, beloved of the gods, Lord of Crowns, TUTAKHAMUN RULER-OF-UPPER-EGYPTIAN-HELIOPOLIS, given life.

101-B. Gaming Board (Cairo Museum No. 541)

Long live the Good God, image of Re, son of Amun upon his throne, master of strength who has taken possession of all lands, the King of Upper and Lower Egypt NEBKHEPRURE, given life and health forever.

Long live the Good God, son of Amun, child of Aten in heaven, the King of Upper and Lower Egypt, NEBKHEPRURE; Son of Re, TUTANKHAMUN RULER-OF-UPPER-EGYPTIAN-HELIOPOLIS, may he live forever.

101-C. Ceremonial Wand

The Good God, beloved one, dazzling like Aten when he shines, the Son of Amun, NEBKHEPRURE, may he live everlastingly.

101-D. Dockets on Wine Jars Deposited in the Tomb

Some of the wine chosen for Tutankhamun's tomb belonged to old stock, dating back to the reign of Amenhotep III:

Number 25: Regnal year 31. Wine of the chamber (?) . . . [of the] western river . . . .

Most of the jars deposited in the tomb, however, have dockets that show the wine to have been produced in Tutankhamun's reign, with the earliest dockets showing that the worship of the Aten still coexisted with the orthodox revival of Amun's cult down to the end of his reign:

Number 1: Regnal year 4. Sweet wine of the Estate of ATEN, l.p.h., of the western river. The chief of the garden (=master vintner), Aper-Reshep.

Number 4: Regnal year 4. Wine of the Estate of TUTANKHAMUN, l.p.h., [of] the western river. By the chief of the gardeners, Kha.

Number 20: Regnal year 9. Wine of the Estate of ATEN of the western river. The chief of the garden, Nebnefer.

Number 23: Regnal year 9. Wine of the Estate of TUTANKHAMUN RULER-OF-UPPER-EGYPTIAN-HELIOPOLIS, l.p.h. from the western river. The chief of the garden, Sennefer.

The highest of these dates indicates, moreover, that Tutankhamun had ruled for some months in excess of nine full years:

Number 24: Regnal year 10. Good wine of the district of Iati.

IV. Reign of Ay

102. Ay's Burial of Tutankhamun, from the Latter's Tomb

Included among the conventional vignettes in Tutankhamun's tomb, which depict the deceased king's burial and his reception by the mortuary gods, is a highly unusual scene which shows The Good God, Lord of the Two Lands, Lord who Performs the Ritual, the King of Upper and Lower Egypt, <KHEPER>KHEPRURE, Son of Re GOD'S FATHER AY, given life like Re forever continually, *wearing the leopard skin of a funerary priest along with the Blue Crown of royalty, as he performs the "Opening of the Mouth" ceremony before the mummy of* The Good God, Lord of the Two Lands, Lord of Crowns, the King of Upper and Lower Egypt NEBKHEPRURE, Son of Re TUTANKHAMUN RULER-OF-UPPER-EGYPTIAN-HELIOPOLIS, given life forever. *Since Ay's accession appears to have been a stopgap measure, put into effect when Tutankhamun died unexpectedly, this representation seems likely to have been designed to establish, at least before the gods, Ay's legal claim, as his predecessor's "heir of burial," to the latter's inheritance.*

103. Miscellaneous Inscriptions of the Reign

103-A. Faience Ring (Berlin Museum)

This modest object is notable in that it associates one cartouche with Ay's name as king, KHEPERKHEPRURE, *with another belonging to his predecessor's widow* ANKHESENAMUN–*most probably in the aftermath of the failed attempt by the queen (perhaps encouraged by Ay himself) to settle Egypt's quarrel with the Hittite Empire by importing a Hittite prince to reign as Ankhesenamun's husband.*[30]

103-B. Dedications

These inscriptions attest to Ay's continuation of Tutankhamun's policy of restoring and embellishing the temples damaged during the reign of Akhenaten.

1. Marginal Inscription from Amenhotep III's Temple at Luxor
Long live the Horus, "Whose Manifestations are Dazzling"; Two Ladies "Mighty in [Strength], Suppressor of the Asiatics"; Horus of Gold, "Rightful Ruler who Brings the Two Lands back into Being"; King of Upper and Lower Egypt KHEPERKHEPRURE, DOER-OF-MAAT. He made, as his monument for his father Amun Pre-eminent in his Private Quarters, the renewing for him of his great and noble portal.

2. Inscription from the Rock-cut Chapel of Ay at Akhmim

Long live the Horus, "Whose Manifestations are Dazzling"; Two Ladies "[Mighty in Strength, Suppressor] of the Asiatics"; Horus of Gold "Rightful [Ruler], Who Brings [the Two Lands] back into Being"; [King of Upper and Lower Egypt, KHEPERKHEPRURE DOER-OF-MAAT; [Son of Re] GOD'S FATHER AY, THE GOD WHO RULES THEBES, beloved of [Min], Lord of [Akhmim], given life like Re forever.

Now it happened, when [the King of Upper and Lower Egypt] KHEPERKHEPRURE DOER-OF-MAAT, the Son of Re GOD'S FATHER AY, THE GOD WHO RULES THEBES, was effective king in [this entire land], that one of these days came to pass, and his Person was seeking benefactions to [propitiate] all the gods, to embellish the shrines of the gods and to make festive their [temples]. . . . doing . . . noble *[things]* before the gods of Upper and Lower Egypt. . . . everybody . . . . *The rest is illegible.*

103-C. Donation Stela from Giza

This document, which confirms the reward of a court functionary, is notable less for its eminently conventional purpose than for the way it attests to Ay's continued support of the orthodox religious establishments suppressed or transferred to the heretic capital during the reign of Akhenaten, and for its oblique reference to the war which Egypt was currently fighting with the Hittite Empire.

Regnal year 3, third month of the Harvest season, day 1. Long live the Horus, Mighty Bull "Whose Manifestations are Dazzling"; Two Ladies "Mighty in Strength, Suppressor of the Asiatics"; Horus of Gold "Rightful Ruler who Brings the Two Lands back into Being"; King of Upper and Lower Egypt, Lord of the Two Lands, KHEPERKHEPRURE DOER-OF-MAAT; Son of Re, GOD'S FATHER AY, THE GOD WHO RULES THEBES, given life.

On this day, when One was in Memphis, His Person commanded that the fields given as a reward to the Overseer of the King's Private Quarters named Isut and to his wife Mutnodjmet be specified, (said fields) having been made in the territory called "Field of the Hittites" upon fields of the Domain of AAKHEPERKARE (=Thutmose I) and the Domain of MENKHEPRURE (=Thutmose IV). The fields [consist of] 54 arouras –

South from the Domain of MENKHEPRURE;

North from the Domains of Ptah and of AAKHEPERKARE, between which its feeder canal (?) runs;

West from the high desert; and East from the Domain of MENKHEPRURE between which its feeder canal (?) runs.

There came on account of it as witnesses the king's scribe and overseer of the double granary Ramose, the scribe Meryre and [the scribe] Tchay; and it was referred to the chief attendant Ra to assign it.

103-D. Dateline on Berlin Museum Stela No. 2074

This monument and its virtual duplicate in the Louvre Museum, Paris, provide the highest known date for Ay's reign.

Regnal year 4, fourth month of the Inundation season, day 1 under the Person of the Horus, Mighty Bull "Whose Manifestations are Dazzling"; Two Ladies "Mighty in Strength, Suppressor of Asia"; Horus of Gold "Rightful Ruler, Who Brings the Two Lands back into Being"; King of Upper and Lower Egypt, Ruler of the Nine Bows,[31] KHEPERKHEPRURE DOER-OF-MAAT; bodily Son of Re, his beloved, Lord of Crowns, GOD'S FATHER AY, THE GOD WHO RULES THEBES, beloved of Osiris, Lord of the Holy Land,[32] given life.

104. Miscellaneous Inscriptions from Ay's Tomb and Mortuary Complex

104-A. Sarcophagus of King Ay from His Tomb in the Valley of the Kings

Surviving fragments of Ay's sarcophagus show that it resembled those of Tutankhamun and Horemheb, with the king's mummy protected by the outstretched wings of the goddesses at each corner. The inscriptions on the lid, in particular, demonstrate the triumph of orthodoxy which had become irreversible under Tutankhamun, and in particular the Aten's return to its traditional role as merely an aspect of the sun-god.

Top: Words spoken by the Osiris King KHEPERKHEPRURE DOER-OF-MAAT, justified: "O mother Nut, may you spread yourself over me and may you place me among the indestructible stars who are in you, and I will not die again." The Osiris King GOD'S FATHER AY THE-GOD-WHO-RULES-THEBES, justified repeatedly forever and forever.

On the upper end of the lid: Atum who is in his disk (=Aten).

On the foot of the lid: The Behdetite who is in the sarcophagus.

104-B. Foundation Deposits from the Mortuary Temple of Ay

Inscribed objects from the foundations of Ay's mortuary temple near Medinet Habu include a number of glazed model bricks. A typical inscription identifies the owner as The Good God, Lord of the Two Lands, KHEPERKHEPRURE DOER-OF-MAAT, the Son of Re, GOD'S FATHER AY, beloved of Amun-Re, Lord of Heaven. *One unusual example should be noted for its odd reversal of names, titles and epithets:* Lord of the Two Lands, GOD'S FATHER AY; Good God, KHEPERKHEPRURE DOER-OF-MAAT, given life.[33]

V. King Horemheb

105. Pre-Royal Monuments

105-A. Tomb at Saqqara

Although the existence of this tomb was long known on the basis of fragments that were later built into the monastery of Apa Jeremias, the site itself was only rediscovered in 1975. Decorated during the reigns of Tutankhamun and Ay, while its owner was still a private citizen, it amply demonstrates the preeminent role which Horemheb elsewhere claimed for himself during his pre-royal career.

1. Horemheb Receives Prisoners of War

In this scene, Horemheb observes the activities of scribes as they register prisoners from Nubia. The inscription describes his career in the following terms: He was sent as the king's messenger to the very limits of Aten's rising, returning when he had triumphed and when his [attack] had taken place. No land could stand before him, but he overwhelmed it in the completion of a moment. His name was pronounced in the land of the Hittites when he traveled northward. And when His Person appeared on the throne of bringing tribute, there was presented to him the tribute of the north and south even as the hereditary prince Horemheb, justified, stood beside the throne of....

2. Horemheb Receives and Passes on Royal Instructions

Horemheb stands at the foot of a dais, before the king and queen, and then turns to address the assembled officials and foreign envoys.

[Words spoken to His Person, when] the chiefs of every foreign country came to beg life from him, by the hereditary prince, sole companion, royal scribe Horemheb, justified. He said, when answering [the king: "... foreigners] who know not Egypt, they are beneath your feet continually forever. Amun bequeaths them to you, though they penetrated [every] foreign country [*and came from* lands] which were not known since the time of Re. Your battle cry is in their hearts as if in one, and your name blazes [... those] who are loyal to you. You are Pre ... and they ... their towns ..., *[and they are fallen to]* your mighty arm through the command of Amun."

[Words spoken by ... Horemheb *to all the king's messengers as they were being sent to*] every foreign country: "Thus says [Pharaoh (?) ... *to all his officials* ...] starting from the southern end of Kush *[and ending at the furthest reaches of Asia]* ... as he [beholds (?)] with his rays, being made .... Now Pharaoh, l.p.h. has placed them upon your hands in order to guard their borders ... of Pharaoh, l.p.h., as in the manner of your fathers' fathers since the very beginning. Now ... *[it had been reported]* that some foreigners who knew not how they might live had come from ... while their countries were hungry and they lived like desert cattle, [and their] children (?) .... [Then arose] the one whose strength is great to send his mighty arm in front of [his army (?) ... to] destroy them while plundering their towns and setting fire *[to their settlements ... to overthrow those]* foreign countries, setting others in their places."

[Words spoken *by these officials*] as they answer [the Lord] of the Two Lands and give adoration to the [Good] God whose strength is great, [NEBKHEPRU]RE ....[34]

105-B. Scribal Statue in the Metropolitan Museum of Art (NewYork)

While most of the texts inscribed on this well-known statue are in praise of the god Thoth, on the right side of the base there is a prayer to Ptah of Memphis (all that is translated here) which mentions the solar globe in a context that demonstrates yet again this figure's resumption of its traditional and innocuous role as the physical manifestation of the sun god's presence.

A "boon which the living king gives" of Ptah South-of-his-Wall, and of Sekhmet, the beloved of Ptah; Ptah-Sokar, Lord of the Mysterious Shrine; and Osiris, Lord of Ro-setchau—may you (*plural*) grant that the Ba may come forth by day to see Aten; may you listen on its (=*the Ba's*) behalf to the daily petition, like the spirits which you have glorified. May you[35] ordain that I follow you at every season as all those whom you favor—because I have been righteous to the god ever since I existed on earth, satisfying him with Maat every day, and I forsook evil before him. There is no instance [of wrongdoing on my part] since my birth, for I am one who is devoted to the god, skillfully- and pleasingly-minded when he hears Maat.

May you cause me to be among the crew of the Neshmet-bark (of Osiris) in its festival of the District of Peqer (at Abydos). For the Ka of the hereditary prince, the sole companion, the deputy of the king in the forefront of the Two Lands, the king's scribe Horemheb, justified.

105-C. British Museum Stela No. 551

In the scene at the top of the tablet Horemheb adores the following divinities:

Re-Harakhty, the unique god, king of the gods as he rises in life and [gives] his beauty ... from (?) him.

[Thoth, Master of the God's Words], preeminent in Hesret, the great god who leads the underworld.

Maat, Daughter of Re, Lady of Heaven, Mistress of the West.

Horemheb addresses these divinities with the following speech: "I have come to you, O lords of continuity, [as one who] carries out commissions at the temple. As you exist and as your images are enduring, day and night, upon the mountains, grant that I may endure on earth while offering [. . .]." [By] the hereditary prince, the fan-bearer at the king's right hand, the generalissimo Horemheb, justified.

Main Text: Adoring Re-Horakhty and making him happy at his rising. The hereditary prince Horemheb—he says:

"Hail to you, who are glorious and effective, O Atum-Harakhty, as you appear from the horizon of heaven! Adoration to you in the mouths of everyone, you being perfect and youthful as Aten within the arm(s) of your mother Hathor! Arise, O lord of <everything?>: may your heart be forever glad, that the double shrines may come to you in obeisance and that they may give worship to your rising. How manifest are you in the horizon of heaven! The Two Lands pour forth turquoise for you, saying 'It is Re-Horakhty, the godly youth, the heir of continuity, who begot himself and fashioned himself by himself; the king of heaven and earth, the ruler of the underworld and chief of the desert, the realm of the dead; [who issued] from the water which brought him, from Nun which reared him, hallowed in his birth!'"

"O mighty king, horizon-manifested, the Ennead jubilates at your rising: everyone is in exultation, rejoicing at your appearing for them."

"O noble god who is in his shrine, lord of continuity occupying his barge, the horizon-dwellers tow you, those who are in the Night Bark convey you, the Eastern Ba's invoke you and the Western Ba's jubilate for you."

"O Good God with shining splendor, who bestrews the Two Lands with electrum; resplendent youth and beloved lord, great in strength, who knows no weariness, quick-running and wide-striding—O you who rises from the eastern horizon and dispels darkness from the entire land: as for everyone who was given over to terror, at your rising they give you adoration, and with jubilation they behold the primeval one while your attendants kiss the ground."

"O you who set in the western horizon and spread darkness over the entire land, brightness occurs when you come forth, and the land darkens when you go to rest in your mansion."

"O goodly youth whom Ptah made distinguished in shape from the other gods, who came forth as a horned falcon, the Two Ladies keeping company on your head; ruler of eternity, sovereign of the gods of continuity! You are the king, lord of the Atef-crown, and your eyes illuminate the lands. You are Re, perfect in shape, and all the living come to you. Your mother Nut lifts you up at dawn, setting the fear of you in the hearts of the Two Lands as they wait for you to reiterate the primeval event—you, the counselor for eternity and prince for the end of continuity, who crosses heaven in the Night Bark and whose manifestation is great in the Day Bark!"

By the hereditary prince Horemheb—he says: "I adore you, for your beauty is in my eyes and your brilliance has come into being upon my breast as I elevate Maat before your person daily in the course of every day."

"Adoration to you, O Thoth, Lord of Ashmunein, who came into being by himself, who had none to give him birth! Unique god, leader of the underworld, who give instructions to the westerners who are in the following of Re and who distinguish the tongue(s) of all the foreign lands: may you cause the king's scribe Horemheb to flourish beside the sovereign, as you do beside the Lord-to-the-Limit, just as you reared him when he issued from the womb!"

"Adoration to you, O Maat, lady of the north wind who open up the noses of the living and give breath to the ones who are in his (=Re's) bark: may you cause the hereditary prince Horemheb to smell the breeze which heaven produces, just as the Lady of Punt smells its smell at the Lake of Myrrh."

"May you (plural) grant entry and exit in the Fields of Iaru, that I may be united there with the Field of Offerings, receiving oblation daily on [the offering tables] of the Lords of Heliopolis—that my heart may cross over, in the ferryboat of the necropolis, to the pure isles of the Fields of Iaru. May you open a good way for me, make plain my path and place <me> in the following of Sokar in Ro-setchau."

For the Ka of the hereditary prince, the sole companion, the generalissimo, revered before Osiris, Horemheb, the justified, possessor of reveredness.

106. Coronation Inscription

The most complete version of the official account in which Horemheb described his accession to the throne is inscribed on the back of a dyad, now in the Egyptian Museum at Turin, which shows the king seated next to his queen, [The King's Chief Wife, Mistress of] the Two Lands, MUTNODJMET, beloved of Isis, the mother of the god—may she live forever.

Main Text: [Long live the Horus, Mighty Bull, "Whose Counsels are Penetrating"; Two Ladies, "For Whom Godly Signs are Great in Karnak"; Horus] of Gold, "Contented with Maat, Who Brings the Two Lands back into Being"; King of Upper and Lower Egypt, Lord of the Two Lands, DJESERKHEPRURE WHOM RE HAS CHOSEN; Son of Re, Lord of Crowns, HOREMHEB BELOVED OF AMUN, beloved of Horus, Lord of Hnes, [given life like Re forever]—[the good god, son of Amun, child of] Kamutef. Amun, King of the Gods, reared him, and Horus Son-of-Isis preserved him with the protection of his limbs. He issued from the womb clothed in awesomeness, the complexion of a god being upon him, and he made . . . him (?). The arm was bent to him respectfully as a youth, and the ground was kissed by great and small. Food and provisions attended him while he was a boy without understanding, *[and he was pointed out among]* the officials at the front of everybody. A god's image was his complexion: one feared when his form was beheld. His father Horus placed himself behind him, the one who created him making his protection.

A generation passed and another [came, *and his father still kept him*] safe, for he knew the day on which he would retire to give him his kingship. So this god was distinguishing his son in the sight of everybody, for he desired to "widen his stride" until the day of his receiving his office would come; and he caused [him to be more respected than anyone else] of his time, the king's heart being satisfied with his dealings and rejoicing at the choosing of him. In order to make fast the laws of the Two Shores he appointed him chief spokesman of the land, being the hereditary prince of this land in its entirety: he was unique, without his equal. The plans [of the Two Lands were under his hand, and] everybody [rejoiced] at what came out of his mouth. When he was called upon in the presence of the sovereign—the palace having fallen into rage—he opened his mouth and answered the king, and made him happy with what came out of his mouth. Unique and effective was he, no [one like him having ever come into being . . .]. All his plans were as the footsteps of the Ibis, and his course was the image of the Lord of Hesret, rejoicing in Maat like the Beaky One[36] and delighting in it like Ptah. When he awakened at dawn he was already burdened with it (=Maat), it being [present at every turn throughout] his dealings while he trod on its path. It is the one that will make his protection on earth for the length of eternity.

So he was administering the Two Lands for a period of many years. [The dues of the Two Lands and the deliveries of Upper and Lower Egypt were] reported [to him], and the councils [came] to him, bowing at the gate of the king's house. The chiefs of the Nine Bows, south as well as north, appealed to him, their arms outspread at his approach, as they did reverence to his face as to a god. All that could be done was done only under [his] command, and . . . his tread, his awesomeness being great in the sight of everybody. On his behalf prosperity and health were beseeched from the gods: "Surely he is the father of the Two Shores, with the excellent wisdom of the god's giving to make fast [the laws of the Two Shores]."

[Now when] many [days had passed] after this—the eldest son of Horus being chief spokesman and hereditary prince in this land in its entirety—then did this noble god, Horus, Lord of Hnes, desire in his heart to establish his son on his continual throne; and [he] commanded *[him to go to the]* monument of Amun. So Horus proceeded, rejoicing, to Thebes, the city of the Lord of Continuity, his son in his embrace, to Karnak, in order to lead him into the presence of Amun, to bequeath to him his kingly rule and make his term of rule.

Now [Amun-Re, Lord of the Thrones of the Two Lands, came out with rejoicing (?)] in his beautiful feast in front of the Southern Sanctum (=Luxor Temple); and he saw that the person of this god, Horus, Lord of Hnes, had his son with him at the "King's Induction,"[37] in order to give him his office and his seat. And Amun-Re became possessed with joy when he saw [the eldest son of Horus] on the day of taking his retirement. Then he addressed himself to this official, the hereditary prince and chief of the Two Lands, HOREMHEB, and he proceeded to the king's house, having placed him in front of him—to the great shrine of his noble daughter Great-[of-Magic]: her [arms] were held out in greeting, and she embraced his beauty and fixed herself upon his forehead. All of the Enneads of the House of Flame were in jubilation at his appearance: Nekhbet and Edjo, Neith, Isis and Nephthys, Horus and Seth, and the entire Ennead which was before the great shrine [made] acclamations to the height of heaven, rejoicing at the pleasure of Amun, and saying: "Behold, Amun has come to the palace, his son in front of him, in order to establish his Crown on his head and to exalt his lifetime like his own! We are gathered together so that we may affix [his crowns] for him and assign to him the insignia of Re and glorify Amun on his account, saying 'You have brought our protector to us! Give him the jubilees of Re and the years of Horus as king. He is the one who shall do what pleases your heart within Karnak, and likewise in Heliopolis and Hikuptah (=Memphis). He is the one who shall enrich them.'"

The Great Name(s) of this good god were then made, his titulary being like that of the Person of Re, consisting of: Horus, Mighty Bull, "Whose Counsels are Penetrating"; Two Ladies, "For Whom Godly Signs are Great in Karnak"; Horus of Gold, "Contented with Maat, Who Brings the Two Lands back into Being"; King of Upper and Lower Egypt, DJESERKHEPRURE WHOM RE HAS CHOSEN; the Son of Re, HOREMHEB BELOVED OF AMUN, given life.

The Person of this noble god, Amun King of the Gods, then went out from the king's house, his son in front of him, crowned in the Blue Crown after he had embraced his beauty, in order to assign to him what Aten encircles, the Nine Bows being beneath his feet. Heaven was in festival and earth laden with joy—and as for the Enneads of the Tilled Land (=Egypt), their hearts were pleased. Indeed, everyone was joyful, and they cried out to the sky. Great and small took up shouting, and the entire land rejoiced.

After this feast in front of the Southern Sanctum was over, Amun King of the Gods returned in peace to Thebes. Then did his Person (=the king) sail downstream with the statue of Re-Horakhty, and he reorganized this land, restoring its customs to those of the time of Re. From the Delta marshes down to the Land of the Bow (=Aswan region) he renewed the gods' mansions and fashioned all their images, they being distinguished from what had existed formerly and surpassing in beauty from what he did with them, so that Re rejoiced when he saw them—they having been found wrecked from an earlier time. He raised up their temples and created their statues, each in their exact shape, out of all sorts of costly gemstones. When he had sought out the gods' precincts which were in ruins in this land, he refounded them just as they had been since the time of the first primeval age, and he instituted divine offerings for them, as regular daily sacrifices—all the vessels of their temples being modeled out of gold and silver. And he equipped them with lay priests and lector priests from the pick of the home troops, assigning them fields and herds, being equipped on all sides, so that they might rise early to pay homage to Re at dawn every day, saying: "As you have extended for us the kingship of your son, who does what pleases your heart, DJESERKHEPRURE WHOM RE HAS CHOSEN, so may you give him millions of jubilees and make his victories against all lands like Horus Son-of-Isis, inasmuch as he satisfies your heart in Heliopolis in unity with your Ennead."

107. Miscellaneous Records of the Reign

107-A. Another Coronation Inscription from Memphis

What remains of this fragmentary inscription seems to follow both the outline and (especially in its latter part) even the exact wording of the version of Horemheb's accession carved on the statue in Turin. In its first preserved section, however, Amun's activities before the coronation proper are recorded in somewhat greater detail than on the Turin text, with the greatest duplication coming in the episodes of the enthronement itself: material common to both texts will be underlined in the following translation; but since much of it is restored, it will not be given in extenso.

The first preserved passage refers to Amun as he was resting in his mansion of the Southern Sanctum (=Luxor Temple), his ennead behind him. When dawn came [and a] second day came [into] being, ... [Then said Amun-Re, King of the Gods]: "You are my son, my heir, who issued from my body. So long as I exist you shall exist, without being distant <from> me . . . . *[And you shall act on behalf of the gods]*, doubling their offerings, so that they might recognize you as my son, who issued from my body, and gather to give you [my kingship]."

[Then Amun addressed himself to his son], and he proceeded to the king's house, having placed him in front of him, to the great shrine of his noble daughter, Great-of-Magic. *The text that follows, albeit fragmentary, follows the Turin version word for word through the proclamation of Horemheb's titulary, after which it concludes rather abruptly:* He made, as his monument for his father, Ptah South-of-his-Wall, the making for him of a "station of the ruler"[38] out of quartzite-stone, right in front of the great hall of . . . , two doorleaves being upon them of genuine pine, in order to make holy the house of the one who made him, to purify the processional way of his father Ptah. He has built a mansion for him anew . . . , . . . of [. . .] cubits, out of every sort of costly stone. Its flag-masts are of genuine pine worked with Asiatic copper, their tips of electrum. A festival court is made for it . . . , [that he might not] be far from him, for he has wished to make him more distinguished than any kings who have come into existence: one acts for the one who has acted, and one reciprocates with a good thing like . . . . *The rest is lost.*

107-B. Monuments of King Horemheb from El-Amarna

Given Horemheb's reputation as an opponent of Akhenaten's heresy, it is remarkable that two fragments from his reign were found in the ruins of the Great Temple of the Aten at El-Amarna. The first (1) bears a cartouche of Horemheb's throne-name on one side, but on the adjoining side there is the lower part of a procession of officials–an incongruous element on a royal monument, which may suggest that this piece was recut from a private monument. The other piece (2) is a conventional statue base, inscribed with this fragmentary text: . . . the one who came forth from his limbs; the King of Upper and Lower Egypt, ruler of the Nine Bows, the Lord of the Two Lands, DJESERKHEPRURE WHOM RE HAS CHOSEN; the bodily Son of Re, his beloved, [HOREMHEB]. . . .

The presence of two separate monuments at the very hub of the Atenist heresy suggests that they are not intrusive materials, deposited later, but deliberate dedications to the Aten's cult.[39] *Even if so, however, such gestures on Horemheb's part seem not to have gone far beyond the borders of the heresy's capital.*

107-C. Dated Inscriptions Attributed to Horemheb

The length of Horemheb's reign is in dispute. Of the documents presented below, the first is notable for reflecting the resumption of activity in the Theban necropolis. The second, found in Horemheb's private tomb at Saqqara, is widely regarded as Horemheb's highest contemporary year date. The third item, while believed by some to date from Horemheb's reign, is just as widely considered to belong to the time of Ramesses II. We omit a fourth inscription, allegedly from the sixteenth year of Horemheb's reign, which is most plausibly to be dismissed as a forgery.[40]

1. Ostracon Dated to Horemheb's Seventh Year

Regnal year 7 of the King of Upper and Lower Egypt, DJESERKHEPERRE [*sic*], l.p.h., HOREMHEB, l.p.h.: the day when the crewman Hay, my father, was allowed to enter into the tomb[41]—when Thutmose, the estate manager of the City (=Thebes), distributed the places which are in the estate of the tomb[42] to the work-gang [of] Pharaoh, l.p.h., and he assigned the tomb chapel of Amen<mose> to Hay, my father, as a charge, since my mother Hener was his born daughter, and he had no male child, and his places had become abandoned.

2. From the Tomb of Generalissimo Horemheb at Saqqara

This docket, written on a jar from the Memphite tomb of Horemheb, dates to Regnal year 13, third month of the Inundation season. Very good wine from the vineyard of the estate of HOREMHEB BELOVED-OF-AMUN in the estate of Amun. *As usual, the provenance of the wine and vintner's name follow.*

3. From the Mortuary Temple of Horemheb in West Thebes

The following graffito was written in ink on the shoulder of a statue at the site of Horemheb's mortuary temple. Since chronological considerations seem to require that Horemheb reigned close to three decades, this text could be contemporary, although the dateline is not specific. On the other hand, many authorities believe that the delivery of a new statue during the reign of Ramesses II is referred to here.

Regnal year 27, first month of the Harvest season, day 9: day of the entering of HOREMHEB, l.p.h., beloved of Amun, who hates his enemies and loves . . . .

108. Edict from Karnak

Horemheb's great edict is one of the most extensive of examples of pharaonic legislation extant. While scholarly opinion no longer regards the contents of this document as being predominantly a reaction against conditions under the Amarna pharaohs, some of its provisions may well have been enacted to counteract abuses that had become entrenched during the time of Akhenaten and his successors.[43]

Preamble

The beginning of the text consisted of a eulogy of the king, of which only a few phrases survive: . . . [effective seed] which proceeded from the god, . . . in the likeness of . . . , [whom no one resisted in (?)] his time, . . . who fills [the storehouses] with [valuable things], . . . , [HOREMHEB BELOVED-OF-AMUN], given life forever continually. On this day, the commencement of continuity and the beginning [of eternity, when the king is given the duration of the solar globe which is in (?)] the sky and the kingship of Re, he was provided with the seat [of his father (?) . . .], and the country was flooded with love of [him]. Maat returned and reoccupied [her place], . . . [and the people] rejoiced, for the Tilled Land (=Egypt) entered a new cycle, as Egypt rejoiced happily *[on account of its king]*. He has come, moreover, laden with prestige, and has filled the Two Lands with his beauty—for, as for this perfect god, it is on behalf of Re that he was created, [and for] the lord of the gods [was he begotten]—a ruler zealous and watchful . . . [against] greedy men. He ordained [laws], achieving justice (Maat) throughout the Two Shores, for he delights in exalting her (=Maat's) beauty.

His Person took counsel in his heart, . . . *[devising plans to]* crush evil and destroy iniquity. His Person's plans are an effective refuge which suppresses rapacity around *[the communities of the land and reverses the bad conditions]* which had come into being among them. His Person was continually watchful, seeking what is useful for the Tilled Land and scrutinizing instances *[of justice which might be implemented by]* his Person. So he took up the scribe's palette and the papyrus roll, and he put it into writing, according to everything his Person had said. The king himself declared, as a decree *[for promoting justice, the following enactments againt these]* instances of greed in the land.

Against Requisitioning Boats Used for State Corvee Duty

If a private individual makes for himself a boat with its on-board shelter,[44] in order to be able to serve Pharaoh, l.p.h., *and if people*] of the army *[come and appropriate it as if it were for (?)]* taxes: then the individual is despoiled of his property and deprived of his abundant means *[of doing service. This is a crime!]* Something like this should not be done [to controvert] his good purposes. As for every boat which is taxable for the offering halls of Pharaoh, l.p.h., by the two deputies [of the army] . . . , *[if someone comes]* and seizes a boat belonging to any member of the army or anybody in the entire land, let the law be applied to him by cutting off his nose and sending him to Tcharu.[45] [As for] an individual who is without a boat, and he gets from someone else a boat for his service obligation, and undertakes on his own to bring wood and is thus fulfilling his obligations [to Pharaoh, l.p.h., . . .]: [should others] seize and plunder his cargo, and steal it, and the individual stands despoiled of his [means of doing service . . . so that] he has nothing— This is not good, this report: it is an abuse indeed! My Person had decreed that one should turn away from it. Indeed, [*this applies to* . . . , and to] those who contribute to the Private Quarters, and similarly to all the gods' offerings when they are taxed by the two deputies of the army and . . . : [*if anyone does this*, let] the law [be applied] against him by cutting off his nose and sending him to Tcharu.

Against Illegally Requisitioning Slaves

Similarly, although the servants of the offering storerooms of Pharaoh, l.p.h., have been going and requisitioning people in the town to gather saffron *[in the season (?), and]* these servants [seize the male and female slaves of an] individual; and these servants send [them on the job of gathering the saffron] for six or seven days, without its being known whether they (=the state employees) are free to dispose of them (=the slaves), this is an overweening abuse: one should not act in this fashion either! As for any place....

[*Moreover,* as] for any servant(s) of the [offerings] storeroom [of Pharaoh, l.p.h., about whom] it will be heard that they are still requisitioning people to gather saffron, and whom someone else comes to denounce, saying, "My male or female [slave] was taken . . . ," [let the law be applied to him by cutting off his nose, sending him to Tcharu, and by assessing from him the service of the male or female slave] for every day which he [*sic*] spent [with him].

Seizure of Hides and Inspection of the Cattle of Pharaoh

[Further] the two corps of the army, when they are in the field—one in the southern district and the other in the northern district—have been appropriating hides throughout the entire land, without ceasing for a single year in order to let [the people] breathe . . . ; [and they seize the hides without] distinguishing the brands on them, and after going from house to house, with beatings and duckings, not leaving a single hide for [anyone], ... And when [the overseer of the cattle] of Pharaoh, l.p.h., goes [to] perform [the cattle-count in the] entire [land], and he . . . , no hide is found with them, so that they can be accused of defaulting even as they fill their hearts by saying, "They have been taken from us!"—This is an instance of cravenness: one should not [behave in] this fashion!

When the overseer of the cattle of Pharaoh, l.p.h., goes to perform the cattle-count in the entire land, he is the one who shall bring the hides of the dead animals which are upon [the . . . in] his usual fashion. And as for any member of the army about whom it will be heard that he goes and still appropriates hides [until] today, let the law be applied against him by beating him with one hundred blows and five open wounds, and by confiscating the hide he has taken by theft.

Reform of the Provisioning of Royal Progresses

Now, as for this other instance of dishonesty [about which] one [hears] in the land: the fact that [the agents] of the queen's estate and the scribes of the offering tables of the royal quarters go after the local mayors, oppressing them and searching for [materiel] for the progress downstream and upstream which used to be sought from the mayors in the reign of King MENKHEPERRE (=Thutmose III)—now, as for that, namely, provisions for the progress downstream and upstream which they have been extorting since [King] MENKHEPERRE used to go [downstream and upstream] each year during [the feast of Opet in] the journey to Thebes, and for which the [agents] of the royal quarters would approach the mayors, saying, "Give [the] materiel for the journey which is lacking, for look, Pharaoh, l.p.h., is making the journey of the feast of Opet each year with nothing lacking!"; so there is prepared before Pharaoh, l.p.h., [everything] which [*should be* at] the quay *[under the authority of the agents]* of the royal quarters; and one goes after [the] materiel [belonging to the mayors] and has them prepared by force. Now what is the meaning of returning again to search for such materiel [from them]? For really, it is through the property of private individuals that the mayors arrange for [the] journey . . . from the contributions of those who are at the head [of . . .]. This is [an instance of cravenness]! My Person has commanded that no one be allowed to act in this way any further, from this day on. As for the materiel which [is] supplied on the quay, that is what should be investigated!

Abolition of the State Tax on Fodder

Similarly, those who gather fodder for the offering halls [and the places of Pharaoh, l.p.h., are going into the *plots* and] the gardens of private individuals, gathering their fodder daily [and saying], "It is for the service obligation [of Pharaoh], l.p.h.," [and thus] they [set] about [depriving] these private individuals of their means of service. This is a bad deed: [one should not act in this way!] It is only among the orchards and the [. . .]s of the dwelling of Pharaoh, l.p.h., [and the . . .] of Pharaoh, l.p.h., which are grasslands, [that those who gather fodder for the offering halls of Pharaoh, l.p.h., may go to gather fodder [for the] service obligation to Pharaoh, l.p.h. If one hears that they are going to the garden of any member of the army or [any] persons [who are in the entire land, and they take its grasses, *those are*] people who are decree-violators.

Against Fraud in Assessing Taxes

Further, regarding the baboon-keepers who are going [*about*] levying taxes in the southern district and/or the northern district, requisitioning grain from the citizenry with the estate *oipe*-measure of 50 *hin* while they undervalue what is required . . . , requisitioning also linen, plants, vegetables [and . . . while] they requisition from estates and boats while other people go in the opposite direction, exacting taxes in the southern district and/or the northern district, exacting an *oipe*-measure from these private individuals, this [being] right for payment . . . . My Person had commanded that one should turn away [from them] entirely to prevent *[them from further injuring]* private individuals by fraud.

The next section, which appears to concern the rights and restrictions laid on employees of the harem, is too badly damaged for consecutive translation.

General Observations on Justice

I have restored this entire land . . . , [and] I have *[traversed]* it. I refashioned Upper Egypt and fortified [Lower Egypt]. . . . . I know its insides completely, I have touched its utmost interior. I examined *[the condition of this land and I chose men who were]* discreet, whose characters were good, who knew how to seek out people's thoughts, obedient to the words of the king's house and to the laws of the council chamber. I appointed them to judge the Two Lands and to gratify those who are in *[Egypt. I selected them and]* I installed them in the two great cities of Upper and Lower Egypt, every man living tranquilly in them, with no exception thereto. I placed instructions in front of them and laws as [their] regular concern. . . . [I caused them to] be active; I guided them to the path of life and I led them to the right place. My instruction to them is: "Don't get too intimate with other people. Don't receive gifts from another. There is no completion (?) [in it]. What is [one] of you worth, more than others, if you commit wrong against the righteous?

Regulations of Local Lawcourts

Now as for the tax of silver and gold . . . , my Person [has commanded] that it be eliminated, to prevent the exacting of a tax of anything from the local courts of Upper and Lower Egypt.

Now, as for any mayor or any priest about whom one hears that he sits down to do business in a local court which has been convened for business, and he deals falsely with a righteous cause in it, it shall count against him as a great crime, worthy of death. Indeed, my Person has done this to perfect the laws of the Tilled Land and to prevent a reoccurrence by another individual *[who behaves in this manner]*.

[As to the people who are to be the] judges of the local court, it is the priests of the temples, the mayors of the interior of the country and the lay priests of the gods who make up each local court according to their pleasure, in order to judge the citizenry of every city. My Person has been concerned with the Tilled Land, in order to make prosperous the lives of those who are in it ever since he appeared on the throne of Re. That is why local court(s) have been established throughout the entire land. [Every priest and] every [mayor shall continue] to make up the local courts in the cities according to the excellent plan *[which the king has devised to implement justice]* completely.

Regulations for the Rewarding of State Employees and the Protocol at Court

I shall observe custom with respect to the guarding of my Person at every first day, when they surround my Person three times per month. It shall become like a feast for them—each man being seated and getting a share of every good thing, consisting of good bread, meat and cakes from royal property, . . . , with voices reaching heaven for him (=the king) while glorifying every good deed *[of theirs–including]* the first-rank leaders of the guard, every officer of the army and every man in [. . . , *without*] limit, while tossing honors to them from the window of appearances and calling each man by his name. It is the king himself before whom they will parade, making acclamation, being provisioned with the property of the king's house even while they continue to draw regular rations from the double granary, each one of them, with wheat and barley. One who does not have his share is not found, [but . . .] in order to make the remainder for him . . . . [They shall return] to their cities without even having completed therein the appointed time (of service?), taking their ease while their body servants hasten behind them to their proper places, carrying all the things which they find there, things worthy of speaking about, giving . . . at the desire of these . . . body servants (?) . . . . [in (?)] the chamber of the Lord of the Two Lands . . . . [The . . . and the] sandal-bearers, they serve in the broad courts of the inner palace, free to go and come through its portals without saying "Would that [*I might have something* . . .]." . . . , [saying] "I am the official!" They enter through the portals of . . . quickly, by horse, to the holy area, with a dog at their feet and an attendant at the rear . . . . [He *enters*] the council chamber, dressed in [*fine clothing*], shod in sandals, with a staff in his grasp like a herdsman . . . . [*I have appointed* . . .] to his place as it was at the primeval occasion. I have arranged the protocol of the inner palace, the custom of the inner quarters of the king's companions. I have set my house to . . . , they . . . the heralds of the council chamber, according to their rank, while "spreading holiness" throughout the entire house, and while the members of the king's entourage are at their exact places and the Thirty[46] are at their customary positions. . . .

Conclusion

As long as the period of my development on earth remains firm, it shall be spent making the monuments of the gods. I shall be renewed continually like the moon. I am . . . , endowed with life, stability and dominion, one whose limbs shed light on the limits of the land like the disk of Re, whose luminous nature is mighty like that of Re when he places himself in the season of the Inundation—his beauty being exceedingly brilliant, and his power being in the heart(s) of the elite. . . . . [*I have done all this*] to cause you to listen to these decrees which my Person has made anew, in order to direct the entire land after my Person called to mind those instances of greed which are done in front of this land. [How] great [is what I have done (?)] . . . . *The last column is destroyed.*

VI. The Amarna Age in Later Records

109. Extracts from the Inscription of Mose

This record of a lawsuit from the time of Ramesses II, in the century following the heresy, illustrates how contemporary writers ignored or vilified Akhenaten and his immediate successors.

Regnal year 59[47] under the Person of the King of Upper and Lower Egypt DJESERKHEPRURE WHOM-RE-HAS-CHOSEN, [the Son of Re] HOREMHEB BELOVED-OF-AMUN. Copy of the examination [made by] the lay priest [of the litter][48] Iniy, who was an officer of the court, of the farming estate of the shipping master Neshi [which was in the] village of Neshi, to wit: "I arrived at the village of Neshi, the place at [which] the fields are and of which the citizeness Wernero and the citizeness Takharu spoke. They assembled the heirs of Neshi together with the important people of the town who make up the lay priests (?) of the farming estate [of] Neshi in order to hear their statement.

List of the names of the witnesses of Neshi:
the citizeness Kakay;
the citizeness Henutwedjebu;
the priest (?) . . . ;
the soldier Baka,
making four persons (*literally,* "men").

List of the names [of] the witnesses who came from the town so that they might swear:
The worker Heriherneferher;
Several more names missing,
[making . . . persons]. What they said with one voice: "As Amun endures, and as the ruler endures, we shall speak truthfully . . . . As for me, I am from the town . . . today (?). I have seen the farming estate of the shipping master Neshi, it being in the possession of [the] heirs [and . . . , which took place (?)] in the time of the enemy of Akhet-Aten, while . . . [in] Akhet-Aten in [which] one was.[49] The citizeness Sheritre, the mother of the citizeness [Takharu] . . . *(the man)* Iry became . . . on the farming estate, cultivating . . . Sheritre the mother of Takharu." Now after . . . . *The rest is lost.*

110. Tax Record Mentioning the Heresy Period

Part of a fragmentary letter from the Ramesside period also illustrates the tendentious manner with which records from the Amarna period continued to be used for state business: Similarly, as to the message you sent me saying, "Give me the death-date of [. . .]nakht," when one arrives in Memphis it is [. . . who shall reply], to wit: "He died in regnal year nine of the rebellion."

111. The Later Eighteenth Dynasty in Historical Memory

King lists from the later New Kingdom, in both royal and private monuments, purged those rulers who had become non-persons in the eyes of their successors: this damnatio memoriae included the female pharaoh Hatshepsut from earlier in the

Eighteenth Dynasty together with Akhenaten, Nefernefruaten, Smenkhkare, Tutankhamun and Ay. The memory of the Amarna age was thus officially suppressed, and in all the lists which covered this period Horemheb is shown as the immediate successor of Akhenaten's father, Amenhotep III.[50] *Necessarily, however, documents of the Amarna Period survived in the archives (see 109-110 above), which may explain how the late priestly tradition found in the Egyptian history of Manetho (third century* B.C.E.*) included these uncanonical pharaohs. Manetho's list, which appears to be a composite drawn from canonical and uncanonical sources, is preserved only in later copies by other authors, each of which differs from the others in detail. As quoted in Josephus's pamphlet "Against Apion," however, his account of the later Eighteenth Dynasty appears to be as follows:*[51]

Then his son Amenophis (=Amenhotep III?), for 30 years, 10 months.

Then his son Orus (=Horemheb?), for 36 years, 5 months.

Then his daughter Akenkheres (=Ankhetkheprure Nefernefruaten?), for 12 years, 1 month.

Then her brother Rathotis (=Tutankhamun?), for 9 years.

Then his son Akenkheres (=Akhenaten?), for 12 years, 5 months.

Then his son Akenkheres the second (=Ankhkheprure Smenkhkare?), for 12 years, 3 months.

Then his son Harmais (=Horemheb again?), for 4 years, 1 month.

Notes

1. The writer regards this explanation as more likely than the alternative, which would have Akhenaten engaged in a homosexual relationship with his male coregent and eventual successor, Smenkhkare: see Samson 1978: 120 for a brief discussion of the controversy.

2. Roughly the same format is employed for Boundary Stela L, which, as we have noted above, is most probably also a private rather than a royal monument.

3. Publication forthcoming by James P. Allen (personal communication).

4. The princess is named below the main texts. While her name may also have been part of the original version, its position here (which would imply that her figure preceded that of her elder sister) violates the norm in this period, by which the daughters appeared in sequence of birth. For this reason we believe that Ankhesenpaaten's name was added to the stela and formed no part of its original version.

5. For analysis of this defective copy, see Newberry 1928:5-6.

6. Section numbers follow Daressy 1916b and Engelbach 1931 rather than those used in the wholly derivative edition of Sandman 1938.

7. In the original version, the beginnings of A-E all consisted of Kiya's most characteristic title, "Wife and Greatly Beloved of the King" etc.

8. No effort was made to harmonize the final version with the original, which probably had "his heart [being glad]" here.

9. Cartouche, completely excised.

10. The seated king hieroglyph was substituted for an original, presumably female, suffix here and in the following clause.

11. The second person singular suffix "your," presumably a mistake in either the original or final version, has been erased, but the first person singular "my," which is required here, was never completed.

12. The female first person suffix of the original version is intact here.

13. The original text of Queen Kiya was doubtless addressed to "m[y lord]," that is, the king in the excised cartouche which follows (i.e., Akhenaten).

14. Probably substituted for "here" in the original.

15. Allen (1988:125) makes a case for restoring "[son of] the King of Upper and Lower Egypt" etc. at this point in the final version. If so, something like "(so says) the son of the King" etc. should be understood here.

16. If the speaker is the son of this ruler, as mooted in the preceding note, restore [NEFERKHEPRURE-WAENRE] here.

17. Here, if nowhere else in the preceding text, the final owner of the coffin was named.

18. The vintner's title, which had been "chief of the garden" up to Akhenaten's year 13, was changed in that year to "chief of the basin." Since it was still in this form during Smenkhkare's first year (see above, 95-B), this docket belongs by default to the beginning of Tutankhamun's reign: see Helck 1961-70:728.

19. Since the king had begun his reign as "Tutankhaten" and reigned for several years from the heretic's capital at El-Amarna, it seems impossible to restore "regnal year 1" as mooted (among others) by Helck 1955-58:2025, line 18, and idem 1961:365.

20. The names in the cartouches throughout this text were usurped by Horemheb.

21. Both divine and royal determinatives are used here, just as they had been attached to the same word ("father") when it was applied to the Aten during the heresy period.

22. I.e., their images, which had been defiled during the heresy.

23. I.e., protected from all normal requisition of temple property by the state.

24. Throughout Egyptian history this phrase was used to connote a new beginning or "renaissance" in political affairs.

25. This was continued by Ay when he decorated the colonnade's façade and represented himself in alternation with Amenhotep III in scenes on its outer doorjambs.

26. Presumably a deity who combined the natures of Amun, Atum, and the moon god is meant.

27. The term is apparently to be read "father of fathers"; but this writer is not convinced that its meaning can be narrowed down either to "grandfather" (Larsen 1985) or "great-grandfather" (Reeves 1982).

28. See preceding note.

29. The variant on the other side of this mostly duplicate text is "King of Upper and Lower Egypt, ruler of joy, <Lord of> Crowns, who has taken possession of the White Crown and assumed the Double Crown in life and dominion; Lord of the Two Lands," etc.

30. For discussions of this episode, see Murnane 1990:22-31; and Schulman 1978.

31. The Paris stela substitutes "Lord of the Two Lands."

32. Paris stela: "Lord of Abydos."

33. These last two words are reversed in the original.

34. This cartouche is badly damaged, but in other scenes from the tomb the king is shown to be Tutankhamun. Here as elsewhere, Horemheb substituted his own royal names once he had become king.

35. Singular.

36. The last three phrases compare Horemheb to the god Thoth.

37. I.e., the ritual in which the king was to be formally brought into the temple by the gods—the point being that there was no properly designated king on hand at this occasion.

38. This is the name given to an emplacement for a royal statue along the axis of a temple.

39. Caution is indicated, however, by the presence of a block dating almost two centuries later, from the reign of Ramesses III, inside the river temple at El-Amarna, proving an otherwise ill-documented reoccupation of the site in the later New Kingdom: see Peet and Woolley 1923:128-29.

40. The case for authenticity, initially made by Redford 1973, has since been doubted by many (see Redford 1981 and Murnane 1990:30-31).

41. That is, he was inducted into the community of workmen at Deir el-Medina in West Thebes.

42. I.e., the account which paid for the work on the royal tomb in the Valley of the Kings, which included the upkeep of the workmen in West Thebes.

43. For this translation I have chosen to follow Kruchten's composite text, omitting most of the plausible but unverified restorations of unplaced fragments that were suggested by Helck.

44. Or "with his knapsack/kit bag"? See Bryan and Meltzer 1978.

45. A border town which divided Egypt from Asia.

46. The royal council.

47. While this figure is generally seen as encompassing the entire period from Akhenaten's accession down to the death of Horemheb, Von Beckerath (1978:44–45) has suggested that it may represent the misreading of a "regnal year 28" from the hieratic of a presumed original text on papyrus.

48. Referring to the transport of a divine image at ceremonial occasions.

49. This expression may well bear the connotation "[which] had been the royal residence."

50. See Redford 1986:21-24, 34-39, 40, 44.

51. The identifications proposed here, while eminently defensible, are still quite debatable: see Krauss 1978:204-56.

Sources

1. Edition: Saghir 1991: 21-27.
2-A. Editions: Blankenberg-Van Delden 1969: 134-45; Helck 1955-58: 1737 (579A).
Translations: Breasted 1906-7: 2:348-49; Helck 1961: 234; Blankenberg-Van Delden 1969: 18.
2-B. Editions: Edwards 1939a: pl. 13; Helck 1955-58: 1923 (716).
Translation: Helck 1961: 320.
2-C. Edition: Legrain 1903.
Translation: Millet 1988.
2-D. Edition: Helck 1955-58: 1881-82 (680).
Translation: Helck 1961: 299.
2-E. Editions: Petrie 1897: pl. ix; Helck 1955-58: 1761 (611A).
Translation: Helck 1961: 245.
2-F. Editions: Gayet 1894: 3-28; Helck 1955-58: 1682-1705 (572).
Translation: Helck 1961: 211-21.
2-G. Edition: Helck 1955-58: 1667-70 (568).
Translations: Helck 1961: 203-5.
3. Editions: Brunner 1964; Helck 1955-58: 1713-21 (573).
Translation: Helck 1961: 224-28.
4. Editions: Edwards 1939a: 22-25, pl. xxi; Helck 1955-58: 1943-47 (732).
Translations: Pritchard 1969: 367-68; Helck 1961: 328-31; Lichtheim 1976: 86-89.
5. Editions: Legrain 1902: 262-66; Sandman 1938: 143-44 [cxxxviii]; Helck 1955-58: 1962 (746). This translation incorporates corrections made by Ricardo A. Caminos and Jürgen Osing for the Egypt Exploration Society's forthcoming publication of the inscriptions at Gebel Silsila, through the kindness of the late Professor Caminos.
Translations: Helck 1961: 336-37; Aldred 1988: 88 (excerpt).

6. Edition: Traunecker 1984 (fragments); full publication by Traunecker is pending.
   Translation: Redford 1984:135-36 (excerpts).
7. Edition: Redford 1981.
8. Edition: Chappaz 1983, with references, for all but the last item: numbers for these selections are the catalogue numbers by which they are listed in this publication. The final item is unpublished and depends on the translator's notes and photographs.
9. Editions: Saad and Manniche 1971; Helck 1983: 139-41.
   Translation: Helck 1973b.

10-A. Editions: Lepsius 1849-58: III: pl. 110d, and idem, 1897-1913: III:49; Sandman 1938: 148 [cxlvi]).

10-B. Editions: Fakhry 1935: 42; Sandman 1938: 150 [cl].

10-C. Editions: Fakhry 1935: 45-46; Sandman 1938: 151 [clv].

10-D. Edition: Helck 1955-58: 1992-93 (752.1).
Translation: Helck 1961: 348-49; Redford 1984:135-36.

10-E. Edition: Helck 1955-58: 1994 (752.2).
Translation: Helck 1961: 349.

10-F. Editions: Redford 1976: 95-121; Helck 1955-58: 1995 (752.3).
Translation: Helck 1961: 349.

10-G. Edition: Redford 1976: 59-63.

10-H. Edition: Redford 1976: 76-94.

10-I.1. Edition: Redford 1988: 29-33, fig. 16.

10-I.2. Edition: Redford 1988: pls. 7, 10.

10-I.3. Edition: Redford 1988: pl. 16.

10-I.4. Edition: Redford 1988: pl. 35.

10-I.5. Edition: Redford 1988: 5, pl. 39.

10-I.6. Edition: Redford 1976: pl. 34.1.

10-I.7. Edition: Redford 1982.

11. Editions: Sandman 1938: 152 [clx]; Aldred 1973: 97 [no. 11].
12. Editions: Legrain 1906; Sandman 1938: 147 [cxlii-iii].
13. Edition: Habachi 1965: 91-92, fig. 13.
14. Editions: Hall 1913: 302 [no. 2868 = British Museum 51084]; Sandman 1938: 148 [cxlv].
15. Editions: Breasted 1908-9: 70-72, fig. 42; Sandman 1938: 151 [clvii].
16. Editions: Daressy 1916; Sandman 1938: 149 [cxlviii].
17. Editions: Knudtzon 1915: 240-41; Schroeder 1914: 17-21; Helck 1955-58: 1995 (754).
    Translations: Helck 1961: 350; Kühne 1973: 43-44; Moran 1992: 90 n. 2.

18-A. Edition: Sandman 1938: 187 [ccxxxv].

18-B. Edition: Sandman 1938: 188 [ccxxxvi].

18-C. Edition: Sandman 1938: 190 [ccxlii].

18-D. Edition: Sandman 1938: 190-91 [ccxliii].
18-E. Edition: Sandman 1938: 195 [cclxii].
18-F. Edition: Sandman 1938: 195 [cclxiv].
18-G. Edition: James 1974: 133 and pl. lxxv (302).
Translation: Löhr 1975: 179.
19. Edition: Gardiner 1906.
20. Editions: Daressy 1918; Sandman 1938: 134-37 [cxxiv]; Helck 1955-58: 2018-22 (767).
Translation: Helck 1961: 361-63.
21. Editions: Schiaparelli 1887: 464-65 (no. 1722); Sandman 1938: 146 [cxl]; Helck 1955-58: 2018 (766).
Translation: Helck 1961: 360.
22. Editions: Griffith 1898: 91-92, pl. xxxviii; Sandman 1938: 17-48 [cxliv]; Löhr 1975: 142-44.
Translations: Wente 1980; idem 1990: 28.
23. Edition: Drioton 1943: 35-43.
24. Edition: Lacau 1909-26: 222-24, pl. lxix; Sandman 1938: 178-79 (ccxii); Helck 1955-58: 2022 (768).
Translations: Helck 1961: 363; Löhr 1975: 176-7.
25-A. Edition: Munro 1981.
25-B. Edition: Aldred 1959: 19-22 with pl. iii.
26-A. Edition: drawn from Zivie 1990: 151-66.
26-B. Editions: Schäfer 1931: pl. 6; Mariette 1884-85: 449; Löhr 1975: 172-75 (Dok. III.2b-c), and pl. vi.1 (Dok. III.2a).
Translations: Löhr 1975: 172-73 (Dok. III.2a)
27. Editions: Bissing 1929; Sandman 1938: 144-45 [cxxxviii].
28. Edition: Drioton 1943: 25-35.
29. Edition: Zivie 1975.
Translation: Löhr 1975: 180-86 (Dok. III.7a-g).
30-A. Editions: Epigraphic Survey 1980: 32-33, pl. 9; Helck 1955-58: 1872 (674).
Translation: Helck 1961: 295.
30-B. Edition: Epigraphic Survey 1980: 34-37, with pls. 12-15.
30-C. Edition: Epigraphic Survey 1980:38, pl. 20.
30-D. Edition: Epigraphic Survey 1980:30-32, pl. 7.
31. Edition: Helck 1955-58: 1995 (753).
Translation: Helck 1961: 349.
32-A. Editions: Davies 1941: pl. xiii; Helck 1955-58: 1778 (634).
Translation: Helck 1961 253.
32-B. Editions: Davies 1941: pl. xxv; Helck 1955-58: 1776 (634).
Translation: Helck 1961: 252.
32-C. Editions: Davies 1941: pl xxx; Helck 1955-58: 1780-81 (634).
Translation: Helck 1961: 254.

32-D. Editions: Davies 1941: pl. xxxiv; Helck 1955-58: 1781-82 (634).
Translation: Helck 1961: 254-55.

32-E. Editions: Davies 1941: pl. xxxvi; Helck 1955-58: 1782-83 (634).
Translation: Helck 1961: 255.

32-F. Editions: Davies 1941: pl. xxvii; Helck 1955-58: 1788-89 (634).
Translation: Helck 1961: 257-58.

33. Editions: Davies 1923: 137-45; Sandman 1938: 140-43; Helck 1955-58: 1996 (755 = extracts).
Translation: Helck 1961: 350 (extracts).

34-A. Editions: Brugsch 1857: 274, pl. 50 (no. 1345); Černý 1973: 51.

34-B. Editions: Bruyère 1937: 98-99, fig. 42.1; Černý 1973: 50-51.

34-C. Edition: Bruyère 1937: 104, pls. x.1, xii.
Translation: Černý 1973: 51.

34-D.1. Edition: Daressy 1901.

34-D.2. Edition: A. Hassan 1976: 235 (4) with pl. vi.3.

35-A. Edition: Goyon 1957:106-7, pls. xxv (90) and xxxi (91).
Translation: Redford 1963.

35-B. Edition: Allen 1994b.

35-C. Edition: Redford and Redford 1989: 44-48 (nos. 6 and 7).

36. Editions: Legrain 1902: 260-62; Sandman 1938: 133-34 [cxxii]; Helck 1955-58: 1963-64 (=B).
Translation: Helck 1961: 337-38 (=B).

37. Editions: Murnane and Van Siclen 1993: 11-68, pls. 2-12, 22, 23A, 31B, 32; Davies 1903-8: 5:28-31, pls. xxix-xxxii, xxxvii-viii; Helck 1955-58: 1965-80 (749); Sandman 1938: 103-118.
Translations: Helck 1961:338-44.

38. Editions: Murnane and Van Siclen 1993: 69-109, pls. 13-15, 17-21, 23B, 24-30, 31A; Davies 1903-8: 5:31-34, pls. xxv-xxviii, xxxiii-iv, xxxvi, xxxix-xliii; Helck 1955-58: 1981-1988 (749); Sandman 1938: 119-31.
Translations: Breasted 1906-7: 2:394-400; Helck 1961: 344-47; Lichtheim 1976: 48-51.

39. Edition: Murnane and Van Siclen 1993: 193-94, pls. 16, 23.

40-A. Editions: Borchardt 1923: 2-24, pl. i; Sandman 1938: 154-55 [clxiii]).

40-B. Editions: Berlin Museum 1924: 255-56 (no. 14145); Sandman 1938: 156 [clxv]; Aldred 1973: 102 (no. 16).

41-A. Editions: Griffith 1926; Sandman 1938: 166 [clxxxix].

41-B. Editions: Frankfort and Pendlebury 1933: 102, pl. xlvii.2; Sandman 1938: 166 [cxc].

41-C. Editions: Pendlebury 1951: 233-35, pl. cviii; Stewart 1976: 21, p. 11 (bottom).

42-A. Editions: Bryant and Reed 1893; Edwards 1939a: 27-28, pl. xxiv (no. 1000).

42-B. Edition: Edwards 1939a: 29, pl. xxvi (no. 935).
42-C. Edition: Bittel and Hermann 1934: 28.
43. Edition: Schäfer 1918: 32-33, Abb. 29; Sandman 1938: 161-62 [clxxxi].
44-A. Edition: Balcz and Bittel 1932: 34-37, Abb. 17; Sandman 1938:153-4 (clxii).
44-B. Edition: Bittel and Hermann 1934: 30.
45-A. Edition: Fairman 1961: 29-30, figs. 1-2.
45-B. Edition: Harris 1974b: 28-29, fig. A.
45-C. Edition: Peet and Woolley 1923: 147-49, 152-54, pls. xxxiv.1-2, lvi (22/273); Sandman 1938: 167 [cxcii]; Hanke 1978: 256 (Abb. 44), 268 (Abb. 46).
45-D. Edition: Roeder 1969: pl. 197 (PC 179), with Hanke 1978: 256 (Abb. 44, upper right).
45-E. Edition: Peet and Woolley 1923: pl. lvii (85), with Hanke 1978: 258 (Abb. 46).
45-F. Edition: Roeder 1969: pl. 19 (207 + 234-VIII A), with Hanke 1978: 260 (Abb. 48).
45-G. Edition: Roeder 1969: pl. 23 (224-VIII), with Hanke 1978: 261 (Abb. 49).
46-A. Editions: Bissing 1911-14: pl. 82; Sandman 1938: 155 [clxiv].
46-B. Edition: Martin 1989a: 37-48, pls. 57-81.
46-C. Edition: Martin 1974: 13-16, pls. 6-9.
46-D. Edition: Martin 1974: 26-30; Sandman 1938: 166-67 [cxci].
46-E.1 Edition: Martin 1974: 88-90, pl. 53.
46-E.2. Edition: Martin 1974: 95-96.
46-E.3. Edition: Loeben 1986; Aldred 1988: 229-30.
46-E.4. Edition: Khouly and Martin 1987: 8, pl. 21 (no. 35).
47-A. Editions: (1) Peet and Woolley 1923: pls. lxiii [170-171], lxiv [2, 8, 23, 75]; Frankfort and Pendlebury 1933: pl. lviii [8, 17, 24, 25, 27]; (2) Sandman 1938: 180-81 [ccxviii-ccxx].
47-B. Edition: Pendlebury 1951: pls. lxxxiv (4).
Translation: Pendlebury 1951: 161; and cf. for others in the same series Wente 1990: 96 (nos. 125-127).
47-C. Edition: Pendlebury 1951: pls. lxxxv-xciv [16, 17, 18, 23, 34, 37, 44, 55, 74, 93, 99, 107, 117, 185, 196-197, 208, 218, 233, 237, 245).
47-D. Editions: Dawson 1924; Sandman 1938: 182 [ccxxi].
47-E. Editions: (1) Petrie 1894: pl. xxi [9, 11, 21, 19]; Frankfort and Pendlebury 1933: pl. lvii [AA]; Peet and Woolley 1923: pl. lv [I, S, V]; (2) Sandman 1938: 182-3 [ccxxii-ccxxiv].
48. Editions: Lacau 1909-26: 214-16, pl. lxv; Sandman 1938: 156-57 [clxvi].
49. Editions: Maspéro 1881: 116; Sandman 1938: 157 [clxvii].

50. Editions: Nicholson 1870: pl. 2; Sandman 1938: 200 [cclxxxiv].

51-A. Edition: Habachi 1965: 82-84, pl. xxvi.

51-B. Edition: Habachi 1965: 79-84, pl. xxv [C].

52. Editions: Gabra 1931: 238-42; Sandman 1938: 161 [clxxi].

53-A. Editions: Habachi 1965: 70-79, pls. xxii-xxv; and for Altar E: Legrain 1901: 62; Sandman 1938: 179 [ccxiii]; Habachi 1965: 74, 78.

53-B. Edition: Habachi 1965: 70-72.

54. Editions: Davis 1910: 13-15, pls. xxxi-xxxiii; idem 1990: 22-24, pls. xxxiii-xxxv; Sandman 1938: 164-66 [clxxxviii]).

55. Editions: Smith 1976: 124-30, pls. 29, 75 [3-4]; Helck 1980.
Translation: Schulman 1982: 301-3.

56. Editions: Gauthier 1910: 122-23; Sandman 1938: 146 [cxxxix]; Helck 1955-58: 1963 (747).
Translations: Helck 1961: 337; Schulman 1982: 302-3.

57. Editions: Sandman 1938: 184-200 [ccxxv-cclxxxi], with references cited.

58-A. Editions: Berlin Museum 1924: 267-68 (no. 17555); Sandman 1938: 176 (ccvi); Helck 1955-58: 2002 (757).

58-B.1. Editions: Davies 1903-8: 6: xxiv; Sandman 1938: 87-89 (cx); Helck 1955-58: 2001 (756: titles only)
Translations: Davies 1903-8: 6: 32-33; Helck 1955-58: 2001 (756: titles only); Helck 1961: 352 (titles only).

58-B.2. Editions: Davies 1903-8: 6: xxv bottom; Sandman 1938: 89-90 (cxi).
Translation: Davies 1903-8: 6: 34.

58-B.3. Editions: Davies 1903-8: 6: xxv top; Sandman 1938: 90-93.
Translations: Breasted 1906-7 2: 408-11; Davies 1903-8: 6: 28-29; Lichtheim 1976: 93-96.

58-B.4. Editions: Davies 1903-8: 6: xxvii; Sandman 1938: 93-96 (cxiii).
Translations: Davies 1903-8: 6: 29-31; Pritchard 1969: 369-71; Simpson 1973: 289-95; Lichtheim 1976: 96-100; Foster 1992: 5-10.

58-B.5. Editions: Davies 1903-8: 6: xxvi, xxviii-xxxi; Sandman 1938: 96-97; Helck 1955-58: 2000-2001 (756).
Translations: Davies 1903-8: 6: 19-23; Helck 1961: 352.

58-B.6. Editions: Davies 1903-8: 6: xxxi; Sandman 1938: 97 (cxv).
Translation: Davies 1903-8: 6: 33.

58-B.7. Editions: Davies 1903-8: 6: xxxii, xxxiv; Sandman 1938: 98-100 (cxvi); Helck 1955-58: 1997-99 (756 = C-E only).
Translation: Davies 1903-8: 6: 33-34; Helck 1961 = 351 (C-E only)

58-B.8. Editions: Davies 1903-8: 6: xxxiii; Sandman 1938: 100-102 (cxviii).
Translation: Davies 1903-8: 6: 34.

59.1. Editions: Davies 1903-8: 3: xxvii; 4: ii; Sandman 1938: 43-44 (li).
Translation: Davies 1903-8: 6: 32.

59.2. Editions: Davies 1903-8: 3: xxvii; Sandman 1938: 44-46 (lii); Helck 1955-58: 2002 (759).
Translations: Davies 1903-8: 3: 32; Helck 1961: 353.

59.3. Editions: Davies 1903-8: 3: xxviii, xxxviii; Sandman 1938: 46-47 (liv).
Translations: Davies 1903-8 3: 32; Breasted 1906-7 2: 414-15.

59.4. Editions: Davies 1903-8: 3: xxix; Sandman 1938: 6-9.
Translations: Davies 1903-8: 3: 31-32; Breasted 1906-7 2: 414.

60-A.1. Editions: Davies 1903-8: 4: xxxii-xxxiii; ibid, 5: 7; Sandman 1938: 10-16 (viii).
Translations: Davies 1903-8: 4: 27-29; Lichtheim 1976: 90-92.

60-A.2. Editions: Davies 1903-8: 5: ix; Sandman 1938: 40-42 (xlvii).
Translation: Davies 1903-8: 5: 17.

60-A.3. Editions: Davies 1903-8: 5: x; Sandman 1938: 64 (lxxxiii).
Translation: Davies 1903-8: 5: 17.

60-A.4. Editions: Davies 1903-8: 5: xi; Sandman 1938: 64-65 (lxxxiv).
Translation: Davies 1903-8: 5: 17.

60-B. Editions: Davies 1903-8: 5: xxi-xxiii; Sandman 1938: 67-68 (lxxxviii-xciii).
Translation: Davies 1903-8: 5: 9-11.

61-A. Editions: Berlin Museum 1924: 399 (no. 19241); Sandman 1938: 158 (clxxi).

61-B.1. Editions: Davies 1903-8: 4: xxxii-xxxiii, xliii; Sandman 1938: 10-16.
Translations: Davies 1903-8: 4: 27-9; Lichtheim 1976: 90-92.

61-B.2. Editions: Davies 1903-8: 4: xxxi, xliv; Sandman 1938: 54-55 (lxx).
Translation: Davies 1903-8: 4: 19-20.

61-B.3. Editions: Davies 1903-8: 4: xxxii; Sandman 1938: 55 (lxxii).
Translation: Davies 1903-8: 4: 31.

61-B.4. Editions: Davies 1903-8: 4: xxxix; Sandman 1938: 57 (lxxv).
Translation: Davies 1903-8: 4: 31.

62. Editions: Legrain 1910: 108; Sandman 1938: 178 (ccxi).

63-A. Editions: Bissing 1914: i; Sandman 1938: 174-75 (cciv); Helck 1955-58: 1942-43 (731); Habachi 1965: 70-92.
Translations: Breasted 1906-7 2: 400-402; Helck 1961: 327-28.

63-B. Edition: Habachi 1965: 89-90.

63-C. Editions: Brugsch 1883-91: 1068-70; Sandman 1938: 175 (ccv).

64. Editions: Maspéro 1909-24: 27-28, pl. xxiii; Sandman 1938: 177 (ccvii).

65. Editions: Frankfort and Pendlebury 1933: xxiii.4; Sandman 1938: 159-60 (clxxiv).
Translation: Frankfort and Pendlebury 1933: 109.

66.1. Editions: Davies 1903-8: 3: ii; Sandman 1938: 33-34 (xxxvi).
Translation: Davies 1903-8: 3: 17-18.

66.2. Editions: Davies 1903-8: 3: iii; Sandman 1938: 6-9 (vii).
Translation: Davies 1903-8: 3: 18.

66.3. Editions: Davies 1903-8: 3: iv-v; Sandman 1938: 34-35 (xxxviii).
Translation: Davies 1903-8: 3: 18.

66.4. Editions: Davies 1903-8: 3: vi-vii; Sandman 1938: 35 (xxxix).
Translation: Davies 1903-8: 3: 7.

66.5. Editions: Davies 1903-8: 3: viii-xii; Sandman 1938: 35-36 (xl); Helck 1955-58: 2006 (764).
Translations: Davies 1903-8: 3: 7-9; Helck 1961: 355.

66.6. Edition: Davies 1903-8: 3: vii, xiii-xv; Sandman 1938: 36-37 (xli); Helck 1955-58: 2006 (764).
Translation: Breasted 1906-7: 418; Davies 1903-8: 3: 9-12; Helck 1961: 355.

66.7. Editions: Davies 1903-8: 3: xvi; Sandman 1938: 37 (xlii); Helck 1955-58: 2007 (764).
Translations: Davies 1903-8: 3: 12-13; Helck 1961: 356.

66.8. Editions: Davies 1903-8: 3: xvii-xviii; Sandman 1938: 37-38 (xliii).
Translation: Davies 1903-8: 3: 13-15.

66.9. Editions: Davies 1903-8: 3: xviii; Sandman 1938: 38 (xliv).
Translation: Davies 1903-8: 3: 15-16.

66.10. Editions: Davies 1903-8: 3: xix, xxxvi; Sandman 1938: 38-40 (xlv).
Translation: Davies 1903-8: 3: 18-19.

66.11. Editions: Davies 1903-8: 3: xx; Sandman 1938: 40 (xlvi).
Translation: Davies 1903-8: 3: 18.

66.12. Editions: Davies 1903-8: 3: xx; Sandman 1938: 40-42.
Translation: Davies 1903-8: 3: 2-4.

66.13. Editions: Davies 1903-8: 3: xxi; Sandman 1938: 43 (xlix).
Translation: Davies 1903-8: 3: 4.

66.14. Editions: Davies 1903-8: 3: xxii; Sandman 1938: 43 (l).
Translation: Davies 1903-8: 3: 16-17.

66.15. Edition: Davies 1903-8: 3: xxiii.
Translation: Davies 1903-8: 3: 17.

66.16. Editions: Davies 1903-8: 3: xxvii; Sandman 1938: 46 (liii).
Translation: Davies 1903-8: 3: 15-16.

67. Editions: Berlin Museum 1924: 127-30 (no. 20376); Sandman 1938: 170-71 (cxcvii); Helck 1955-58: 2023-24 (768).
Translation: Helck 1961: 363-64.

68.1. Editions: Davies 1903-8: 5: ii-iii; Sandman 1938: 59-60 (lxxvii).
Translations: Breasted 1906-7 2: 411-13; Davies 1903-8: 5: 16.

68.2. Editions: Davies 1903-8: 5: iv; Sandman 1938: 60-61 (lxxix).
Translation: Davies 1903-8: 5: 2-4.

68.3. Editions: Davies 1903-8: 5: ii; Sandman 1938: 60 (lxxviii).
Translation: Davies 1903-8: 5: 18.

68.4. Editions: Davies 1903-8: 5: iv; Sandman 1938: 62-63 (lxxx).
Translation: Davies 1903-8: 5: 17-18.

68.5. Editions: Davies 1903-8: 5: v; Sandman 1938: 63 (lxxxi).
Translation: Davies 1903-8: 5: 1.

69.1. Editions: Davies 1903-8: 4: xxviii; Sandman 1938: 53-54 (lxviii).
Translation: Davies 1903-8: 4: 30-31.

69.2. Editions: Davies 1903-8: 4: xxvii; Sandman 1938: 52-53 (lxvii).
Translation: Davies 1903-8: 4: 31.

69.3. Editions: Davies 1903-8: 4: xxiv-xxvi; Sandman 1938: 51-52 (lxvi); Helck 1955-58: 2005 (763).
Translations: Davies 1903-8: 4: 16-18; Helck 1961: 355.

69.4. Editions: Davies 1903-8: 4: xx-xxii; Sandman 1938: 51 (lxiv).
Translation: Davies 1903-8: 4: 15-16.

69.5. Editions: Davies 1903-8: 4: xvii-xix; Sandman 1938: 50-51 (lxiii).
Translation: Davies 1903-8: 4: 14-15.

69.6. Editions: Davies 1903-8: 4: xvi, xxiii, xxix, xxxii-xxxiii; Sandman 1938: 10-12 (viii).
Translation: Davies 1903-8: 4: 28.

70.1. Editions: Davies 1903-8: 1: vi-ix; Sandman 1938: 1-2 (i); Helck 1955-58: 2003-4 (762).
Translations: Breasted 1906-7 2: 405-6; Davies 1903-8: 1: 20-23; Helck 1961: 354.

70.2. Editions: Davies 1903-8: 1: x-xix; Sandman 1938: 2 (ii); Helck 1955-58: 2004 (762).
Translations: Davies 1903-8: 1: 23-30; Helck 1961: 354.

70..3. Editions: Davies 1903-8: 1: xxv, xxix-xxxii; Sandman 1938: 2-3 (iii); Helck 1955-58: 2004-5 (762).
Translations: Davies 1903-8: 1: 33-42; Helck 1961: 355.

70.4. Editions: Davies 1903-8: 1: xxxiv; Sandman 1938: 3-4 (iv).
Translation: Davies 1903-8: 1: 15-16, 52-53.

70.5. Editions: Davies 1903-8: 1: xxxv; Sandman 1938: 5-6 (v).
Translation: Davies 1903-8: 1: 52.

70.6. Editions: Davies 1903-8: 1: xxxv, xl; Sandman 1938: 6 (vi).
Translation: Davies 1903-8: 1: 52.

70.7. Editions: Davies 1903-8: 1: xxxvi; Sandman 1938: 6-10 (vii).
Translations: Breasted 1906-7 2: 405-6; Davies 1903-8: 1: 49-50.

70.8. Editions: Davies 1903-8: 1: iv, xxxvii; cf. ibid. 4: xxxii-xxxiii; Sandman 1938: 10-16 (viii).
Translations: Davies 1903-8: 1: 50-52; Lichtheim 1976: 90-92.

70.9. Editions: Davies 1903-8: 1: xxxviii; Sandman 1938: 16-17 (ix, x).
Translation: Davies 1903-8: 1: 49.

70.10. Editions: Davies 1903-8: 1: xxxix; Sandman 1938: 17-20 (xi).
Translation: Davies 1903-8: 1: 52-53.

70.11. Editions: Davies 1903-8: 1: xli; Sandman 1938: 20-21 (xiii, xiv).
Translation: Davies 1903-8: 1: 49.

71.1. Editions: Davies 1903-8: 2: xxix, xxxvii-xl; Sandman 1938: 29-30 (xxviii); Helck 1955-58: 2003 (761).
Translations: Davies 1903-8: 2: 38-43; Helck 1961: 353.

71.2. Editions: Davies 1903-8: 2: xxix; Sandman 1938: 30 (xxix).
Translation: Davies 1903-8: 2: 45.

71.3. Edition: Davies 1903-8: 2: xxx-xxxi; Sandman 1938: 30-31 (xxx, xxxi).
Translation: Davies 1903-8: 2: 45.

71.4. Editions: Davies 1903-8: 2: xxxvi; Sandman 1938: 32 (xxxii, xxxiii).
Translation: Davies 1903-8: 2: 45.

71.5. See 95-A below.

72. Editions: Berlin Museum 1924: 234-35 (no. 14123), as corrected by Rammant-Peeters 1983: 6-7 with pl. ii, and through the kind assistance of Dr. Rolf Krauss (Ägyptisches Museum, Berlin-Charlottenburg).
Translation: Rammant-Peeters 1983: 6-7 (titles only).

73-A. Editions: Frankfort and Pendlebury 1933: vii.4, 6; Sandman 1938: 173-74 (cci-cciii).
Translation: Frankfort and Pendlebury 1933: 144-45.

73-B. Edition: Davies 1903-8: 5: 12-13.

74. Editions: Davies 1903-8: 4: xxxvii; Sandman 1938: 56 (lxxiv).
Translation: Davies 1903-8: 4: 31 (5).

75-A. Edition: Borchardt and Ricke 1980: 346-47 (Cairo Museum 20/6/28/9: left side of lintel), joined to Cairo Museum JE 37505 (right side) by Rolf Krauss (Ägyptisches Museum, Berlin-Charlottenburg): to be published by Krauss, and included here by his permission.

75-B. Edition: Stewart 1976: 19, pl. 10.2.

76. Editions: Davies 1903-8: 5: xiii; Sandman 1938: 65-66 (lxxxvi).
Translation: Davies 1903-8: 5: 15.

77-A. Editions: Frankfort 1927: 213, with pls. xlv.2, 3, xlvii; Sandman 1938: 162 (clxxxiii).

77-B.1. Editions: Davies 1903-8: 2: vii; Sandman 1938: 23-24 (xx).
Translation: Davies 1903-8: 2: 29-30.

77-B.2. Editions: Davies 1903-8: 2: viii; Sandman 1938: 24-25 (xxi).
Translation: Davies 1903-8: 2: 30.

77-B.3. Editions: Davies 1903-8: 2: ix; Sandman 1938: 25-27 (xxii).
Translation: Davies 1903-8: 2: 31.

77-B.4. Editions: Davies 1903-8: 2: x-xi; Sandman 1938: 27 (xxiii).
Translation: Davies 1903-8: 2: 16-17.

77-B.5. Edition: Davies 1903-8: 2: xi (bottom), xii.

Translation: Davies 1903-8: 2: 17.

77-B.6. Editions: Davies 1903-8: 2: xx; Sandman 1938: 27 (xxiv).
Translations: Davies 1903-8: 2: 19.

77-B.7. Editions: Davies 1903-8: 2: xxi; Sandman 1938: 27-28 (xxv).
Translations: Davies 1903-8: 2: 30-32.

77-B.8. Editions: Davies 1903-8: 2: xxi; Sandman 1938: 17-20 (xi).
Translation: Davies 1903-8: 2: 31-32.

77-B.9. Editions: Davies 1903-8: 2: xxi; Sandman 1938: 28-29 (xxvi).
Translation: Davies 1903-8: 2: 30-31.

77-B.10. Editions: Davies 1903-8: 2: iv; Sandman 1938: 21-22 (xv); Helck 1955-58: 2002 (760).
Translation: Davies 1903-8: 2: 15-16; Helck 1961: 353.

77-B.11. Editions: Davies 1903-8: 2: iv; Sandman 1938: 22 (xvi-xvii); Helck 1955-58: 2002 (760).
Translations: Davies 1903-8: 2: 30; Helck 1961: 353.

77-B.12. Editions: Davies 1903-8: 2: v; Sandman 1938: 22-23 (xviiii).
Translation: Davies 1903-8: 2: 30.

77-B.13. Editions: Davies 1903-8: 2: v; Sandman 1938: 33 (xix).
Translation: Davies 1903-8: 2: 15.

77-B.14. Editions: Davies 1903-8: 2: xxiii; Sandman 1938: 29 (xxvii).
Translation: Davies 1903-8: 2: 28-29.

78.1. Editions: Davies 1903-8: 6: vii; Sandman 1938: 70 (xcvi).

78.2. Editions: Davies 1903-8: 6: iii, viii; Sandman 1938: 69 (xciv).
Translation: Davies 1903-8: 6: 25.

78.3. Editions: Davies 1903-8: 6: vi; Sandman 1938: 69-70 (xcv).
Translation: Davies 1903-8: 6: 5-6.

78.4. Edition: Davies 1903-8: 6: iv-v.
Translation: Davies 1903-8: 6: 3-5.

79. Editions: Berlin Museum 1924: 126 (no. 20375); Sandman 1938: 172 (cxcviii).

80.1. Editions: Davies 1903-8: 4: ii; Sandman 1938: 43-44 (li) and 47-48 (lvi).
Translation: Davies 1903-8: 6: 30.

80.2. Editions: Davies 1903-8: 4: iii; Sandman 1938: 33-34 (xxxvi).
Translation: Davies 1903-8: 4: 29.

80.3. Editions: Davies 1903-8: 4: iv; Sandman 1938: 48-49 (lviii); Helck 1955-58: 2002 (758).
Translation: Davies 1903-8: 4: 29-30; Helck 1961: 353.

80.4. Editions: Davies 1903-8: 4: v-vii, xi-xii; Sandman 1938: 49 (lix).
Translations: Davies 1903-8: 4: 2-3.

80.5. Editions: Davies 1903-8: 4: viii-ix; Sandman 1938: 49-50 (lx).
Translation: Davies 1903-8: 4: 4.

80.6. Editions: Davies 1903-8: 4: viii; Sandman 1938: 50 (lxi).
Translation: Davies 1903-8: 4: 5.

81. Editions: Legrain 1910: 107-8; Drioton 1943: 15-25; Sandman 1938: 177 (ccviii).
82. Editions: Wiedemann 1885: 201-2; Sandman 1938: 177 (ccix).
83. Editions: Frankfort 1927: 210, with pl. xlvi; Sandman 1938: 164 (clxxxvii).
84-A. Editions: Borchardt 1914: 16-18, with fig. 5; Sandman 1938: 172 (cxcix).
84-B. Editions: Davies 1903-8: 4: xxxv; Sandman 1938: 55-56 (lxxiii).
85-A. Editions: Peet and Woolley 1923: 10, pl. ix-3
85-B. Editions: Peet and Woolley 1923: 8, fig. 1.
86. Editions: Davies 1903-8: 2: xlii; Sandman 1938: 33 (xxxv).
Translation: Davies 1903-8: 2: 3.
87. Editions: Davies 1903-8: 4: xxxviii-xxxix; Sandman 1938: 57-59 (lxxvi).
Translation: Davies 1903-8: 4: 31.
88. Editions: Davies 1903-8: 5: xv; Sandman 1938: 66 (lxxxvii).
Translation: Davies 1903-8: 5: 17.
89.1. Editions: Davies 1903-8: 6: xiii, xv, xxxiv; Sandman 1938: 71-75 (xcviii, cii, ciiii).
Translation: Davies 1903-8: 6: 31.
89.2. Editions: Davies 1903-8: 6: xiv; Sandman 1938: 72 (c).
Translation: Davies 1903-8: 6: 32.
89.3. Editions: Davies 1903-8: 6: xii; Sandman 1938: 70-71 (xcviii).
Translation: Davies 1903-8: 6: 32.
89.4. Editions: Davies 1903-8: 6: xiv; Sandman 1938: 72 (xcix).
89.5. Editions: Davies 1903-8: 6: xiv; Sandman 1938: 72-73 (ci).
Translation: Davies 1903-8: 6: 32.
89.6. Edition: Davies 1903-8: 6: xvi (cf. ibid. 4: xxxii-xxxiii); Sandman 1938: 10-16 (cv).
Translation: incorporated into composite text translated in Davies 1903-8: 4: 27-29; and by Lichtheim 1976: 90-92.
89.7. Edition: Davies 1903-8: 6: xv; Sandman 1938: 75-78 (civ).
Translations: Davies 1903-8: 6: 25-26; Breasted 1906-7 2: 416-17.
89.8. Editions: Davies 1903-8: 6: xvii-xviii; Sandman 1938: 78-80 (cvi); Helck 1955-58: 2008-11 (765).
Translations: Davies 1903-8: 6: 10-12; Helck 1961: 356-58.
89.9. Editions: Davies 1903-8: 6: xix-xx; Sandman 1938: 80-83 (cvii) and 201; Helck 1955-58: 2012-16 (765).
Translations: Davies 1903-8: 6: 12-14; Helck 1961: 358-59.
89.10. Editions: Davies 1903-8: 6: xix; Sandman 1938: 83-84 (cviii); Helck 1955-58: 2016-17 (765).
Translations: Davies 1903-8: 6: 27; Helck 1961: 360.
89.11. Editions: Davies 1903-8: 6: xxi; Sandman 1938: 84-87 (cix).
Translation: Davies 1903-8: 6: 27-28.

90-A. Editions: Spiegelberg and Erman 1898: 126-29 with pl. xvii; Sandman 1938: 180 (ccxvii).
90-B. Editions: Berlin Museum 1924: 266 (no. 13239); Sandman 1938: 160 (clxxv).
90-C. Editions: Davies 1903-8: 5: xiii; Sandman 1938: 65 (lxxxv).
90-D. Editions: Berlin Museum 1924: 518 (no. 15099); Sandman 1938: 178 (ccx).
90-E. Editions: Pendlebury, 1951: pl. cii (49).
91. Editions: Berlin Museum 1924: 115; Sandman 1938: 168 (cxcv).
92. Editions: Newberry 1928: 4-5; Sandman 1938: 168 (cxciv).
93-A. Editions: Pendlebury 1951: 231-33, pl. lxxiii 8-9; Stewart 1976: pls. 12, 52.2, and p. 22.
Translations: Samson 1978: 103-6; Allen 1988: 117-21; Krauss 1989; Gabolde 1990.
93-B. Edition: Pendlebury 1951: pl. xcv, no. 279.
93-C. Editions: Samson 1978: 108-32; Krauss 1978: 30-6, 84-90; idem 1990.
94. Edition: Gardiner 1928; Helck 1955-58 = 2024 (771 = titles only)
Translation (titles only): Helck 1961: 368.
95-A. Edition: Lepsius 1849-58 3: 99; Davies 1903-8: 2: 43-44, pl. xli.
95-B. Edition: Pendlebury 1951: lxxxvi (35).
96-A. Edition: Loeben 1991.
96-B. Edition: Davis 1910: 16-19, pl. xxx; idem 1990: 25-29, pl. xxxii; Sandman 1938: 168-69 (cxcvi).
Translations: Daressy 1916b; Engelbach 1931; Hanke 1978: 171-74, 269-70; Allen 1988: 121-26.
97. Edition: Erman 1900: 113.
98-A. Edition: Roeder 1969: pl. 106 (831-VIIIC).
98-B. Edition: Pendlebury 1951: pl. lxxxvi (55).
99. Editions: Lacau 1909-26: 224ff and pl. 70; Helck 1955-58: 2025-32 (772).
Translations: Bennett 1939; Pritchard 1969: 250-51; Helck 1961: 365-68.
100-A. Edition: Helck 1955-58: 2034-36 (774).
Translation: Helck 1961: 368-69.
100-B. Edition: Amer 1985.
100-C. Edition: Helck 1955-58: 2078 (798).
Translation: Helck 1961: 389.
100-D.1. Edition: Epigraphic Survey 1994: pls. 3, 119.
Translations: ibid., pp. 1, 43.
100-D.2. Edition: Epigraphic Survey, forthcoming. The translation in this book is based on the author's notes.
100-E. Edition: Edwards 1939a, p. 14 with pl. xv.
Translation: Edwards 1939b.

100-F. Editions: Reeves 1981; Larson 1985, 1992.
100-G. Editions: Glanville 1929: 5-6, pl. ii (4); Helck 1955-58: 2083 (802).
Translation: Helck 1961: 391.
100-H.1. Editions: Davies and Gardiner 1926: pl. 14; Helck 1955-58: 2068 (792).
Translation: Helck 1961: 385.
100-H.2. Editions: Griffith 1921-22: pls. 24.9, 28.1; Helck 1955-58: 2074-75 (794 B, D); Karkowsky 1981: 115-39.
Translation: Helck 1961: 387-88.
100-I.1. Edition: Davis 1912: 128-29.
100-I.2. Edition: Schaden 1977: 148, 162-66.
100.J.1. See 105-A below.
100-J.2. Edition: Helck 1955-58: 2103-5 (809).
Translation: Helck 1961: 399-400.
100-K. Edition: Schaden 1977: 139-41.
101-A. Edition: Helck 1955-58: 2052-54 (781-E).
Translation: Helck 1961: 376-78.
101-B. Edition: Helck 1955-58: 2055 (781-G).
Translation: Helck 1961: 378.
101-C. Editions: Carter 1933: pl. 42-A; Helck 1955-58: 2063 (789).
Translation: Helck 1961: 382.
101-D. Edition: Černý 1965 (nos. 1, 4, 20, 23-25).
102. Edition: Beinlich and Saleh 1989: 1.
103-A. Editions: Newberry 1932: 50; Helck 1955-58: 2108 (817); Krauss and Ullrich 1982.
103-B.1. Editions: Gayet 1894: pl. xxii, fig. 79; Helck 1955-58: 2106 (810).
Translation: Helck 1961: 400.
103.B.2. Editions: Lepsius 1849-58: 3: 114a; Helck 1955-58: 2106-7 (811).
Translation: Helck 1961: 400-1.
103.C. Edition: Helck 1955-58: 2109-10 (818).
Translation: Helck 1961: 402.
103-D. Editions: Berlin Museum 1924: 122-25; Helck 1955-58: 2110-11 (820).
Translation: Helck 1961: 403.
104-A. Edition: Schaden 1984: 50-53.
104-B. Edition: Hölscher 1939: pls. 52-56 (especially Cairo Museum 6058-59); Helck 1955-58: 2107 (813: titles only).
Translation: Helck 1961: 401 (titles only).
105-A.1. Edition: Martin 1989b: 78-84, pl. 91.
105-A.2. Edition: Martin 1989b: 94-97, pls. 111-115.
105-B. Edition: Winlock 1924; Helck 1955-58: 2089-94 (804).
Translations: Helck 1961: 393-95; Lichtheim 1976: 100-103.
105-C. Editions: Edwards 1939a: pl. 28; Helck 1955-58: 2094-99 (805).
Translation: Helck 1961: 395-97.

106. Editions: Gardiner 1953: pl. ii; Helck 1955-58: 2113-20 (825).
Translations: Gardiner 1953: 14-16; Helck 1961: 404-7.

107-A. Editions: Petrie 1909: pl. 6; Helck 1955-58: 2121-24 (826).
Translation: Helck 1961: 407-8.

107-B.1. Edition: Petrie 1894: 43, pl. xi.5.

107-B.2. Editions: Pendlebury 1951: 12, pl. lx.3; Bierbrier 1982: 9, pls. 1 (bottom), 2 (bottom).

107-C.1. Editions: Blackman 1926: 177, pls. xxxiv-v; Helck 1955-58: 2162 (844).
Translation: Helck 1961: 423-24.

107-C.2. Edition: Martin 1979: pl. 3.2.

107-C.3. Edition: Hölscher 1939: 106-8 with fig. 90, and pl. 51c.

108. Edition: Kruchten 1981; Helck 1955-58: 2140-62 (843).
Translation: Helck 1961: 416-23.

109. Editions: Gardiner 1905: 127-40; Gaballa 1977: pls. lviii-lxiii.
Translations: Gardiner 1905: 93-109; Gaballa 1977: 22-27.

110. Edition: Gardiner 1938: 124.

111. Edition: Waddell 1940: 100-19.

Concordance

Davies 1903-8	*Writings from Ancient World*
1:vi-ix	70.1
x-xix	70.2
xxv	70.3
xxix-xxxii	70.3
xxxiv	70.4
xxxv	70.5, 70.6
xxxvi	70.7
xxxvii	70.8
xxviii	70.9
xxxix	70.10
xli	70.11
2:iv	77-B.10, 77-B.11
v	77-B.12, 77-B.13
vii	77-B.1
viii	77-B.2
ix	77-B.3
x-xi	77-B.4
xi bottom - xii	77-B.5
xx	77-B.6
xxi	77-B.7, 77-B.8, 77-B.9
xxiii	77-B.14
xxix top right	71.1
xxix bottom right	71.2
xxx-xxi	71.3
xxxvi	71.4
xxxvii-xl	71.1
xli	95-A
xlii	86
3:ii	66.1
iii	66.2
iv-v	66.3
vi-vii	66.4
viii-xii	66.5
xiii-xv	66.6
xvi	66.7
xvii-xviii	66.8
xviii top	66.9
xix	66.10
xx	66.11, 66.12
xxi	66.13
xxii	66.14
xxiii	66.15
xxvii	59.1, 59.2, 66.16
xxviii	59.3
xxix	59.3
4:ii	80.1
iii	80.2
iv	80.3
v-vii	80.4
viii	80.6
viii-ix	80.5
xi-xii	80.4
xvi	69.6
xvii-xix	69.5
xx-xxii	69.4

xxiii	69.6
xxiv-vi	69.3
xxvii	69.2
xxviii	69.1
xxix	69.6
xxxi	61-B.2
xxxii left	61-B.3
xxxii-iii	60-A.1, 61-B.1, 69.6, 70.8
xxxv	84-B
xxxvii	74
xxxviii-ix	87
xxxix	61-B.4
5:ii	68.1, 68.3
iii	68.1
iv	68.2, 68.4
v	68.5
ix	60-A.2
x	60-A.3
xi	60-A.4
xiii	90-C
xv	88
xxi-iii	60-B
xxv-viii	38
xxix-xxxii	37
xxxiii-vi	38
xxxvii-viii	37
xxxix-xliii	38
6:iii	78.2
iv-v	78.4
vi	78.3
vii	78.1
viii	78.2
xii	89.3
xiii	89.1
xiv left	89.4
xiv middle	89.2
xiv right	89.5
xv left	89.1
xv right	89.7
xvi	89.6
xvii-xviii	89.8
xix right	89.10
xix-xx	89.9
xxi	89.11
xxiv	58-B.1
xxv	58-B.2, 58-B.3
xxvi	58-B.5
xxvii	58-B.4
xxviii-xxxi	58-B.5
xxxi	58-B.6
xxxii	58-B.7
xxxiii	58-B.8
xxxiv	58-B.7, 89.1

Helck 1955-58

1667-70 (568)	2-G
1682-1705 (572)	2-F
1713-21 (573)	3
1737 (579 A)	2-A
1761(611 A)	2-E
1776-89 (634)	32-A - F
1872 (674)	30-A
1881-82 (680)	2-D
1923 (716)	2-B
1942-43 (731)	63-A
1943-47 (732)	4
1962 (746)	5
1963 (747)	56
1963-64 (748)	36-B
1965-80 (749)	37
1781-88 (749)	38
1992-93 (752.1)	10-D
1994 (752.2)	10-E
1995 (752.3)	10-F
1995 (753)	31
1995 (754)	17
1996 (755)	33
1997-2001 (756)	58-B.1 (titles), B.5, B.7 (C-E)
2002 (757)	58-A
2002 (758)	80.3
2002 (759)	59.2
2002 (760)	77-B.10-11
2003 (761)	71.1
2003-5 (762)	70.1-3
2005 (763)	69.3
2006 (764)	66.5-7
2008-17 (765)	89.8-10
2018 (766)	21
2018-22 (767)	20
2022 (768)	24
2023-24 (768)	67

2025-32 (772)	99
2034-36 (774)	100-A
2052-54 (781 E)	101-A
2055 (781 G)	101-B
2063 (789)	101-C
2068 (792)	100-H.1
2074-75 (794 B, D)	100-H.2
2078 (798)	100-C
2083 (802)	100-G
2089-94 (804)	105-B
2094-99 (805)	105-C
2103-5 (809)	100-J.2
2106 (810)	103-B.1
2106-7 (811)	103-B.2
2107 (813)	104-B
2108 (817)	103-A
2109-10 (818)	103-C
2110-11 (820)	103-D
2113-20 (825)	106
2121-24 (826)	107-A
2140-62 (843)	108
2162 (844)	107-C.1

Sandman 1938

1-2 (i)	70.1
2 (ii)	70.2
2-3 (iii)	70.3
3-4 (iv)	70.4
5-6 (v)	70.5
6 (vi)	70.6
6-9 (vii)	59.4, 66.2, 70.7
10-16 (viii)	60-A1, 61-B.1, 69.6, 70.8, 89.6
16-17 (ix-x)	70.9
17-20 (xi)	70.10, 77-B.8
20-21 (xiii-xiv)	70.11
21-22 (xv)	77-B.10
22 (xvi)	77-B.11
22-3 (xviii)	77-B.12
23 (xix)	77-B.13
23-24 (xx)	77-B.1
24-25 (xxi)	77-B.2
25-7 (xxii)	77-B.3
27 (xxiii)	77-B.4
27 (xxiv)	77-B.6
27-28 (xxv)	77-B.7
28-29 (xxvi)	77-B.9
29 (xxvii)	77-B.14
29-30 (xxviii)	71.1
30 (xxix)	71.2
30-31 (xxx-i)	71.3
32 (xxxii-iii)	71.4
33 (xxxv)	86
33-34 (xxxvi)	66.1, 80.2
34-35 (xxxviii)	66.3
35 (xxxix)	66.4
35-36 (xl)	66.5
36-37 (xli)	66.6
37 (xlii)	66.7
37-38 (xliii)	66.8
38 (xliv)	66.9
38-40 (xlv)	66.10
40 (xlvi)	66.11
40-42 (xlvii)	60-A.2, 66.12
43 (xlix)	66.13
43 (l)	66.14
43-44 (li)	59.1, 80.1
44-46 (lii)	59.2
46 (liii)	66.16
46-47 (liv)	59.3
47-48 (lvi)	80.1
48-49 (lviii)	80.3
49 (lix)	80.4
49-50 (lx)	80.5
50 (lxi)	80.6
50-51 (lxiii)	69.5
51 (lxiv)	69.4
51-52 (lxvi)	69.3
52-53 (lxvii)	69.2
53-54 (lxviii)	69.1
54-55 (lxx)	61-B.2
55 (lxxii)	61-B.3
55-56 (lxxiii)	84-B
56 (lxxiv)	74
57 (lxxv)	61-B.4
57-59 (lxxvi)	87
59-60 (lxxvii)	68.1
60 (lxxviii)	68.3
60-61 (lxxix)	68.2
61-63 (lxxx)	68.4
63 (lxxxi)	68.5
64 (lxxxiii)	60-A.3
64-65 (lxxxiv)	60-A.4
65 (lxxxv)	90-C

65-66 (lxxxvi)	76
66 (lxxxvii)	88
67-68 (lxxxviii-xciii)	60-B
69 (xciv)	78.2
69-70 (xcv)	78.3
70 (xcvi)	78.1
70-71 (xcvii)	89.3
71-72 (xcviii)	89.1
72 (xcix)	89.4
72 (c)	89.2
72-73 (ci)	89.5
73-75 (cii-ciii)	89.1
75-78 (civ)	89.7
78-80 (cvi)	89.8
80-83 (cvii)	89.9
83-84 (cviii)	89.10
84-87 (cix)	89.11
87-89 (cx)	58-B.1
89-90 (cxi)	58-B.2
90-93 (cxii)	58-B.3
93-96 (cxiii)	58-B.4
96-97 (cxiv)	58-B.5
97 (cxv)	58-B.6
98-100 (cxvi)	58-B.7
100-102 (cxviii)	58-B.8
103-18 (cxix)	37
119-31 (cxx)	38
132 (cxxi)	19
133-34 (cxxii-iii)	36
134-37 (cxxiv)	20
137-40 (cxxv-xxx)	32
140-43 (cxxxi-vi)	33
143-44 (cxxxvii)	5
144-45 (cxxxviii)	27
146 (cxxxix)	56
146 (cxl)	21
147 (cxlii-iii)	12
147-48 (cxliv)	22
148 (cxlv)	14
148 (cxlvi)	10-A
149 (cxlviii)	16
150 (cl)	10-B
151 (clv)	10-C
151 (clvii)	15
152 (clx)	11
153-54 (clxii)	44-A
154-55 (clxiii)	40-A
155 (clxiv)	46-A
156 (clxv)	40-B
156-57 (clxvi)	48
157 (clxvii)	49
158 (clxxi)	61-A
159-60 (clxxiv)	65
160 (clxxv)	90-B
161 (clxxix)	52
161-62 (clxxxi)	43
162 (clxxxiii)	77-A
164 (clxxxvii)	83
164-66 (clxxxviii)	54
166 (clxxxix)	41-A
166 (cxc)	41-B
166-67 (cxci)	46-D
167 (cxcii)	45-C
168 (cxciv)	92
168 (cxcv)	91
168-69 (cxcvi)	96-B
170-71 (cxcvii)	67
172 (cxcviii)	79
172 (cxcix)	84-A
173 (cc)	85-A
173-74 (cci-iii)	73-A
174-75 (cciv)	63-A
175 (ccv)	63-C
176 (ccvi)	58-A
177 (ccvii)	64
177 (ccviii)	81
177 (ccix)	82
178 (ccx)	90-D
178 (ccxi)	62
178-79 (ccxii)	24
179 (ccxiii)	53-A
180 (ccxvii)	90-A
180-82 (ccxviii-xx)	47-A
182 (ccxxi)	47-D
182 (ccxxii-xxiv)	47-E
184-87 (ccxxv-xxxiv)	57
187 (ccxxxv)	18-A
188 (ccxxxvi)	18-B
188-90 (ccxxxvii-xli)	57
190 (ccxlii)	18-C
190-91 (ccxliii)	18-D
191-95 (ccxliv-lxi)	57
195 (cclxii)	18-E
195 (cclxiv)	18-F
195 (cclxv-lxxxi)	57
200 (cclxxxiv)	50
201 top	89.9

Bibliography

Aldred, Cyril

1959 "The Beginning of the el-ᶜAmarna Period." *JEA* 45: 19-33.

1973 *Akhenaten and Nefertiti.* Brooklyn: The Brooklyn Museum.

1976 "The Horizon of the Aten." *JEA* 62: 184.

1988 *Akhenaten, King of Egypt.* London: Thames & Hudson.

Allen, James P.

1988 "Two Altered Inscriptions of the Later Amarna Period." *JARCE* 25: 117-26.

1989 "The Natural Philosophy of Akhenaten." Pp. 89-101 in *Religion and Philosophy in Ancient Egypt.* Ed. by W. K. Simpson. Yale Egyptological Studies 3. New Haven, CT: Yale Egyptological Seminar.

1994a "Nefertiti and Smenkh-ka-re." In *Tell el-Amarna 1887-1987.* Ed. by Gordon D. Young and Barry J. Beitzel. Winona Lake, IN: Eisenbrauns.

1994b "Further Evidence for the Coregency of Amenhotep III and IV?" *GM* 140: 7-8.

Amer, Amin A. M. A.

1985 "Tutankhamun's Decree for the Chief Treasurer Maya." *RdE* 36: 17-20, with pl. 1.

Assmann, Jan

1972 "Die 'Häresie' des Echnaton: Aspekte der Amarna-Religion." *Saeculum* 23: 109-26.

1975 "Aton." *LÄ* 1: cols. 526-40.

1980 "Die 'Loyalistische Lehre' Echnatons." *SAK* 8: 1-32.

1989 "State and Religion in the New Kingdom." Pp. 55-88 in *Religion and Philosophy in Ancient Egypt.* Ed. W. K. Simpson. Yale Egyptological Studies 3. New Haven: CT: Yale Egyptological Seminar.

Balcz, Heinrich, and Kurt Bittel

1932 "Grabungsbericht Hermopolis 1932." *MDAIK* 3: 9-45.

Barta, Winfried
1975 "Zur Darstellungsweise der Kolossalstatuen Amenophis' IV. aus Karnak." *ZÄS* 102: 91-94.
Beckerath, Jürgen von
1978 "Nochmals die Regierungsdauer des Haremhab." *SAK* 6: 43-49.
1984 "Eine Bemerkung zu der vermuteten Koregenz Amenophis' III. und IV." *GM* 83: 11-12.
Beinlich, H., and M. Saleh
1989 *Corpus der Hieroglyphischen Inschriften aus dem Grab des Tutanchamun.* Oxford: Griffith Institute.
Bell, Lanny
Bell, Lanny
1985a "Luxor Temple and the Cult of the Royal Ka." *JNES* 44: 251-94.
1985b "Aspects of the Cult of the Deified Tutankhamun." Pp. 31-59 in *Mélanges Gamal Eddin Mokhtar.* Vol. 1. Bd'E 97.1. Cairo: Institut Français d'Archéologie Orientale.
Bennett, John
1939 "The Restoration Inscription of Tutᶜankhamun." *JEA*: 25: 8-15.
Berlin Museum
1924 *Ägyptische Inschriften aus den Königlichen Museen zu Berlin.* Vol. 2. Leipzig: J. C. Hinrichs.
Bierbrier, M. L.
1982 *The British Museum: Hieroglyphic Texts from Egyptian Stelae etc.* Vol. 10. London: British Museum.
Bilolo, M.
1984 "De la portée révolutionnaire des nouveaux noms d'Aménophis IV." *GM* 77: 7-12.
Bissing, Wilhelm von
1911-14 *Denkmäler Ägyptischer Skulptur.* Munich: F. Bruckmann.
1914 "Denkmäler zur Geschichte der Kunst Amenophis IV." *SBAW* 3: 3-7.
1929 "Stele des Nachtmin aus der Amarnazeit." *ZÄS* 64: 113-17.
Bittel, Kurt, and Alfred Hermann
1934 "Grabungsbericht Hermopolis 1933." *MDAIK* 5: 11-44.
Blackman, A. M.
1922 "A Study of the Liturgy celebrated in the Temple of the Aton at El-Amarna." Pp. 505-27 in *Recueil d'études égyptologiques dediées à la mémoire de Jean-François Champollion.* Bibliothèque Sciences historiques et philologiques 234. Paris: École des Hautes Etudes.
1926 "Oracles in Ancient Egypt." *JEA* 12: 176-85.
Blankenberg-Van Delden, C.
1969 *The Large Commemorative Scarabs of Amenhotep III.* DMOA 15. Leiden: Brill.

Boddens-Hosang, F. J. E.

1988 "Akhenaten's Year Twelve Reconsidered." *DE* 12: 7-9.

Bongionanni, A.

1983-4 "Consideration sur les 'noms' d'Aten et la nature du rapport souverain-divinité à l'epoque amarnienne." *GM* 68: 43-51, with addendum in *GM* 71: 93.

1986 "Giubileo di Akhenaten: verità storica o finzione letteratia?" *Atti della Accademia delle Scienze di Torino, Classe di Scienze Morali, Storiche e Filologiche* 120: 161-71.

Borchardt, Ludwig

1914 "Ausgrabungen in Tell el-Amarna 1913/14." *MDOG* 55: 3-39.

1923 *Porträts der Königin Nofretete aus den Grabungen 1912/13 in Tell el-Amarna.* WVDOG 44. Leipzig: J. C. Hinrichs.

Borchardt, L. and H. Ricke

1980 *Die Wohnhäuser in Tell el-Amarna.* WVDOG 91. Berlin: Mann.

Breasted, James Henry

1906-7 *The Ancient Records of Egypt.* 5 vols. Chicago: University of Chicago Press.

1908-9 "Second Preliminary Report of the Egyptian Expedition." *AJSL* 25: 1-110.

Brugsch, Heinrich

1857 *Geographische Inschriften altägyptischer Denkmäler*, vol. 1. Leipzig: J. C. Hinrichs.

1883-91 *Thesaurus Inscriptionum Aegyptiacarum.* Part 5: *Historisch-biographische Inschriften altaegyptischer Denkmaeler.* Leipzig: J. C. Hinrichs.

Brunner, Hellmut

1964 *Die Geburt des Gottkönigs.* ÄA 10. Wiesbaden: Harrassowitz.

Bruyère, Bernard

1937 *Rapport sur les fouilles de Deir el-Médineh, 1933-1934.* Part 1: *La Nécropole de l'Ouest.* Cairo: Institut Français d'Archéologie Orientale.

Bryan, B.

1991 *The Reign of Thutmose IV.* Baltimore: The Johns Hopkins University Press.

Bryan, B., and E. S. Meltzer

1977-78 "A Note on an Obscure Title *ṯꜣy ṯnfyt pḏ(t) n nb tꜣwy.*" *JSSEA* 8: 60-65.

Bryant, A. C., and F. W. Reed

1893 "An Inscription of Khuenaten." *PSBA* 15: 206-15.

Bryce, Trevor R.

1990 "The Death of Nipḫururiya and its Aftermath." *JEA* 76: 97-106.

Carter, Howard

1933 *The Tomb of Tut-Ankh-Amen.* Vol. 3. London: Cassell and Co.

Černý, Jaroslav

1965 *Hieratic Inscriptions from the Tomb of Tutᶜankhamun*. Tutᶜankhamun Tomb Series 2. Oxford: Griffith Institute.

1973 *A Community of Workmen at Thebes in the Ramesside Period*. BdE 50. Cairo: Institut Français d'Archéologie Orientale.

Chappaz, Jean-Luc

1983 "Le premier édifice d'Aménophis IV - Karnak." *BSEG* 8: 13-46.

Daressy, Georges

1901 "Rapport sur la trouvaille de [Hatiay]." *ASAE* 2: 1-13.

1902 "Le temple de Mit-Rahineh." *ASAE* 3: 22-31.

1916a "Une scarabée d'Amenhotep IV." *ASAE* 16: 178.

1916b "Le cercueil de Khu-en-Aten." *BIFAO* 12: 145-59.

1918 "Deux statues de Balansourah." *ASAE* 18: 53-57.

Davies, Nina, and Alan Gardiner

1926 *The Tomb of Huy, Viceroy of Nubia in the Reign of Tutankhamun (No. 40)*. EES-TTS 4. London: Egypt Exploration Society.

Davies, Norman de Garis

1903-8 *The Rock Tombs of El Amarna*. EES-ASE 13-18. 6 vols. London: Egypt Exploration Society.

1923 "Akhenaten at Thebes." *JEA* 9: 132-52.

1941 *The Tomb of the Vizier Ramose*. Mond Excavations at Thebes 1. London: Egypt Exploration Society.

Davis, Theodore

1910 *The Tomb of Queen Tiyi*. Theodore M. Davis' Excavations, Biban el Moluk. London: Constable and Co.

1912 *The Tombs of Harmhabi and Toutankhamanou*. London: Constable and Co.

1990 *The Tomb of Queen Tiyi*, reissued with an introduction and bibliography by C. N. Reeves (and with different pagination). San Francisco: KMT Communications.

Dawson, Warren R.

1924 "Note on some Ostraca from el-ᶜAmarnah." *JEA* 10: 133.

Derchain, Philippe

1988 "Encore le monotheisme." *CdE* 63: 77-83.

Drioton, Etienne

1943 "Trois documents d'epoque amarnienne." *ASAE* 43: 15-43.

Drury, Allen

1976 *A God against the Gods*. Garden City, NY: Doubleday.

Eaton-Krauss, Marianne

1985 "Tutanchamun." *LÄ* 6: cols. 812-16.

1990 "Akhenaten versus Akhenaten." *BiOr* 47: cols. 541-59.

Edwards, I. E. S.

1939a *Hieroglyphic Texts from Stelae etc. in the British Museum*. Vol. 8. London: British Museum.

1939b "The Prudhoe Lions." *AAA* 26: 3-9.

Engelbach, Reginald

1931 "The so-called Coffin of Akhenaten." *ASAE* 31: 98-114, pls. i-ii.

1940 "Material for the Revision of the History of the Heresy Period of the XVIIIth Dynasty." *ASAE* 40: 133-55.

Epigraphic Survey

1980 *The Tomb of Kheruef*. OIP 102. Chicago: University of Chicago Press.

1994 *Reliefs and Inscriptions at Luxor Temple*. Vol. 1: *The Festival Procession of Opet in the Colonnade Hall*. OIP 112. Chicago: Oriental Institute.

199- *Reliefs and Inscriptions at Luxor Temple*. Vol. 2: *Columns, Upper Register Scenes, Portals, Marginalia and Graffiti in the Colonnade Hall*. Chicago: Oriental Institute (forthcoming).

Erman, Adolf

1900 "Geschichtliche Inschriften aus dem Berliner Museum: Aus der Ketzerzeit." *ZÄS* 38: 112-26.

Fairman, H. W.

1960 "The supposed year 21 of Akhenaten." *JEA* 46: 108-9.

1961 "Once Again the So-called Coffin of Akhenaten." *JEA* 47: 25-40.

Fakhry, Ahmed

1935 "Blocs decorés provenant du temple de Louxor." *ASAE* 35: 35-51.

Foster, John L.

1992 *Echoes of Egyptian Voices: An Anthology of Ancient Egyptian Poetry*. Norman and London: University of Oklahoma Press.

Frandsen, Paul

1979 "Egyptian Imperialism." Pp. 167-90 in *Power and Propaganda*. Ed. by M. T. Larsen. Mesopotamia 7. Copenhagen: Akademisk Forlag.

Frankfort, Henri

1927 "Preliminary Report on the Excavations at el-ᶜAmarnah, 1926-7." *JEA* 13: 209-18.

Frankfort, Henri, and J. D. S. Pendlebury

1933 *The City of Akhenaten*. Part 2: *The North Suburb and the Desert Altars*. MEES 40. London: Egypt Exploration Society.

Fritz, W.

1991 "Bemerkungen zum Datierungsvermerk auf der Amarnabrief Kn. 27." *SAK* 18: 207-14.

Gaballa, G. A.

1977 *The Memphite Tomb-Chapel of Mose*. Warminster: Aris & Phillips.

Gabolde, Marc

1990 "Le droit d'ainesse d'Ankhesenpaaton." *BSEG* 14: 33-47.

Gabra, Sami

1931 "Un temple d'Aménophis IV à Assiout." *CdE* 6, no. 12: 237-43.

Gardiner, (Sir) Alan H.

1905 *The Inscription of Mes.* UGAÄ 4: 89-140. Leipzig: J. C. Hinrichs.

1906 "Four Papyri of the 18th Dynasty from Kahun." *ZÄS* 43: 27-47, pls. 1-3.

1928 "The Graffito from the Tomb of Pere." *JEA* 14: 10-11, pls. v-vi.

1938 "A Later Allusion to Akhenaten." *JEA* 24: 124.

1953 "The Coronation of King Haremab." *JEA* 39: 13-31, pl. ii.

Gauthier, Henri

1910 "Quelques fragments trouvés à Amada." *ASAE* 10: 122-24.

Gayet, Albert

1894 *Le Temple de Louxor.* Fasc. 1. MMAF 15. Paris: E. Leroux.

Glanville, (Sir) Stephen

1929 "Some Notes on Material for the Reign of Amenophis III." *JEA* 15: 2-8.

Glass, Philip

1987 *Akhenaten* (Opera). Complete recording on CBS Masterworks M2K 42457 (compact disks).

Gohary, Jocelyn

1992 *Akhenaten's Sed-Festival at Karnak.* London: Kegan Paul International.

Goyon, Georges

1957 *Nouvelles inscriptions rupestres du Wadi Hammamat.* Paris: Imprimerie Nationale.

Griffith, Francis L.

1898 *The Petrie Papyri: Hieratic Papyri from Kahun and Gurob.* London: Bernard Quaritch.

1921-22 "Oxford Excavations in Nubia." *AAA* 8: 1-19, 65-104.

1926 "Stela in honour of Amenophis III and Taya from Tell el-Amarnah." *JEA* 12: 1-2.

Gunn, Battiscombe

1923 "Notes on the Aten and his Names." *JEA* 9: 168-73,

Habachi, Labib

1965 "Varia from the Reign of King Akhenaten." *MDAIK* 20: 70-92.

Hall, H. R. H.

1913 *Catalogue of Egyptian Scarabs, etc., in the British Museum.* Vol. 1. London: British Museum.

Hanke, Rainer

1978 *Amarna-Reliefs aus Hermopolis: Neue Veröffentlichungen und Studien.* HÄB 2. Hildesheim: Gerstenberg Verlag.

Harris, J. R.

1973a "Nefernefruaten." *GM* 4: 15-17.

1973b "Nefertiti rediviva." *AO* 35: 5-13.
1974a "Nefernefruaton regnans." *AO* 36: 11-21.
1974b "Kiya." *CdE* 49: 25-30.

Hassan, Ali
1976 *Stöcke und Stäbe im pharaonischen Ägypten bis zum Ende des Neuen Reiches.* MÄS 33. Berlin and Munich: Deutschen Kunstverlag.

Hassan, Selim Bey
1938 "A Representation of the Solar Disk with Human Hands and Arms and the Form of Horus of Behdet as seen on the Stela of Amenhotep IInd in the Mud-brick Temple at Giza." *ASAE* 38: 53-61.

Helck, Wolfgang
1955-58 *Urkunden der 18. Dynastie.* Berlin: Akademie-Verlag.
1961 *Urkunden der 18. Dynastie. Übersetzung zu den Heften 17-22.* Berlin: Akademie-Verlag.
1961-70 *Materialen zur Wirtschaftsgeschichte des Neuen Reichs.* AMAW. Wiesbaden: Franz Steiner Verlag.
1969 "Amarna-Probleme." *CdE* 44: 200-213.
1973a "Probleme der Zeit Haremhabs." *CdE* 48: 251-65.
1973b "Zur Opferliste Amenophis' IV." *JEA* 59: 95-99.
1980 "Ein 'Feldzug' unter Amenophis IV gegen Nubien." *SAK* 8: 117-26.
1983 *Historisch-Biographische Texte der 2. Zwischenzeit und Neue Texte der 18. Dynastie.* 2nd ed. Wiesbaden: Harrassowitz.
1984 "Kije." *MDAIK* 40: 159-67.

Hölscher, Uvo
1939 *The Excavation of Medinet Habu.* Vol. 2: *The Temples of the Eighteenth Dynasty.* OIP 41. Chicago: University of Chicago Press.

Hornung, Erik
1971 "Gedanken zur Kunst der Amarnazeit." *ZÄS* 97: 74-8.
1982 *Conceptions of God in Ancient Egypt. The One and the Many.* Translated by John Baines. Ithaca, N.Y.: Cornell University Press.

James, T. G. H.
1974 *Corpus of Hieroglyphic Inscriptions in the Brooklyn Museum.* Vol. 1. Brooklyn: Brooklyn Museum.

Janssen, J. J.
1975 *Commodity Prices from the Ramessid Period.* Leiden: Brill.

Johnson, W. Raymond
1990 "Images of Amenhotep III at Thebes: Styles and Intentions." Pp. 26-46 in *The Art of Amenhotep III: Art Historical Analysis.* Ed. by L. M. Berman. Cleveland: Cleveland Musuem of Art.

Kamal, Ahmed Bey
1911 "Rapport sur les fouilles executés dans la zone comprise entre Deirout au nord et Deir el-Ganadlah au sud." *ASAE* 11: 3-37.

Karkowski, Janusz
1981 *Faras. Vol. 5: The Pharaonic Inscriptions from Faras.* Warsaw: Panstwowe Wydawnictwo Naukowe.

Kemp, Barry
1978 "Imperialism and Empire in New Kingdom Egypt." Pp. 7-58 in *Imperialism in the Ancient World.* Ed. by P. D. A. Garnsey and C. R. Whittacker. Cambridge: Cambridge University Press.
1987 "The Amarna Workman's Village in Retrospect." *JEA* 73: 21-50.

Khouly, Aly el-, and G. T. Martin
1987 *Excavations in the Royal Necropolis at El-ʿAmarna, 1984.* SASAE 33. Cairo: Institut Français d'Archéologie Orientale.

Kitchen, Kenneth A.
1962 *Suppiluliuma and the Amarna Pharaohs.* Liverpool Monographs in Archaeological and Oriental Studies. Liverpool: Liverpool University Press.

Knudtzon, J. A.
1915 *Die El-Amarna Tafeln.* 2 vols. VAB 2. Leipzig: J. C. Hinrichs.

Kozloff, Arielle P., Betsy M. Bryan, and Lawrence M. Berman
1992 *Egypt's Dazzling Sun: Amenhotep III and his World.* Cleveland: Cleveland Musuem of Art, in association with Indiana University Press.

Krauss, Rolf
1978 *Das Ende der Amarnazeit.* HÄB 7. Hildesheim: Gerstenberg Verlag.
1986 "Kiya—Ursprüngliche Besitzerin der Kanopen aus KV 55." *MDAIK* 42: 67-80.
1989 "Neues zu den Stelenfragmenten UC London 410 + Kairo JE 64959." *BSEG* 13: 83-7.
1990 "Einige Kleinfunde mit Namen von Amarnaherschern." *CdE* 65: 206-18.

Krauss, R., and D. Ullrich
1982 "Ein gläserner Doppelring aus Altägypten." *JPK* 19: 199-212.

Kruchten, Jean-Marie
1981 *Le Décret d'Horemheb.* Université Libre de Bruxelles, Faculté de Philosophie et Lettres, no. 82. Brussels: Éditions de l'Université de Bruxelles.

Kühne, Cord
1973 *Die Chronologie des Internationalen Korrespondenz von El-Amarna.* AOAT 17. Neukirchen-Vluyn: Verlag Butzon & Bercker Kevelaer and Neukirchener Verlag.

Lacau, Pierre
1909-26 *Stèles du Nouvel Empire.* Fascicles 1-2. CG. Cairo: Institut Français d'Archéologie Orientale.

Larson, John

1985 "The Tut-ankh-amun Astronomical Instrument (Oriental Institute 12144)." *Oriental Institute Museum Featured Object Number One.* Chicago: Oriental Institute.

1992 "The Tutankhamen Astronomical Instrument." *Amarna Letters* 2: 76-86.

Lefebvre, Gustave

1929 *Histoire des Grands Prêtres d'Amon de Karnak jusqu'à la XXIe Dynastie.* Paris: Librairie Orientaliste Paul Geuthner.

Legrain, Georges

1901 "Notes prises à Karnak. VI. Sur un temple d'Aton à Hermonthis." *RecTrav* 23: 61-65.

1902 "Les stèles d'Amenothes IV à Zernik et à Gebel Silsileh." *ASAE* 3: 260-66.

1903 "Fragments de canopes." *ASAE* 4: 138-145.

1906 "Sur quelques monuments d'Amenothes IV provenant de la cachette de Karnak." *ASAE* 7: 228-31.

1910 "Notes d'inspection. LXV. Sur un oushabti du temps de Khouniatonou et le scarabée 5993 de Turin." *ASAE* 10: 108.

Leprohon, Ronald J.

1985 "The Reign of Akhenaten seen through the Later Royal Decrees." Pp. 93-101 in *Mélanges Gamal Eddin Mokhtar.* BdE 97.2. Cairo: Institut Français d'Archéologie Orientale.

Lepsius, Karl Richard

1849-58 *Denkmäler aus Ägypten und Äthiopien.* 12 vols. Berlin: Nicolaische Buchhandlung.

1897-1913 *Denkmäler aus Ägypten und Äthiopien, Text.* Ed. by Edouard Naville. 5 vols. Leipzig: J. C. Hinrichs.

Lichtheim, Miriam

1976 *Ancient Egyptian Literature: A Book of Readings.* Vol. 2: *The New Kingdom.* Berkeley, Los Angeles, and London: University of California Press.

Loeben, Christian

1986 "Eine Bestattung der Grossen Königlichen Gemahlin Nofretete in Amarna? Die Totefigur des Nofretete." *MDAIK* 42: 99-102.

1991 "No Evidence of Coregency: Zwei getilgte Inschriften aus dem Grab von Tutanchamun." *BSEG* 15: 81-90.

Löhr, Beatrix

1975 "Ahanjati in Memphis." *SAK* 2: 139-87.

Mariette, Auguste

1884-85 *Les mastaba de l'ancien empire.* Paris: F. Wieweg.

Martin, Geoffrey Thorndike

1974 *The Royal Tomb at El-ᶜAmarna.* Vol. 1: *The Objects. The Rock Tombs of*

El ʿAmarna. Part 7.1. EES-ASE 35. London: Egypt Exploration Society.

1979 "Excavations at the Memphite Tomb of Horemheb, 1978: Preliminary Report." *JEA* 65: 13-16.

1989a *The Royal Tomb at El-ʿAmarna*. Vol. 2. *The Rock Tombs of El ʿAmarna*. Part 7.2. EES-ASE 39. London: Egypt Exploration Society.

1989b *The Memphite Tomb of Horemheb, Commander-in-Chief of Tutʿankhamun*. Vol. 1: *The Reliefs, Inscriptions, and Commentary*. MEES 55. London: Egypt Exploration Society.

1991 *A Bibliography of the Amarna Period and its Aftermath*. London: Kegan Paul International.

Maspéro, Gaston

1881 "Notes sur quelques points de grammaire et d'histoire." *ZÄS* 19: 116-31.

1909-24 *Le Musée Égyptien*. 3 vols. Cairo: Institut Français d'Archéologie Orientale.

Meltzer, Edmund S.

1989 "Herodotus on Akhenaten?" *DE* 15: 51-55.

Millet, Nicholas

1988 "Some Canopic Inscriptions from the Reign of Amenhotep III." *GM* 104: 91-93.

Moran, William L.

1992 *The Amarna Letters*. Baltimore: Johns Hopkins University Press.

Munro, Peter

1981 "Frühform oder Deckname des Jati (Aton) in Heliopolis?" *MDAIK* 38: 359-67.

Murnane, William J.

1977 *Ancient Egyptian Coregencies*. SAOC 40. Chicago: Oriental Institute.

1979 "The Bark of Amun on the Third Pylon at Karnak." *JARCE* 16: 111-27.

1990 *The Road to Kadesh*. 2nd ed. rev. SAOC 42. Chicago: Oriental Institute.

1991 "Servant, Seer, Saint: Amenhotep, Son of Hapu." *KMT* 2.2: 9-13, 56-59.

1994 "Some Datelines from El-Amarna Reconsidered." In *Tell el-Amarna 1887-1987*. Ed. by Gordon D. Young and Barry J. Beitzel. Winona Lake, IN: Eisenbrauns.

Murnane, William J., and C. C. Van Siclen III

1993 *The Boundary Stelae of Akhenaten*. London: Kegan Paul International.

Navailles, R., and F. Neveu

1989 "Qu'entendait-on par 'journée d'esclave' au Nouvel Empire?" *RdE* 40: 113-23.

Newberry, Percy E.
1928 "Akhenaten's Eldest Son-in-law ʿAnkhkheprure." *JEA* 14: 3-9.
1932 "King Ay, The Successor of Tutʿankhamun," *JEA* 18: 50-52.
Nicholson, Sir C.
1870 "On the Disk-Worshippers of Memphis." *TRSL*, ser. 2: 9: 197-214.
O'Connor, David
1987-88 "Demarcating the Boundaries: An Interpretation of a Scene in the Tomb of Mahu at El-Amarna." *BES* 9: 41-52.
Otto, Eberhard
1955 "Monotheistische Tendenzen in der Ägyptischen Religion." *Welt des Orients* 2: 99-110.
Peet, T. E., and Sir Leonard Wooley
1923 *The City of Akhenaten.* Part 1: *Excavations of 1921 and 1922.* MEES 38. London: Egypt Exploration Society.
Pendlebury, J. D.
1951 *The City of Akhenaten.* Part 3. *The Central City and the Official Quarters.* MEES 44. London: Egypt Exploration Society.
Perepelkin, G.
1978 *The Secret of the Gold Coffin.* Moscow: "Nauka" Publishing House.
Peters, Elisabeth
1968 *The Jackal's Head.* New York: Tor Books [1988].
Petrie, W. M. F.
1894 *Tell el Amarna.* London: Methuen.
1897 *Six Temples at Thebes 1896.* London: B. Quaritch.
1909 *Memphis.* Vol. 1. London: School of Anthropology in Egypt.
Porter. B., and R. L. B. Moss
1964 *Topographical Bibliography of Ancient Egyptian Hieroglyphic Texts, Reliefs and Paintings.* Vol. 1: *The Theban Necropolis,* Part 2: *Royal Tombs and Smaller Cemeteries.* 2nd ed. Oxford: Griffith Institute.
Pritchard, James B.
1969 *Ancient Near Eastern Texts Relating to the Old Testament.* 3rd ed. Princeton: Princeton University Press.
Rammant-Petters, Agnes
1983 *Les pyramidions égyptiens du Nouvel Empire.* OLA 11. Leuven: Departement Orientalistiek.
Ray, John
1985 Review article of Redford 1984. *GM* 86: 81-93.
Redford, Donald B.
1963 "The Identity of the High Priest of Amun in the Beginning of Akhenaten's Reign." *JAOS* 83: 240-41
1967 *History and Chronology of the Eighteenth Dynasty of Egypt.* University of Toronto Near and Middle East Series 3. Toronto: University of Toronto Press.
1973 "New Light on the Asiatic Campaigning of Horemheb." *BASOR* 211: 36-49.

1976 *The Akhenaten Temple Project*. Vol. I. *Initial Discoveries*. Warminster: Aris & Phillips.

1981 "A Royal Speech from the Blocks of the 10th Pylon." *BES* 3: 87-102.

1982 "An Offering Inscription from the 2nd Pylon at Karnak." Pp. 125-31 in *Studies in Philology in Honour of Ronald James Williams*. SSEA(P) 3. Toronto: Benben Publications.

1984 *Akhenaten, The Heretic King*. Princeton: Princeton University Press.

1986 *Pharaonic King-Lists, Annals and Day-Books*. SSEA(P) 4. Mississauga: Benben Publications.

1988 *The Akhenaten Temple Project*. Vol. 2: *Rwd Mnw, Foreigners and Inscriptions*. Aegypti Texta Propositaque 1. Toronto: University of Toronto Press.

1992 *Egypt, Canaan and Israel in Ancient Times*. Princeton: Princeton University Press.

Redford, Susan, and D. B. Redford

1989 "Graffiti and Petroglyphs Old and New from the Eastern Desert." *JARCE* 26: 3-49.

Reeves, C. N.

1981 "The Tomb of Tuthmosis IV: Two Questionable Attributions." *GM* 44: 49-55.

1982 "Tuthmosis IV as 'great-grandfather' of Tutᶜankhamun." *GM* 56: 65-69.

Roeder, Gunther

1969 *Amarna-Reliefs aus Hermopolis*. Hildesheim: Pelizaeus-Museum.

Romano, James F.

1990 "A Second Look at 'Images of Amenhotep III in Thebes: Styles and Intentions' by W. Raymond Johnson." In *The Art of Amenhotep III: Art Historical Analysis*. Ed. by L. M. Berman. Cleveland: Cleveland Museum of Art.

Saad, Ramadan, and Lise Manniche

1971 "A Unique Offering List of Amenophis IV Recently Found at Karnak." *JEA* 57: 70-72.

Saghir, Mohammed el-

1991 *The Discovery of the Statuary Cachette of Luxor Temple*. SDAIK 26. Mainz: Philipp von Zabern.

Samson, Julia

1978 *Amarna, City of Akhenaten and Nefertiti*. 2nd ed. *Nefertiti as Pharaoh*. Warminster: Aris & Phillips.

Sandman, Maj

1938 *Texts from the Time of Akhenaten*. BAe 8. Brussels: Fondation Égyptologique Reine Élisabeth.

Schaden, Otto

1977 *The God's Father Ay*. Ph.D. Dissertation, University of Minnesota. Ann Arbor: University Microfilms.

1984 "Clearance of the Tomb of King Ay (WV-23)." *JARCE* 21: 39-64.

Schäfer, Heinrich
1918 "Altes und Neues zur Kunst und Religion von Tell el-Amarna." *ZÄS* 55: 1-43.
1931 *Amarna in Religion und Kunst*. Leipzig: J. C. Hinrichs.

Schenkel, Wolfgang
1985 "*Zꜣt*, "Kindchen," und *ṯꜣ.t*, "Jüngchen." GM 84: 65-70.

Schiaparelli, Ernesto
1887 *Museo archeologico di Firenze: Antichità egizie*, Part 1. Catalogo generale dei musei d'antichità, Ser. 6, vol. 1. Rome: Academia dei Lincei.

Schroeder, Otto
1914 *Die Tontafeln von El-Amarna in akkadischer Sprache*. Vorderasiatische Schriftdenkmäler der Königlichen Museum zu Berlin 11.1. Leipzig: J. C. Hinrichs.

Schulman, Alan R.
1964 "Some Observations on the Military Background of the Amarna Period," *JARCE* 3:51-69.
1978 "Ankhesenamun, Nofretity and the Amka Affair." *JARCE* 15: 43-48.
1982 "The Nubian War of Akhenaten." Pp. 299-316 in *L'Égyptologie en 1979*. Vol. 2. Paris: Éditions du Centre National de la Recherche Scientifique.

Simpson, William Kelly
1973 *The Literature of Ancient Egypt*. New edition. New Haven: Yale University Press.

Smith, H. S.
1976 *The Fortress of Buhen: The Inscriptions*. MEES 48. London: Egypt Exploration Society.

Spiegelberg, W., and A. Erman
1898 "Grabstein eines Syrischen Söldners aus Tell Amarna." *ZÄS* 36: 126-29.

Stadelmann, Rainer
1969 "*Šwt-Rꜥw* als Kultstätte des Sonnengottes im Neuen Reich." *MDAIK* 25: 159-78.

Stewart, H. M.
1976 *Egyptian Stelae, Reliefs and Paintings from the Petrie Collection*. Part 1: *The New Kingdom*. Warminster: Aris & Phillips.

Tawfik, Sayed
1973 "Aton Studies. 1. Aton before the Reign of Akhenaten." *MDAIK* 29: 77-86.
1975 "Aton Studies. 2. Back again to Nefer-nefru-Aton." *MDAIK* 31: 159-68.
1981 "Aton Studies. 6. Was Nefernefruaten the Immediate Successor of Akkhenaten?" *MDAIK* 37: 469-73.

Traunecker, Claude
1984 "Données nouvelles sur le début du règne d'Aménophis IV et son oeuvre à Karnak." *JSSEA* 14.3: 60-69.
Trigger, Bruce
1981 "Akhenaten and Durkheim." Pp. 165-82 in *Bulletin du Centennaire. BIFAO* Supplement 81. Cairo: Institut Français d'Archéologie Orientale.
Van Dijk, Jacobus
1993 "Horemheb, Prince Regent of Tutᶜankhamun." Pp. 11-64 in idem, *The New Kingdom Necropolis of Memphis. Historical and Iconographic Studies.* Groningen: Rijksuniversiteit Groningen (Ph.D. Dissertation).
Waddell, W. D.
1940 *Manetho.* Loeb Classical Library. Cambridge, MA: Harvard University Press.
Wente, Edward F.
1980 "The Gurob Letter to Amenhotep IV." *Serapis* 6: 209-15.
1990 *Letters from Ancient Egypt.* SBL-WAW 1. Atlanta: Scholars Press.
Wente, Edward F., and James E. Harris
1992 "Royal Mummies of the Eighteenth Dynasty. A Biologic and Egyptological Approach." Pp. 2-20 in *After Tutᶜankhamun: Research and Excavation in the Royal Necropolis at Thebes.* Ed. by C. N. Reeves. London and New York: Kegan Paul International.
Werner, Edward K.
1975-84 "The Amarna Period of Eighteenth Dynasty Egypt: A Bibliography." *NARCE* 95: 15-36; 97-98: 29-40; 101-2: 41-65; 106: 41-56; 110: 24-39; 114: 18-34; 120: 3-20; 126: 21-38.
Wiedemann, K. A.
1885 "On a Monument of the Time of King Chu-en-iten." *PSBA* 7: 201-3.
Wilson, John A.
1973 "Akh-en-Aton and Nefert-iti." *JNES* 32: 235-41.
Winlock, H. E.
1924 "A Statue of Horemheb before his Accession." *JEA* 10: 1-5.
Wolf, Walter
1924 "Vorläufer der Reformation Echnatons." *ZÄS* 59: 109-19.
Yoyotte, Jean
1981 "Le géneral Djéhouty et la perception des tributs syriens." *BSFE* 92: 33-51.
Zivie, A.
1990 *Découverte à Saqqarah: Le Vizir Oublié.* Paris: Editions du Seuil.
Zivie, C. M.
1975 "À propos de quelques reliefs du Nouvel Empire au Museé du Caire." *BIFAO* 75: 285-310, pls. li-lvi.

Glossary

Aakheperkare. Throne-name of Thutmose I (ca. 1493-1479 B.C.E.).

Aakheprure. Throne-name of Akhenaten's great-grandfather, Amenhotep II (ca. 1426-1400 B.C.E.)

Akhet. Translated conventionally (and for convenience here) "horizon," this was actually the space between the earthly horizon and the underworld (*Duat*).

Akhet-en-Aten. "Horizon of Aten," a name that apparently designated the domains of Amenhotep IV's god at Thebes. A different version of the same name, Akhet-Aten, was later given to the heresy's new capital at El-Amarna.

Amun. Divine lord of Thebes and (as "Amun-Re") the leading figure of the Egyptian pantheon during the New Kingdom.

Ankhkheprure. Throne name used by both Nefernefruaten and Smenkhkare, Akhenaten's immediate successors (reigned ca. 1336-1332 B.C.E.).

Ankhesenpaaten. Third daughter of Akhenaten and Nefertiti, she bore a daughter of the same name while living at El-Amarna. She later wed Tutankhamun, changed her name to "Ankhesenamun," and became queen of Egypt.

Ankhtowy. "Life of the Two Lands," a subsidiary name for Memphis.

Anubis. The jackal god who was patron of the embalming house.

Aten. The "disk" of the sun, visible manifestation of Akhenaten's god.

Atum. The primeval creator god, whose main cult center was at Heliopolis.

Ay. Royal counselor, whose service spanned the reigns of Akhenaten and Tutankhamun, and who succeeded the latter as king.

Ba. The dynamic component of an individual's spiritual identity. The Bas of a locality are assumed to be the divinized ancient kings of those places.

Baketaten. Apparently the youngest daughter of Queen Tiyi and Amenhotep III.

Baking ratio. The number of baked or brewed goods extracted from each measure of grain, generally calculated against the *oipe*.

Behdetite. The god Horus of Edfu (=Behdet), shown in the form of a winged sun-disk.

Benben. A cult object, associated with the primeval creator god, which resided in each of the principal temples to the Aten in Egypt.

Black Land. The Nile River valley, contrasted with the desert or "Red Land."

Cubit. The standard short measure of length, 20.6 inches (=52.3 centimeters).

Deben. The standard weight for metals, about 91 grams.

Deir el-Medina. Modern name for the village occupied by the workmen employed to build the royal tombs on the west bank of Thebes.

Dja. A measure of capacity: about a third of a liter.

Djahy. Name given to the southern part of Western Asia, corresponding to Palestine, the Lebanon, and southern Syria.

Djeserkheprure. Throne-name of King Horemheb.

Eight. Name given to the "Ogdoad," a group of eight primeval gods who resided in Hermopolis (modern Ashmunein).

Ennead. "The Nine" major gods and goddesses, originally composed of the creator god Atum and the first generations of his children, but also a name that referred to local pantheons of deities throughout Egypt.

Geb. The earth god, son of Shu and married to the sky goddess Nut.

God's Father. A middle-grade priestly title. It was also used by Ay during his career as an official and subsequently as king, perhaps to describe his personal relationship with and/or his advisory role to the crown

Great Green. Term that most often refers to the ocean.

Greatest of Seers. Title of the Aten's chief priest at El-Amarna, modeled on the similar title of the high priest of the sun god Re at Heliopolis.

Great-of-Magic. Serpent goddess who is identified with the crowns.

Hathor. Cow goddess, one of the king's divine "mothers" who was associated with the sky, as well as with music and dancing.

Hatshepsut. Daughter of Thutmose I and wife of Thutmose II, who usurped the throne during the minority of her nephew, Thutmose III, and reigned (ca. 1472-1458 B.C.E.) until he reached maturity.

Heka-Aten. Abbreviation used in this book for the later didactic name of the Aten, "The living one, sun, ruler of the horizon, who becomes excited in the horizon in his name which is sunlight which comes from the disk," in use from about year 9 of Akhenaten's reign

Hekau. "Magic," the god who embodied that power and was one of the deities who presided over the king's birth as a god.

Heliopolis. Cult center of the sun-god, located a short distance northwest of Memphis. "Upper Egyptian Heliopolis" refers to Armant, not far southwest of Thebes.

Hesret. The necropolis area which adjoined Hermopolis; sacred to Thoth and the "Eight."

Hikuptah. "Mansion of the Ka of Ptah," referring to the temple of the god Ptah and by extension to his city of Memphis.

Hor-Aten. Abbreviation used in this book for the early didactic name of the Aten, "the living one, sun, Horus of the horizon who becomes excited in the horizon, in his name which is light (=*Shu*) that is in the Aten," in use throughout most of the first decade of the reign of Amenhotep IV/Akhenaten.

Horakhty. "Horus of the Double Horizon," the earliest identity of Akhenaten's god, which identified him with the traditional figure of the heavenly falcon.

Horus. A falcon god, originally the sky god par excellence, who is also the the primary divine identity of the pharaoh.

House of Flame. Term designating the regional shrine of Lower Egypt, in the Delta; and, secondarily, the room inside a temple which represented that shrine during re-enactments of the king's coronation.

Iaru. Location of the fields in which the blessed dead live in the next world.

Isheru. The precinct of the goddess Mut, consort of Amun, located south of her husband's temple at Karnak in Thebes.

Isis. Wife of the god Osiris (q.v.) and mother of Horus.

jubilee. See Sed Festival.

Ka. One of the spiritual components of a mortal or a divinity which carries the force of the individual. Gods had as many as fourteen Kas, and their superiority over mere mortals is conveyed in epithets such as "foremost of the Kas of the living."

Kamutef. "Bull of his Mother," a name given to the god of fertility which implies that he generated himself.

Karnak. Modern name of the precinct of the god Amun at Thebes, called *Ipet-suwet*, "Reckoner of Places," in Egyptian.

Kharu. A term for Asia, literally meaning "Hurrian country" but referring indefinitely to Asia, as distinct from Nubia.

Kheperkheprure. Throne-name of King Ay (ca. 1322-1319 B.C.E.).

Khepri. "He who develops," the form of the sun-god which is born at dawn in the form of a beetle (which in Egyptian hieroglyphic represents the power of transformation).

Khnum. The ram-god, resident at Aswan; the lord of potters, who shapes the king and his Ka on the potter's wheel.

Khonsu. The moon-god of Thebes, son of Amun and Mut, often referred to with the added epithet Neferhotep, "(Whose) setting is good."

Kiya. Akhenaten's "other wife": she bore her husband a daughter, but both she and her child were eclipsed and her monuments usurped by Queen Nefertiti's daughters, Meritaten and Ankhenpaaten.

Kush. A term designating southern Nubia, but which often is used to refer to the lands south of Egypt *in toto*.

l.p.h.. Abbreviation (as in Egyptian) of "may he/she live, prosper, and be healthy!"

Lake of Myrrh. Semi-mythological lake, located in the African country of Punt, at the source of the myrrh which was among this region's major exports to Egypt.

Lower Egypt. The northernmost of the "Two Lands" of Egypt, in the Delta.

Luxor. Temple, located 1.5 km. south of the Karnak Temple and named "Southern Sanctum." Rebuilt by Amenhotep III, it was dedicated to an ithyphallic form of Amun-Re.

Maat. The goddess, daughter of Re, who is identified with the principle of harmony in the cosmos.

Manu. Name given to the western mountain(s) on which the western side of heaven rests.

Maru-Aten. "Viewing Place (?) of Aten," a temple located at the southern end of El-Amarna.

Medjay. A people from the desert fringes of Nubia, brought to Egypt as mercenaries during the sixteenth century B.C.E. and retained as the pharaonic police force.

Meketaten. Second daughter of Akhenaten who died (perhaps in childbirth) in or about her father's thirteenth regnal year.

***men*-container**. A measure of capacity, ca. 4.8 liters.

Menkheperre. Throne-name of Akhenaten's great-great- grandfather Thutmose III (ca. 1479-1425 B.C.E.).

Menkheprure. Throne-name of Akhenaten's grandfather Thutmose IV (ca. 1400-1390 B.C.E.).

Meretaten (or **Meritaten**). Eldest daughter of Akhenaten and Nefertiti, and mother of a daughter by the same name; married Akhenaten's successor, Smenkhkare.

Min. The ithyphallic fertility god, native of Coptos in Upper Egypt.

Mitanni. Kingdom on the Upper Euphrates River in Syria: formerly a rival of Egypt, its royal family later formed a marriage alliance with the pharaohs until their kingdom was broken up by the Hittites during Akhenaten's reign.

Montu. Falcon-headed warrior god, native of Armant (southwest of Thebes).

Mut. "The Mother," consort of Amun-Re and mother of Khonsu.

Mutemwia. Wife of Thutmose IV and mother of Amenhotep III.

Mutnodjmet. Sister of Queen Nefertiti and eventually queen, as consort of Horemheb.

Naharin. Territory around the Euphrates River in North Syria, virtually coterminous with the land of Mitanni.

Naune. See **Nun**.

Nebkheprure. Throne-name of Tutankhamun (ca. 1332-1322 B.C.E.)

Nebmaatre. Throne-name of Akhenaten's father, Amenhotep III (ca. 1390-1353 B.C.E.).

Nefernefruaten. (1) Formal extension of Queen Nefertiti's name; (2) fourth daughter of Akhenaten and Nefertiti; (3) personal name of Akhenaten's immediate successor, who is probably to be identified with the former Queen Nefertiti.

Neferkheprure-Waenre. Throne-name of Amenhotep IV/Akhenaten (ca. 1353-1336 B.C.E.).

Nefernefrure. Fifth daughter of Akhenaten and Nefertiti.

Nekhbet. Vulture-goddess of Elkab in southern Upper Egypt; also one of the protecting deities which stands guard on the pharaoh's crown.

Nekhen. Egyptian name of Hierakonpolis, the city across the river from Elkab, which possessed a special sacredness as one of the primeval capitals in earliest Egypt.

New Kingdom. Period which is roughly coterminous with the period of the Egyptian empire, comprising the Eighteenth, Nineteenth and Twentieth Dynasties.

Nine Bows. A group of foreign peoples (mostly Nubian or Libyan) which represented, as a group, the traditional enemies of Egypt.

Nun. The primeval waters in the underworld.

Nut. Sky-goddess, wife of Geb and mother of Osiris, Isis, Seth, and Nephthys.

Oipe. The standard grain measure, about 76.8 liters = ca. 70 dry quarts.

Osiris. God of vegetation, but primarily regarded as king of the dead, who presided over the ethical judgment of the deceased in the underworld. Dead individuals were identified with him (as "The Osiris NN") in the orthodox religion, but he had no role in Akhenaten's system.

Pe. One of the sister cities which made up the urban area of Buto in the Delta and represented, in some contexts, the northern half of Egypt.

Piece. This unit of weight (in the shape of a flat round piece of metal) was a widely used measure of value during the New Kingdom. A number of "pieces" made up the *deben*, but the relation of these two units apparently depended on the value of the materials.

Pre. See Re.

Prophet. (Literally, "god's servant" in Egyptian) Term used for a member of the higher clergy. The first four prophets of a divinity were the chief managers of his/her cult, with the "first prophet" being the high priest.

Ptah. Creator god of Memphis, husband of Sekhmet.

Punt. Area on the Sudanese coast, visited by the Egyptians since the Pyramid Age, from which exotic African products were obtained.

Re. God "Sun," sometimes referred to with the definite article as *Pre*, whose cult center was in Heliopolis.

Red Crown. One of the components of the Double Crown, and conventionally identified as the crown of Lower Egypt.

Red Land. The desert, contrasted with the fertile "Black Land" of the Nile Valley.

Red Mountain. The quartzite quarry located northeast of Cairo. Its ancient name is still preserved by its modern Arabic name, *Gebel Ahmar.*

River mile. Usually reckoned at 10.5 km., but at El-Amarna it must be ca. 2.625 km. (assuming it was a fixed measure of distance and not, as is also suggested, a variable one, representing a unit of travel time between points on the river).

rod. A measure of length, consisting of 100 cubits.

Ro-inty. The "mouth of the valley" at Elkab.

Ro-setchau. Term used as a name for the necropolis to the west of Memphis, embracing the regions of Giza and Saqqara.

Sea of Knives. Region of the underworld through which the sun-god passes in his nightly journey.

Sed Festival. Program of rites in which the king renewed his lease on life and the royal power.

Sefkhet-abwy. "She of the seven sets of horns," a goddess of writing.

Sekhmet. "Female Power," a goddess in the form of a lioness who was viewed as a bringer of pestilence. She was also the wife of Ptah and mother of the third figure in the Memphite triad, the god Nefertem.

Selkis. Scorpion goddess, one of the four female deities who stood guard at the corners of the king's sarcophagus.

***Sem* priest**. A type of priest who served as a royal deputy in temple ritual, and who also officiated at the rite of "opening the mouth" for the deceased.

Serekh. Hieroglyphic "palace façade" which encloses the first of the king's "great names," which defines him as a manifestation of Horus.

Setepenre. Sixth daughter of Akhenaten and Nefertiti.

Sety I. Second king of the Nineteenth Dynasty (ca. 1290-1279 B.C.E.), under whom the damage done by the iconoclasts during Akhenaten's reign was still being repaired.

Shabti. Servant figurine, taken into an individual's tomb to serve him as a substitute worker in the next world.

Shu. God of the illuminated void and son of Atum, understood in the New Kingdom as a god embodying the light that emanated from the sun.

Sitamun. Daughter of Amenhotep III and his chief queen, Tiyi; full sister of Amenhotep IV/Akhenaten.

Smanebbehdet. City in the Delta, representing the northern extremity of Egypt.

Sokar. Underworld god, closely associated with Ptah and Osiris.

Tatenen. "Rising Land," one of the manifestations of the god Ptah.

Tcharu. Town on Egypt's northern border.

Tefnut. Sister-wife of Shu and daughter of Atum.

Thoth. Ibis god of Hermopolis, scribe of the gods.

"Tilled Land." Term (*To-mery*) for the cultivated land of the Egyptian Nile Valley.

Tiyi. (1) Chief queen of Amenhotep III, mother of Akhenaten; (2) Wife of Ay and nurse of Queen Nefertiti.

Tushratta. Last king of Mitanni, a contemporary of Amenhotep III and Akhenaten.

Tutankhaten. Prince of uncertain parentage, who became king (reigned ca. 1332-1322 B.C.E.), changed his name to Tutankhamun, and fully restored the orthodox cults which Akhenaten had suppressed.

Two Ladies. Serpent goddess Edjo of Buto and vulture goddess Nekhbet of Elkab, both protectors of the king, as the second of his "great names" and as the figures who stand guard upon his brow.

Two Lands. Upper and Lower Egypt.

Two Shores. Another synonym for Egypt.

Upper Egypt. The Nile Valley, running from the first Nile cataract at Aswan to the base of the Delta.

vizier. The prime minister of the pharaoh's administration, answering only to the king. By the later Eighteenth Dynasty there were two viziers, for Upper and Lower Egypt respectively.

Waenre. "Only One of Re," part of Amenhotep IV/Akhenaten's throne-name and occasionally employed alone as a sobriquet of the king.

Weret-hekau. See Great-of-Magic.

White Crown. One of the pair which made up the Double Crown, and since late predynastic times identified as the crown of Upper Egypt.

Indexes

Deities

Royalty

Private Individuals
(*Principally Owners of Tomb and Monuments*)

Places

Subjects